DEMOCRATIZING FRANCE

DEMOCRATIZING FRANCE

The political and administrative history of decentralization

VIVIEN A. SCHMIDT
University of Massachusetts
at Boston

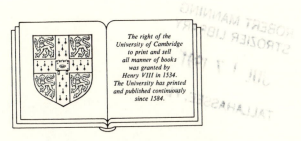

The right of the
University of Cambridge
to print and sell
all manner of books
was granted by
Henry VIII in 1534.
The University has printed
and published continuously
since 1584.

CAMBRIDGE UNIVERSITY PRESS

Cambridge

New York   Port Chester   Melbourne   Sydney

Published by the Press Syndicate of the University of Cambridge
The Pitt Building, Trumpington Street, Cambridge CB2 1RP
40 West 20th Street, New York, NY 10011, USA
10 Stamford Road, Oakleigh, Melbourne 3166, Australia

First Published 1990

Printed in the United States of America

Library of Congress Cataloging-in-Publication Data
Schmidt, Vivien Ann, 1949–
Democratizing France : the political and administrative history of
decentralization / Vivien A. Schmidt.
p. cm.
Includes bibliographical references.
ISBN 0–521–39156–3
1. Decentralization in government – France – History. 2. Local
government – France – History.   I. Title.
JS4895.S36 1990
354.4407′3 – dc20
90-1639
CIP

British Library Cataloging-in-Publication
applied for.

ISBN 0–521–39156–3 hardback

Contents

Preface   *page* ix

PART I
THE POLITICAL HISTORY OF
DECENTRALIZATION FROM THE FRENCH
REVOLUTION TO THE PRESENT

Introduction: When political interest leads to disinterested
politics   3

  1 The legislative history of recurring centralization from the
     French Revolution to the Third Republic   10
     The triumph of decentralization from before 1789 to
       1815   12
     The continuing history of centralization between 1815
       and 1871   25

  2 The triumph of decentralization during the Third
     Republic   41
     The legislative debates on decentralization   43
     Continuing decentralization in the Third Republic and
       recentralization under the Vichy regime   60

  3 The unsuccessful push for decentralization from the
     Fourth Republic through the conservative Fifth Republic   70
     The Fourth Republic's return to the status quo ante   72
     The consistent failure of reform efforts in de Gaulle's
       Fifth Republic   77
     The slowdown of reform initiatives in the conservative
       Fifth Republic after de Gaulle   91

v

Contents

4 Legislating decentralization in the administration of
   local government: The reforms of the Socialist Fifth
   Republic   105
   The passage of the framework law of March 1982   107
   The transfer of executive powers and the end of the
      tutelle   115
   The transfer of administrative functions and civil service
      reform   120
   The transfer of financial resources   132

5 Legislating decentralization in the politics of local
   government   138
   The new legislation focused on local politics   140
   Toward a new electoral balance?   152

PART II
THE IMPACT OF DECENTRALIZATION ON LOCAL
POLITICS AND ADMINISTRATION

Introduction: When informal rules become formal roles   181

6 When informal rules counter formal roles: Local
   government before the Socialist reforms of the Fifth
   Republic   187
   The institutions and processes of local government from
      the Third Republic to the Fifth Republic   188
   The local politico-administrative system   207

7 Rhetoric versus reality in local government: Local politics
   and administration before the Socialist Fifth Republic   222
   The rhetoric of centralization   223
   The rhetoric of nonpartisanship   247

8 When informal rules become formal roles: The new
   pluralism in the institutions and processes of local
   government   264
   The new politics in the periphery   267
   The new decentralized *dirigisme* in local economic
      development   289

9 Unblocking society by decree: The transformation of the
   politico-administrative system   310
   Changing the politico-administrative system   312
   Changing the roles, rules, and relationships   316

Contents

10 A new rhetoric and a new reality in local government:
   Local politics and administration in the Socialist Fifth
   Republic and beyond   342
   The new rhetoric of the limits of decentralization   344
   The new rhetoric of good management and the
      politicization of the periphery   371

Conclusion   389

Bibliography   393

Index   399

Preface

In recent years, decentralization has become extremely popular as a means of governmental reform, with national governments around the world seeking to devolve·more power and responsibility to local governments in efforts to encourage greater political participation and democracy and to increase administrative efficiency and costs. In this, France has been no exception. But the way in which the Socialists in power from 1981 to 1986 went about decentralization was exceptional indeed. Instead of the usual piecemeal reforms leading to gradual change, the Socialists "revolutionized" center-periphery relations by redefining the role of the state in the periphery and giving extensive new powers to territorial units of government through a series of laws that by 1986 encompassed over forty laws and close to three hundred decrees.

Most scholars of French politics and administration were taken completely by surprise by the Socialists' decentralizing reforms. And understandably so. Since the French Revolution, the legislative history had been one of endless parliamentary debates and countless failed initiatives. The only lasting, major decentralizing reform of the local governmental system was already close to a century old, having been passed at the beginning of the Third Republic. Although it had ended the century-old pattern of recurring centralization begun with the French Revolution, it had restricted itself to making the mayor an elected official and the executive power in the communes, or municipalities. Centralization remained in the person of the prefect and in the formal and legal institutions of local administration, even though decentralization was nevertheless ever present in the informal process of local government, promoted by the relationship of complicity between prefects and local elected officials that permitted the latter to engage in a rhetoric that hid their informal power and influence from public view. In short, local officials' basic satisfaction with the local politico-administrative system as it was, combined with the long history of piecemeal, failed attempts at reform by legislators more concerned with their own political interests than with principle, made any thoroughgoing reform appear highly unlikely. But the Socialists did decentralize. This book explains why and how.

More specifically, *Democratizing France* seeks to lend new insight into the changing nature of the French state and its relationship to local society by combining a historical analysis of the parliamentary debates and legislation related to decentralization with an examination of the impact of such legislation on local politics and administration. Part I traces the legislative history of decentralization from the Revolution to the present, focusing in particular on the reforms at the beginning of the Third Republic and of the Socialist Fifth Republic. It explains these two successes, and the many failures, as much in terms of the concepts and institutions of the Revolution as in terms of legislative patterns of behavior. For Part I, in addition to the standard sources of information, I have interviewed the principal politicians and upper-level civil servants involved in the policy-making processes that produced the Socialist decentralization laws. These include the chief architect of the reform, the late Gaston Defferre, Minister of the Interior and Decentralization and Socialist mayor of Marseilles; one of the primary figures involved in the floor debate, Jean-Pierre Worms, Socialist member of the National Assembly and a vice-mayor of Macon; and the main civil servants charged with formulating, revising, and implementing the reforms, Michel Cotten and Eric Giuily, successive directors of the Office of Local Government (*Direction générale des collectivités locales*) in the Ministry of the Interior.

Part II combines three different approaches in its examination of the impact of the decentralizing reforms of the Third Republic and the Socialist Fifth Republic: (1) the historian's as it traces the development of the institutions and processes of local government over time; (2) the political sociologist's as it outlines the system of interrelationships among actors in the periphery before and after the Socialist reforms; and (3) the cultural anthropologist's or even ordinary language analyst's when it considers the shifts in language in response to changes in practice. In Part II, for evidence of more recent changes, I have interviewed officials of the central ministries and conducted field research in the Lorraine and Provence-Alpes-Côte d'Azur with a sample of elected officials (on the right and left) and civil servants (from the highest to the lowest ranks) drawn from every level of local government. My list includes such local notables as Jean-Marie Rausch, at the time centrist mayor of Metz, president of the regional council of the Lorraine, and Senator, but more recently also minister in Rocard's government; Philippe Séguin, at the time Gaullist mayor of Épinal, regional councilor of the Lorraine, general councilor of the Vosges, and member of the National Assembly, but more recently also a minister in Chirac's government; Christian Pierret, at the time Socialist mayor of St. Dié, general councilor of the Vosges, and general reporter of the budget in the National Assembly; and Jacques Médecin, at the time right-wing Gaullist mayor of Nice, president of the department of the Alpes-Maritimes, member of the regional council, and member of the National Assembly.

I owe a debt of gratitude to all the above-mentioned officials for their willingness to take time from their busy schedules to share their views with me. Also, I am indebted to Jean-Pierre Worms, whose conversations about the politics of the reform and its potential impact on local administration provided me with much food for thought, and added immeasurably to this book. I would also like to express my appreciation to the countless civil servants interviewed, many of whose comments have of necessity gone unattributed, although I must single out three whose inside views of the system, contacts, and sources of information proved invaluable: Dominique Schmitt, director-general of the region of the Lorraine; Christian Serradji, secretary-general of the Commission on the Organization of Central Administration in the Office of the Prime Minister; and Philippe de Lara of the *École des ponts et chaussées*, but at that time at the Observatory on Decentralization in the Ministry of Transport.

Special thanks are also in order for Bernard Chenot, president of the Institute of French Administrative Sciences, and Céline Wiener, its secretary-general at the time, without whose help this study would have been much impoverished, and for Michel Basex, whose invitation to teach at the University of Paris X (Nanterre) came at a propitious moment for my research. And I should not fail to mention the French government, which provided me lo these many years ago with a predissertation fellowship for work on decentralization during the Third Republic, and the *Institut d'Études politiques* with which I was affiliated at the time.

Among scholars, I owe a special debt to Martin Schain, whose careful reading of the full manuscript, along with his constant encouragement, made this book much better than it might have been. In this same vein, my appreciation goes to Alfred Diamant, Douglas Ashford, and Yves Mény. I also wish to thank the Center for European Studies at Harvard University, where I was in residence for my sabbatical year of 1985. I should not forget Aristide Zolberg, who piqued my interest in the topic when I was his graduate research assistant at the University of Chicago. Last, but by no means least, I thank Susanne Rudolph, Alan Ryan, Theodore Lowi, and Candace Hetzner for their support, encouragement, advice, as well as friendship over the long haul.

The political history of decentralization from the French Revolution to the present

Introduction: When political interest leads to disinterested politics

When the Socialists passed decentralizing legislation from 1982 to 1986 that redefined the role of the state in the periphery and gave extensive new powers to territorial units of government, they fulfilled one of the last imperatives of the French Revolution. The history of decentralization over the previous two centuries had not been a very successful one. Only once before the Socialist reforms, one hundred years ago during the beginning years of the Third Republic, had Parliament passed significant, lasting decentralizing legislation. Before the Third Republic, the legislative pattern was one of recurring centralization, which from the first years of the Revolution consisted of short periods of decentralization in times of governmental crisis followed by long periods of recentralization in times of relative governmental stability. Between the laws passed at the beginning of the Third Republic and those at the beginning of the Socialist Fifth Republic, although the century-old pattern of recurring centralization did end, formal decentralization itself did not advance much; the legislative history was one of endless parliamentary debates and countless failed initiatives on an ever expanding list of reforms.

However, each time Parliament did pass decentralizing legislation, no matter how minor it might have been in terms of the formal exercise of power, local autonomy and political participation increased, producing local elected officials who were more representative of, and responsive to, the local electorate. What is more, the major piece of decentralizing legislation at the beginning of the Third Republic promoted a shift in the local balance of power, which in turn encouraged a critical realignment of the national electorate, and the new groups favored by decentralization at the local level became the new, all-important constituency at the national level. There is every possibility that such a critical realignment may come about again, promoted by the Socialists' decentralizing legislation of 1982–6.

Why has decentralization had such a dramatic impact on national and local politics each time it has occurred? And why have major decentralizing reforms been successful only twice in the legislative history of France since 1789? The answers to these questions have much to do with the Revolution itself, which not only set the parameters of the legislative debate on decentralization, conceptually and institutionally, but also initiated the self-interested pattern of legislative behavior on the issue.

The Revolution, first of all, fixed the terms of the debate when it formulated the primary question regarding decentralization as, To what extent are the requirements of national unity and the dictates of principles of equality before the law compatible with local liberty? To this day, no debate on decentralization has conceptualized the issue of decentralization in terms other than these; this has, for the most part, had detrimental consequences for local democracy. For example, the principle of universal suffrage in elections for leaders of the nation was granted relatively early on (1848). That principle, however, took much longer to be extended to local leaders (1884 for the mayors of communes, 1986 for the presidents of the regions), mainly because national elections were seen as promoting national unity and local ones, as weakening it. What is more, although the prefects controlled the communes through their appointment of the mayors—with brief respites—until the 1870s, they continued to exercise powers of oversight (*tutelle*) in the communes along with executive powers in the departments and regions, up until the 1980s, in all cases in order to ensure that the principles of equality before the law were not undermined by local liberty. They continue to retain certain powers of review over local governments for the same reason. Finally, proposals for new intermediate structures such as the regions were resisted for a very long time, principally because they were seen as threats to national unity and equality, even when they didn't promote local liberty – whether they represented a return to the traditional provinces, a means for achieving regional self-determination, or a functional solution to the problems of regional economic development. In short, by assuming an opposition between unity and equality on the one hand and local liberty on the other, the Revolution ensured that local democracy lagged far behind national democracy.

Secondly, the Revolution determined the institutional context within which all future reforms would have to fit. By radically altering the structure and size of local governments, putting "republican" departments and communes in the place of the royal provinces and parishes, the Revolution consecrated institutional forms that subsequent regimes could do little to reform, let alone replace. It is telling that whereas the structure of the national government has been altered over a dozen times, the structure of local government has been left essentially untouched since the Revolution. New institutions may very well have been created (in

4

particular, the regions), but these have in no way threatened the basic organization of the periphery, and the communes remain almost as numerous as at the time of the Revolution.

Lastly, the Revolution established the primary pattern of legislative response to the issue of decentralization, one in which questions of political interest consistently outweighed those of political principle. Legislators time and again voiced their principled support for local liberty while out of power or unsure of governmental control and their pragmatic opposition to decentralization once certain of such power and control. This has led to some curious contradictions. In the first century following the Revolution, the legislative answer to the question of how much local liberty is compatible with national unity was always more liberal in times of crisis, when national unity was most in doubt, than in times of governmental stability. In the next century the legislative answer to the question of how much local liberty is compatible with principles of equality before the law was always "very little," despite the increasing inequalities among local governments in financial resources and in the relative degrees of freedom they experienced in their administrative functions.

Legislators' underlying reasons for their self-interested opposition to decentralization did shift over time, though. Between 1789 and 1871, the failure of decentralization resulted in large measure from the continuing, if understandable, distrust of the general population by those in power who, having gained power as a result of popular upheaval in most instances, feared losing power in consequence of such upheaval. Between 1884 and 1981, the failure of reform efforts reflected less and less the distrust of the general population by those in power than it did a distrust of those in power by local elected officials and administrators who had been developing informal means of getting around the formal, centralized system. These self-interested reasons have helped ensure that, however decentralizing the debates, legislators have rarely seriously challenged the Jacobin principles of centralization, which put the concerns of national unity and the demands of equality before the law first and the Girondin desire for local liberty second.

Thus, although decentralization in the Third Republic ended the pattern of recurring centralization, decentralization itself remained quite narrowly defined, in large measure because of legislators' pragmatism. Their main question was how to decentralize within the confines of the administrative system set up by Napoleon and of the administrative organization of the countryside established by the Revolution. Their answer was to leave the prefect the executive power in the departments and make the elected mayor the executive power in the communes.

The legislators of the Socialist Fifth Republic, although similarly pragmatic and equally careful to remain true to the organizing principles of local government established by the Revolution and in the Napoleonic era, nonetheless managed to go a good deal further than had their confreres of the century before. They ended a century-old pattern of much talk about decentralization and little action, with reforms that progressively altered, replaced, or revised almost every law related to center–periphery relations. These reforms, among other things, abolished the prefects' *tutelle,* transferred the prefects' executive powers to the presidents of the departments and regions, turned over state administrative functions and financial resources to the locality, and proposed to reform the territorial civil service. In addition, they made the region another regular level of local government with directly elected officials and limited the *cumul des mandats,* or accumulation of offices, which allowed mayors to be presidents of departments and regions as well as deputies, senators, or ministers at the same time.

The Socialists, in brief, revised almost every aspect of local government. But although they went very far with the reform, they did not go nearly as far as they originally intended. Pragmatism was very much at play here. For only by pushing the reforms through swiftly, all the while building a consensus based on wide consultation and compromise, could the Socialists be certain to make their reforms irreversible. But, as with many consensus-building efforts, in France as elsewhere, the search for consensus meant sacrificing many of those aspects of the reform that were not generally agreed upon and leaving other aspects of the reform vulnerable to those organized groups with a vested interest in the new system. This is why the more innovative reforms in the area of local democracy and the sweeping changes originally planned for the social services area and for local finances were set aside. And it is also why the Socialists failed to rationalize the basic structures of local government either by reducing the number of communes or by choosing between the departments and regions. But however pragmatic the reforms, the question that remains to be answered is: How were legislators in the Third as well as the Fifth Republics able to decentralize at all?

The only two successes of decentralizing legislation, one per century since the Revolution, actually follow the pattern begun during the Revolution, one in which political interest and the politics of the moment more than political principle determined the fate of decentralizing legislation. It so happens that at the start of both the Third Republic and the Socialist Fifth Republic, political circumstance helped ensure that political interest would support the disinterested politics represented by decentralizing reforms. In both cases the governing majority's support for local liberty was part of a reasonable political calculation to retain power in the short term as well as a component in a brilliant political strategy to forge a new electoral coalition to retain power in the long term.

In both the 1870s and in the 1980s, the ground had already been prepared for decentralization by a century's worth of discussion and a decade's worth of intensive debate, all of which had come to nought. In each case, it was the left that, having become the standard-bearer for decentralization during the preceding decade of increasing agitation for reform and having come to national power only after many years in opposition, put through lasting reforms. In both centuries, most members of the left supported decentralization as much, if not more, for pragmatic reasons, as a way of limiting the right's potential central control while ensuring the left's continued access to local power, than for principled ones.

The left's strong interest in decentralization, however, cannot be understood if we see it simply as a way of maintaining power in the face of an uncertain future. For there are surely more efficient ways of retaining power, as French history has amply demonstrated. Indeed, this political calculation cannot be fully explained except as part of a larger political strategy to gain and retain the allegiance of a changing electorate.

In both centuries, more specifically, support for decentralization was part of a political strategy by the left to forge a new electoral coalition made up of ascending sociopolitical groups in the periphery. Léon Gambetta set out to gain the allegiance of the *couche nouvelle,* or new social stratum of middle-income peasants and shopkeepers, making this the key theme of his electoral campaigns, beginning in 1872. So too Mitterrand, quite consciously echoing Gambetta, sought to appeal to the new social stratum of *salariés,* or wage earners, made up of the *cadres moyens,* or middle-level managers, and workers.

In the Third Republic, decentralization helped produced the "revolution of the mayors," which, by making the mayor the choice of the popularly elected municipal council, served to enfranchise on the local level the middle-income peasants and shopkeepers at the expense of the formerly all-powerful rural aristocracy. It is this new electorate that at the national level has been credited with stabilizing and republicanizing France; at the same time it has been blamed for making the Third Republic a "stalemate society," incapable of promoting the kind of industrialization necessary to keep up with the modern world. Moreover, although France by the Fourth and Fifth Republics was no longer a nation of peasants and shopkeepers, its local governmental institutions continued to favor these groups and thus to act as a brake on industrial development and as an impediment to increased local democracy, at least until the Socialists' reforms.

The questions for the Socialist Fifth Republic, then, are: Will decentralization today help produce a new "revolution," this time by making the presidents of the departments and regions elected executives and by enfranchising on the local level the new electorate of workers and middle managers at the expense of the previous coalition? And will the new electorate bring with it at the national level a "recentering" of France, or will it be blamed for further polarization and continuing economic crisis?

Whether the Socialists themselves will benefit the most from this "revolution" remains open to question. The new electorate is still clearly in the process of formation: Witness the recent back and forth in the various elections. Meanwhile, the Socialists as much as the moderate right and even the extreme right have all been in search of new ideologies or policies likely to appeal to this new electorate or at least portions thereof. For now, given the results of the 1988 presidential and legislative elections, it looks as if Mitterrand may have won his gamble seven years down the road, just as Gambetta did, with a center-left coalition. Mitterrand's success was due to a combination of factors: (1) the Socialists' pre-1981 electoral strategy, which involved refashioning their traditional ideology and rhetoric to appeal to a new, emerging portion of the electorate, the wage earners; (2) their post-1983 ideological flexibility, which included a move toward more pragmatic politics along with an opening to the center; and (3) the failure of their rivals on the moderate and the extreme right to mount a lasting challenge with their own counter-ideologies and policy initiatives.

In the long run, whichever party or coalition gains the upper hand, decentralization is likely to have served the interests of new sociopolitical groups in the periphery. In turn, these may become the foundation for a new, national electoral coalition supporting a new, more progressive elite, a more modern economy, and a more democratic polity. But even if these changes are a long time in coming, decentralization will have fulfilled one of the last imperatives of the French Revolution by democratizing the institutions of local government, giving citizens at the local level the same political rights they exercise at the national level while increasing the accountability and powers of their local representatives. As such, decentralization will remain the Socialists' crowning achievement.

Part I of *Democratizing France,* in sum, offers a historical analysis of decentralization from the French Revolution to the present. It focuses in particular on the parliamentary debates and legislation related to decentralization, considering the impact the concepts and institutions of the Revolution have had on those debates and on the ensuing laws. By examining the patterns of legislative behavior with regard to decentralization, it serves to explain the few successes as well as the many failures of decentralizing initiatives.

Chapter 1 traces the political history of recurring centralization from the French Revolution to the Third Republic. Chapter 2 takes a close look at the legislative politics during the beginning years of the Third Republic, when the first set of lasting decentralizing reforms was passed, and then proceeds to consider the history of inactivity through the rest of the Third Republic and during the Vichy interlude. Chapter 3 examines the endless parliamentary debates and failed initiatives that characterized the Fourth Republic's return to the status quo ante, the Fifth Republic's consistent failure of reform efforts under de Gaulle, and the slowdown in reform initiatives under his successors. Chapter 4 brings us to the Socialist reforms of 1982–6, detailing the ways in which the Socialists legislated decentralization in the administration of local government with the transfer of executive powers, administrative functions, and financial resources, as well as the minimal changes wrought by the opposition when it returned to power between 1986 and 1988. Finally, Chapter 5 examines the impact of Socialist decentralization on the politics of local government, considering not only the effect of specific legislation on local elites and elections but also the relationship of Socialist decentralization to national politics and the possibility of a critical realignment of the electorate.

I

The legislative history of recurring centralization from the French Revolution to the Third Republic

Alexis de Tocqueville, writing in the mid-1800s, perhaps best described the outlines of the legislative history of decentralization that began with the Revolution of 1789 when he suggested that, time and time again, there was "in the beginning, invariably, a push toward decentralization . . . in the end, an extension of centralization. In starting one follows the logic of one's principles; in finishing one follows that of one's habits, of one's passions, of power. In sum, the last word always remains with centralization which, to be honest, increases in depth at the same time it diminishes in appearance."[1] The reason for this recurring pattern, he found, was that legislators' only real concern was for their own power and incumbency, whether they argued in favor of centralization, claiming that it was necessary for national unity, or against it. For "the majority of those who in France speak against centralization . . . do not basically wish to destroy it, some because they hold power, others because they count on gaining it."[2] On the question of decentralization, political principle continually gave way to the pragmatism of those who, once in power, saw their political interests furthered by continuing, or even increasing, governmental centralization.

This pattern of recurring centralization reflected a continuing and understandable, distrust of the local population by those in power who had gained power as a result of local upheaval in most instances, but feared losing it in consequence of such upheaval. It was only in periods of governmental crisis that legislators, uncertain of their own tenure in office, tended to respond positively to the demands of the populace for increased local democracy and greater power over local affairs. But this

[1] Alexis de Tocqueville, *L'Ancien Régime et la Révolution, fragments et notes inédites* (Paris: NRF, Gallimard), p. 343, quoted in Bela Farago, "De la décentralisation," *Commentaire* vol. 6, no. 21 (Spring 1983).
[2] Alexis de Tocqueville, quoted by H. de Ferron, *Institutions municipales et provinciales comparées* (Paris: L. Larose & Forcel, 1884), p. 176.

lasted only as long as power remained uncertain. Although the first few years of the Revolution brought decentralizing laws, starting with those of the Constitutional Monarchy and ending with the unimplemented ones of the Girondins, recentralization came in the years to follow, first with the Jacobins, then with the Directory, and then with Napoleon, whose centralized system was continued through the Restoration of 1815 and was only slightly modified in the first years of the July Monarchy beginning in 1830. Decentralization reappeared for a short time with the Revolution of 1848, to be replaced by the highly centralized system of the Second Empire, which was to end again in another crisis in 1870 with the government of National Defense. This pattern of recurrent centralization was to change, however, with the beginning of the Third Republic.

In the meantime, the terms of the debates about decentralization remained extremely narrow, limited conceptually and institutionally by the Revolution. By conceptualizing the issue of decentralization only in terms of the question, To what extent are the requirements of national unity and the dictates of principles of equality before the law compatible with local liberty? the Revolution created an opposition that put any attempts to institute local democracy at a distinct disadvantage. It is significant that, as of 1848, whereas the popular election of the head of state finally came to be accepted as a means of promoting national unity, the popular election of the mayor continued to be rejected as a threat to such unity. Curiously enough, only during the times when national unity was most in doubt, in times of crisis, did legislators allow the popular election of the mayor. But even in those times, legislators felt the need to counterbalance this local liberty, such as it was, by reducing the powers of local governments, reinforcing the role of the agents of the central government, or restricting the franchise. In times of stability such limitations on local liberty were only increased by ending the system of local election of the mayor and revising the system of municipal council elections in ways guaranteed to benefit the party in power. During such times, from the Napoleonic era forward, the prefects were exercising executive powers in the departments, all in the name of ensuring that principles of equality before the law be respected.

The institutions of the Revolution, like its concepts, had a very strong hold on legislators, especially because the institutions came to embody those very concepts. The radical break with the royal provinces and the parishes of the ancien régime through the creation of departments and communes that, in theory at least, were to be equal in size and importance was in large measure a rejection of the inequalities inherent in the previous structures and an attempt to institute local liberty. Starting at this time, moreover, the defense of these new institutions became tantamount to protecting national unity. One of the main reasons for the consistent rejection of the numerous proposals for the creation of territorial divisions akin to regions is that they evoked the old provinces and the "federalism" that from 1789 on most legislators saw as the greatest threat to national unity. What is more, given the instability of national governmental structures, the very persistence of local governmental structures somehow seemed a guarantee of the maintenance of national unity. This was certainly one, but by no means the only, reason why subsequent regimes never challenged the basic organization of local government. Equally important was that, once Napoleon had completed the administrative restructuring of local governmental institutions set up by the Revolution and established the prefectoral system, central government after central government found the existing local governmental system an efficient tool for maintaining itself in power in the periphery. So why change it?

The concepts and institutions of the Revolution, together with the political interest of the legislators, seemed to conspire to promote centralization. The notion that local liberty could be compatible with national unity and equality before the law was accepted only in moments of crisis or by members of the opposition. From the Revolution to the Third Republic, as decentralizing as the debates were, there was never any serious challenge to the Jacobin principles of centralization that put the concerns of national unity and the demands of equality before the law first, the Girondin desire for local liberty second.

THE TRIUMPH OF CENTRALIZATION FROM BEFORE 1789 TO 1815

The Revolution of 1789 marks the beginning of the pattern to which de Tocqueville referred: short periods of decentralization in times of crisis followed by long periods of recentralization in times of relative stability by governments intent on keeping as much power for themselves as possible. In the first years of the Revolution, under the Constitutional Monarchy, legislators fearful of the king sought to limit his powers over local government by producing moderately decentralizing legislation with elected mayors, municipal councils, departmental councils, and even elected government representatives, but with a highly restricted electorate.

The Girondins, whose political support was in the countryside, went much further than this with the Constitution of 1793, which called for the election of all local governmental officials by universal suffrage. It was never implemented, however, and the Jacobins instituted a highly centralized system in its place, in which elections were suspended and local governments essentially were put in the hands of governmental agents. With this system they felt they would be better able to control the country, administer the Terror, and maintain themselves in power. Under the Directory another centralized system emerges for similar reasons, although one with a proliferation of generally useless and powerless, albeit elected, administrative bodies alongside the all-powerful governmental agents.

It was during the Napoleonic era, however, that centralization reached its zenith, with prefects in complete control of the departments, mayors appointed by the central government, and only the illusion of universal suffrage retained for the election of members of local governmental councils. What had begun in the first days of the Revolution as an attempt to replace the ancien régime's inconsistent and unequal local administrative system with something more democratic and efficient ended with the systematization of centralization under Napoleon and a highly efficient and undemocratic local governmental system.

Centralization and decentralization under the ancien régime

Under the ancien régime six hundred years of local liberty were followed by two hundred years of slow, but progressive, centralization. By the twelfth century most villages were both democratic and self-governing, run by a local assembly consisting either of all the local population or only a privileged portion of it, which elected its own municipal officials. By the late seventeenth and early eighteenth centuries this communal liberty began to lose ground to an absolute monarchy intent on completing political unity by administrative unity. With the imposition of a financial system, the loss of communal powers of taxation, and the rise of the system of royal intendants, most traditional local liberties were abrogated.[3]

In many cases the diminution of local powers was the unintended consequence of actions meant to rationalize local finances and strengthen national finances. Colbert's attempt to end the financial mismanagement and abuse of local officials and notables by placing municipal finance under the supervision of the *contrôl général* and the intendants, for instance, spelled the beginning of the *tutelle* and the beginning of the end of municipal independence and control over local revenue and expenditure. This, together with the increasing number and variety of taxes, sales of offices, and so forth, ensured that by the time of the Revolution the mismanagement and abuse by local notables had simply been replaced by

[3]For early, detailed discussions of the early administrative history, see de Ferron, *Institutions*, pp. 2–4; Th. Ducrocq, *Études sur la loi municipale du 5 avril 1884* (Paris: Ernest Thorin, 1886), p. 116; and Émile Monnet, *Histoire de l'Administration* (Paris: Rousseau, 1885), pp. 36–7. For more recent accounts, see Pierre Goubert, *L'Ancien Régime*, vol. 2 (Paris: Colin, 1973); Maurice Bordes, *L'Administration provinciale et municipale en France au XVIIIe siècle* (Paris: Société d'edition d'enseignement supérieur, 1972); Gérard Sautel, *Histoire des institutions publiques* (Paris: Dalloz, 1974).

that of the state.[4] And what often began as a way of raising revenue, as in the case of the law of 1692 abolishing free municipal elections, was generally rationalized into a principle of government,[5] because the monarchy had come to regard municipal liberty as a threat to national unity.

Despite all of its efforts, centralization by the monarchy was not the uniform and uncontested success many thought.[6] Commercial and provincial capitals conserved most of their liberty, and villages maintained theirs in exchange for higher taxes.[7] The administrative division of the country was varied and incoherent, including *généralités* and *intendances, baillages* and *sénéchaussées, pays d'élection* and *pays d'État*, ecclesiastical provinces and dioceses, military governments and chief command posts, all with different administrative arrangements and taxes. This meant that the heavy hand of the central state was felt unequally, with the differences depending upon the administrative structure and the history of the area in which a town was located.[8] France was highly centralized in name, but quite decentralized in fact.

In the last years of the monarchy, the inequities and inefficiencies of this local governmental system occasioned a great deal of criticism and recommendations for administrative reorganization and reform. As early as 1764 d'Argenson had proposed the reorganization of local government through the division of the kingdom into "departments." In 1787 the monarchy had considered creating departments, or "subdelegations," at an intermediate level between the communes and the provinces, and the physiocrats had suggested that these be no larger than one day's journey from the local governmental seat for any inhabitant of the region. Finally, numerous reformers had proposed geometrical divisions of the country in a manner reminiscent of the United States, for example, Letrosne who in 1779 suggested that France be divided as squarely as possible into 25 generalities, 250 districts, 4,500 boroughs; Robert de Hesselm who in 1780 published a map of France consisting of 9 regions, 81 counties, 729 cantons, etc.; and Sieyès who in 1788 proposed a division of France into 50 provinces, each divided into 40 boroughs, each in turn made up of 20 parishes, but then modified this in August 1789 to recommend 89 departments made up of 9 communes, plus Paris.[9]

[4]Nora Temple, "The Control and Exploitation of French Towns during the Ancien Régime," in *State and Society in Seventeenth Century France*, ed. Raymond F. Kierstead (New York: New Viewpoints, 1975), pp. 67–87.
[5]De Ferron, *Institutions*, p. 13.
[6]See comments by Goubert, *L'Ancien Régime*, vol. 2, p. 18.
[7]Ibid., pp. 81–2. See also Bordes, *L'Administration;* and Sautel, *Histoire*, pp. 78–97.
[8]See Temple, "Control and Exploitation," for an account of the differences in the kind and weight of taxation in the *pays d'élection* and *pays d'État*.
[9]Jacques Godechot, *Les Institutions de la France sous la Révolution et l'Empire*, 2d ed. (Paris: Presses universitaires de France, 1985), pp. 94–5.

Recurring centralization, 1789 to 1871

The general issue of administrative reform had been a matter of great concern since the middle of the century. This was reflected both in the plethora of works by such thinkers as d'Argenson, Mirabeau, Dupont de Nemours, and Le Trosne, who were recommending local elected bodies and discussing their proper relationship with the central government, and in the weak reforms that were establishing elected assemblies in various provinces during the last years of the monarchy.[10] This concern was even reflected in the popular fiction of the time, in countless utopian novels (generally in the form of extraordinary voyages), which envisioned ideal governments that were located in a France of the future or at the antipodes of France and were based on principles of equality, ruled by elected assemblies or enlightened despots, and divided geometrically into units of equal size, all governed by a single, uniform set of laws.[11]

Nothing, however, came of all of this during the monarchy. It took the Revolution of 1789 to reform the local governmental system of France effectively. The Revolution ultimately substituted an efficient, uniform, centralized administrative system for the less efficient, unequal framework of the ancien régime. As de Tocqueville explained, "the Revolution pronounced at the same time against royalty and against provincial institutions."[12] But in so doing, according to Pierre Goubert, the ancien régime gained a posthumous victory, because the mainly verbal absolutism of the kings was put into practice, with the Revolution actualizing the desires of the monarchy in the names of liberty, equality, and fraternity.[13]

Decentralization under the Constituent Assembly and the Girondins

The Revolution and the various systems of government it produced between the years 1789 and 1799 did more damage to municipal liberty in those ten years than had the centralizing monarchy in the preceding two hundred. In the first months of the Revolution, all municipalities were placed under one common law. In one fell swoop, the traditional boundaries, liberties, and community ties of the communes were legally destroyed, even though certain practices persisted long afterward. The com-

[10]For an excellent discussion of the views of these philosophers, as well as of the debates at the time more generally, see François Burdeau, *Liberté, libertés locales chéries* (Paris: Cujas, 1983), pp. 14–26.

[11]See, for example, Abbé Morelly, *Code de la nature* (Paris: 1775); Simon Tyssot de Patot, *Voyages et aventures de Jacques Massé* (Amsterdam: 1710); Bernard le Bovier de Fontenelle, *La République des philosophers, ou histoire des Ajaciens* (Geneva: 1789).

[12]Alexis de Tocqueville, *Democracy in America* (New York: Doubleday, 1969), p. 87.

[13]Goubert, *L'Ancien Régime*, p. 247.

munes, however, did remain in large measure coextensive with the parishes they replaced, whereas the districts into which the departments were divided did have some affinity with the old *pays*. And even the original eighty-three departments, historically viewed as having violated traditional provincial divisions, actually respected the basic outlines of the provinces to a great extent, with the larger provinces divided into three, four, or five departments, the midsize ones encompassing single departments, and the smaller ones grouped together into departments.[14]

This administrative reorganization of the periphery was not something that the legislators of the Constituent Assembly created out of whole cloth, however. The influence of political thinkers and utopians under the ancien régime was quite strong, especially as regards the main outlines of the administrative reorganization. But utopia is one thing and reality, another. Although the original proposal for administrative reorganization by Thouret, building on that of Sieyès, very much reflected utopian ideals with a plan calling for eighty departments divided into squares measuring eighteen leagues per side, each with nine equal-sized communes divided further into four cantons, reality interceded as legislators objected to the resulting inequalities in electoral representation, the violation of traditional divisions and natural boundaries, and so forth. Ultimately, the Constitutent Assembly abandoned any notion of the geometrical division of the countryside and decided to respect the traditional divisions of the provinces wherever possible by setting up seventy-five to eighty-five departments in which any inhabitant was to be able to get to the *chef-lieu,* or department seat, from anywhere in the department within a day's journey (approximately forty kilometers).[15]

The actual division, however, ended up being even further from utopia than the legislators intended, in large measure because of the often heated responses by the periphery to proposed divisions of the countryside and decisions about which commune was to become the departmental or district seat. In what were to become the departments of the Nord and the Pas-de-Calais, for example, the Lille forces successfully fought the initial proposal to divide the area into an interior department and a maritime one, but lost to Douai in the battle to gain the departmental seat in the Nord (Lille had to wait until 1804 for victory in this matter).[16] In most divisions of the countryside, although the main outlines of the traditional boundaries were kept, a close look reveals a good deal of readjustment.

[14]Godechot, *Institutions,* pp. 97–8.
[15]Ibid., p. 97.
[16]Louis Trenard, "Provinces et départements des Pays-Bas français aux départements du Nord et du Pas-de-Calais," in *Régions et régionalisme en France du XVIII siècle à nos jours,* ed. Christian Gras and Georges Livet (Paris: Presses universitaires de France, 1977), pp. 75–85.

This was a response not only to local political pressures but also to the desire to create areas of relatively equal size, especially in the smaller provinces (for example, in the creation of the department of the Haute-Loire, where Velay was attached to one part of the Auvergne and Brioude); to respect certain traditional boundaries (for example, in the Basse-Pyrénées, where two enclaves remained from the Haute-Pyrénées because they were part of communal pasturelands); and to ensure that major cities be made departmental seats even if they were not the requisite distance for all inhabitants (for example, Toulon in the Var).[17]

The administrative reorganization of the countryside, in brief, was a compromise between the impetus of pre-Revolutionary ideals proposing radical reorganization according to principles of equality and geometric "rationality"; the weight of history and tradition, a drag on any kind of reform; and the politics of the moment, which demanded a quick resolution of the problem, acceptable to most groups in the Assembly. Compromise, moreover, was also involved in the reform of local administration.

Although there was general agreement on the left and the right about the importance of creating a strong executive power with local administration subordinated to it in the interests of national unity, most feared putting the king in control of a local system that, if truly subordinated, would effectively bring back the intendants. The final compromise was a system that actually left local government largely independent of the central government. Although the principle of subordination of authority was retained – with departments placed under the authority and inspection of the king for administrative matters, districts placed under the departmental administrations, and the communes placed under the two above levels – the king had no power in financial matters because the legislature had control in this area and the king in any case had no agents capable of making departments, let alone the districts or communes, obey his will.[18]

The debates in the Constituent Assembly over administrative reform centered on the question, To what extent could national unity and equality before the law be reconciled with local liberty? The answer tended to have much more to do with political interest resulting from the politics of the moment than with political principle. The right, which could have been expected to defend the traditional privileges of the provinces, saw instead a golden opportunity to strengthen the power of the king, thus achieving under a constitutional monarchy what had been impossible under the absolute monarchy. It tended to see any local liberty as a threat to national unity, with the royalist newspapers complaining that the France resulting

[17]Godechot, *Institutions*, pp. 98–102.
[18]See discussion in Burdeau, *Libertés*, pp. 44–7.

from the decentralizing laws reflected "the picture of a multitude of small states, each with its own leaders, judges, army, treasury."[19] The extreme left, by contrast, for the most part downplayed its own centralizing principles to support a reasonable modicum of decentralization because it feared the monarchy and found local liberty considerably more compatible with national unity and equality before the law than they would only a few years later. Thus, it was Robespierre who rose in objection to a proposal by the right that, in response to the troubles in the provinces in February 1790, went so far as to recommend that the king be put directly in charge of local administration. The extreme left, in effect, consistently resisted all attempts to strengthen the powers of the central government. For example, in the beginning months of 1791 they opposed, albeit unsuccessfully, the moderates' initiatives to reinforce the authority of the king over the district and the department and to enhance the Ministry of Interior's ability to exercise oversight over the municipalities.[20]

The final result of these debates was a system that, although centralized in the sense that it set up a single, uniform set of rules for all local governmental units subordinated to the central authority, nevertheless allowed for a reasonable amount of decentralization. Under the moderate Constitutional Monarchy established in 1789, the decrees of December 14 and 22, 1789, and the Constitution of 1791 legislated an elective mayor and municipal council (joined by "notables," twice the number of councilors, for certain functions) with little *tutelle*, or administrative oversight, allowed. Under the law of January 8, 1790, moreover, each department was to have an elected assembly of thirty-six councilors who nominated an eight-member executive committee responsible for administration, tax assessments, tax collection, and the departmental budget. The only supervision was to be by an elected *procureur général syndic*, an itinerant officer responsible to the king. Each of the districts was also to have an elective council.

Moderating the effects of this generous decentralization was a highly restrictive franchise: only "active" citizens could vote, that is, those who paid a *contribution*, or tax, equivalent to three days' wages or more. (For the departments, the *contribution* came to ten days' wages.) The vote was in consequence bestowed only on the wealthier members of the bourgeoisie and the upper classes. (The electorate in the departments, for example, would be restricted to about five hundred voters.)[21] Implicit in this restriction of the franchise was the understanding that, if universal suffrage

---

[19]Ibid., p. 48.
[20]Ibid., pp. 45, 48.
[21]It is important to note, however, that the monetary value of a day's wages differed considerably from one district to the next, depending in many cases on the political leanings of those in positions of power. See Godechot, *Institutions*, p. 103.

were to be introduced, it would have to be counterbalanced by an increased *tutelle* or by decreased local liberty. Even so, within the limits of a restricted suffrage, a large degree of decentralization was allowed. The results of this system, by all accounts, were terrible disorganization and a steady increase in the powers of the local collectivity.[22]

The Constituent Assembly's system of decentralized local government was not to last very long. By 1793 two opposing political currents were present in the National Convention: the Jacobins and the Girondins. The Girondin current, in favor of municipal liberty, sought to increase the decentralization demanded by the population at large by destroying all distinctions between "active" and "passive" citizens. The Girondins' Constitution of June 24, 1793, was extremely democratic, demanding universal suffrage and total decentralization. The committee drafting the Constitution was focused more on the ideas of Rousseau, and thus on equality and fraternity, than on the ideas of Montesquieu, separation of powers, and liberty, which were the primary preoccupations of the Constituent Assembly. And it was also concerned with the Girondins' own political interest. The system was one designed to facilitate their stay in power and to undermine the Jacobins' political strength, based mainly in the center. This meant favoring local government in general, but especially the departments, because the October 1792 elections of departmental administrations – the first by universal suffrage, i.e., males of at least twenty-five years of age, residents of the departments for a year, and not servants – produced pro-Girondin majorities in most departments.[23]

The Constitution increased the powers of the departments by adding to their functions and by abolishing the districts at the same time that they reduced the number of members of the general council from thirty-six to eighteen (and the *directoire*, or executive committee, from eight to four). It replaced municipal administrations with *grandes communes*, or large municipalities, measuring four square leagues, which were to mix the Jacobin urban population with the more moderate, rural population, thus diluting the strength of the Jacobins' power base. All of this reinforced the powers of administrative officials. But there was an important counterbalance to this: All administrative officials were to be elected by universal suffrage through a complicated system starting with primary assemblies made up of small groups of citizens numbering between four hundred and nine hundred. These assemblies had the right to censure or hold a referendum on any law or other action taken by local government.[24] This was decentralization with a difference, therefore, because although the

---

[22]Monnet, *Histoire*, p. 160.
[23]Godechot, *Institutions*, pp. 317–19.
[24]Ibid., pp. 276–7.

principle of subordination of the departments to the central government and the communes to the departments was retained, the two levels had a good deal of autonomy in deciding their own affairs, with the citizenry at large as active participants.

The Girondins' Constitution, in brief, democratized as it decentralized local government. But it was never put into operation, despite the fact that it was approved by the population at large by referendum. It was nevertheless to be an important document in the history of French decentralization and democracy, because it was used as a guide by the republicans of 1848 and, in terms of principles and ideas, even the drafters of the 1946 Constitution.[25]

Recentralization under the Jacobins and the Directory

The Girondins' fall from power ended the short legislative history of decentralization under the revolutionaries. In the years to follow, first the Jacobins and then the Directory were to institute highly centralized systems of local government. In each case, the justification was that national unity was paramount and that this required central control in order to fight enemies outside and inside the country. The result was a periphery subject to authoritarian governments with less and less freedom in local government.

The Jacobins opposed the Girondins and their constitution, which they felt was bound to set up a system of federated republics that would destroy national unity and state sovereignty. They reasoned that because the central government was elected by universal suffrage, it necessarily expressed the will of the people. Decentralization would fragment that popular will into its constituent parts. It would also diminish the Jacobins' power, because the Jacobins were much stronger in the center than in the periphery, where they were being challenged not only by the invading armies outside of the new republic, but by the enemies from within. Thus, once certain of their power, they proceeded to reform local government in a way guaranteed to further their own political interests. As opposed to their previous position in the Constituent Assembly, where they pushed for a high degree of decentralization, this meant recentralizing power.

With the organic law of 14 Frimaire, Year II (December 4, 1793), the Jacobins took away most of the departments' powers (the domain of rich bourgeois who had in many instances violently protested the Jacobins' victory over the Girondins in June, 1793), suppressing the general coun-

[25]Ibid., p. 288.

cils, the presidents, and the *procureurs généraux syndics* and leaving only the executive committees with very limited duties. The departments' loss was the more radical districts' gain. They were given wider powers, but put directly under the authority of the Convention, while the elected *procureurs syndics* were replaced with government-appointed agents. The municipalities, which reported to the districts, also found their powers increased as they gained responsibility for public safety and thus the Terror in the provinces. At the same time, however, the districts lost much of their autonomy of action when the elected *procureurs* were replaced with government-appointed agents. By now, local elections had been suspended and the Jacobins, therefore, had total control over the appointment of local governmental officials in the departments, districts, and communes. The Jacobins had put into place a totally centralized system in which local administration was essentially in the hands of governmental agents.

After Thermidor, however, with the end of Jacobin power, local administration changed again, although not to the benefit of democracy or efficiency. Under the Directory, local government lost most of its autonomy. There was no attempt to actualize the goals of the Constitution of 1793. The bourgeoisie had returned to power and would have no truck with the ideas of Rousseau. The Constitution of 5 Fructidor, Year III (August 22, 1795) established a two-tier system of voting: universal suffrage by all citizens (restricted to men, over twenty-one years of age residing in France) who were grouped in cantons (of no more than nine hundred voters) for municipal elections but not for departmental elections. Departmental elections were the sole purview of second-level electors (chosen by universal suffrage), who were of necessity rich, because one of the requirements for candidacy was owning property equivalent to 200 days' labor (or 150 in rural areas).

The Constitution of the Year III nevertheless softened the municipal organization of the previous year by granting some of the municipal liberty demanded by local electorates. The municipal council and the mayor were to be elected by universal suffrage; but now, the mayor could not represent the state. The powers of the mayor were therefore significantly reduced, whereas *commissaires* were appointed by the government to oversee the actions of the mayor and to represent the state in all communes. The mayor was subject to review by a *commissaire* himself subject to hierarchical supervision.

This new dual system of local government was designed to avoid the problems created by the mayor's dual role as representative of the state and executive organ of the commune. But in effect, the decentralized system was almost inoperative, and the *commissaire* had major control over the municipality. It was generally very difficult to find individuals who, even if elected, were willing to serve in the departments and the municipalities. This was especially the case in communes with fewer than five thousand inhabitants, where all that was required was a municipal agent and a deputy (only communes with more than five thousand inhabitants could have a municipal council and a mayor). Often even those who did serve were dismissed for a variety of reasons, whether because of royalist sentiments, for voting against the Constitution in the referendum, or for some other reason.[26]

By now there were eighty-nine metropolitan departments (and eleven colonial departments), which in the meantime had regained their pre-Jacobin powers as well as gained new financial ones. But they were essentially controlled by the government-appointed *commissaire central*, although they did not always accept this control happily.[27] Moreover, the *districts* had disappeared, mainly because of their role in the Terror of the Year II, with their functions taken over to some extent by cantonal administrations with an elected president and the ever-present government-appointed *commissaire*. These new cantonal administrations, though, were an unmitigated disaster, which functioned very poorly. According to Godechot, their sole contribution was a negative one, because they only hastened the end of any real rural communal political life by accustoming the peasants to the administration from afar that they would experience under the military dictatorship of Napoleon.[28] These cantons, in any case, did not outlast the Directory.

The system established by the Directory in the Constitution of the Year III, designed to avoid the disorganization of the Constitution of 1791 and the extreme centralization of the organic law of the Year II, succeeded only in maintaining extreme centralization and extreme disorganization with the proliferation of many useless administrative bodies.[29] Nonetheless, it was with this system, along with the previous one of the Jacobins, that centralization took hold. It is important to note that in 1794, the word "centralization" entered the French political vocabulary.[30] The word "decentralization," by contrast, would not enter the vocabulary until the 1820s.[31] Decentralization was nearly inconceivable in the period in-between, especially during the Napoleonic era.

[26]Ibid., pp. 472–4.
[27]Ibid., pp. 470–2.
[28]Ibid., p. 476.
[29]This period saw a tremendous increase in the number of personnel in local administration, as well as a real change in who was in office. See Denis Woronoff, *La République bourgeoise de thermidor à brumaire 1794–1799* (Paris: Seuil, 1972), pp. 51–5.
[30]Burdeau, *Libertés*, p. 49.
[31]Ibid., p. 69.

The systematization of centralization under Napoleon

Napoleon, under the Consulate and the Empire, accomplished what the Jacobins and the Directory could not: the systematization of centralization. Napoleon continued the pattern of increasing centralization in the periphery begun by the Jacobins in 1793 and extended by the Directory, although he returned to the basic outlines of the administrative organization and structure of 1790.

During the Consulate, the Constitution of the Year VIII (December 15, 1799) and the law of 28 Pluviôse, Year VIII (February 17, 1800) established that all communes were to have a mayor and municipal council, with the number of deputy mayors varying according to the size of the commune. After the Year XII only Paris was left outside of the common law – divided into twelve municipal arrondissements, each with its own mayor and two deputy mayors. These laws gave back to the mayor his dual role, but simultaneously destroyed even the appearance of decentralization. Napoleon's newly created prefect, now the executive power in the department, chose the mayors and the deputy mayors (from within the municipal council, as of the Year X) in communes with fewer than five thousand inhabitants and recommended names to the emperor for the larger communes. He had the power to suspend mayors, deputy mayors, and municipal councils in communes with fewer than five thousand inhabitants. He also had the *tutelle administrative*, or a priori review power, over all decisions of the communes.

Universal suffrage remained as a symbol without any true effect: Sieyès devised a system as of the Year VIII in which the citizens elected a tenth of their number (approximately six hundred thousand) to an electoral list from which the government would choose its municipal officials. The tenth elected by universal suffrage would in turn elect a tenth of their number (between fifty and sixty thousand) from which departmental officials would be chosen. These in turn would elect a tenth of their number to make up the national list from which national officials would be chosen. Because these *listes de notabilités* were large, the government had virtual freedom in its choice of mayor, municipal council, and general council of the department.

The Constitution of the Year X introduced a small measure of democracy into this system by changing the election procedures. Napoleon disliked the *listes de notabilités,* preferring to give the citizenry more of an illusion of popular sovereignty in order to make his dictatorship more palatable. In this new system all citizens of a canton became electors in a cantonal asssembly responsible for choosing the members for life of the electoral colleges of the arrondissements (numbering between 120 and 200 and responsible for electing two candidates for each vacant seat in

the legislative corps, in the *Tribunat,* and in the council of the arrondissement) and of the departments (numbering 600 and responsible for electing two candidates for each vacant seat on the legislative corps, in the
Senate, and in the general council of the department). In addition, the
cantonal assemblies elected two candidates for the positions of justice of
the peace and of municipal councilor in communes of more than five
thousand inhabitants, whereas they directly elected muncipal councilors
in smaller communes.[32]

But these were small concessions in a system in which the prefect, often
dubbed the *empereur au petit pied* because of his authoritarian role, was
in complete control of the local governmental system as head of the
department. Although Napoleon retained the departmental organization
of 1790, even imposing it on the newly conquered territories as well, he
completely revised the department's administrative structure. The prefect
(carefully chosen from the *listes de notabilités*) was in sole command of
what continued to be the key level of government in the periphery. He
was assisted by a general council (elected by the departmental electoral
college consisting mainly of former administrative officials and rich landowners) and by a prefectoral council appointed by the head of state, but
of similar composition. Neither council, however, had any administrative
powers or any real impact on local government.[33]

The prefect was the department. He extended his control over the
locality through the subprefect, who was appointed by Napoleon and
was in charge of a new intermediate level between the departments and
the communes: the arrondissement, which recalled the districts of 1790
but was somewhat larger. The subprefect was charged with carrying out
the orders of the prefect and with overseeing the administration of the
municipalities. He was to be assisted by the council of the arrondissement
(chosen from the two candidates elected by the electoral college of the
arrondissement and consisting, again, mainly of former administrative
officials and of large-scale farmers). But this council was as inconsequen-
tial as those at the departmental level.[34]

The mayors of the communes were last in the chain of command that
went from Napoleon through the prefects and subprefects. Their role was
an important one, because the mayors retained all the powers gained in
previous periods. They, too, were assisted by a council, the municipal
council, which was as ineffective as the other councils. But the mayor had
no real independence, because he was beholden to the prefect for his job,
and he was closely watched by the prefecture or the subprefecture. This

[32]Godechot, *Institutions,* pp. 573–4.
[33]For further detail, see ibid., pp. 589–92.
[34]Ibid., pp. 592–5.

meant that the mayorality, lacking the appeal of local election, looked like a job with few rewards and many headaches, especially in the smaller communes. Rural mayors often felt caught between their loyalty to their fellow villagers and their obligation to follow the directives of the central government, especially in cases such as conscription, which they generally did everything in their power to thwart, thereby running afoul of the prefect.[35] In consequence, it was relatively easy to find mayors for the larger communes (recruited from among former administrative officials and merchants). It was much more difficult, just as under the Directory, in the rural communes (numbering approximately forty thousand to begin with and only slightly diminished after attempts to consolidate them).[36] It is telling that, when Napoleon returned in the One Hundred Days, intent on gaining as much support as possible in the periphery, he established the election of mayors and deputy mayors in communes of fewer than five thousand inhabitants.

In the years after the Revolution a centralized system of local government was instituted that went far beyond that of the monarchy. But Napoleon had really only streamlined a system put into effect by the Jacobins in 1793. And this system was to last for a very long time.

THE CONTINUING HISTORY OF CENTRALIZATION BETWEEN 1815 AND 1871

Between the years 1815 and 1830, under the Restoration, the essentials of the Napoleonic system of local government were retained despite the fact that there was a great deal of debate favoring decentralization, with the right seeking to expand the powers of the departments, the left to institute local elections. Even though some loosening up of the system did occur under the July Monarchy between 1830 and 1848, it did not significantly reduce governmental centralization or alter the organizing principles underlying the Napleonic legislation of the Year VIII.[37] The mayor continued to be appointed by the government (albeit from within the municipal council) and the prefect continued to control local affairs through the department. The fact that a restricted local electorate gained the right to elect members of the municipal council during this period, however, did make a difference for local government. It opened up local politics to a significant portion of the population and gave local elected

[35] See Stephen Van Holde, "Recruitment in Revolutionary France." Paper prepared for delivery at the National Meetings of the American Political Science Association, Atlanta, Ga. (Aug. 31–Sept. 3, 1989).
[36] Godechot, *Institutions,* pp. 595–9.
[37] Ducrocq, *Études,* p. 116.

officials a political legitimacy that offset the prefect's administrative powers, thus spelling the beginning of the relationship of mutual dependence that was to come into its own during the Third Republic.[38]

Only during the Second Republic was the general history of continuing centralization to change, but just for a short time. Once again, decentralizing laws were passed in the initial moments of crisis, only to be followed by recentralizing legislation as soon as governmental control was no longer in doubt. The one lasting gain was that local councils were to be elected by universal suffrage. But this had little significance, because in the Second Empire the prefects' powers were reinforced and the mayors were again appointed by the government, now from outside or inside the municipal council.

Throughout this period legislators' attitudes toward decentralization and their failure to reform the Napoleonic system continued to be related to questions of personal power and incumbency, with the very same politicians who argued for decentralization while out of power opposing it once in power. Political interest, in brief, was elevated to principle, with support for decentralization dependent upon the various parties' sense of how it would first and foremost affect their own prospects.

Continuing centralization under the Restoration

Under the Restoration the basic organization of the Napoleonic system was maintained and, in some respects, intensified, because even the illusion of universal suffrage in local council elections was set aside. The central government appointed the general councilors, councilors of the arrondissements, municipal councilors, mayors (from outside or inside the municipal council – as it saw fit), and, of course, the prefects and subprefects.

During this period there was much debate over the need to reform this system, but little action. Between 1817 and 1820 the Chamber of Deputies discussed the matter of decentralization a great deal and seriously considered a decentralizing proposal in 1821 and again in 1829; but all of this came to nought. The liberal proposals of the parliamentary commission in 1819, which considered allowing the local election of municipal and departmental councilors, were abandoned as a reaction to the assassination of the duc de Berry and to the fall of Descazes, the minister responsible for promoting reform. The government's 1821 proposal only complicated the system without liberalizing anything and was ultimately tabled.[39] The Martignac proposal of 1828–9 recommended the local

[38]See the discussion in Part II, Chapter 6, under "The informal decentralization of local governmental processes."
[39]Monnet, *Histoire*, pp. 359–63.

election of municipal and general councilors by a restricted electorate – in communes of fewer than five hundred there would be no more than thirty voters from those who paid the highest taxes. However, it went too far for the right, which was against even the idea of election, and not far enough for the liberal left. The project was so modified by the left, which demanded an electorate of all citizens over twenty-one years of age (twenty-five for departmental councilors) who paid taxes of three hundred francs or more as well as an end to the arrondissements pure and simple, that the minister himself withdrew it.[40]

During the Restoration as a whole, members of the ultra right were the most vocal in support of decentralization, focusing mainly on increasing the power of the periphery at the departmental level. Members of the liberal left, by contrast, were much less heard on the topic until the very end of the regime, although when they did speak, it was primarily in favor of municipal power and local elections.

The ultras on the right, in particular, were concerned with decentralization, seeing the Napoleonic system of centralization, especially after the One Hundred Days, as the single most dangerous threat to the monarchy. Between 1816 and 1820, the ultras in the Chamber of Deputies such as Villèle, Corbière, and others condemned the size, cost, and power of the administrative bureaucracy, as well as the predominance of Paris to the detriment of the rest of the country. Although the ultras would have preferred that the departments be grouped into larger units reminiscent of the traditional provinces, the departmental level was nevertheless where they focused their arguments for increased local power, specifically the power of the general council. As nobles based primarily in the periphery, they felt this would help solidify the hold of the monarchy over the countryside and, quite naturally, their own hold as well. And they were therefore disappointed with the projected law on municipal and departmental organization presented to the Chamber on February 22, 1821, because it made no reference to the general councils. Only Villèle and Corbière were satisfied with the projected law, having become ministers without porfolio and, following the typical pattern, no longer so keen on decentralization.[41]

By the end of the year, once Villèle became Minister of the Interior and Corbière, Minister of Finance, they made clear their opposition to decentralization, with Corbière stating that, for the moment, "it is impossible to change the administration of France," and with Villèle insisting that administrative reform had to wait until the moral and social forces in the provinces were reequilibrated. As François Burdeau recently put it, "A

[40]Ibid., pp. 363–70.
[41]Burdeau, *Libertés*, pp. 75–80.

decentralizer turned minister is not necessarily a decentralizing minister."[42] And the reason, as usual, was that decentralization was no longer in the legislators' political interest. In 1815 Villèle had been the head of the majority in opposition to the government: decentralization, therefore, would have served his purposes well. In 1821, by contrast, it could not, because he was a minister governing against a majority composed of liberals and moderates.[43] Needless to say, the rest of the ultras were not at all pleased with Villèle's turnabout and throughout the 1820s pushed for more radical reform involving the replacement of the departments with "larges centralisations provinciales" to become real intermediary powers between Paris and the communes.[44]

Whereas the goal of the right, as the liberal de Girardin put it at the time, was to "displace centralization, displacing it from the government in order to replace it in the *chefs-lieux* of our departments," that of the left, he suggested, was not to destroy national centralization but simply to harmonize it with constitutional institutions.[45] The liberal left, in effect, put most of its faith in local elections and municipal power. But it was generally much less of a presence in the debates on decentralization throughout the Restoration, in part because of an unwillingness to appear to make common cause with the ultras. There are many examples of liberals who, like Benjamin Constant, wrote in favor of municipal power and local elections but did little in the Chamber of Deputies to promote these views. J. M. Duvergier de Hauranne was an exception when, in the Chamber in 1818 and 1819, he repeatedly called for reforms involving local elections for the municipal council, although not for the general councils of the departments, but to no avail.[46] This lack of concern about the departmental level was to change only with the debate on the Martignac proposal in 1829, when the liberal left pushed for a wider franchise in departmental elections than the government would allow.

Nothing was to come of these discussions, however, until the change in regime. Interestingly enough, the debate in society at large over decentralization was much more significant under the Restoration than under the July Monarchy. Whereas during the Restoration forty-five works appeared on administrative organization (twenty-six of these in its very last years), only seventeen appeared through the July Monarchy.[47] This is probably because the modest reforms that were put through seemed to satisfy most parties to the debate, even though they did not go nearly as

[42]Ibid., pp. 80–1.
[43]Monnet, *Histoire*, pp. 360–1.
[44]Burdeau, *Libertés*, p. 82.
[45]Ibid., p. 89.
[46]Ibid., pp. 83–6.
[47]Ibid., pp. 96–7.

far as many had demanded under the previous regime. The liberals, in opposition throughout the Restoration, gained power in the July Monarchy and, much like previous governments, were no longer as keen on decentralization as before. Again, the more certain a government became of its power, the less willing it was to make decentralizing concessions. But in this instance the reversal was not as dramatic because the liberals had never been very radical in their proposals for reform.

Minor reform under the July Monarchy

In any event, it was under the July Monarchy of Louis Philippe that the first decentralizing laws were promulgated since the Girondin Constitution of 1793. The laws of March 21, 1831, June 22, 1833, and the organic law of 1837 gave a restricted local electorate the right to elect the municipal council in the commune and gave the commune itself separate legal status, with its own attributes, with the right to settle certain matters on its own and to deliberate on others, and with the right to buy, sell, and own property. But although the commune was no longer an administrative unit of the state, the government retained the right to nominate the mayor, albeit now from within the municipal council, and maintained a strict *tutelle* over the actions of the mayor. Any mayoral directive, for example, had to wait one month for prefectoral approval before it could be put into application. Paris, as usual, remained outside the common law, divided into twelve arrondissements, each with its own mayor and two deputy mayors.

At the departmental level, the prefect remained the executive power, although the decision-making powers of the general council were extended by the law of May 10, 1838, at the same time that the department was legally turned into a true local collectivity from the administrative unit it had been since 1811. But the recommendation that the general council be allowed to exercise some *tutelle* over the municipal councils in the place of the prefect was rejected, as were many other recommendations for extending its powers. The departments continued to be perceived as a threat, this time from the legitimist right; the perennial fears of the departments becoming federated republics resurfaced. The law in consequence contained proscriptions against general councils meeting outside of regular sessions, against general councils from different departments meeting together, and against general councils discussing issues outside their particular sphere of competence.[48]

The delays in voting the laws reflected the divisions among the liberal majority as to how much power to give local governments. These delays

[48]Sautel, *Institutions*, pp. 489–90.

were further helped by the government, which the more time passed and memories of 1830 receded, was less willing to change the system. Thus, the reforms it would allow in 1833, such as giving municipal councils decision-making powers in six areas, were not acceptable in 1834, when such powers were reduced to only two areas. The Chamber of Peers, moreover, tended to support the government in its efforts to undermine the reforming zeal of the Chamber of Deputies.[49] In addition, those who had recently come to power argued as usual against many aspects of decentralization even though they had themselves demanded them during the Restoration.[50] The opposition to any attempt to abolish the councils of the arrondissements was the best example of this.

The only consensus among the legislators of the majority was on the principle of election for local government; but even here there was a great deal of disagreement as to how it should translate in terms of the size and nature of the electorate. Odilon Barrot, the great promoter of decentralization, wanted to allow municipal governments increased powers and an expanded electorate consisting of all the *contribuables,* or taxpayers, for the election of all local councils. Thiers, the apostle of administrative centralization, by contrast, found that any such decentralization would risk creating "thirty-seven thousand small states" and would allow the birth of new fiefdoms. Barrot's response was that centralization had already destroyed communal existence, "leaving nothing but individuals, nothing but 33 million Frenchmen in the presence of an all-powerful government."[51]

Outside of the rhetorical flourishes, of which there were many, the discussion remained quite vague, with little definition of terms as centralizers and decentralizers on both the left and right talked past one another. On the republican left, there were actually many more centralizers in the Jacobin tradition than decentralizers, and understandably so, given a history in which the periphery had shown itself to be much less republican than the center. Cormenin, for example, wrote a book in 1842 that warned people against decentralization, maintaining that "centralization is France itself" and that while Paris is the intellectual head of the country, the provinces "are nothing but the feet."[52] And although Louis Blanc did want an end to the "suffocating regime" resulting from the Orleanist administrative centralization, he was concerned about national unity and admiring of centralization, certain that if properly administered it could coexist with communal liberty. In the end the republican left was quite moderate in its support for local liberty, focusing more on decentraliza-

[49]Burdeau, *Libertés,* pp. 98–9
[50]Monnet, *Historie,* p. 444.
[51]Burdeau, *Libertés,* p. 100.
[52]Ibid., pp. 115–16.

tion at the communal level, but never suggesting that local governments become powers in their own right, because this would entail that they become counter-powers to the national government.[53]

By contrast, the decentralizers on the right, made up of the legitimists who were the successors to the ultras under the Restoration, were the only ones interested in giving local governments real powers. They now saw decentralization as a way of ensuring the return of the legitimate monarch to national power and of the nobles to local power.[54] Among decentralizing liberals on the right we find de Tocqueville condemning centralization in principle but doing little to fight it and finding the reforms of the July Monarchy themselves quite adequate.[55] Despite the fact that he had roundly condemned centralization by implication in *Democracy in America,* de Tocqueville actually numbered himself among those ambivalent about centralization. In commenting on his own verbal liberalism and that of his friends, he requested not to be asked "to explain this subtle taste; it must be experienced." Others, however, did not find this taste so subtle, among them Georges Hanotaux, who writing in 1903 insisted that "if we go to the bottom of things, this means that the opposition is constrained by the excesses of governmental authority, finding them unjust and intolerable up until the moment at which the opposition itself is in a position to commit them in turn."[56] This certainly appeared to be the case for the Orleanists, who opposed any decentralization that could undermine their hegemony.

The main question for the majority was, To what extent will local elections help expedite administrative business and maintain the stability of the regime? The answer was a compromise that essentially consecrated the reform proposals of 1829, primarily because the particular electorate it selected ensured the liberals' control of the local councils. For municipal elections, as of the law of 1831, the electorate consisted of those eligible to vote on the basis of two kinds of qualifications. First, there were those eligible by virtue of their payment of the *cens* (direct taxes), which in the smallest communes was set at an amount that would include the most highly taxed tenth of the inhabitants and in the larger communes was set to include decreasing proportions of the inhabitants. These electors were joined by those eligible by virtue of their *capacité,* that is, members of the liberal professions such as lawyers, professors, and doctors, as well as governmental officials, military officers, judges, merchants and members of the chambers of commerce, and so forth. (Paris

[53]Ibid., pp. 116–18.
[54]Ibid., pp. 108–13.
[55]Ibid., pp. 118–26.
[56]Georges Hanotaux, *Histoire de la France contemporaine* (Paris: Société d'éditions contemporaines, 1903), vol. 3, p. 123.

had to wait until 1834 to be able to vote by this system.) For departmental elections, as of the law of 1833, the electorate was to be the same as that for deputies, that is, citizens paying a *cens* of two hundred francs and those eligible by virtue of their *capacité,* thereby increasing the electorate by another eighth.

Even with this restricted electorate, the new laws made a difference. According to Tudesq, "the electoral law of March 21, 1831, contributed more than any other piece of legislation to the democratization of political life under a regime that was not at all democratic and to the apprenticeship for a representative regime."[57] The municipal law enfranchised close to 2 million electors and democratized in many instances the electorate and their elected representatives, bringing the *petite bourgeoisie* (lower middle class) as well as the *bourgeoisie moyenne* (middle-middle class) into local politics, especially in the more rural areas where the eligibility requirement of the *cens* often fell well below twenty francs. The politicization of this electorate was apparent from the first municipal elections, which eliminated the largest landowners from the municipal council in a number of departments. But it was even clearer from the number of *petits bourgeois* and *moyens bourgeois* agitating for the extension of the right to vote in 1839 and from the increasing politicization of urban municipal elections toward the end of the regime.[58]

Thus, even though a reasonable amount of apathy remained in municipal elections (in 1834, only 56 percent of the electors voted), the change in the law governing municipal elections opened local politics up to a significant portion of the local population. This democratization, according to André-Jean Tudesq, explains why the transition in 1848 to universal suffrage was not the abrupt shift at the communal level that it was at the national level.[59] It was, in the words of Maurice Agulhon, the beginning of the "descent of politics toward the masses,"[60] even if it didn't descend very far and even if the results in the first municipal elections of the Second Republic produced conservative municipal councils in the rural regions and small towns that encompassed the large majority of the population.[61]

Establishing the local election of the local councils and allowing those with *capacités* and those with property to sit, as well as to vote, ensured a modicum of democratization in local government. But this was still basi-

---

[57]André-Jean Tudesq, *La Démocratie en France depuis 1815* (Paris: Presses universitaires de France, 1971), pp. 50–1.

[58]Ibid., pp. 59–60. For the continuing electoral strength of the very rich in municipal government, see André-Jean Tudesq, *Les Grands Notables (1840–1849)* (Paris: Presses universitaires de France, 1964), pp. 1,108–39.

[59]Ibid., pp. 50–2.

[60]Maurice Agulhon, *La République au village* (Paris: Plon, 1970), p. 259.

[61]Tudesq, *Démocratie,* p. 54.

cally decentralization to the benefit of the highly privileged, if no longer always titled.

Decentralization under the Second Republic

Only with the Revolution of 1848 and the short-lived Second Republic did decentralization really take hold again, if only for a very short time. Universal suffrage became effective for all local elections. For a brief period, between February and May 1848, the prefectoral corps was even abolished in name, with prefects now called *commissaires de la République* and responsible for several departments. The decree of July 3, 1848 established that general councilors were to be elected by canton, whereas the decrees of July 3–11, 1848, determined that in communes of fewer than six thousand inhabitants, the mayor would be elected by the municipal council and in larger communes, the mayor would be appointed by the government from within the municipal council.[62] Although the *tutelle* was retained, some modicum of local freedom was ensured.

The government was considering further reform when the coup d'état of Louis Napoleon intervened. The commission on decentralization, set up to revise all the laws governing local administration and to create a new code of interior administration, had proposed greater powers for the various local councils, although it had basically left the administrative structures as they had been established by the decrees of 1848. As a result, the great promise of the Revolution of 1848, which many initially thought would produce a highly decentralized system, thus fulfilling the desires of the Girondins, was never realized, even on paper.

Part of the reason for the lack of radical decentralizing reform during the Second Republic was that the support for reform came more from the periphery than from the center. The movement in favor of decentralization was based primarily in the provinces. Newly certain of their own powers as a result of the conservative victory in the elections by universal suffrage of the Constituent Assembly in April 1848, the provinces were reacting against the continued violence in Paris, especially during the June days. According to Burdeau, the provinces rejected centralization because it concentrated national authority in a city that threatened the maintenance of legal order.[63] The results were calls by some to move the seat of government from the city and threats by others that the departments would secede if order was not restored. The less extreme, however, saw the only answer to the problem as that of increasing the powers of local

[62]Ducroq, *Études*, p. 119; Monnet, *Histoire*, p. 444; and Léon Morgand, *La Loi municipale* (Paris: Berger-Levrault, 1906), p. 498.
[63]Burdeau, *Libertés*, p. 139.

governments, for example, by giving the departments legislative powers or, at least in times of crisis, by allowing them to form a high council with political powers in cases in which the constitutional powers could not properly exercise their functions.[64] None of these suggestions bore fruit.

As the threat of violence in Paris receded, so did enthusiasm for decentralization. A year later, the Conseil d'Etat, which was charged with preparing the projected law on local administration, consulted with the prefects, general councils, and municipalities with over twenty thousand inhabitants. It found that a majority of local elected officials did not want any increase in their powers nor even their own election by the popularly elected municipal council, but that they did favor an increase in the powers of the prefects.[65] The notables wanted deconcentration, not decentralization. And this should not be too surprising, given that the notables were themselves empowered by this particular system and that most had become used to the particular balance of power between the prefects and themselves – under the July Monarchy as much as under the Second Republic. Giving the prefects greater deconcentrated powers and authority thus would make the centralized system more responsive to the local notables and more efficient by virtue of its being closer to the periphery.

At the center the response to decentralization was cautious from the beginning. The main concerns when the debates on the decrees of July 1848 took place were ones involved in coordinating the laws of 1831 and 1833 with universal suffrage. The debates about local government during the discussion of the Constitution of November 4, 1848, although they were much more involved because they took up all the old arguments, ended with no basic changes in the system. Thus, even though Odilon Barrot's proposal to solve the problem of the proliferation of communes by regrouping them into cantons while abolishing the arrondissements (a replay of the 1830 discussions) was written into the constitution, it was never implemented.[66]

Part of the reason for the timidity of the reforms was the divisions within both the right and the left. On the right, the conservative republicans, who had been liberals under the previous regime, were divided. Although some such as Barrot actively sought to promote decentralization, others did very little, such as de Tocqueville, who was in a position to put his anti-centralization ideas into practice as a member of the constitutional commission, but again did nothing to promote decentralization. Yet others remained defenders of centralization, such as Vivien, who was also a mem-

[64]Ibid., pp. 138–42.
[65]Ibid., p. 142. For the report of the *Conseil d'État*, see *Moniteur Universel*, Supplement to no. 358 (Dec. 24, 1850).
[66]Sautel, *Institutions*, pp. 498–9.

ber of the constitutional commission, and Thiers. For the liberals in general, decentralization was conditioned by the tension between their interest in defending liberty and and in maintaining social order. Because they trusted the central power more than local governments to maintain order, decentralization remained a secondary consideration.[67]

By contrast, for the legitimists on the right, decentralization was a central concern. Now, more than ever, they found local liberty to be the key to the salvation of a France that had gone socialist, nay communist, at the center, in Paris. The legitimist response to the election in Paris of the "communist" Eugène Sue was to ask, "How much longer must we be subjected to this shameful yoke of the new Sodom? Are we to wait until the poison from this infected center has circulated all the way to the extremities and corrupted the whole of France?"[68] During the debates on the Constitution, legitimists such as Béchard spoke eloquently for allowing local elected officials sole responsibility for the administration of local interests. But this suggestion came to nothing, as did the later one of the legitimist Raudot, who proposed a highly decentralized system that separated national from local interests at the departmental level by making the prefect an exclusive agent of the government and by having the general council, together with a delegate elected by it as executive agent, represent the department and exercise the *tutelle* over the communes. Mayors were to be chosen by the municipal council in all communes. The proposal was sent for study to the commission on decentralization, and buried.[69]

As time passed many of the legitimists lost their faith in decentralization as the countryside became more republican and socialist. By February 1851 a portion of the "troops of the Comte de Chambord" no longer supported the local election of the mayor. Political interest, even for some on the far right, had already replaced political principle. But to be fair the main principle for the legitimists was to conserve themselves by reinforcing the authority of the land-owning classes and the influence of the clergy. Decentralization remained a principle only insofar as it could further this end.[70]

On the left, just as much as on the right, there was considerable division. Although there were those who favored decentralization, the Jacobins were still well represented, and understandably so. The provinces had just voted for a conservative government and were generally hostile to Paris and to the left. Moreover, in the face of an extreme right claiming decentralization for itself, even the more decentralizing leftists were hard

---

[67]Burdeau, *Libertés,* pp. 147–50, 155.
[68]*Journal de Rennes,* May 4, 1850, quoted in Burdeau, *Libertés,* p. 143.
[69]Sautel, *Institutions,* p. 500; and Burdeau, *Libertés,* pp. 144–5.
[70]Burdeau, *Libertés,* pp. 146, 156.

put to defend their position. This was clearly easier for revolutionaries in the provinces, where one social democrat complained: "The provinces are the Ireland of France."[71] Even at the center, however, a number of decentralizers remained, such as Lamennais, who felt that centralization produced apoplexy at the center and paralysis in the periphery; he therefore argued for an elected mayor and municipal council as well as an elected departmental president and administration with the equivalent of powers of the *tutelle* over the communes.[72] In the debates on the Constitution, numerous members of the left criticized the government's centralizing tendencies, just as they did later in the discussion of the work of the commission on decentralization.

Nonetheless, the majority of the left was in favor of centralization and defended it, for example, in the constitutional commission. For most the attacks on Paris in the first months set the stage for a continued defense of Jacobinism. Blanqui in the first months of the Second Republic, for example, proclaimed: "Paris is the head, the provinces the intestines."[73] Even Louis Blanc, who had been hostile to Paris and centralization during the July Monarchy, didn't find it so bad under the current set of circumstances. For the centralizing left, liberty and equality could best be defended by a strong state, especially because the state that identified with Paris appeared to be more to the left, or at least more enlightened, than local governments during this period.

In any event, despite the divisions on the left and the right on the issue of centralization, a reasonable amount of decentralization was legislated, helped by the fact that governmental control remained uncertain. But this situation was not to last for long. Nevertheless, as long as it lasted, it assured much more local liberty than the system that was to follow under the Second Empire.

Recentralization under the Second Empire

After the coup d'état of Napoleon III, local liberties were again suspended. Louis Napoleon in many respects went back to the system of the First Empire. This time, however, universal manhood suffrage was retained for the election of the municipal and general councils. But it was accompanied by a highly centralized system of mayoral selection and an extremely heavy-handed prefectoral role as executive of the department. By Article 57 of the Constitution of January 4, 1852, and the law of July 7, 1852, the executive gained the power to appoint the mayor even from

---

[71]E. Gorges, *Organisation de la commune en France* (1848), p. 14, quoted in Burdeau, *Libertés*, p. 150.

[72]Burdeau, *Libertés*, p. 151.

[73]Ibid., p. 150.

outside the municipal council.[74] The central government had the power to dissolve the municipal councils and to replace them with an ad hoc commission until the next set of elections. Paris had even less liberty, because its municipal council was to be appointed by the emperor and, in 1859, it was cut into twenty arrondissements, each with its own appointed mayor and two deputy mayors.

During the Second Empire the prefects became the *préfets à poigne,* famous for dominating local politics and administration as electoral agents for the central government and as keepers of the peace. Throughout the Second Empire, the powers of the prefect tended only to grow and those of local elected governments to decline. With the law of March 25, 1852, the prefect's powers at the departmental level were expanded through deconcentration. Successive legislation in such areas as public works, highways, water, railways, game, hospitals, local finance, and communal affairs only added to those powers.[75] By the law of May 5, 1855, the *tutelle* was reinforced. The prefect could now suspend or revoke any mayor for a period of one year. This period was extended to three years by the law of July 24, 1867.[76]

By the 1860s, in response to this extreme centralization, a lively set of debates had started on the issue of decentralization. Between 1860 and 1870, twenty-four books were published with the word decentralization in the title, and seventy-seven works addressed the issue of administrative reform of local government.[77] The interest in decentralization was especially high in the provinces, where a number of reform proposals originated. Primary among these was the Nancy program, published by a number of notables from the Lorraine in 1865, who proposed radical reforms of local government. This program gained the support of a wide variety of members of the opposition, from legitimists, to Orleanists and republicans, and started a nationwide debate on the issue of decentralization. The proposal recommended the reinforcement of the powers of the commune; the replacement of the arrondissement with the canton; the "liberation" of the department, which was to administer itself and to exercise, along with the canton, the *tutelle* over the communes; and the limitation of the prefect's role to "politics," i.e., only those things related to relations with the central government.[78]

In the legislature, on the right, the legitimists were, as always, in favor

[74]Monnet, *Histoire*, p. 445; and Morgand, *Loi*, p. 499.
[75]Brian Chapman, *The Prefects and Provincial France* (London: George Allen & Unwin, 1955), p. 44.
[76]Ducroq, *Études*, p. 201; and Monnet, *Histoire*, p. 446.
[77]Burdeau, *Libertés*, p. 162.
[78]Sautel, *Institutions*, pp. 504–5. For the reaction to the program, see Burdeau, *Libertés*, pp. 168–74. See also Odette Voilliard, "Autour du programme de Nancy (1865)," in *Régions*, Gras and Livet, pp. 287–302.

of decentralization. And their arguments remained the same as in the past. The Orleanists were again somewhat divided on the issue, with Thiers, for example, remaining true to centralization and Barrot to decentralization. Some liberals, however, who were lukewarm at best on decentralization in the Second Republic and before, became proponents of it. Thus, Vivien, a defender of centralization during the Second Republic, was one of the first to switch sides, arguing in the 1852 edition of his *Études administratives* that decentralization was necessary to develop the seeds of liberty contained in the legislation of the July Monarchy, to extend the proposals of the Commission on Decentralization of the Second Republic, to give more power to the departments, and to create a regional level of government. And Vivien was followed by others, including the duc de Broglie, who in a book written in 1859, seized by the police in 1861, and finally republished in 1870, praised the British system of self-government and argued for giving local elites responsibility not only for functions emanating from local administration but also for those traditionally considered part of the state purview at the local level.[79]

Most on the left also rallied around decentralization, which is not to say that the left agreed with the right on the exact form decentralization was to take. Many members of the left were wary, for example, of the Nancy program, because it recommended giving tremendous powers to the departments, which were traditionally controlled by the aristocracy and the upper *bourgeoisie*. Instead, they argued primarily in favor of communal liberties.[80] Jules Simon, for one, wrote in 1859 that: "There will be no liberty in France until there are men; there will be no men until there are communes; there will be no communes until we have in reality efficaciously decentralized."[81] Jules Ferry similarly stated in 1858: "France will not have liberty so long as she lives under the chains of administrative centralization."[82] The left's principled stance in favor of decentralization was only reinforced by the Second Empire's use of the official candidature, which sought to mobilize the administration to ensure that the elections would return a progovernment majority.

Even Louis Napoleon claimed to be in favor of decentralization, starting in 1858. But he, just as most Bonapartists, was not interested in any significant amount of decentralization. Most Bonapartists' views were reflected in the book by Dupont-White entitled *L'Individu et l'État,* a panegyric for centralization. Nevertheless, the government itself set the study of reform in motion in 1863, with members such as Rouher a year

[79]Burdeau, *Libertés,* pp. 160–1.
[80]See the discussion in Burdeau, *Libertés,* pp. 173–4.
[81]Ibid., p. 161.
[82]Ibid., p. 177.

later praising the reform in the works.[83] The result was the law of July 18, 1866, which provided for some liberalization of local government by conferring on the general councils of the departments increased decision-making powers not always subject to prior ministerial approval. But it did not allow them to choose their own presidents and executive bureaus. The municipal law of July 24, 1867 did much the same for the communes by enlarging the municipal councils' decision-making powers and allowing many decisions of the mayor to be immediately put into effect, without prior approval of the prefect.[84]

It was only with the law of July 22, 1870, in response to a deteriorating political situation, that the government diminished municipal centralization very slightly by allowing the appointment of the mayor solely from within the municipal council.[85] It similarly increased the powers of the general council of the department with the law of July 23, 1870, by allowing that council to elect its *bureau*, or executive committee. But the government would not give in on a variety of other issues, such as a left-inspired proposal that mayors be elected by the municipal council, the demand that the sessions of local councils be made public, or that political opinions be allowed to be heard in such sessions.[86] The measures the government did give in on, in any event, did not save it from defeat.

The Government of National Defense, by the decree of September 25, 1870, set up a highly decentralized administrative system. The mayor was to be elected by the municipal council in all communes and the municipal council was to be elected by universal suffrage. But the government, after having dissolved all municipal and general councils, suspended all elections, given the state of war, and actually proceeded to appoint all members of provisional municipal and departmental commissions. Although the appointees were republicans in the main, the action was seen as highly centralizing and was roundly condemned throughout the country, especially by notables on the right.[87] The response was the most extreme in Paris, already in a state of siege, where rioting followed calls for free local elections and municipal freedom on October 31, 1870. In November, by way of appeasement, Paris was allowed to hold local elections for its mayors and deputy mayors by universal suffrage. The administration of the city, however, was still controlled by the central government by means of the appointment of a central mayor.[88] Paris, in any event, was soon to

[83]Ibid., p. 164.
[84]Sautel, *Institutions*, pp. 505–6.
[85]Monnet, *Histoire*, p. 447; and Morgand, *Loi*, p. 501.
[86]Sautel, *Institutions*, pp. 506–7.
[87]See the discussion in Burdeau, *Libertés*, pp. 189–90.
[88]Sautel, *Institutions*, pp. 507–9.

take matters into its own hands, with the declaration of the Paris Commune on March 18, 1871.

In the Paris Commune, the extreme left was completely behind decentralization insofar as it represented support for local autonomy and a protest against imperial and monarchical centralization. Most members of the municipal government of the Commune of Paris, however neo-Jacobin some of them might have been with regard to the exercise of power within Paris, agreed as to the necessity of a thoroughgoing decentralization in France once it was pacified. They felt that political unity would be based on the federation of all emancipated urban centers with Paris.[89]

The Commune of Paris was eventually defeated. The Government of National Defense was disbanded. And the Third Republic, which took its place while the Commune was still raging, returned to power a much more conservative set of legislators, much less enamoured on the whole of local freedom, at least in the form it had taken with the Paris Commune. Once again, as a commentator fifteen years later pointed out, "in the most troubled times, during the most violent crises, the nomination of the mayors is given to the municipal council."[90]

[89]Burdeau, *Libertés*, pp. 191–2.
[90]Monnet, *Histoire*, p. 448.

2

The triumph of decentralization during the Third Republic

The beginning years of the Third Republic marked the end of the pattern of recurring centralization that had plagued France for nearly a century. The pattern in the very first years of the Republic followed that of previous regimes: recentralizing legislation replaced the decentralizing legislation passed during the initial crisis period. But for once this was not the end of it. A prolonged period of crisis, characterized by constant shifts in policy, began in 1871 and continued through 1877. It was followed in 1884 by the organic law on municipal decentralization, which significantly increased the importance of the mayor by making him the choice of the popularly elected municipal council and the executive power in the commune. As a result of this law and the law of 1871 on departments formalizing the powers of the popularly elected general councils, the local governmental system was significantly decentralized. And although this system did not completely satisfy most legislators, it was to remain essentially intact during the rest of the Third Republic – to be replaced only for the brief interlude of the Vichy regime with a highly centralized system.

Legislators from the center-left to the extreme left during the beginning years of the Third Republic must take the credit for reversing the pattern of recurring centralization by putting into place a reasonably decentralized system of local government. The left, however, cannot therefore claim any greater principled attachment to local liberties than the right. For political interest combined with political circumstance – more than political principle – helps explain the left's promotion of the disinterested politics of decentralization. Support for decentralization represented a reasonable political calculation of a left faced with an uncertain future in power, which was intent on limiting the potential centralized power a future right-wing government could exercise and on ensuring its continued access to power on the local level even if it were lost on the national level. Decentralization was also a component of a brilliant political strategy on the part of Gambetta and the parties of the left to forge a new electoral coalition between two politically ascendant socioeconomic groups: the *paysans moyens,* or middle-income peasants, and *petits-bourgeois,* or shopkeepers, who made up what Gambetta called the *couche nouvelle sociale,* or new social stratum.[1]

Decentralization in the Third Republic, coming at a time when the electorate had finally reached political maturity with regard to universal suffrage, engendered what Daniel Halévy called *la révolution des maires.*[2] This revolution, which made the mayor into the locally elected executive power, republicanized the communes, bringing Gambetta's new social stratum of middle-income peasants and shopkeepers into national politics on the side of the left, which had supported decentralization.

Finally, it is the relationship between the middle-income peasants and the shopkeepers that created the "celebrated community of values," which on the one hand, has been credited with democratizing France – establishing what Stanley Hoffmann has called the "republican synthesis," which flourished from 1878 to 1934 – and with stabilizing it, by ending its pattern of recurring revolution.[3] It is this same relationship, on the other hand, that has been blamed for making the Third Republic, in the words of Hoffmann, a "stalemate society," in which the balance between agrarian and industrial interests left the government incapable of promoting the kind of economic development necessary for France to keep up with the modern world and, especially by World War II, with a rapidly industrializing and expansionist Germany.[4] Nevertheless, regardless of the end result of the "republican synthesis," the interim period ensured the greatest governmental stability and local democracy France had seen since before the Revolution of 1789.

Decentralization at the beginning of the Third Republic, thus, capped one hundred years of effort, but the definition of decentralization remained narrow. The legislative debates focused primarily on the manner of selection of the mayor by government appointment or local election and only secondarily on the prefect's powers in the department as opposed to those of the general council. This was mainly because the parameters of the debates had already been set by the Revolution, which had resolved the issue of the administrative reorganization of the countryside with its division into departments and communes, and by the Napoleonic era, which had established the administrative institutions of local

[1]Daniel Halévy, *The End of the Notables* (Middletown, Conn.: Wesleyan University Press, 1974), p. 135.
[2]Daniel Halévy, *La République des ducs* (Paris: Grasset, 1937), p. 370.
[3]Stanley Hoffmann "Paradoxes of the French Political Community," in *In Search of France,* ed. S. Hoffmann, C.P. Kindleberger, L. Wylie, et al. (New York: Harper and Row, 1963), pp. 8–9.
[4]Ibid., pp. 1–32.

government, with the prefects in the departments as the focal point of centralization.

What remained was to determine how to decentralize within the confines of this administrative system. For many legislators, this meant without challenging the system's organizing principles and, thus, centralization itself. The main question, as always, was: How much local liberty was compatible with national unity and equality before the law? Unlike in the past, however, when the first liberal, decentralizing response in a time of crisis was quickly succeeded by centralization, there was much more back and forth due to the prolonged uncertainty at the beginning of the Third Republic. And it was this prolonged period that made decentralization possible, because the left became convinced that a reasonable measure of local liberty was indeed compatible with national unity, that is, with a nation unified behind itself.

The success of decentralizing legislation during the beginning years of the Third Republic did not spell the end of the debates about decentralization, although it did mark the end of any successful legislation. The topic continued to reemerge as a major legislative issue in the years subsequent to the decentralization law of 1884, primarily in the last decade of the nineteenth century and then in the early interwar years. But the definition of decentralization reflected in the reform initiatives with regard to the communes and departments remained quite narrow, with legislators increasingly tending to be less intent on promoting local liberty than on instituting administrative reforms, primarily as an effort to alleviate the burdens the state was imposing on the locality. Beginning with the turn of the century, however, regionalism began to supplant much of the attention on communal government, with calls for regional decentralization focused primarily on proposals for an elected, regional level of local government, as well as on demands for greater regional self-determination. But although some laws were passed reforming local finances and administration, none were passed on the region, which was, as always, regarded as a threat to national unity. For the Third Republic, the major reforms came at the beginning. And the Vichy regime, for a short time, was to reverse even these.

THE LEGISLATIVE DEBATES ON DECENTRALIZATION

The long period of crisis at the beginning of the Third Republic was largely responsible for ending the pattern of recurring centralization France had experienced since the end of the ancien régime. Although most of the left, confronted with a conservative majority in Parliament throughout much of this period, consistently supported decentralization, most of the right opposed it after 1871, once its members started losing elections in town and country alike. Thus, in the period between 1871 and 1884, the left reintroduced mayoral selection by the popularly elected municipal council in communes of ever increasing size every time it regained power; whenever the right took over, however, it revoked republican mayors or produced recentralizing legislation that gave the government the right to appoint and revoke mayors in all communes.

The first piece of legislation related to local government was, as always, decentralizing, with almost all factions of the left and right, from the center to the extremes, taking a principled stance in favor of local liberty. This soon ended, however, just as it had traditionally, in this case with the right abandoning political principle and moving to recentralize. In the face of an increasingly republican electorate, its strategy was to seek to consolidate its control over the government in any way possible. As in the past, however, its various attempts to retain power, including the use of appointed mayors as electoral agents, backfired. Because the electorate of the Third Republic had become politically mature, the actions of the right served only to reinforce electoral support for the left by an increasingly politicized peasantry, at the same time that it increased the left's faith in decentralization.

The left's support for decentralization was a testimony more to the pragmatism of the majority of left-leaning legislators who found decentralization for once in their political interest than to their unwavering principled support for local liberty. Although the left had become a standard-bearer for decentralization during the preceding decade of increasing debates about, and agitation for, decentralization, such as in the 1860s, this in no way ensured that it would continue to support it. That it did was the result of a short-term political calculation and a long-term political strategy.

Its experience of many years outside of power as well as its uncertainty of staying in power convinced the left that decentralization was a way of limiting the central power of the conservative majority for the moment, while guaranteeing for itself continued access to power on the local level. This political calculation proved wrong at first, because decentralization initially led to an increase in the power of the right in the periphery and no significant diminution in its power in the center. The left nevertheless continued to support decentralization, trusting in its assumption that, in the end, this would help it gain and retain the allegiance of the increasingly republican electorate of the countryside. And this political strategy worked.

From the very beginning of the Third Republic, the left had had a much clearer sense of the political maturity, or at least of the political educability, of the electorate than the right. As early as 1872, Gambetta had been out campaigning, calling on the *couche sociale nouvelle,* made up of the *travailleurs des villes et des campagnes,* or the workers of the cities and the countryside, to rally behind the new Republic.[5] By workers, Gambetta did not mean the proletariat. Rather, he meant not only, as René Rémond suggested, the petite-bourgeoisie and the middle class of new professionals who were to experience the greatest social and political mobility in the Republic,[6] but also, as Hoffmann made clear, "the peasantry and middle classes composed largely of 'independents' (non–wage earners)."[7] These were the groups to which Gambetta appealed in his electoral campaigning; and these were the groups that responded, as the increasing republican victories demonstrate, culminating in the results of the 1876 Chamber elections. The left, with its support of decentralization, helped ensure the republicanization of the periphery.

Decentralization in 1871

In the first years of the Third Republic, legislators were not solely focused on narrow considerations of political interest related to concerns about their own personal power and incumbency. They also addressed more general considerations such as fears related to the possibility of a monarchist takeover or a proletarian revolution, worries over the vagaries of universal suffrage, and speculations about the allegiance of two socioeconomic groups of new political importance, the middle-income peasants and the shopkeepers.

The middle-income peasants and shopkeepers were the political unknowns of the new Republic. Whereas the proletariat, associated in the minds of most legislators with the Paris Commune, was a revolutionary element to be controlled and suppressed, the middle-income peasants and the shopkeepers were potentially revolutionary only if certain traditional alliances to be revived. More specifically, if the middle-income peasants were to ally themselves with the aristocracy and the rich peasants they could precipitate a monarchist takeover; whereas if the shopkeepers were to ally themselves with the workers, as in the Revolution of 1848, they could start another proletariat revolution.[8] One or both eventualities made the demands of these two ascendant social groups for some political franchise an important element in all legislators' considerations. And because these groups were situated mainly in the small towns and villages

---

[5]For the text of Gambetta's speech, see Frédéric Bon and Michel-Antoine Burnier, *Les Nouveaux Intellectuels* (Paris: Seuil, 1971), pp. 59–60.

[6]René Rémond, *La Troisième République cours I.E.P.* (Paris: Les cours du droit, 1959-60), footnoted in Bon and Burnier, *Intellectuels*, p. 60 n. 1.

[7]Hoffmann, "Paradoxes," p. 5.

[8]Such traditional alliances are discussed in Karl Marx, *Le 18 brumaire de Louis Bonaparte* (Paris: Editions sociales, 1969), p. 49. See also Hoffmann, "Paradoxes," pp. 3–7.

throughout France and would be most affected by any new municipal laws, the answer to the municipal question gained even greater importance, as it would have an impact not only on the individual politician's power and incumbency, but on the future of the Republic itself.

The manner of selection of the mayor was one of the first items on the agenda in the beginning of the Third Republic. Against the backdrop of the still raging Paris Commune, legislators clearly felt the urgency of regularizing local government and restoring the principle of election for local councils. Many of those elected owed their victory in large measure to the provinces' reaction against the centralization of the Government of National Defense and the violence of the Paris Commune.

But concern about the future of the Republic and interest in repaying the loyalty of the provinces were not the only reasons for proceeding so quickly to the matter of municipal decentralization. The legislators were also worried about the mayor's potential role as an electoral agent – in favor of the government if appointed, in favor of the group of his choice if elected. Experience of previous regimes had taught most legislators that because the mayor directed the drawing up of electoral lists and presided over balloting, his potential for political influence and abuse was almost unlimited.[9] Adolphe Thiers, the first president of the Third Republic, had perhaps best expressed this view in 1869 under the Second Empire, when he declared that the appointed mayor held the election in his hands.[10] Because legislators were in reaction against the system of the Second Empire and uncertain over the allegiances of the electorate, they voted for a reasonably decentralizing municipal law.

All parties of the left, including the center left represented by Dufaure, the moderate left led by Jules Ferry, and the extreme left of Gambetta, were in favor of decentralization for the communes.[11] Repudiating their Jacobin past, they all now saw decentralization as one of the unaccomplished republican imperatives of 1848 and 1870 – as well as a way of keeping absolute power out of the hands of the conservative majority in the National Assembly. Ernest Picard, the first Minister of the Interior under Thiers (from October to May 1871) and a member of the center left, was quite open about the left's political interest, given the uncer-

[9] Joseph Barthélemy, *Le Gouvernement de la France* (Paris: Payot & Cie, 1919), p. 165.
[10] Jean-Paul Charnay, *Le Suffrage politique en France* (La Haye: Mouton & Co., 1965), p. 230.
[11] For a discussion of the party groupings, see J. Gouault, *Comment la France est devenue Républicaine* (Paris: A. Colin, 1954), pp. 17–18; and Alain Bomier-Landowski, "Les Groupes Parlementaries de l'Assemblée Nationale et de la Chambre des Députés de 1871 à 1940," in François Goguel, *Sociologie electorale* (Paris: Colin, 1954), p. 76.

tainty of its continuation in government under Thiers. His argument, which was intended to appeal to all sides, was that decentralization would deny any future government the means to influence elections and to entrench itself in power by controlling the nomination of the mayor. Only one member of the extreme left objected to the law and argued instead in favor of regionalism on the grounds that the law would split citizens' loyalty between the commune and the nation.[12]

Most parties of the right, consisting of the Orleanist center right led by the duc de Broglie and the the two legitimist parties – Ernoul's moderate right and Cazenove de Pradine's extreme right – also supported municipal decentralization, mostly for pragmatic reasons similar to those of the left. Unlike the left, however, they justified their position on the basis more of principle than of politics. Thus, de Meaux of the Orleanist center right, typical of rightists, maintained that decentralization would bring back the vigorous kind of municipal life abrogated by the Empire at the same time as it would restabilize the countryside.[13] In actuality, because the right owed its majority in the National Assembly to a peasantry still politically tied to the aristocracy and violently opposed to the Paris Commune, most members of the right voted for decentralization in order to retain peasant support and to undercut the decentralizing thrust of the Paris Commune.[14] A secondary consideration was their desire to limit the electoral power of Thiers.

Thiers, as a candidate of the center left and a constitutional monarchist soon to become a conservative republican, was put at the head of government by the conservatives only because they were divided among themselves and Thiers had received the greatest number of votes in the general election. With Thiers at the head of government, the various parliamentary groups of the right were convinced that even if their own interests were not satisfied, at least no one else's would be either.

The only group opposed to the decentralization of local government was that part of the extreme right consisting of twenty Bonapartists led by Rouher who were waiting for an early return of the deposed emperor. Remaining true to the centralizing ideology of the First and the Second Empires, they all agreed with their spokesman in the debates on the provisional municipal law, Prax-Paris, who echoed the concerns of the monarchy during the ancien régime as much as those of the Jacobins of the Revolution. Thus, he declared that decentralization would be a great threat to national unity not only because it would set up many small republics within the larger one, but also because it would turn Paris into a

---

[12]*Le Temps*, Apr. 7, 1871.
[13]Ibid.
[14]Daniel Halévy, *La Fin des notables* (Paris: Grasset, 1930), p. 52.

power equal to the national government and, therefore, capable of rising up against it.[15]

In any event, no one really listened to the Bonapartists. Legislators, however, did pay attention to the protestations of Thiers, who, when presented with the first draft of the provisional municipal law that would have allowed for the election of the mayor by the municipal council in all communes, complained that he would be unable to maintain order with such a law and that the legislators were not, as he was, "charged with saving society."[16] Bowing to his protest, the legislators, after debates that went from March 31 to April 14, 1871, passed a moderately decentralizing provisional law (497 pro and 160 con) that, although not as extensive as the law promulgated by the Government of National Defense, was nevertheless more decentralizing than that passed during the Revolution of 1848. This law allowed for the selection of the mayor by the popularly elected municipal council in all communes with fewer than twenty thousand inhabitants, but left to the government the power to appoint the mayor in all larger communes as well as in the *chef-lieux* of the departments and the arrondissements.

Once the municipal law was passed, a departmental law was next on the agenda. The Commission on Decentralization had proposed expanding the department's powers in a number of important ways, such as giving the general councils the *tutelle* over the communes and the right to meet whenever two-thirds of their members so desired, and making the departmental commission close to the equivalent of the executive power in the department. In the debate in the legislature, however, although most on the left and the right argued for greater liberty, there was not nearly the same agreement on the left and the right as to the form the law should take.

The left, after all, had never been very keen on giving departments extensive powers. Most of its members were concerned about the amount of power that was to be accorded a small number of notables in the departmental commissions, with Henri Brisson claiming that the proposed law itself was an "aristocratic" piece of work and Ernest Picard (no longer Minister of the Interior) insisting that it set up a "veritable oligarchy." Tolain, in explaining the left's opposition to the law as it stood, made clear that it was because it saw it as "a political arm put into the hands of the parties to fight both the central power and the demands of the populace."[17] This time the left made common cause with Thiers, who, for different reasons, opposed the Commission's proposals on the *tutelle* and on spontaneous meetings, and managed to convince the Commission

[15]*Le Temps*, Apr. 7, 1871.
[16]Halévy, *Le Fin*, p. 53; and *Le Temps*, Apr. 10, 1871.
[17]François Burdeau, *Libertés*, p. 195.

to give these up. The left, nonetheless, was not about to support the reinforcement of the central power, with some on the left even arguing for the election of the prefect by the general council.

Most members of the right, by contrast, were favorable toward the reform, mainly because they felt that it could only increase their own powers. The content of their remarks was much the same as in the debates on municipal reform. And most remained true to their positions under previous regimes, such as Raudot who asked, "After seventy years of excessive centralization, where is the French nation, where is French energy?" whereas others quoted de Broglie's work of over a decade before. Nevertheless, some were still worried about the Paris Commune and were willing to moderate the proposed reform because of the need to retain central control throughout the prefects. Thus, the viscount d'Haussonville expressed the fear that powerful general councils would become "veritable parliaments," able to destroy the unity of France.[18]

The law that was ultimately passed introduced very little significant change. The law of August 10, 1871 left the centrally appointed prefect as the executive power in the department, although it did increase the powers of the general council by setting up a *commission départementale*, or elected standing committee, to oversee the administrative actions of the prefect and by giving the general council alone the authority to pass the budget and to decide how to spend any monies not specifically mandated by national legislation. The change was enough, then, to enable Thiers to protest that these departmental commissions were "so many enemas in the backside of my prefects" ("autant de clystères dans le derrière de mes préfets").[19] However vexing the new departmental commissions, they clearly did not interfere much with the prefect's freedom. This explains why the departmental law, once passed, was left essentially as it was, whereas the municipal law underwent a series of changes related to changes in the government.

Recentralization in 1873 and 1874

By the middle of 1873, the rightist majority in the Assembly was no longer content to take the back seat to an executive power (Thiers) more and more in league with the republicans and in support of a *République de droit* (republic based on law). As the Paris Commune receded into history, so did the unquestioning conservative thrust of the country as a whole. The parties of the right, in effect, had found that they were no longer able to count on the traditional allegiance of the peasants to keep

[18]Ibid., pp. 194–7.
[19]Paul Bernard, *L'État et la décentralisation – Du préfet au commissaire de la République* (Paris: Documentation française, 1983), p. 39.

them in power. For the first time, they were confronted with what François Goguel has called the *véritable avènement* of universal suffrage.[20] Only in 1871, according to Goguel, did universal suffrage attain political maturity in fact as well as in law. Before, it was at first immature and inexperienced, then manipulated and maintained in half slavery.[21] Now it had become a political reality.

Most significantly, for the first time the peasantry had become truly politicized even if, according to Eugen Weber, this politicization was not as sudden as Goguel and his followers would have it. Whereas in some areas rural political awareness predates this period, as Maurice Agulhon has shown for the Var under the Second Empire and Philippe Vigier for the Alpine country to the north, Weber himself finds that many other rural areas "remained in an archaic stage – local and personal – into at least the 1880s."[22] What brought them out of that archaic stage, as Weber himself makes clear, was politics itself.[23]

In the beginning years of the Republic, politics had become one of the most important topics of discussion in rural areas – even before the socio-economic benefits of the Republic in the 1880s that made the peasants' interest in politics a certainty.[24] The extended period of crisis in those beginning years, with the constant shifts of power in Paris, kept the peasants mostly fascinated – and sometimes alarmed. One of the factors contributing to solidifying peasant support behind the Republic was the incident with the comte de Chambord. When the legitimist pretender to the throne refused the tricolor in favor of the white flag of his ancestors, it brought back the peasants' recurring fears of everything a return to the monarchy could mean in terms of higher taxes and tithes, restricted hunting privileges, and loss of lands.[25]

Of the many different peasant groups that became politicized at this time, probably the most important group for the future of the Republic was that of the middle-income peasants. This was the group of small proprietors who worked their own lands and had benefited most from the economic changes that had brought about the rural exodus and technical progress.[26] This was the group most influenced by Gambetta's electoral campaigns and that voted for the Republic over and over again.

[20]François Goguel in the preface to Gouault, *France*, p. 12.
[21]Ibid., p. 10.
[22]Eugen Weber, *Peasants into Frenchmen* (Stanford, Calif.: Stanford University Press, 1976), p. 241. See also Agulhon, *La République*; Philippe Vigier, *La Seconde République dans la région Alpine*, 2 vols. (Paris: Presses universitaires de France, 1963); and Marcel Faure, *Les Paysans dans la société française* (Paris: Colin, 1966).
[23]Weber, *Peasants*, p. 271.
[24]Ibid., pp. 274–5.
[25]Ibid., pp. 241–4.
[26]Georges Dupeux, *La Société française (1789–1960)* (Paris: Colin, 1964), p. 178.

This was the case even in right-wing western France, which was effectively controlled by the surviving land-owning nobility; for here, as André Siegfried noted, the strength of the right was limited in areas where there were peasant proprietors who almost always voted for the left.[27]

Of course, not all middle-income peasants voted for the left. Generally, those who did were from areas where villages were compact units, such as in the north and northeast, where "the village community of independent peasant proprietors formed a natural foundation for a democratic political culture and for emancipation from dominance from the notables."[28] For similar reasons, republicanism took hold in the south, such as in Provence, where the large "urbanized villages" had already ensured rural politicization. Where farms were scattered and villages few and far between as in the Massif Central and the Pyrenées, by contrast, politicization was long in coming, hampered by the slowness in communications and the intellectual backwardness of the area.[29] Poverty and illiteracy, in fact, are most useful in explaining the lack of rural politicization, even in the more urbanized areas of the countryside such as those of the Lorraine.[30] Even though the Lorraine had fairly large villages, it had far fewer of the social clubs that in Provence, for example, brought republican politics to the village.[31]

The spread of republicanism in the countryside, in short, was related to the politicization of those middle-income peasants who were found for the most part in the more urban villages. And this politicization, in turn, was tied in large measure to the influence of the towns and thus to the already long-politicized *petite-bourgeoisie*, which moreover had recently been enlarged by the rise of small enterprises and the artisanry.[32] It was the influence of the *petite-bourgeoisie* that led J. Gouault to argue that the *République des ducs* was succeeded by a *petit-bourgeois* political democracy: a democracy that was political, not social; *petit-bourgeois*, not proletarian.[33] This alliance between the peasants and shopkeepers, this "celebrated community of values," in effect, stabilized the republic by isolating the industrial proletariat while reducing monarchist support.[34] Put another way, by bringing politics to the periphery, decentralization

[27]André Siegfried, *Géographie électorale de l'Ardèche sous la IIIème République* (Paris: 1949), p. 57.
[28]R.D. Anderson, *France 1870–1914* (London: Routledge & Kegan Paul, 1977), p. 50.
[29]Ibid., p. 51.
[30]Serge Bonnet, *Sociologie politique et religieuse de la Lorraine* (Paris: A. Colin, 1972), p. 256.
[31]Weber, *Peasants*, p. 269.
[32]Dupeux, *Société*, p. 175.
[33]Gouault, *France*, pp. 192–3.
[34]Hoffmann, "Paradoxes," pp. 6–10.

effectively enfranchised two groups in the periphery: the middle-income peasants and the shopkeepers, at the expense of the aristocracy on the one hand, and the urban proletariat on the other.

Even at the time, the aristocratic right had some sense of their impending loss of power. The politicization of the peasantry, in particular, left members of the right uncertain about their own tenure in office. And it was this very uncertainty that led the right to pass the recentralizing law of 1874, with which it intended to counterbalance universal suffrage by using mayors as electoral agents.

The right had been losing ground to the left in the various by-elections since 1871. With the symbolic victory of the extreme left in the election of Barodet (in the partial elections in Paris), the right took fright. It catapulted itself into executive power on May 24, 1873.[35] The right then sought to maintain itself in power through a system that, according to the center left, brought back the *candidature officiel* of the Empire.[36] In addition, it operated with a *tutelle administrative* aggravated by dispositions that significantly restricted the powers and attributions of the mayor in effect since 1790.

In the Commission on Decentralization, during this time, there was a good deal of back and forth on the organic law it was charged to produce. In March 1872, when the Commission approved the election of the mayor by the municipal council in all communes except for Paris, members of the right were already beginning to have trepidations. There was talk of being willing to allow the liberal reform to proceed only on the condition that the electorate be restricted, with a two-stage process for municipal elections. There were suggestions for "moralizing" universal suffrage by allowing family men two votes or by allowing the most highly taxed members of the commune to choose a certain number of municipal councilors.[37] But ultimately, the right decided not to enmesh itself in the issue of universal suffrage, and instead decided to propose that the government be given the right to appoint mayors in all communes.

In the debates in the legislature on the municipal law at the beginning of 1874, the arguments with which most parties of the right sought to justify the reversal of their own policy of two and a half years before were again ones of principle. But now, instead of citing the dangers to traditional municipal life of centralization, the center right talked only of the dangers to traditional life of decentralization, as well as of its dangers to national sovereignty. In so doing, they addressed not only the concerns of the Bonapartists, who, as always, were convinced that only a centralized

---

[35] Jean-Jacques Chevalier, *Histoire des institutions et des régimes politiques de la France moderne (1789–1958)* (Paris: Dalloz, 1967), pp. 304–5.
[36] *L'Année politique*, vol. 1 (Paris: Charpentier & Cie., 1875), pp. 79–80.
[37] Burdeau, *Libertés*, p. 197.

France could remain powerful, but also more particularly, the concerns of the moderate right, fearful for the "tranquillity of the villages."[38] Even before the legislative debates, de Broglie had declared to the commission on the municipal law that, without government appointment of the mayor, "it will be impossible to remedy the moral disorder [of the country]."[39] One of the first tasks of the *ordre moral* was to pass a centralizing municipal law. For without such a law, according to de Broglie, he would be unable to fulfill his ministerial obligations.[40]

As always, though, the real reason for the change in policy on decentralization had more to do with questions of political interest rather than principle. With this change, the conservative majority, according to the *Année politique* of 1874, hoped to alter the results of future elections, turning possible defeats into successes by placing municipal government in the hands of friends.[41] The allegations by the right about the moral disintegration of certain communes was, in fact, a thinly veiled protest against the presence of partisan mayors not partisan to the executive power. As Louis Blanc, president of the extreme left and hero of the 1848 revolution, pointed out in the legislative debates on the law, the right was using a lame excuse since it had dismissed only ninety-eight out of seventy-two thousand mayors in the previous two and a half years. Its real reason for recentralizing, according to Blanc, was to stem the rising tide of republicanism even among its former supporters, the peasants, by setting up a counterbalance to universal suffrage with government-appointed mayors. Ever since the "villages voted like the cities," he insisted, the government "has thought of nothing else but to construct barriers between itself and this great sea that rises: universal suffrage." And as if to confirm the accuracy of Blanc's statement, a member of the right yelled out in response: "Yes, the Red Sea."[42]

On the right, only the legitimist, extreme right sided with the left in support of decentralization. In its view, the rest of the right had miscalculated. According to the marquis de Franclieu, anticipating themes to become popular in the following century, the only way to counterbalance universal suffrage was with a nonpartisan mayor, not with centralization. This would only be possible with a decentralization that would allow for competition for office by a diversity of (corporatist) interests at the local level.[43]

The protests of the left and the extreme right were useless. The duc de

[38]*Journal Officiel de la République française* (Paris), Jan. 14–20, 1874; and *Le Temps,* Jan. 20, 1874.
[39]*Le Temps,* Dec. 10, 1873.
[40]The right had in fact engineered a ministerial crisis in order to ensure that new municipal legislation would be put on the agenda.
[41]*L'Année politique,* vol. 1, p. 61.
[42]*Journal Officiel,* Jan. 14, 1874.
[43]*Journal Officiel,* Jan. 16, 1874.

Broglie threatened to resign if he did not get his way. The center right, concerned about its continuation in power, passed the provisional municipal law by a vote of 359 to 318. The "law of January" conferred upon the central government the right to nominate the mayors and adjuncts of all communes; and it resulted in the revocation of many republican mayors solely because of their opinions.[44] With this law, and a subsequent law in 1875 diminishing the review powers of the general council of the department, the rightist majority of the 1871 Assembly lived up to its epitaph suggested by Hector Pessard: "Outrageously monarchical, it made the Republic despite the republicans; liberal and decentralizing, it died having used up the arsenal of Jacobin and Bonapartist weapons."[45]

As it turned out, the municipal law did not serve the right's interests well. Coming close on the heels of the incident with the comte de Chambord, the law only increased the population's fears in general of a monarchist takeover. The peasants in particular were alienated by the new law, which relegated them to the passive role of the past, which they were no longer willing to play because they had begun to enjoy their municipal freedoms. Whereas the more prosperous peasants saw the competition for political office as an opportunity to better their own status, the resulting "open political market" increased the less prosperous peasants' self-respect by enabling them to choose among their peers rather than, as traditionally, among the aristocratic notables.[46]

The right had no idea of how much its action had alienated the increasingly politicized peasantry. Despite the right's demonstrated disappointment in the peasants, it had not completely lost its faith in them. The Constitution of 1875 established that, whereas the Chamber was to be elected by universal suffrage, the Senate was to be elected by members of the Chamber and by electors nominated by the municipal council – mayors, for the most part.[47] As Halévy explains, the conservatives thought that "by making the electoral base of the Senate the village ... they would install the village – the traditional idea of the village that they retained – in the heart of the Republic. In reality, they brought the Republic to the village."[48] The politicization of the peasantry, together with its attachment to decentralization, could only increase when the peasants themselves could elect senators indirectly, through their own directly elected mayors. Together this produced what Halévy termed *la révolution des maires,* which ended the rule of the aristocratic notables and the

[44] *L'Année politique,* vol. 1, p. 115.
[45] Hector Pessard, *Mes petits papiers,* 2d ser. 1871–3 (1888), p. 125, quoted in Burdeau, *Libertés,* p. 199.
[46] Weber, *Peasants,* pp. 263–4.
[47] Ducrocq, *Études,* p. 111.
[48] Halévy, *La République,* p. 369.

République des ducs of the first years of the Republic by bringing politics to the village and the village into national politics.[49]

The republicanization of the peasantry emerged quite clearly in the legislative elections of 1876: Universal suffrage declared overwhelmingly in favor of the republican left. In this election, the left triumphed in large measure because while Gambetta was out stumping the country, calling on the *couche nouvelle sociale* of workers of the cities and countryside for support, the right-wing Prime Minister Buffet sat back, counting on the appointed mayors and prefects to exert the electoral pressure necessary to maintain his side in power. But although the mayors in their new role as senatorial electors did help produce a conservative majority for the newly constituted Senate in the elections of 1876, in the 1876 elections for the Chamber of Deputies, they "held themselves aloof and avoided compromising themselves for a government of uncertain future."[50] The political maturity of the electorate had made the mayors much more reluctant and much less able to manipulate the population or to tamper with the results of their votes.

Gambetta's political strategy, which was lost on the conservatives, had worked. When he declared: "To work, republicans; to the conquest of the municipality to the detriment of the notables," he initiated the all-out republican effort to gain influence over the countryside and to create a wedge between the peasants and their traditional allies, the aristocracy.[51] In this undertaking, however, he received considerable help from the aristocratic members of the right, who did as much to alienate the peasants as the left did to gain their allegiance. In effect, the left drew a large amount of political capital from the actions of the center right during the election campaign. The left now felt perfectly justified in claiming credit for the decentralizing law of 1871 and in presenting itself as the sole champion of municipal liberty. And its members pledged themselves to decentralizing municipal reform, should they be elected.

Decentralization in 1876, recentralization in 1877, and regularization in 1882 and 1884

The republican victory in the 1876 elections of the newly constituted Chamber of Deputies put municipal legislation back at the top of the agenda. The manner of selection of the mayor had become even more important, because the new Constitution of 1875 established that whereas the Chamber was to be elected by universal suffrage, the Senate was to be selected by electors nominated by the municipal councils (generally may-

[49] Ibid., pp. 369–70.
[50] Chevalier, *Histoire*, p. 319.
[51] Ibid., p. 335.

ors) as well as by the members of the Chamber of Deputies. In the Senate elections of 1876, a conservative majority won, elected by the mayors appointed under the 1874 law.

The Opportunists, the center-left and moderate-left majority in the Chamber, were newly schooled in Gambetta's formula for the passage of the Constitution: a substitution of *la politique des résultats* (pragmatic politics) for *la politique des chimères* (the politics of illusion). They proposed only a moderately decentralizing provisional law, reasoning that the conservative Senate would not support anything more decentralizing.[52] In so doing, the Opportunists turned against Gambetta himself, who felt pragmatic politics inappropriate in this case. Representing the views of the extreme left, Gambetta argued for a more decentralizing law, maintaining that with a law limited to the smaller and less important communes, liberty would be given to the hamlets and not to the other communes in which "one finds the agglomeration of intelligence, the epicenter and cradle of democracy."[53] In any event, Gambetta failed to win over the center and moderate left led by Ferry. All the amendments to the government project that were proposed by members of the extreme left, which would have given the municipal council the power to select the mayor in all communes, failed.

For the most part, the right in the Chamber, opposed the decentralizing legislation. The marquis de Valfons of the legitimist moderate right, for example, declared that the law of 1874 was as good under the *ordre moral* as under the *ordre républicain,* because it alone would ensure that the mayor was above party politics.[54] Only the Bonapartists in the Chamber changed their previous position and now favored full-scale decentralization, siding with the consistently decentralizing legitimist extreme right and with the extreme left. Needless to say, they did this less out of a sincere change of heart than out of their own brand of pragmatic politics that involved their desire to keep as much power as possible out of the hands of the left. They insisted that their own pragmatism was at least as justifiable as that of the center left. Thus, Robert Mitchell declared: "Just as we distance ourselves from the imperial tradition, so you distance yourselves from the republican tradition; and one of these days, perhaps, we will meet."[55] He went on to accuse Ferry, not completely unfairly, of considering questions involving only his own personal power and incumbency when he spoke against full decentralization.

The Chamber voted for the moderately decentralizing proposed law

[52] *L'Année politique,* vol. 3 (1877), p. 223.
[53] *Journal Officiel,* July 12, 1876.
[54] Ibid.
[55] Ibid.

after the debates in July 1876. The Senate approved it following the debates in August 1876. In the Senate, interestingly enough, the position of members of the moderate right was different from the one taken by their fellows in the Chamber. The duc de Broglie spoke of the politics of conciliation, and of the changed circumstances that enabled him to support reversing the law he himself had put through in 1874. After all, he said, the election had produced a conservative majority in the Senate.[56] The Senate, therefore, endorsed the Chamber's recommendation for a law in which the mayor was to be elected by the municipal council in all communes except the *chef-lieu* of the department, the arrondissement, and the canton. In these latter cases (affecting the three thousand largest communes), the executive was to appoint the mayor from within the municipal council; the government retained the *tutelle*.

The decentralizing law of 1876 thus was the product more of political interest than of principle for the right and the left. Obviously, the right was happy to keep as much power as possible out of the hands of the left, which was now running the government. For the left, not so differently, the threat of a conservative return to executive power made attractive a measure that would reduce state control over local government, even though it was the left that was denying itself that control in the short term. But the left felt little need to exercise such control because local government was becoming increasingly republican – in part as a result of the left's consistent support of decentralization. In fact, it was in the left's interest to decentralize, if only to fulfill its electoral promises. And thus, the conjunction of the political interests on the left and right, at a time when governmental instability continued to be a problem, meant that decentralization held the day.

With the crisis of May 16, 1877, the left became only more convinced of its wisdom in supporting decentralization. In this period the center right returned to executive power and proceeded to revoke most republican mayors. The mayors were replaced by Bonapartists for the most part, who reintroduced the *candidature officiel*. In all, 54 out of 90 prefects were replaced, as were numbers of mayors, all of liberal and left tendencies, and most of the 363 leftist deputies in the Chamber, who were also mayors.[57] Thus, when the elections of 1877 returned only a slightly diminished republican majority to the Chambers, despite the efforts of the right, decentralization was secured. The left was now fully committed to putting through decentralizing laws, but it had to wait until the Senate elections of 1879 produced a republican majority that

---

[56]*Journal Officiel,* Aug. 10, 1876.
[57]*L'Année politique,* vol. 3, p. 251.

agreed with the Chamber on the need for further decentralization. By that time, decentralization was no longer the burning issue it had been in earlier years.

Although important to decentralization, the years 1882 and 1884 were essentially anticlimactic. The major decision to support decentralization had been settled in 1876 for most parties. What was left was the municipal freedom of only three thousand communes and the organic municipal law to fix decentralization for all time. And these two issues provoked little debate.

There nevertheless had been repeated complaints by the Radicals, especially about the slowness of the government in proceeding to the decentralizing reform. In 1880, Georges Clemenceau expressed his regrets that no movement had occurred on municipal reform. In the cantonal elections of August 1880, the Radical left campaigned for a thorough-going municipal reform. In the legislative elections of 1881, the Radicals chastised the Opportunists for their inertia in the domain of local administrative institutions. The Radicals, in effect, were much more determined to push for real reform than the Opportunists who were in power. The Radical Goblet, as Minister of the Interior in 1882, demonstrated this when he proposed a law that went much farther than the law that was to be passed in 1884: It suggested a considerable enlargement of the functions of the municipal council; an end to the state's *tutelle* over the communes in all matters that didn't concern it; and the use of the canton to create big, strong communes.[58]

In 1882 the government, responding to pressures to move the issue of decentralization along, brought a piece of the organic municipal law in preparation to the Chamber of Deputies for deliberation. The Chamber was asked mainly to resolve the question of the election of the mayors. Political interest, once again, was the primary issue; legislators asked about the impact of the election by the municipal council of the mayors in the three thousand communes that were departmental, arrondissement, and cantonal seats, and Goblet responded that the five hundred republican mayors would not be lost, because in most places there were few mayors chosen by the government contrary to the wishes of the majority of the council.[59] In fact, mayors were picked from the majority of the council in 10 percent of the local governments in question. In any event, the law of 1882 easily passed, revising the law of 1876 by putting the three thousand communes that were outside the common law within it – all, except for Paris, which was to remain outside the common law. The government still retained the *tutelle*.[60]

[58]Burdeau, *Libertés*, pp. 200–1.
[59]*Le Temps*, Feb. 17, 1882.
[60]*L'Année politique*, vol. 9 (1882), p. 64.

The organic municipal law of 1884 occasioned little general discussion.[61] The extreme left expressed its disappointment that the reform did not go far enough and suppress the *tutelle*. According to Lanesson, it would have liked "to make the communes the kind of independent political unit which they have always been denied, in giving them in addition the right to oversee their resources in complete independence."[62] The response by de Marcère of the center left was to marvel that one could be a centralizer and anarchist at the same time.[63] The government refused to end the *tutelle*. Except for this refusal, no major questions arose, and even this question was cursorily considered.[64] The Senate had even less discussion. The law was promulgated on April 5, 1884, as the *loi organique municipale*.

Everywhere, except for Paris, the mayor was to be elected by the municipal council. Mayors could be suspended for not more than one month by a decree of the prefect. The suspension could last three months only by action of the Minister of the Interior. The mayor could be revoked only by a decree of the president of the Republic.[65] This was itself a considerable reduction of the *tutelle*. The prefect, however, was still to exercise the *tutelle*, or a priori administrative and financial review of all decisions of the mayor, whose dual role ensured that, as the representative of the state, he came under the direct authority of the state, whereas as the executive power of the commune, he came under the surveillance and control of the state.

Even with this *tutelle*, the mayor had significant powers. Specifically, as the representative of the state the mayor was responsible for the publication and execution of laws and regulations; the execution of general security measures; and the special functions attributed to the mayor by law. As the executive representative of the commune, the mayor had his own powers, first, which put him in charge of the organization of the services of municipal police; the appointment, promotion, and revocation of municipal employees; the regulatory powers that the rural and municipal police exercise over citizens of the commune; the public domain of the municipality; and the administration of goods in the private domain. Secondly, the mayor had the powers of execution of the deliberations of the municipal council encompassing execution of the budget; execution of sales and contracts; representation of the commune as plaintiff or

---

[61]The organic municipal law of 1884 was first deliberated in the Chamber of Deputies from Feb. 8 to Mar. 1 and then between June 29 and Nov. 10, 1883. It was deliberated in the Senate, first, from Feb. 5 to Feb 18, 1884, and, second, from Feb. 28 to Mar. 15, 1884.

[62]Chamber of Deputies, Apr. 24, 1883, quoted in Burdeau, *Libertés*, p. 201.

[63]*Journal Officiel*, July 1, 1883.

[64]*Le Temps*, Feb. 10, 1883.

[65]Ducroq, *Études*, p. 200.

defendant; direction of communal works; and organization of all services created by the municipal council.[66]

The organic municipal law of 1884 set the parameters of communal government for most of the next century, because it remained, with only minor modifications, operative until the Socialist reforms of 1982.[67] With this new law, the left succeeded in ending the pattern of recurring centralization that had plagued France for nearly a century. A testimony to the importance of this new law are the remarks of Émile Monnet, attached to the presidency of the Senate, who voiced his concern that, now "decentralization and municipal liberties are running at full steam." He went on to express the hope that, "given the impossibility of the government reinstituting the *tutelle* so imprudently abandoned . . . the confidence of the governors in the wisdom of the governed would never again be betrayed by events."[68]

CONTINUING DECENTRALIZATION IN THE THIRD REPUBLIC AND RECENTRALIZATION UNDER THE VICHY REGIME

After the passage of the organic municipal law of 1884, decentralization did not vanish as an issue of public or parliamentary concern. On the contrary, public and legislative debate was often extensive, sometimes outdoing in intensity that preceding the reforms of 1871 and 1884. Throughout the last decade of the nineteenth century and then again in the early interwar years, decentralization was a major legislative issue. But it resulted in very little legislation of note, despite the fact that royalists, Bonapartists, liberals, Radicals, and Socialists were all supporters, albeit for different reasons. For most, decentralization now meant administrative reform: a way to simplify administration, to reduce the number of civil servants, and to diminish public expenditures. For a few, the abolition of the subprefects remained an important consideration, as did the creation of cantonal and regional levels of administration. Regionalism also began to take on great importance at this time. From 1900, when Charles-Brun founded the regionalist movement, regionalism became a hotly debated issue, with demonstrations, interventions in parliamentary campaigns, and reform proposals in Parliament that demanded an elected, regional level of local government, greater freedom in local educa-

[66]Maurice Hauriou, *Précis élémentaire de droit administratif* (Paris; Sirey, 1938), pp. 143, 176–81.

[67]For modifications, see Walter Rice Sharp, *The French Civil Service: Bureaucracy in Transition* (New York: Macmillan, 1931), pp. 416–30; and Jean de Savigny, *L'État contre les communes?* (Paris: Seuil, 1971), pp. 16–17.

[68]Monnet, *Histoire*, p. 454.

tion, culture, and language, and even regional autonomy. In the early 1920s, when much legislative attention was again devoted to decentralization, it was hard to find a proponent of decentralization who did not favor regionalism as well.

Here, a piece of the old pattern recurred, with those in power resisting decentralization even though they were the ones to push for it while out of power. The difference from the past was that centralization was not deliberately reinforced by those in power, and certainly no recentralizing laws were put into place except, of course, under the Vichy regime. There was little legislation during the rest of the Third Republic and that was decentralizing. An increase in centralization did occur, nevertheless, although generally as the unintended consequences of the professionalization of the civil service, the expansion of the field services of the state, the modernization of the economy, and the increase in the size and importance of the state itself. This was countered to some extent by the decentralization resulting from the growing strength of local government and by the developing complicity between prefects and local notables in the periphery, which ensured that, as a result of the informal processes of local government, local elected officials had more informal power and autonomy than the formal institutions would, at least on the surface, allow.[69]

The debate on decentralization for the remainder of the Third Republic

By the 1890s, the recently passed decentralizing reforms no longer seemed sufficient to most parties. Although the political issue of the local election of the mayor had been resolved to the satisfaction of most legislators, the administrative issues involving the powers and attributions of local government had not been. Moreover, because Parliament was having increasing trouble in balancing its budget beginning in the 1890s, decentralization appeared to be a perfect way to save money and to shift the burden of any number of services from the center to the periphery. There was, in fact, a consensus as to the need for reform. But the various parties to the debate nevertheless differed as to their justification for reform, as well as to the specific form it was to take.

In the center, Paul Deschanel, representing the views of the moderate republicans in power from 1876 until 1902, sought to make the case for further decentralization by arguing that it took matters out of the hands of functionaries and put them into the hands of citizens, thereby setting

[69]See Part II, Chapter 6, under "The institutions and processes of local government from the Third Republic to the Fifth Republic," for the details of this relationship.

up the government of the country by the country.[70] For Deschanel, the commune was the "real school of self-government"[71] and also a forum in which the mayor had comparatively more power than in most other countries. He insisted that, whereas elsewhere the power was collective, in France it was "personnel et unitaire" and therefore gave the mayor personally significant, unitary powers.[72] In an impassioned speech in the Chamber of Deputies in 1890, Deschanel rekindled interest in the issue of decentralization by arguing that if France was to be strong and healthy, it would have to have "self-government" at all levels, with "the progressive substitution of the actions of citizens for those of civil servants," and the "gradual disappearance of the bureaucratic institutions of Caesarism."[73]

Deschanel's speech began a decade of intense public and parliamentary debate about decentralization. Twenty years later, though, not much had been accomplished. In 1910 Deschanel declared: "We have the Republic at the summit, the Empire at the base – it is a question of putting the Republic everywhere."[74] None of Deschanel's recommendations for reform, which included enlarging the municipal councils, expanding their powers, and putting them under the *tutelle* of departmental commissions, were implemented. This was due in large measure to the resistance of the moderate republicans who, although equally willing to engage in the rhetoric of decentralization, were unwilling to translate this into action.

To listen to the moderates in power talk, one would have assumed that further decentralization was to be quickly and easily legislated, because it was presented as a panacea for all governmental ills. The progressive liberals, when arguing in favor of regional decentralization, insisted that it would make local administration more efficient and cost-effective by reducing taxes, by increasing consumption, and by enhancing the competitiveness of merchants in international markets.[75] In summing up the views of the liberals in a book written in 1899, Émile Fontaine contended that decentralization, meaning government by the countryside for the countryside, would (1) lead to solutions conforming to the immediate needs of the locality; (2) avoid red tape and the slowness of the state administrative apparatus; (3) avoid the costs of the state apparatus and

[70]Paul Deschanel, *La Décentralisation* (Paris: 1895), pp. 44–5. It is important to note that, although Deschanel represented the views of the moderate republicans, he himself did not join any parliamentary parties throughout his long career, which included an eight-month stint as president of the Republic in 1920.
[71]Ibid., p. 4.
[72]Ibid., pp. 13–15.
[73]Burdeau, *Libertés,* p. 224.
[74]Ibid., p. 232.
[75]Ibid., p. 223.

the deficits of the central government; (4) avoid the army of functionaries engendered by centralization; (5) provide freedoms allowed even in many authoritarian regimes; and (6) remedy the paradoxical situation in which the electorate has the power to vote the highest offices directly but not the lowest, namely, the mayor.[76]

In addition to all of their principled reasons for promoting decentralization, as listed above, the moderate republicans had self-interested ones. They supported reform, in part as a way of challenging the left, and insisted that they alone could succeed with the reform, because it demanded the "tolerance" that was the very basis of their philosophy. Despite all their arguments, they did little while in power to promote decentralization and to respond to the increasing demands for decentralization. When push came to shove, the moderates equivocated, for example, by linking decentralizing reform to electoral reform and insisting on delaying the former in anticipation of the latter.[77] Once they had lost to the Radicals, however, the moderates also became determined supporters of decentralization. Thus, we find Méline, who had ample opportunities while he was prime minister or while his party was in power to promote decentralization, arguing in 1910 that centralization had very much killed even minimal municipal liberties, whereas the prefect's powers in the matter of civil service appointment in the departmental services had become excessive.[78]

This was not the pattern only of the moderate republicans; the Radicals were also guilty of being more supportive of decentralization while out of power than while holding it. Thus, in the 1890s while out of power, the Radicals proclaimed themselves the leaders of the movement for decentralization, making it the first article in their parliamentary program in 1894 and lamenting the fact that, four years later, it had not gotten very far because "we still have the same administration, the same judicial organization, the same number of prefects, subprefects, and magistrates. Instead of diminishing, the number of civil servants doesn't stop growing along with the taste for bureaucracy."[79] The Radicals' attack on the prefects and other functionaries was not so much because they represented the centralized power of Paris, but because they served a government of moderates and progressives who used these governmental agents to the Radicals' disadvantage. This was confirmed by the first congresses of the Radicals in 1902 and 1903, in which they called for a houseclean-

[76]Émile Fontaine, *Décentralisation et déconcentration* (Saint-Malo: Lagadec, 1899), pp. 9–15.
[77]See the discussion in Burdeau, *Libertés*, pp. 234–6.
[78]Léon Jacques, *Les Partis politiques sous la IIIème République* (Paris: Sirey, 1913), p. 211.
[79]"Manifeste du groupe radical-socialiste de la Chambre des députés," Mar. 30, 1898, quoted in Burdeau, *Libertés*, p. 221.

ing of the administrative service and a reform of the magistrature in order to put both in the hands of republicans.[80]

Once the Radicals gained power in the early 1900s, although they continued to give lip service to decentralization, they did little to promote reform. Only a few Radicals such as Beauquier and Clemenceau continued to push for reform. Although interest in decentralization was revived by Clemenceau in 1906, the overhaul of local administration that he had envisioned came to nothing. The Radicals on the whole considered that decentralization, as it was envisioned especially by the regionalists, could not be reconciled with a centralization that ensured national unity and equality before the law. In the early part of the century, many feared that too much decentralization would favor local notables, whose republicanism was not very deeply rooted. And in the early interwar years, most Radicals remained cautious on the issue of regionalism, supporting the creation of regions only as economic units. They claimed to be concerned about the threat to national unity presented by the regional separatists, especially in Alsace, but in fact the Radicals saw regionalism as a threat to the government of which they were a part, especially from the right, which had taken up the regionalist cause with a vengeance. Beyond this, the Radicals were unlikely to support decentralization during a time when they were seeking to establish a Jacobin centralization in their own party structure over the opposition of many of their supporters in the periphery.[81]

The Socialists, by contrast with others on the left and in the center, had no such history of going back on political principle with regard to decentralization. And for good reason, given their own growing political power in the cities where, by the 1890s, they had begun to win municipal elections and where, by the 1900s, municipal socialism was in full swing.[82] By the turn of the century, it had become clear that decentralization had encouraged, not only rural politicization, but also a more radical urban politicization, with the proletariat the main beneficiaries. The proletariat in most of the larger urban communes (except of course for Paris, which would have to wait nearly another full century for its political freedom), were not left completely without power, even though they were not favored for the most part by the continuing "republican synthesis" in the periphery.

For the Socialists, decentralization was to assure the improvement of the human condition, especially with the end of capitalism. Some even insisted that "the conquest of the municipal council, this molecule of

[80]Serge Berstein, "Le parti radical et le problème du centralisme (1870–1939)," in *Régions*, Gras and Livet, pp. 226–9.
[81]Ibid., pp. 236–40.
[82]Anderson, *France*, pp. 123–30.

society, is the first stage of the proletariat in its liberation."[83] As early as 1886, moreover, the program of the Republican Socialist Alliance took up the old refrain: "Division of governmental power: to the Chamber of Deputies, national interests; to the general councils, regional interests; to the municipal councils, communal interests." In the Chamber of Deputies in 1888, the Socialists adopted a program in which the first article supported: "Individual liberty, communal autonomy." And by 1895 the group of Socialist deputies proposed a constitutional reform extending communal liberty.

In addition, when the issue came up again after World War I, the Socialists declared in favor of regional reform as well as, as always, the expansion of communal powers. But here, they were as cautious as the Radicals on the role of the region.[84] It is only just before World War II that one finds a clear statement of support for an elected, regional level of government as well as for increased power to the departments with the elimination of the prefects when Léon Blum, in 1939, declared:

I do not see, for example, any reason to maintain in the departments or organized regions the representatives of the central power, the appointed prefects and subprefects, and I believe firmly that the application of the principle of election to local or regional powers would contribute singularly to revive energies, bringing back a sort of vital ardor [to local government].[85]

Even the revolutionary left was unquestionably behind decentralization. Significantly enough, Jules Guesde dedicated two of his nine major speeches in the legislative session of 1893–8 to the defense of local liberty. For the Guesdists, the attainment of local power would, at the very least, weaken class enemies, even if municipal socialism would not in and of itself bring about a social revolution.[86] Later, in the 1920s, the Communists also came out in favor of a program of emancipation of local governments, determined to eliminate "the political and administrative servitude" of the communes and departments, and to allow them political and administrative autonomy, control over their own budgets, their own administration, the raising of their own revenues and the determination of their own expenditures, control of their police, and the freedom to intervene in the local economy by the extension of the municipality's indus-

[83]E. Massard, *Le citoyen de Paris*, 18/6/1888, cited by Michèle Perrot, *Les Ouvriers en grève* (Paris: Mouton, 1974); and Yves Mény, "Partis politiques et décentralisation," in *L'Administration vue par les politiques*, ed. Institut français des sciences administratives (Paris: Cujas, 1978), p. 112.
[84]Burdeau, *Libertés*, pp. 224, 248–9.
[85]Léon Blum, *L'action régionaliste*, (Feb., 1939), quoted in Yves Mény, *Centralisation et décentralisation dans le débat politique français* (Paris: Librairie générale de droit et de jurisprudence, 1974), p. 120.
[86]Mény, *Centralisation*, pp. 223, 234.

trial and commercial capacity."[87] Moreover, in contrast with the radicals, the Communists were in the main supportive of regional autonomy in Alsace.[88]

Finally, on the right, the monarchists, whether legitimist or Orléanist, remained true to decentralization. Even the Bonapartists supported decentralization, claiming that the emperor himself, at the end of his life, had expressed interest in an ambitious reform. For most conservatives, decentralization was synonymous with regionalism, and retained echoes of the old provincial divisions. But the decentralization envisioned was often very different for different factions on the right. Most Christian Democrats, for example, sought to promote what they felt would be the true democratization of the country through elected regional governments with greatly enhanced powers, although, for the members of the *Parti démocrate populaire* (PDP), regional interests were not political and the election of members of the regional council, therefore, was to be by "different corporatist groupings."[89] Most notable among the corporatist projects for the region was that of the deputy Hennessy, who, starting in 1913, submitted several proposed laws in which the elected officials of a new regional level of local government were to represent the professions. Much of the authoritarian right, by contrast, wanted a regional decentralization that was really deconcentration, often recommending giving greater powers back to the representatives of the central power in the periphery, and thus eliminating what they considered the deleterious effects of universal suffrage on local government. For this, the authoritarian right felt it necessary to wait until the return of the monarchy.[90]

The legislation affecting decentralization for the remainder of the Third Republic

In the end, however, although there was considerable debate on decentralizing reform, there was much less legislative action. Whatever action there was, it favored decentralization up until the 1930s. Thus, the reforms encompassed a variety of measures intended to make local government more efficient and effective, such as the law of March 22, 1890, which intended to solve the age-old problem of the unwieldy number of

[87]Ibid., p. 248.

[88]For the ins and outs of Communist party support in Alsace, and how the regional question played itself out in the divisions of the CP in Alsace, see Bernard Reimeringer, "Un communisme régionaliste? Le communisme alsacien," in *Régions,* Gras and Livet, pp. 360–92.

[89]Jean-Marie Mayeur, "Démocratie Chrétienne et régionalisme," in *Régions,* Gras and Livet, pp. 454–5.

[90]For details, see Burdeau, *Libertés,* pp. 236–44, 249–51.

communes in France by allowing neighboring communes to consolidate, forming syndicates of communes to provide certain local services. This worked no better than previous solutions. By 1915, no more than forty were created.[91]

Other laws increased decentralization by expanding the administrative and financial powers of local governments at both the communal level, for example, with the act of 1902, which enlarged the borrowing powers of the commune, and at the departmental level, for example, with the laws on public assistance passed between 1890 and 1906 involving welfare, hospitals, and social service establishments. The departments also benefited from deconcentration, mainly with Premier Poincaré's legislative decrees in 1926, which deconcentrated the control of Paris over departmental and communal affairs in such areas as the setting up of municipal service corporations and the establishment of joint departmental services for economic and social welfare purposes.

Yet other laws seemed more in the line of increased democracy: the law of 1899 gave the departmental commission the right to elect its president and the act of 1908 restricted the rights of the government to dismiss or suspend mayors and *adjoints* or deputy mayors. There was even legislation on the regions in 1919, for example, the establishment of regional economic groupings led by the chambers of commerce – the "Clémentel regions" of April 5, 1919.

Needless to say, none of these reforms satisfied the decentralizers. They were, in any case, minimal when judged against the increasing weight of the state. The state, after all, was encroaching on local governments in a variety of ways. This resulted in a certain amount of state recentralization in center–periphery relations. But in discussing the diminution in the powers of the locality, it is important to distinguish between what were conscious efforts by the state to recentralize and what were simply the unintended consequences of ministerial actions or prefectoral practices, of the professionalization of the civil service, of the deconcentration of the field services of the state, of legislation that responds to pressures from various segments of the population, and of the requisites of modernization.[92]

Thus, one of the first increases in state centralization came soon after 1884, when prefects began to exercise their veto power and to control more rigidly the purse strings of the communes. In 1914, due to pressures from professional organizations of civil servants, the mayors' powers were decreased when a personnel code was put into effect. By 1919, the mayors' freedom to appoint and promote as they pleased was reduced in cities of over five thousand inhabitants when a code was adopted with legal regula-

[91]Sautel, *Histoire*, p. 521.
[92]See Part II, Chapter 6, under "The formal centralization of local governmental institutions," for the details.

tions for recruitment on merit.[93] Add to this the myriad laws and decrees beginning at the turn of the century that led to the proliferation of the field services of the state in the periphery, and it becomes clear why legislators at various reprises called for new decentralizing measures.[94]

The formal restrictions in the powers of local elected officials resulted more from an increase in the powers of other authorities and groups in the center and in the periphery than from any deliberate legislative attempt to decrease local elected officials' powers. Only in the 1930s were there deliberate attempts to restrict local powers, and these were few. The law of 1930 substituted a system of interdepartmental understandings for the freer system of departmental syndicates. The crisis of local finances brought a reinforcement of the *tutelle* on local collectivities.

Until the Vichy regime, there was little legislative recentralization, although there was mounting centralization as a result of the encroachments of the state in the periphery. This centralization, however, was offset to some extent by an increase in local elected officials' informal power and influence. A cozy relationship was in fact developing at this time between prefect and local elected officials, which gave the latter much more say in local matters than the formal and legal system would suggest.[95]

The Vichy interlude

All this was to change during the Vichy regime, which represented a real break in the Third Republic's history of legislative inactivity since 1884 and the much longer history of progressive decentralization. The laws of October 12, 1940, and August 7, 1942, on the departments, and those of November 16, 1940, on the communes, basically undid the advances made since the French Revolution. Mayors were now appointed. The local election of municipal councilors was retained only for communes with populations under two thousand. In all the other communes and in the departments, commissions were appointed with a strictly consultative role. The major innovation was the law of April 1941, which constituted the regions and created a regional prefect. But this did little even in the

[93]For the professionalization of the civil service and its impact on local government, see Jean-Claude Thoenig, "La politique de l'État à l'égard du personnel des communes," *Revue française d'administration publique* no. 23 (July–Sept. 1982). Also see the discussion of this in Part II, Chapter 6, under "The formal centralization of local government institutions."

[94]See Jean-Marc Virieux, "Les tendances longues de la décentralisation," *Futuribles*, no. 56 (June 1982).

[95]See Part II, Chapter 6, under "The informal decentralization of local governmental processes."

way of deconcentration, because the regional prefect's new powers were taken from the departmental prefect, and not from the center.

Nevertheless, the men of Vichy described their reforms as "authoritarian decentralization." And initially, at least, the reforms, especially as they related to the regions, thrilled the regionalists on the authoritarian right who thought their dreams of fifty years before were about to be actualized. They were soon disillusioned, when they found that the new regions simply constituted a new level of administration in the service of the central state rather than local governments with their own powers and attributions. The reality of the Vichy regime was of regional centralization, despite the rhetoric that included Marshal Pétain himself remarking that the institution of governors at the head of the reconstituted provinces established an administration that was to be at the same time "concentrated and decentralized."[96]

In the Resistance, needless to say, there was much opposition to this system, and some discussion of what kind of transitional organization was necessary once the war was won. For most, it was to be a deconcentrated system based in the departments, with *commissaires de la République* in charge. As for the permanent system of the future, most anticipated something more democratic than that of the Third Republic, which they saw as retaining Napoleonic or monarchist elements. Thus, the Communists proposed that communes and departments be given financial and political autonomy, to be guaranteed by putting an end to the prefects and subprefects. The Socialists similarly expected an end to the *tutelle* and the freedom of the communes and departments. Together, toward the end of 1945, they even called for the creation of a mayor of the department.[97] In this, and in other decentralizing reforms, however, they were to be sorely disappointed by the Fourth Republic.

Under the Vichy government, in sum, there was considerable centralizing legislation accompanied by minimal debate. But most of this legislation was rescinded at the end of the war. The Fourth Republic essentially returned to the system established at the beginning of the Third Republic.

[96]See Burdeau, *Libertés*, pp. 255–7. For a discussion of how regional administration worked, see Yves Durand, "La politique régionale de Vichy dans la pratique: La préfecture régionale d'Orléans," in *Régions*, Gras and Livet, pp. 506–27.

[97]Burdeau, *Libertés*, pp. 257–9.

3

The unsuccessful push for decentralization from the Fourth Republic through the conservative Fifth Republic

The legislative history of decentralization during the Fourth Republic and the conservative Fifth Republic under Charles de Gaulle and his conservative successors was one of failed attempts at reform. Whereas in the Fourth Republic, no real reforms were passed, during the Fifth Republic, the reforms that were passed remained basically ineffective. In the meantime, the periphery had been changing. Decentralization in the beginning of the Third Republic, as we have seen, essentially enfranchised the middle-income peasants and shopkeepers at the expense of the proletariat and of the formerly all-powerful aristocracy, thereby setting the stage for a new balance of local political power. But by the Fourth and especially the Fifth Republics, France was no longer a nation of peasants and shopkeepers, even though these groups continued to hold the balance of power in the periphery. They were increasingly challenged by newer, more progressive groups made up of the *salariés*. These wage earners consisted of middle-level managers and workers who, living in the rapidly growing urban agglomerations that were essentially left out of the rural-dominated complicity in center–periphery relations, were intent on creating a more diverse set of local institutions and on demanding an equal share of local power.[1] These are the groups that were turning more and more toward the Socialists and Communists, first in local elections and finally in the national elections of 1981. Throughout the Fourth and the conservative Fifth Republics, however, their desires were largely ignored, with the politicians of the Fourth Republic focusing more on the traditional groups in the periphery and the Gaullists of the Fifth looking to the *forces vives*, or socioprofessionals, to break the "conservative complicity" in the periphery.

The issue of decentralization reappeared as a major legislative issue at

[1]Marc Abélès, "Les Chemins de la décentralisation," *Les Temps Modernes* no. 463 (February 1985): 1,402.

70

the beginning of the Fourth Republic, and then again at regular intervals throughout the Fifth Republic to become an almost constant topic of discussion from the 1960s on. The Fourth Republic, like the Third, was on the whole characterized by legislative inactivity after a beginning flurry of activity; the conservative Fifth Republic, by continued activity that came to very little. In the meantime, the definition of decentralization had come to be more and more broadly defined and to include such topics as: (1) alleviating if not abolishing the prefect's *tutelle;* (2) giving more administrative and financial autonomy to the communes, the departments, and the regions created after World War II; and (3) increasing the mayor's executive power and transferring the prefect's executive power to the presidents of the departments and regions. But whereas the definition of decentralization was becoming broader, the primary focus of the bulk of the reform initiatives, as in the Third Republic, remained quite narrow. Legislators tended to be much less often intent on promoting local liberty than on instituting administrative reforms, and the consolidation of the communes was one of the major initiatives. It was not until the 1970s that the issue of local democracy again began to be seriously conjoined with the topic of administrative reform in the arguments of most parties to the debate.

This pattern was equally true for the regions, which, especially for the conservative governments of the Fifth Republic, had become almost exclusively a vehicle for administrative reform and a means of creating a counterweight to local power, even though the regionalist movement had been gaining increasing strength in a variety of areas. The discrediting of the regions as a result of Vichy and their subsequent revival as an administrative arm of the central government, even leaving aside the traditional objections to regionalization, made the idea of instituting the region as a regular level of government suspect. It was only in the 1970s that the regionalists' call for regional self-determination (in watered-down form) joined the mainstream of the debate.

With the lack of significant reforms, the need for decentralization came to be felt more and more acutely, given the centralization attendant upon the exponential growth in the size and weight of the state. But the resistance to formal decentralization was great, coming from local administrators, whose powers would naturally decline with decentralization; from local elected officials who feared that any change might jeopardize the large measure of informal power and autonomy they had come to enjoy as a result of a relationship of complicity with the prefect and other representatives of the central government in the periphery;[2] and from national politicians. On the one hand, the lack of significant reform in

[2] See Part II, Chapter 6 for the details of this relationship.

Parliament reflected the disagreement among rival parties as to the best way of solving the problem. On the other hand, it attested to the combined strength of those who opposed the various proposed solutions, either because they were Jacobins on the right and the left, convinced of the need for centralization, or because they were participants, as local elected officials, in the cozy set of relations developing between prefects and local notables. National politicians were increasingly also mayors or municipal, departmental, and regional councilors as a result of the *cumul des mandats,* or accumulation of offices, and thus the beneficiaries of a system they might otherwise have wished to destroy. Despite their concerns about the administrative inefficiencies and costs, members of the political elite were basically satisfied with the informal rules and relations at the basis of local government, which helps explain the failure of decentralizing reform efforts.

The growing number of groups with a vested interest in the existing local administrative system meant that those who promoted reform had to overcome what appeared to most scholars to be by the late 1970s insurmountable odds. Until the Socialist reforms of 1982, political interest ensured against any real decentralization that went significantly further legislatively than the decentralizing legislation of 1884 for the communes and 1871 for the departments.

THE FOURTH REPUBLIC'S RETURN TO THE STATUS QUO ANTE

The Fourth Republic essentially continued the pattern of legislative inactivity characteristic of the Third Republic after its beginning years. But, unlike the Third Republic, the Fourth Republic did not produce even one significant piece of decentralizing legislation in its first years. Scholarly consensus is that the only contribution of the Fourth Republic was an attempt to diminish the prefect's *tutelle* by substituting the term "control," a change in words only.

With the end of World War II and the Vichy interlude, the legislators had to reconstruct the polity and the economy. The rallying cry, "the return to republican legality," for local government meant a return to the institutions of the Third Republic, the departments and the communes. The reaction against Vichy spelled the death knell for regional reform, especially because its strongest supporters on the extreme right had been discredited. But even at the departmental and communal levels, both the disagreements among proponents of decentralizing reforms and the strength of their opponents ensured that, during the Fourth Republic, no real reforms were ever passed. The moment was really lost due to the delay in reform resulting from the need to stabilize the country during the liberation period. Whereas the first Constituent Assembly actually contemplated some significant reform, the less left-wing, second Constituent Assembly ensured that the Fourth Republic would return to the institutions of the Third, nothing more.

In the first months of the liberation, the left replaced the regional prefects of Vichy with regional *commissaires de la République* charged to restore republican legality. This experience, along with that of Vichy, inspired a few Deputies to propose regionalization projects. Among them was that of F. L. Closon, who in 1946 recommended replacing the departments with regions consisting of two councils, one either directly or indirectly elected by the local population, the other "economic council" made up of socioprofessionals, representing managers, workers, farmers, and artisans.[3] Others suggested that the region be kept at the very least for the purposes of the deconcentration of the central ministries. But these suggestions were quickly thrust aside, due to the reaction against the regions, which had their origins in the Vichy regime. Even the Christian Democrats of the *Mouvement républicain populaire* (MRP) (the successors of the PDP), despite their previous history of support for the regions, made only a brief reference to administrative decentralization in their program of 1945, and in pamphlets denounced the "federalism that was such a threat to national unity in times of crisis."[4] All in all, the arguments favoring the regions were dismissed out of hand by an Assembly intent on putting an end to "regional anarchy."[5]

Most parties to the debate, opposing any and all forms of regionalism, argued one and all for a return to "republican legality" and to the institutions of the Third Republic. For the Communists, the only significant departure from the past was that the president of the department was to be the departmental executive in place of the prefect, whom they saw as the agent of the exploitative, monopoly-controlled state and as the arm of local, private economic interests. The Communists, though, were the only ones to go so far as to suggest the elimination of the prefect, and they continued to support this after the initial piece of legislation was passed in 1946 (that is, in 1947, 1957, and 1963). However, lest we mistakenly assume that the ordinarily centralizing Communists were truly decentralizing in this case, we must note that in the law proposed in 1957, they recommended substituting a "delegate of the government" for the prefect, leaving open the likelihood that the prefect would have retained significant

---

[3]For the range of regional projects proposed during the Fourth Republic, see Mény, *Centralisation*, pp. 182–98.
[4]Mayeur, "Démocratie chrétienne," in *Régions*, Gras and Livet, p. 458.
[5]Mény, *Centralisation*, p. 76.

powers even with the transfer of executive power to the departmental president.[6] Nevertheless, in their support of empowering the departments, the Communists went further than any other parties to the debates.

The Socialists did not push for as significant a change as the Communists. Many were afraid that "federalism, more or less anarchical" would occur if the Communist-inspired legislation were voted. Although the Socialists also proposed that the president of the general council be its executive head, they wanted to retain the prefect to represent the central government and to exercise "administrative control" rather than the *tutelle*. Moreover, other than this somewhat ambiguous proposal, the *Section française de l'internationale ouvrière* (SFIO), despite its traditional decentralizing views and its own decentralized party organization, did little to promote decentralization; and they suggested nothing to adapt the institutions of the Third Republic to the new realities of the Fourth. This cautiousness was in part due to the fact that the members of the SFIO, well established at the local level, were already satisfied with the local system as it was, in part to the fact that the left in power had a lot of other things to think about besides decentralization. Reconstruction, economic problems, and decolonization took up the energies of the left.[7]

The Radicals, too, once they became more important actors in the debate during the second Constituent Assembly (in the first, the Communists and the Socialists were dominant), soon became preoccupied with things other than decentralization. In particular, they were concerned with the maintenance of public order and the limitation of the Communists' potential power, which any decentralizing legislation would enhance. Thus, the Radicals continued their traditional ambivalence with regard to decentralization, appearing more decentralizing in word than in deed. Although in the debates Pierre Cot exhorted them: "Put trust in the people of the department. Put more democracy in the organization of public power and do not fear the future," the Radicals were instrumental in ensuring that the local government system of the Third Republic would be reinstituted, essentially unchanged.[8]

On the right and among moderates, the demand was quite simply for a return to the pre-Vichy laws and institutions and for an end to the regions in any shape or form. This was the demand that won the day.

By March 1946 the Constituent Assembly had agreed to get rid of the regional *commissaires* and the regional services in order, in the words of the Socialists, to restore to its former position the "department of the republic . . . the cement of French unity."[9] This did not, however, lead to

[6]Ibid., pp. 94–9.
[7]Ibid., pp. 119–22.
[8]*Journal Officiel*, Sept. 5, 1946, quoted in Mény, *Centralisation*, p. 119.
[9]Mény, *Centralisation*, p. 76. For a full account of the debates, see ibid., pp. 68–80.

any greater powers for the departments since the Radicals, supported by the right and with the tacit approval of the Socialists, opposed the Communists' proposal to transfer the powers of the prefect to the president of the general council.[10] The Radicals and the right saw the immediate elimination of the prefects and the creation of a departmental president with executive powers as leading France down the path to anarchy, federalism, even "a federalism of colors," viz., of different political sides. According to E. Herriot, this would be a threat to "the unity and indivisibility of the Republic."[11]

The final result of the debate in the second Constituent Assembly was a compromise in which almost everyone was satisfied, despite the fact that nothing was won. Whereas Article 87 of Title X of the Constitution of 1946 actually stated that the executive head of the department was to be the president of the general council and not the prefect, Article 89 postponed the implementation of this until a later organic law could work out the details – which never happened. Moreover, despite the initial moves to replace the prefect, Title X only provided for the legal substitution of the word *tutelle* with *contrôle administratif.* This was barely even a change in words, because *tutelle* continued to be employed, and the actual administrative control was not significantly reduced.

The failure of decentralization during the beginning years of the Fourth Republic was also influenced by the uncertainties of the *après-guerre* and the need to reestablish order. It also had to do with resistance to reform by the prefectoral corps and by local notables. Brian Chapman, commenting in the mid-1950s on the resistance of the notables, found that the reasons were mainly political: some politicians feared the creation of "red fiefs" in departments such as Haute Vienne, whereas others feared competition from newly powerful local presidents of the general councils. Among the presidents themselves, some were loathe to take on the administrative burdens, and others "feared that such an increase in authority would render them personally responsible before the public; they would be compelled sometimes to take unpopular decisions and their political position with the electorate would be endangered."[12]

The prefects were happy to feed the uncertainties of local notables, presenting themselves as the guarantors of local autonomy. The prefects were understandably hostile to a reform that would have transferred their executive powers in the department to the president of the general council. As a result, from the very beginning of the Fourth Republic, they focused all of their efforts on neutralizing Title X of the Constitution. In

[10]Ibid, pp. 80–7. See also Michel Phlipponneau, "La Gauche et le régionalisme," in *Régions*, Gras and Livet, pp. 530–1.
[11]Mény, *Centralisation*, pp. 86–7.
[12]Chapman, *Prefects* p. 174–5.

this, they were able to enlist the support not only of the central government by way of Léon Blum, who, as president of the Council of Ministers, encouraged the prefects to consolidate their powers over the field services of the state and to exert their administrative control over local collectivities in order to ensure "in all circumstances the superior interest of the nation over all particularist tendencies, productive of anarchy," but also of the press.[13] *Le Monde* published the views of a member of the prefectoral corps and *Le Figaro* published André Siegfried's defense of the "modus vivendi" of the Third Republic, with its tradition of collaboration between prefects and general councilors.[14]

The result of this resistance to the implementation of departmental reform on the part of local notables and prefects, combined with the general opposition to regional reform, was that the departments returned to their prewar status, with no more and no less power than before, and no longer threatened by the possibility of a new regional level of local government. But for all this, the push for some form of regionalization was not at all dead. Its focus, however, became much more functional – concentrating on resolving economic and social programs through regional planning – than institutional, the focus of efforts from the turn of the century through the Vichy regime. Most influential in this regard was the book by Jean-François Gravier, *Paris and the French Desert,* which struck a chord throughout France. It insisted that Paris had blighted all of France and that centralization and the central position of Paris in economic development were the major causes of the slow growth of France in general and the lack of regional industrial development in particular.[15] The resulting public discussions spurred on the economic decentralization policies of the central ministries and the creation of regional bodies with specialized functions.

Even in the very beginning of the Fourth Republic, at a time when the region was officially eliminated in favor of the departments, some regional services of the central ministries were nevertheless allowed to persist, despite the expressed intentions of the legislators to wipe out all vestiges of regionalization.[16] Moreover, the need to keep public order led in 1948 to the installation in the military regions of specialized administrative regions headed by inspectors general of the administration in extraordinary mission, the IGAMEs. The new central planning system initiated during this period brought with it demands for a regional compo-

[13]Unpublished circular by Léon Blum, Jan. 17, 1947, cited in Mény, *Centralisation,* p. 345 n. 15.
[14]A. Siegfried, "Défense du département et du préfet," *Le Figaro,* Sept. 24–5, 1949, cited in Mény, *Centralisation,* p. 345.
[15]Jean-François Gravier, *Paris et le désert français* (Paris: Portulan, 1947; Flammarion, 1958).
[16] Mény, *Centralisation,* pp. 79–80.

nent. By 1955 and 1956, twenty-three economic regions were administratively designated to serve as the framework for the elaboration of regional land-use plans, with the regional action programs set up (as a result of the decree of June 30, 1955) under the supervision of the IGAMEs which were to "coordinate the activities of the administrative services and private initiatives in order to favor the economic fabric and to complete the plan of modernization."[17] In addition, the *comités d'expansion,* or expansion committees, found in all regions as of 1950 and made up of local elected officials and socioprofessionals (consisting of industrialists, merchants, managers, agricultural and industrial union leaders, and academics), were given, as of 1954, an official consultative role in the planning process.[18] Little actual regional consultation occurred, however, before the plans of 1957, when a preliminary plan was submitted to a Committee on Regional Planning, to the regional prefects, and the *comités d'expansion.* Local consultation and specific regional policies for development and investment, however, had to wait until 1964 and the creation of the *Délégation à l'aménagement du territoire et à l'action régionale* (DATAR) and of regional commissions made up of local representatives.

The regions, in brief, began to take form out of functional necessity, even though the legislators of the Fourth Republic had sought to deny them any existence whatsoever. It was not until the Fifth Republic of de Gaulle that the regions were to be consecrated officially as deconcentrated levels of governmental action, and not until de Gaulle's successors that they were to become semiautonomous entities, with attributes of their own. In the meantime, the commune and the department were left essentially unchanged. Throughout the conservative Fifth Republic, the prefect was to remain the departmental executive, with the provisions of the Constitution of the Fourth Republic left a dead letter.

THE CONSISTENT FAILURE OF REFORM EFFORTS IN DE GAULLE'S FIFTH REPUBLIC

The Fifth Republic under de Gaulle from 1958 to 1969 engaged in constant efforts to reform local government, which nevertheless resulted in consistent failure. There were innumerable laws, decrees, and ordinances intended to change the administrative structure, finances, and even elites of local government. De Gaulle was intent not only on economic revival and administrative reform, but also on rebalancing forces in the periph-

[17]Paul Camous, "La génèse du project gouvernemental," in *La Réforme régionale et le referendum du 27 avril 1969,* ed. J. L. Bodiguel et al. (Paris: Cujas, 1970), p. 22.
[18]For a full discussion of the regional reforms related to economic development, see ibid., pp. 198–212.

ery to produce a Gaullist majority in local governments. Most of his reforms, however, were more technocratic and deconcentrating in nature than they were democratic and decentralizing. And they met with tremendous resistance not only from members of the opposition but even from the traditionalist members of de Gaulle's own majority and from local administrators, all of whom had been growing increasingly comfortable with the local government system as it stood and had little desire to change it. The local notables were an almost unbeatable force against change, and every resulting law was watered down by them.

The government's approach to reform under de Gaulle

Unable to gain the cooperation of the notables or to proceed to a radical reform, de Gaulle took another route to reform by seeking to create new structures with the regions and with the communes. The ineffectiveness of regional reform was matched by the failure of the efforts to rationalize local government, either by significantly reducing the number of communes or by alleviating the congestion at the center by increasing the prefects' deconcentrated powers.

Instead of focusing his reform efforts on the long-established institutions of local government, de Gaulle attempted to set up a direct link between the central state and the periphery by adding another level of local administration, the region. De Gaulle's interest in the region was primarily as an instrument for economic revival, administrative reform, and political rebalancing. The region, according to de Gaulle's calculations, was to become a counterweight to local power by waking up the socioprofessional groups at the periphery, which were to take power from the conservative complicity of prefects and notables holding the departmental and municipal levels of local government hostage. The reform was essentially corporatist, aimed at deconcentrating rather than decentralizing mainly economic decision-making power in the periphery in order to favor the more dynamic elements of the local population.

De Gaulle set up the regions in 1959–60, grouping the departments into twenty-one *circonscriptions d'action régionale,* or regional action areas. They became functional administrative units in 1964 with a consultative assembly, the CODER, or regional economic development commission. The CODER was made up one-half of representatives of socioprofessional interest groups and one-fourth each of local elected officials and government appointees, charged to consult on the plan and public investment affecting the region. They also gained a regional prefect assisted by a regional mission (the equivalent of an economic think tank) and a regional administrative conference (an advisory body consisting of departmental prefects and regional heads of the field services of the state).

This regional structure, however, was only a beginning for de Gaulle. In 1966 he was already considering democratizing it, by linking it with a reform of the Senate to create a "single assembly uniting the representatives of local collectivities and regional activities with the big economic and social organizations of the country in order to deliberate economic questions before the National Assembly votes on the laws." It was only in March 1968, however, that de Gaulle made completely clear his dissatisfaction with the regional structure as it stood. The events of May 1968 intervened. De Gaulle then tried, but failed, to turn the regions into political units with the referendum of 1969, as we shall see below.

The department, too, gained power throughout the postwar period with the expansion of the departmental administrations by the state in the 1950s and 1960s. The decree of March 14, 1964, was an attempt to rationalize the organization of the field services of the state by putting them under the authority of the prefect. But this was generally regarded as ineffective. Otherwise, the basic organization of the department was left essentially untouched.

The communes also failed to be reformed as needed. The primary focus was on administrative reform, and the primary problem was the unwieldy number of communes, with only the largest able to confront adequately the difficulties of modern urban planning and development. In order to remedy this situation, rather than seeking to alter existing structures, the government sought to superimpose new structures on the old. Thus it passed such measures as the decree of 1958, authorizing the establishment of *districts urbains,* and the ordinance of 1959, facilitating the creation of multipurpose syndicates (SIVOM: *syndicats intermunicipales à vocation multiple*), which together allowed communes to group together in voluntary associations to provide common services.

On the whole, these innovations were very slow in getting off the ground, hampered by local rivalries, fears, and general lack of cooperativeness. Of these reforms, only the communal syndicates achieved some measure of success. By 1970, there were more than 1,000 syndicates, grouping together 11,205 communes, representing one-fourth of the population.[19] The least successful reforms were the districts, which mayors generally opposed because they saw them as taking powers away from the communes and because they could be established without the full agreement of the communes involved.[20] The inadequacy of the districts in particular led to the law of December 1966, which forced the creation of "urban communities" out of four large urban agglomerations (Bordeaux, Lille, Lyons, and Strasbourg) and allowed others to be cre-

[19]Mény, *Centralisation,* p. 288.
[20]Ibid., p. 306.

ated elsewhere on a voluntary basis.[21] These urban communities gained
super councils, which were elected by the municipal councils of the member communes and dealt with the major questions affecting the grouped
communes. By July 1976, however, only 9 urban communities, 163 districts, and 1,800 syndicates of communes had been formed.[22] The attempt to encourage the fusion of communes voluntarily through greater
financial incentives had also met with little success. By 1969 the number
of communes had been reduced by only 1,000, from 38,000 to 37,000.[23]

Paris, too, was the focus of administrative reform throughout this
period, beginning with its division into a *district de la région de Paris* in
1961. The district, incorporating three departments and 8 million inhabitants, was primarily responsible for planning and development. Although
it was composed of elected members of local governments, half were
nominated by the government and were thus Gaullist-dominated, especially because its head was appointed by the government and responsible
to the prime minister. Obviously, this met with resistance by local elected
officials. But they could do little then, just as they could do little in 1964,
when the government, without consultation with local officials, reorga-
nized the Paris region and district by redividing it into five departments as
of 1968 and by replacing the two-tier system of municipal and departmental councils in the department of Paris with a single elected assembly.
Although in 1968, as in 1964, the ostensible reason for reorganization
was the need for administrative reform, the fact that the Seine departmental council had an opposition majority or that the Communists were
powerful in the so-called red belt around Paris played no small role, as
evidenced by the creation of departmental boundaries designed to diminish the Communist party's effectiveness in the region.

The initiative to reform local finances, which had begun in 1958, had
still not seen the light of day.[24] In 1968, however, the *tutelle* was alleviated to a small extent in financial matters, when a number of communes
were allowed to introduce their budgets without the prefect's prior approval (increasing from 646 to 3,083 communes, all larger than two
thousand inhabitants). The mayor's powers and responsibilities were also
slightly increased. These reforms, however, as those at the departmental
and regional levels, did little to alleviate the increasingly serious problems

[21]The Bordeaux urban community was relatively easy to accomplish by contrast
with Lyon, where the attempt to consolidate led to a long, drawn-out court battle.
[22]Howard Machin, "All Jacobins now? The growing hostility to local government
reform," *West European Politics* vol. 1, no. 3 (Oct. 1978): 148.
[23]For the way in which the fusions affected the communes, see Mény, *Centralisation,*
pp. 289–98.
[24]Yves Mény, "Financial transfers and local governments in France: National policy
despite 36,000 communes," in *Financing Urban Government in the Welfare State,* ed.
D. E. Ashford (London: Croon Helm, 1980), pp. 142–57.

of the local governmental system. The problem was that all attempts at reform were met with resistance by local elected officials and administrators as well as by national politicians.

The response to de Gaulle's initiatives

The resistance of local administrators, local elected officials, and national politicians on both the left and the right made significant reform almost an impossibility. To begin with, civil servants, responsible for local administration, represented one of the main sources of resistance to decentralization, especially in its regional form. Part of the reason for the slowness and timidity of the reforms resulted directly, as Charles Debbasch explained, from "the position of functionaries in the decision-making process. It is clearly difficult to ask those very people to transform the administrative system that they themselves represent."[25] The prefects in particular were openly hostile to regionalization in the 1960s, seeing it as a threat to their own traditional career patterns, to their independence in the department, and to their traditional relationship with local notables. Even the few prefects who supported regionalization wanted to make certain that the regions in no way supplanted the departments and thus they envisaged, at best, a limited role for the regions with a regional prefect who would be departmental prefect at the same time and, therefore, "first among equals," rather than a higher authority.[26]

Ultimately, the prefects accommodated themselves to the regional reform, recognizing that there was little they could do to stop it. But they viewed it, just as most of the other reforms that were passed, as only having complicated their tasks. The field services of the state basically shared these views.[27]

Local elected officials, like the administrators, tended to oppose any and all reforms, albeit for somewhat different reasons. Any Gaullist reform effort was certain to be greeted with suspicion by local elected officials, because a vast majority of the opposition dominated local government. Whereas in 1967, 41 percent of the national deputies were members of the Gaullist *Union pour la nouvelle République* (UNR), in 1965 after the municipal elections only 9 percent of all municipal councilors were. And this number further diminished after the March 1971 municipal elections. These figures are all the more significant when one remembers that national politics was split on the right–left divide, but

[25]Charles Debbasch, *L'Administration au pouvoir* (Paris: Calmann-Lévy, 1969), p. 214.
[26]Mény, *Centralisation*, pp. 357–60.
[27]Machin, "All Jacobins," pp. 143–4. See also idem, *The Prefect in French Public Administration* (New York: St. Martin's, 1977), pp. 89–90.

local politics often involved alliances toward the center from the moderate right to the moderate left.

The central government's focus on regional reform was very much an attempt by de Gaulle to circumvent the powers in the periphery. Local notables were not likely to respond kindly to such a strategy and thus agree to give away their own local power, especially because a majority of them didn't even share in such power at the national level. They only diminished in their hostility to the regions once they had essentially colonized the regional establishments themselves.

Local elected officials from the communes and the departments, on the left or the right, saw themselves alone as representative of the local population and, therefore, the only legitimate interlocutors with the central government. Of course, they considered the regional reform, with its emphasis on planning and its use of technocrats and socioprofessionals, to be a direct attack on their own positions. Their "technophobia" led them to insist that the technical competence of the agents of the central state did not offset their mediocrity as administrators and their ignorance of local conditions.[28] They found the socioprofessionals in particular to be a challenge to their own representativeness. Already in 1955, with the *comités d'expansion,* but certainly with the creation of the CODER in 1964, the reaction of local general councilors was extremely negative. The extent of the perceived threat was such that one usually moderate general council president, M. Abel-Durand, asked in 1964 at the yearly meeting of the Assembly of Presidents of General Councils whether the government didn't have a "more or less conscious design . . . to progressively undermine the authority of departmental and municipal administrators elected by universal suffrage, to finish by smothering the personality of local collectivities under new organisms that would be nothing other than barely disguised instruments of an omnipotent state."[29]

Faced with the fact of the regional reform of 1964, though, the general councilors decided that because they couldn't beat it, they would join it. Despite their hostility, the general councilors made haste to participate once the CODERs were set up, to make certain that they didn't find themselves without any influence at all. And they very quickly came to dominate them. It was only one year later, in 1965, that Abel-Durand congratulated his fellow presidents on having made a "conquest" by taking their places in the CODER, because they had no guaranteed representation on the *comités d'expansion,* which the CODER had replaced.[30]

[28]Mény, *Centralisation,* p. 315.
[29]XXXVth Congress of the APGC (Assembly of Presidents of General Councils), *Départements et Communes* (Sept–Oct. 1964), p. 15, cited in Mény, *Centralisation,* p. 317.
[30]*Départements et Communes* (June 1965), p. 17, cited in Mény, *Centralisation,* p. 323.

In the end, the regional reform of 1964 only reinforced the powers of the department.[31] The 1969 proposed regional reform was another matter. Having colonized the regional establishments, local elected officials were certainly unwilling to give up their newly acquired powers.

National politicians were also not always keen on reform, even when they were members of the Gaullist majority. Some were convinced Jacobins like Michel Debré who felt that strong regions would be a danger to the unity of the nation, stating: "Those who wish to humble the nation seek first to humble Paris."[32] Debré favored instead the creation of forty-seven department-regions in place of the old departments, because they could be more efficiently administered and would avoid the major problems of centralization without at the same time threatening national unity – his obsession.[33]

The bulk of the Gaullist supporters who resisted decentralization, however, did so less out of Jacobin concerns than because they themselves were also local elected officials as a result of the *cumul des mandats*. The growing localization of national politics, seen in the rise of the number of national deputies with a local base from 63 percent in 1958 to 80 percent in 1967, together with the relative weakness of national parties, meant that national politicians would be most likely to focus their attention on responding to local needs.[34] This, in turn, would ensure that they would do little to upset the complicity at the base that guaranteed that they personally, at least, would not be held responsible for any unpopular decisions. At the same time, they could always take credit for taking care of local needs on the basis of their personal proximity to power as national politicians. The situation, in effect, left politicians profoundly ambivalent toward reform.

This ambivalence comes out most clearly in legislators' political debate in general on the topic of decentralization. According to Yves Mény, the dramatic political language of the debates themselves, which stated issues in terms of their extremes, became an impediment to action – or an excuse for inaction.[35] Whereas many were sincere in their arguments for or against decentralization, others used them to resist reform, for example, when legislators talked of preserving local liberties as a way of resisting any structural reforms that might jeopardize their powers.[36]

[31]See Pierre Grémion and Jean-Pierre Worms, *Les Institutions régionales et la société locale* (Paris: Centre de Sociologie, 1969).

[32]Philip M. Williams and Martin Harrison, *Politics and Society in de Gaulle's Republic* (New York: Anchor, 1971), p. 294.

[33]For a full account of Debré's views, see Mény, *Centralisation*, pp. 153–73.

[34]Pierre Birnbaum, Francis Hamon, and Michel Troper, *Réinventer le parlement* (Paris: Flammarion, 1977), pp. 30–5.

[35]Mény, *Centralisation*, pp. 50–2.

[36]Ibid., pp. 52–6.

Mény found that the general support for decentralization was both its strength and its weakness. Because everyone agreed, it was hard to muster the troops for battle and hard to get particular programs of reform.[37] He contended, moreover, that a continuing, profoundly centralizing attitude coexisted with a decentralizing rhetoric, something possible only through the ambiguity of the political language. This attitude, he insisted, came from the fact that all still held dear the idea of the unitary state, regardless of their ideology. Thus, at the same time that they all defended decentralization, none would consider challenging the national statute of the civil service, the national diplomas, national regulation, and the uniformity of the law.[38]

Against the backdrop of general legislative resistance to reform, there were nonetheless numerous groups pushing for change. But they were extremely diverse and, as a result, unable to make common cause in favor of reform. Among these groups, most importantly, were, on the one hand, those who proposed radical change in the institutional structures of government, whether because they were ethnic regionalists or supporters of a united Europe, and, on the other hand, those who wanted only to reform the existing structures, primarily progressive civil servants. Both sides, however, were dissatisfied with de Gaulle's reforms.

The most radical of the groups demanding changes in the nation-state as it currently existed were the ethnic regionalists of Bretagne, Corsica, and "Occitan," agitating for local autonomy, fueled by the revival of a regionalism not seen since the early years of the Third Republic.[39] The ethnic regionalists found their strongest support in the work of Pierre Fougeyrollas, who attacked head-on the preoccupation of over two centuries of legislators, and argued for a European unity based on the federalization of France into regions as a way of getting rid of centralist despotism and of "deprefectoralizing." Robert Lafont picked up on this theme and described the prefect as a "monarch by delegation" and proposed giving the regions full powers as local governments within the context of a federated Europe.[40] But the ethnic regionalists also found reinforcement from an entire series of regional groups, whose demands were more moderate, among them associations seeking greater economic resources for their regions, whether they were underdeveloped regions or ones benefiting from an economic takeoff. Finally, at the margins were the

---

[37]Yves Mény, "Le débat politique et la décentralisation," in *La Décentralisation pour la rénovation de L'État,* ed. Charles Debbasch (Paris: Presses universitaires de France, 1976), p. 41.
[38]Ibid., p. 44.
[39]For the development of the regionalist movement, see Mény, *Centralisation,* pp. 371–98.
[40]Pierre Fougeyrollas, *Pour une France fédérale* (Paris: Denoël, 1968); Robert Lafont, *La Révolution régionaliste* (Paris: NRF Collection Idées, 1969), p. 37.

84

peasants of the "inefficient" agricultural regions, which had organized successful protest movements at the beginning of the 1960s.[41]

The goal of the ethnic regionalists, in short, was to destroy the nation-state and establish the regions as the new primary structure, with Europe merely as the necessary secondary, federative level required to organize the regions. By contrast, for the Europeanists, who also wanted to destroy the nation-state, Europe was the primary structure, the regions simply technical divisions necessary for economic and administrative reasons. The Europeanists gave no thought to regional self-determination, especially because their entire purpose was to get away from the particularisms already too pronounced in the division of Europe into nation-states.[42]

Whereas the Europeanists and ethnic regionalists wanted to destroy the nation-state, many progressive civil servants wanted to reform it more moderately, by reconciling the nation with the state, making the state more democratic as well as more efficient.[43] For most of these civil servants, this meant promoting the "nationalization of the state," by opening up access to the state by the nation, that is, the citizenry at large, through greater deconcentration at the regional and departmental levels and, to a lesser degree, greater decentralization to the benefit of the communes. The state through the mediation of its functionaries, in other words, was to remain coordinator and *tuteur*, but was to leave to a more active and participative citizenry the direction and development of local activity.[44]

In the more enlightened, upper levels of the civil service, there was also a focus on regionalization, but in this case as a way of increasing the flow of economic resources to the regions in order to ensure economic efficiency. Thus, progressive technocrats at the *Commissariat général au Plan* and at the DATAR, among others, proposed numerous plans for the overhaul of the country's territorial administration. The DATAR talked of a "growing industrial desert," of "social costs," and of "external diseconomies," while seeking "integrated" economic development.[45] On the left, the upper-level civil servants of the *Club Jean Moulin*, linking communal reform to re-

[41]See the discussion in Sidney Tarrow, "Decentramento incompiuto o centralismo restaurato? L'esperienza regionalistica in Italia e in Francia," *Rivista di Scienza Politica* vol. 9, no. 2 (August 1979): 232.
[42]See Mény, *Centralisation*, pp. 399–436.
[43]The apposition of "destroying the nation-state" versus reconciling the nation with the state is that of Mény in *Centralisation*, pt. II.
[44]C. Alphandéry et al., *Pour nationaliser l'État* (Paris: Seuil, 1986), pp. 24–6.
[45]Guillaume Hannezo and Jean Rondin, "La décentralisation: Une passion d'opposant?" *Échange et Projets* no. 41 (Mar. 1985): 48–9; and Cathérine Grémion, "Decentralization in France: A historical perspective." Paper presented at the conference, "Continuity and Change in Mitterrand's France" (Cambridge, Mass.: Dec. 5–8, 1985), p. 6.

gional reform, proposed a new structure of twelve regions and two thousand communes with directly elected, salaried mayors.[46]

These views tended to remain outside the political mainstream, though, and were taken up only by a minority party on the left, the *Parti socialiste unifié* (PSU) of Michel Rocard, which alone among the political parties provided innovative contributions early on to the debate on decentralization.[47] At the Congress of Grenoble (in May 1966), Rocard, in particular, brought together concerns for increased local democracy with the promotion of local economic development, mixing a managerial theme with democratic imperatives. Here, the focus was still on reconciling the state with the nation, not on destroying the nation-state; but now the answer was to be found at the regional level, through an end to the "colonization of the provinces," the "unequal exchange," and the "confiscation of added value," with "development centered around each locality."[48] This remedy, although based on an analysis that interpreted regional underdevelopment as the regional expression of the class struggle – one in which Paris came to represent the bourgeoisie and the provinces, the proletariat – was nonetheless similar to that of the upper-level civil servants in that the local community was to be able to revitalize itself and master its own development.[49]

With the exception of the PSU, the political parties on the left were, on the whole, comparatively quiet on the matter of decentralization during much of de Gaulle's tenure in office, mainly responding negatively to the Gaullist initiatives. They began to have a siege mentality, and saw most of de Gaulle's reforms as attacks on the last of the "republican bastions" in the periphery. Thus they saw the 1964 regional reforms as attacks on the departments, the creation of the districts and the urban communities as attempts to deny local freedom to the communes, and both of these, together with the electoral law on cities of over thirty thousand, as clear efforts to dilute the left's own strength.[50] They opposed, in particular, the CODER, with its socioprofessional composition titled in favor of management rather than union representation and, with the reform of 1964, the extremely limited departmental representation in comparison with that of socioprofessionals and appointed members. Nevertheless, left-wing

[46]Club Jean Moulin, *Les citoyens au pouvoir* (Paris: Seuil, 1968).

[47]For the intricacies of the internal debates and the resulting proposals, see Mény, *Centralisation*, pp. 475–86.

[48]Michel Rocard, "Décoloniser la province." Report to the Congress at Grenoble (May 1, 1966), Fondation nationale des sciences politiques, Br. 8° 480 (11). See also Hannezo and Rondin, "Décentralisation," pp. 48–9; and Cathérine Grémion, "Decentralization," p. 6.

[49]For an account of this analysis, see Mény, *Centralisation*, pp. 479–85.

[50]Ibid., pp. 123–9, for the left's views on the urban districts.

general councilors preferred to go along with the reform, inserting themselves into the system rather than fighting it.[51]

Very few national leaders on the non-Communist left were favorable to
regionalization at this time. Two notable exceptions were Pierre Mendès-
France and Gaston Defferre. In 1962, Mendès-France published a book
in which he recommended an innovative model of regional organization
that did not, however, challenge the traditional political structures: the
ten to twelve regions, delimited on the basis of economic criteria more
than of historical or ethnic, had no political role and were to consist of a
regional economic council made up of socioprofessionals and an executive power delegated by the central government.[52] Gaston Defferre went
beyond this when, as part of the presidential election of 1965, he included
in his platform, Horizon '80, a somewhat vague recommendation that
the regions have elected assemblies with real powers and even the possibility of a regional executive "if the experience reverals itself positive." Not
all Socialists went quite this far, however; François Mitterand, when
asked about the possibility of a regional executive for Brittany, rejected
the idea completely.[53] Nonetheless, not long after this in 1969, Mitterand
claimed to want rid of the prefects, seeing them as governors.[54]

By the late 1960s, in any event, the non-Communist parties of the left
had become much more actively supportive of decentralization, picking
up on the demands of the various social movements for new relations
between governors and the governed by calling for participation and
autogestion. The non-Communist left was influenced not only by the
PSU, but also by Michel Phlipponneau, a regionalist from Bretagne who
came to socialism and ultimately joined the *Parti socialiste* (PS) because,
unlike the radical ethnic regionalists, he was interested in promoting a
regionalism that would reconcile, not destroy, the nation-state.[55] The
model appropriated by the Socialists grouped together in the *Féderation
de la gauche démocrate et socialiste* (FGDS) was largely inspired by the
one proposed by Phlipponneau and the Breton regionalists of the *Club
Bretagne et Démocratie* in 1967. It called for the regularization of the
region as a local collectivity with planning, administration, and regula-

---

[51]Phlipponneau, "La Gauche," p. 532.

[52]Pierre Mendès France, *La République moderne* (Paris: Gallimard, 1963). See
discussion in Phlipponneau, "La Gauche," pp. 535–6; Mény, *Centralisation,* pp.
133–42.

[53]Phlipponneau, "La Gauche," pp. 536–7. See also Gaston Defferre, *Un Nouvel
Horizon* (Paris: 1965); and Mény, *Centralisation,* pp. 143–6.

[54]*Le Monde,* Feb 7, 1969.

[55]For Phlipponneau's views, see *Debout Bretagne* (St. Brieuc: P.U.B., 1970); and
Mény, *Centralisation,* pp. 475–502. For his role in introducing a regional focus into
the parties of the non-Communist left, see Phlipponneau, "La Gauche," pp. 539–41.

tory powers, with its own budget and resources (transferred from the state), with an assembly elected by universal suffrage, an economic and social council, an executive elected by the assembly, a regional prefect, and its own administrative and technical personnel.[56]

By this time the Communists, too, had become favorable to regionalization, although certainly not the kind promoted by the central government. In addition to the general criticisms on the left with which they agreed, the Communists opposed government regional economic policy and land-use planning on the grounds that it didn't solve the problems in the disparities between the regions in salaries, employment, and so forth, and it failed to promote the decongestion of Paris.[57] But in their recommendations for reform, they were more cautious than the Socialists, fearing federalism. For them, regionalism was supposed to reequilibrate the "material and human productive forces" in the nation as a whole, and thus they were not very sympathetic to the ethnic minorities pushing for regional self-determination.[58]

By 1968, then, the left as a whole had become convinced of the need for regional reform, albeit not the corporatist and functionalist kind promoted by the central government. And their response to de Gaulle's referendum on the region in 1969 was, therefore, quite predictable.

The regional referendum of 1969

By 1968, even de Gaulle had begun to talk of the need for more participation and decentralization in local government. Thus, in early 1968, de Gaulle announced that "the centuries-old effort of centralization that was so long necessary to achieve and maintain [national] unity . . . is now no longer indispensable."[59] After the events of May, when regional reform took on even greater importance as a response to demands for increased participation, de Gaulle became intent on turning the regions into political units. The impetus behind this move, as Couve de Murville explained, was "to put an end to the centralism which, carried to the excessive degree we have now, paralyzes initiative, dilutes responsibility, and puts a brake on development."[60]

In the fall of 1968, wide consultation occurred, with local councilors, interest groups, academics, and other interested parties making their opinions known through the CODER. This came to nothing when the deci-

[56]For details, see Mény, "Le débat politique," p. 75.
[57]Mény, *Centralisation*, pp. 105–10.
[58]Ibid., pp. 110–14.
[59]*Le Monde*, Mar. 26, 1968.
[60]*Le Monde*, Mar. 25, 1969, quoted in Williams and Harrison, *Politics and Society*, p. 295.

sion to have a referendum rather than to legislate reform was taken. The same fate befell the planners' proposals for eight to twelve regions based on the current departments, and the regionalists' dreams for independent regional executives and directly elected regional assemblies able to levy their own taxes. Rather, the existing regions were to be kept, the regional prefects were to be given new powers; the new regional councils (to be composed of 60 percent Deputies and indirectly elected councilors, 40 percent socioprofessionals chosen by associations of farmers, industrial and white-collar workers, liberal professions, industry and commerce, families, and higher education) were to take over the advisory functions of the CODER as well as to gain new powers over such matters as planning, investment in education, transport, communications, health services, and tourism.[61]

Although this model certainly went a good deal further than the region of 1964, it was quite moderate, reflecting the government's concerns about the possible reactions of national and local elected officials. Thus, the "father" of the reform, Jean-Marcel Jeanneney, made a point of assuring national deputies that their presence on the regional councils would make the region "understand national imperatives" and of telling local elected officials that the region would be more a "federation of departments and a federation of communes."[62] The region, in brief, would have representatives from the other levels of government (thus promoting the *cumul des mandats* with yet another level at which to seek public office), but it was not to have any directly elected representatives of its own. These concessions to elected officials, however, were not enough to gain their support. Local elected officials had decided that they could no longer continue to accommodate themselves to reforms that threatened their representativeness and their own positions. And they were instrumental in the failure of the referendum.[63] But this is not the only reason why de Gaulle lost the referendum.

Primary among the reasons for de Gaulle's defeat was the fact that the population at large saw the referendum more as an issue of confidence in the regime than as one of regional reform.[64] A poll in September 1968, asking whether respondents were favorable or hostile to de Gaulle's proposals for regionalization, found 59 percent favorable, 33 percent without a reply, and only 8 percent hostile. Other polls found that whereas

[61]Williams and Harrison, *Politics and Society*, pp. 294–5. See also Bernard Pouyet, "Le région selon le project de la loi référendaire du 27 avril 1969," in *La Réforme régionale*, ed. Bodiguel et al., pp. 239–75. For an account of the range of problems with the reform, see Mény, *Centralisation*, pp. 230–40.

[62]*Journal Officiel*, Dec. 12, 1968, quoted in Mény, *Centralisation*, p. 232.

[63]Mény, *Centralisation*, pp. 337–9.

[64]Fifty-three percent of the voters replied "no," with 80.6 percent of the electorate voting, the highest referendum turnout since 1958.

people understood very little of the reform, only 6 percent expressed hostility to regionalization as their reason for voting "no" in the referendum. Fifty-eight percent, however, gave their reason as hostility to government policy.[65] By the end of the period leading up to the referendum itself in April 1969, it was clear to all that the main issue was confidence in de Gaulle, with the future of the regime the primary question. This was emphasized by de Gaulle himself, who declared that the choice lay between "progress and disorder," and by members of the majority, who talked of the threat of "unspecified disturbances" (Couve de Murville and Georges Pompidou), "a Communist regime" (Michel Debré), and "a takeover by the mob" (Raymond Marcellin).[66] Regional reform was no longer the issue except, of course, for the political elites.

The political elites were unhappy with the referendary nature of the reform, with the way in which regional reform was envisioned, as well as with its tie-in with Senate reform. Most importantly, de Gaulle lost the support of many of his own governing coalition, in particular the traditionalists, who opposed the kind of regional reform proposed because it threatened their own power bases in the periphery by interposing another level of government between themselves and Paris.[67] Interestingly enough, moreover, although de Gaulle's regional reform proposal reflected the basic outlines of the reforms demanded by the Christian Democrats in the 1920s – mainly in the linkage between the renewal of the Senate and the creation of the regional councils – as well as by the representation of socioprofessional categories, the Christian Democrats on the whole opposed the reform.[68] In the traditional center and among moderates, in effect, the response could have been a "yes" on regionalization but a "no" on Senate reform had the votes been separated (most defended the Senate as it was and opposed the attempt to turn it into a corporatist body, politically unrepresentative as well as less powerful). But even the "yes" on regionalization would have been an uncertain one, as many in the center called for the direct election of regional councilors and for assurances that the new region would not increase local tax burdens. In any case, these parties would have preferred a parliamentary reform to the referendum, which left no room for discussion.[69]

[65]Sofres, *Sondages* no. 3 (1969): 20, cited in Machin, "All Jacobins," p. 145.
[66]Williams and Harrison, *Politics and Society,* p. 402.
[67]Peter Gourevitch, "Reforming the Napoleonic State: The Creation of Regional Governments in France and Italy," in *Territorial Politics in Industrial Nations,* ed. Sidney Tarrow, P. J. Katzenstein, and L. Graziano (New York: Praeger Special Studies, 1978), pp. 39–46. See also Peter Gourevitch, "The reform of local government: A political analysis," *Comparative Politics* (1977).
[68]Mayeur, "Démocratie chrétienne," in *Régions,* Gras and Livet, p. 459.
[69]Marie-Françoise Souchon, "La campagne référendaire," in *Le Réforme régionale,* ed. Bodiguel et al., pp. 286–7, 292.

The left similarly objected to the referendary form, the corporatist nature of the Senate reform, and the lack of choice in the structures of regional reform. The Communists, for example, called for a regional assembly elected by universal suffrage and proportional representation, for councils given real powers in terms of the planning or the creation and administration of certain public services, for executive powers given to the president of the regional council, and for the transfer to the region of a part of the budgetary resources of the state. The socialists of the PSU called for similar reforms and proposed a common battle by all socialist forces for the "establishment of democratic organisms at the level of the region," which meant regional assemblies elected on the basis of universal suffrage with an elected executive.[70] At the same time, Mitterand, while asking for an end to the prefects, nonetheless reiterated the old concern that "the division of France into twenty-one regions is dangerous for the unity of the nation and for the autonomy of local collectives."[71] And the non-Communist left in general saw the regional model as presented by de Gaulle as a threat to the "republican bastions," the communes and departments.[72]

With the defeat of the regional proposal in the referendum, it was another three years before the region was established as a new level of local administration. And when it was established, it in no way threatened the traditionalists whom Pompidou now courted. On the whole, if significant local governmental reform was minimally successful under de Gaulle, it was even less so under his successors, who sought much more to court rather than to combat the national politicians of the center who were also the most well ensconced at the local level.

THE SLOWDOWN OF REFORM INITIATIVES IN THE CONSERVATIVE FIFTH REPUBLIC AFTER DE GAULLE

The push for reform, which culminated in failure under de Gaulle in the referendum of 1969, represented the end of any concerted central governmental attempt to significantly alter the functioning of local government. As in the past, the fact that members of the government and the members of Parliament upon whom the government depended for support were for the most part themselves mayors and members of municipal councils, presidents and members of regional councils and general councils of departments, made reform highly unlikely. The *cumul des mandats* ensured that members of the government and the parliamentary majority were themselves part of the informal network of relations in the periph-

[70]Ibid., pp. 294–5.
[71]*Le Monde*, Mar. 9–10, 1969, quoted in Mény, *Centralisation*, p. 148.
[72]Mény, *Centralisation*, pp. 148–51.

ery, which they might otherwise have wished to destroy because of the resulting administrative inefficiencies and high costs.

The problems de Gaulle sought to address with his failed reforms only worsened under his successors. The rising costs and increasing inefficiencies of local government made reform even more of a necessity, whereas the demographic shifts in the periphery rendered the institutions of local government more and more unrepresentative. During the 1960s and 1970s, in effect, approximately 10 million moved to the towns and the cities in one of the largest urban migrations in the postwar period. The result was that nine-tenths of the communes had a population of fewer than two thousand inhabitants, encompassing only one-fourth of the total population. By contrast, thirty-nine communes with a population of over one hundred thousand contained over one-half the population.[73] The depopulation of the countryside and the significant decrease in the size of the peasantry had left the large departments elected on a cantonal basis even less representative than in the past, with the rural communes predominating and the urban communes to a large extent disenfranchised in this context.

De Gaulle's successors did little to remedy these problems, although they did pass some reforms, including making the region a "public establishment." What is more, although de Gaulle sought to appeal to the socioprofessionals in the periphery, the Gaullists and conservatives who followed him in office were much more cautious and continued to cater to the interests of the Third Republic coalition, which, although less and less sizable as an electoral constituency, remained nevertheless an electoral force. The increasing marginality of these two declining socioeconomic groups had not concomitantly decreased their influence because, as the political margins between left and right diminished, these two groups began to exercise increasing electoral power.[74] The conservative governing majority tended increasingly to support the status quo as it sought to appease these groups, for example, by appealing to the shopkeepers with the *loi Royer* (a law limiting the proliferation of supermarkets and department stores) and to the peasantry with continued protectionist measures for farm produce and vinicultural products. The Socialist–Communist alliance, by contrast, took over the innovative role in calling for reforms and in representing the interests of the new electorate in the periphery (the new middle classes of *salariés*, or wage earners, made up of workers and middle managers concentrated in the urban connurbations), with a set of

---

[73]Douglas Ashford, *Policy and Politics in France* (Philadelphia: Temple University Press, 1982), pp. 111–12.

[74]Suzanne Berger and Michael J. Piore, *Dualism and Discontinuity in Industrial Societies* (Cambridge University Press, 1980), p. 89; and Sally Sokoloff, "Socialism and the Farmers," in *Socialism, the State, and Public Policy in France,* ed. Martin Schain and Philip Cerny (London: Frances Pinter, 1985), p. 248.

policy recommendations and programs to implement at the local level, together known as *autogestion,* or self-management.[75]

But the more the left pushed for reform and won local elections, the less the right was convinced of the necessity of decentralizing reform. The result was that whereas there was almost continual debate over the issue of decentralization, with calls for local liberty increasingly conjoined with discussions of the need for administrative reform, there was little in the way of real legislative action.

The government's approach to reform under Pompidou and Giscard d'Estaing

The most significant government reform after de Gaulle was the region. The attempts to rationalize local government by reducing the number of communes, to alleviate the congestion at the center by putting the prefects officially in charge of all the field services of the state, and to diminish the prefects' *tutelle* were all abject failures: the thirty-seven thousand communes were reduced at the most by only one thousand, the prefects' power over the field services of the more powerful technical ministries remained for the most part in name only, and the complicity between prefects and notables had in any case already alleviated most of the unpleasant aspects of the *tutelle.* Thus, the laws of 1970 and of 1971 (the *loi Marcellin*) on the communes, which reduced the *tutelle* in a variety of ways, contained a number of provisions intended to make the mayor a more effective manager, and included some inducements to encourage communal grouping, had little effect on communal government.[76]

The one measure that did have a significant impact on communal government was the law of December, 31, 1975, giving Paris its municipal freedom. A full century after all other cities in the country, Paris was presumably deemed safe (read "nonrevolutionary") enough to have its own elected mayor. And as if to demonstrate the conservative victory over Paris, Jacques Chirac, having resigned as prime minister in a falling out with Giscard d'Estaing, ran and won as the first elected mayor of Paris in 1977.

Most important among the local government reforms, however, was the law of July 5, 1972, institutionalizing the regions as regional public institutions, because this reform, however weak, at least gave the regions a political as well as an economic identity, setting the stage for the future expan-

[75]For a discussion of the Socialists' new electorate, see Part I, Chapter 5, "Gaining the allegiance of the new electorate."

[76]For a detailed account of the reforms, see Philip Mawhood, "Melting an iceberg: The struggle to reform communal government in France," *British Journal of Political Science* vol. 2 (1972); 506–8.

sion of its powers. This is the most one can say for the reform, however, because in terms of its impact on local government it did little more than complicate further the complicity in the periphery. Although following the legacy of de Gaulle, Pompidou was careful not to upset the local balance of power.[77] Pompidou himself allowed as how some would find his project "too prudent, not to say too timorous," but he was not about to pretend to make a revolution.[78] Quite the contrary, as Alain Peyrefitte chronicled, since Pompidou was relatively hostile to the region, as evidenced by his negative response to the 1970 project for autonomous regions (in which two regions on an experimental basis were to be allowed an elected assembly with a regional executive, with the experiment to be extended to other regions if successful), which was prepared in response to the failure of the 1969 referendum. For Pompidou, such an operation represented a threat to national unity. His primary goal, he insisted, was industrialization, and regionalization was not necessary for that.[79] The most important of laws, he remarked on another occasion in response to a journalist's query about regionalization, "is the preservation of the Republic. It is not without relation to the regional question. There is the issue of national unity; it is necessary to protect it to the highest degree, and what has been going on lately can only encourage us in this."[80]

The *loi Frey* (as the regional reform law was called) certainly reflected Pompidou's concerns, as it turned the regions into federations of departments, to distribute funds rather than to make policy. It made them legally inferior to the departments by denying them status as local governments and by allowing only indirect elections for its two advisory bodies. In place of the CODER, there was now the *Conseil régional,* or regional council – one-half consisting of all the Deputies and Senators of the region, the other half made up of representatives of the local governments elected by the general councils, the municipal councils, and the councils of the urban communities – and the *Comité économique et social* (CES), or Economic and Social Committee, made up of the socioprofessionals of the region. Moreover, the reform only gave the regions limited powers, minimal financial means, and made the prefect the executive power.[81] It

[77]See the discussion in Yves Mény, "Central Control and Local Resistance," in *Continuity and Change in France,* ed. V. Wright (London: George Allen & Unwin, 1984), pp. 203–14.
[78]Speech by Pompidou in Brest, October 22, 1971, quoted in "Les présidents et la décentralisation," *La Décentralisation, Cahiers français,* no. 204 (Jan.–Feb. 1982), pp. 43–4.
[79]Alain Peyrefitte, *Le Mal français* (Paris: Plon, 1976), pp. 452–3.
[80]*Le Monde,* Jan. 23, 1971, cited in Mény, *Centralisation,* p. 67.
[81]Gourevitch, "Reform," p. 77. For a full account of the reform, see Vincent Wright and Howard Machin, "The French regional reforms of July 1972," *Policy and Politics* vol. 3, no. 3 (March 1975): 3–5.

did, however, finally give the region the right to elaborate regional programs of its own, independent of the deconcentrated field services of the state, even though the programs had to fall within the lines established by the DATAR.

Needless to say, there were innumerable criticisms of the reform. These included protests about the regional boundaries, complaints about the restricted sphere of action of the regions and their limited financial resources, concerns about the resulting politicization of local government, and even the questions about the regional assemblies and the amount of power given to the departments on the regional councils.[82] Alain Savary, president of the regional council of Midi-Pyrénées, complained that not one person sitting on the regional council actually represented the region, because their positions depended upon their election to another level of government.[83] This situation, in turn, protested André Chandernagor, ensured that the composition of the regional council would change at every municipal, cantonal, or legislative election, adversely affecting the ability of the regional council to carry on sustained work.[84]

As Vincent Wright pointed out, here again it was "the reticence or hostility of certain powerfully placed political and administrative veto groups, some of which are highly vulnerable to any radical change in local governmental structures," which explains the timidity of regional reform.[85] But this was not all. The regions were not very important politically, because they were coequal with departments, and their members (unlike departmental councilors) were not even elected by universal suffrage. The problem for Pompidou was that they nevertheless continued to be met with tremendous resistance from those of the "Caesarian right and the statist left," who, echoing the sentiments of their confreres of a century before, feared that universal suffrage might turn regional assemblies into "small-scale parliaments" and were convinced, like Jacques Chirac in 1975, that the region was "a dramatic element confronting and challenging national unity."[86]

Nevertheless, the debate on decentralization was kept alive, with the government setting up commissions to study the possibility of decentralization and putting individuals noted for their interest in reform at the

[82]See Wright and Machin, "French regional reforms," pp. 13–20.
[83]Alain Savary, *La Région en question? Cahiers de l'I.F.S.A*, no. 17 (Paris: Cujas, 1978), p. 132, cited in Pierre Sadran, "Les accommodements avec la loi de 1972," in *Cahiers français*, no. 204 (Jan.–Feb. 1982) p. 31.
[84]*Le Monde*, June 27, 1979, cited in Sadran, "Les accomodements," p. 31.
[85]Vincent Wright, "Regionalization under the French Fifth Republic: The Triumph of the Functional Approach," in *Decentralist Trends in Western Democracies*, ed. L.J. Sharpe (London: Sage, 1979).
[86]Jacques Caroux, "The end of administrative centralization?" *Telos* no. 55 (Spring 1983): 112.

head of the Ministry for Administrative Reforms. Pompidou was the first to do this, appointing Alain Peyrefitte Minister for Administrative Reforms. But Pompidou, having told Peyrefitte that his reform would have to wait until his second term in office, died before anything could be achieved, and Peyrefitte's report was ignored by Pompidou's successor.[87] Peyrefitte's proposed reforms, in any case, were not likely to have done much for the region, because he anticipated keeping the region only as a multipurpose, interdepartmental syndicate. In other ways, though, Peyrefitte's recommendations would have brought about significant change, because he proposed having only two levels of local government, each with an elected executive: the department and a new structure, the district, which was to take over daily local administration without replacing the communes. The prefect would have been turned into the *commissaire de la République,* representing the government in the periphery.[88]

Pompidou's successor, Giscard d'Estaing, although elected on a proregionalist platform, did little or nothing with the reforms already in place. Initially, Giscard appeared to be following Pompidou's lead when he appointed Jean-Jacques Servan-Schreiber, a major proponent of regional power, Minister for Administrative Reforms, and promised "rapid, radical reforms." But Servan-Schreiber resigned after a week in office. Once Chirac became prime minister, hopes for decentralization diminished, given Chirac's Jacobinism.[89] Moreover, by November 1975, Giscard had come down squarely in favor of the department as the preeminent level of local administration, which "should be affirmed and used as such." At the same time, as regards the democratization of the regions, he found France "too divided to be able to introduce new political jousting in an arena where reflection and concerted effort are needed."[90] Finally, by 1977, Giscard was even defending the communes as they were, insisting that "36,394 communes in France is a precious trump card for local democracy," even though he felt they should be encouraged to cooperate more systematically.[91]

Nonetheless, yet another commission was set up, that of Olivier Guichard, which, as a result of the number of old establishment personalities in its midst, made moderate recommendations intended to reinforce the traditional levels of government – the communes and the departments, over and against the regions. The Guichard report recommended voluntary federations of communes, which would give communes and communi-

[87]Peyrefitte, nonetheless, subsequently came out with a report on the subject. See Alain Peyrefitte, ed., *Décentraliser les Responsabilités: Pourqoi? Comment?* (Paris: Documentation française, 1976).
[88]See Alain Peyrefitte, "Pour un pouvoir provincial," *Le Monde,* Nov. 23–4, 1975.
[89]See discussion in Machin, "All Jacobins," pp. 138–40.
[90]Quoted in *Le Monde,* Nov. 26, 1975.
[91]Quoted in *Le Monde,* July 22, 1977.

ties of communes responsibility for urban planning and development, end the *tutelle,* reorganize the local tax system, and strengthen the departmental councils.[92] These recommendations, however, were generally ignored in the electoral season 1977–8, when the left, with its common front in which nine-tenths of the communes had united lists, took control of 154 of the 221 cities with more than thirty thousand inhabitants.

The next commission, chaired by Jacques Aubert, had somewhat more success than the Guichard commission, because its findings were considered in the drafting of new, proposed legislation beginning in 1978. The Aubert report, based on the results of consultations with interested parties (for example, the Association of Mayors and of Presidents of General Councils) as well as a questionnaire sent out to all mayors in June 1977, found that local government was ridiculously complex and inefficient. The resulting proposed legislation, however, suggested no major reforms and no greater powers to the region; and only some laws related to the reform of local finances were passed.

The proposed *loi Bonnet,* or Bonnet bill, moreover, passed by the Senate in 1980 and awaiting consideration by the Assembly, did not even go as far as the Guichard report. In particular, it did not recommend a federation of communes or a change in the departmental councils, nor did it consider any limitation in the *cumul des mandats,* as recommended by the Peyrefitte report. Nonetheless, the Bonnet bill would still have reinforced the autonomy of the existing structures in a variety of areas: by giving mayors control over building permits where the commune had an approved *Plan d'occupation du sol* (POS), or land-use plan (the existing system involved the mayor being the first to sign building permits, with subsequent approval required by the prefect and the *direction départementale d'équipement* [DDE]); by creating a block grant (*dotation globale d'équipement*) in place of sectoral subsidies (*subventions sectorielles*); by establishing a statute for local elected officials that would provide certain benefits (for example, retirement and accident insurance) and protections (for example, of employment leaves and absences), as well as regularize and increase their pay; and by alleviating certain aspects of the *tutelle.*[93]

The reforms anticipated in the Bonnet bill were even more moderate than those proposed by previous commissions. They therefore had a good chance of passing had the conservatives not lost power in 1981; but the law would have done little to alter center–periphery relations or the

[92]Commission de développement des responsabilités locales, *Vivre Ensemble* (Paris: Documentation française 1976). See the discussion in Mény, "Central Control," pp. 206–7.

[93]See Jean-Marc Virieux, "Les projets de décentralisation de 1972 à 1981," in *La Décentralisation, Cahiers français,* no. 204 (Jan.–Feb. 1982), pp. 34–9.

practice of local government. The conservative governments following de Gaulle had clearly given up on de Gaulle's push to reform local government; and even their own commissions' recommendations on decentralization appeared too radical.

Part of the reason for the conservative governments' resistance to the decentralization reforms proposed by its many commissions was their interest in wooing the local notables, who were satisfied with the status quo. The regional reform served the purposes of local elected officials who found their own positions in no way threatened; they had already gained influence over the CODER and had developed a very good set of relations with the DATAR. It also served the purposes of the central government, because, by enabling it to continue to carry on in the normal way with local notables, it served to attenuate local and regional tensions while avoiding the rise of a strong regionalist movement.[94] Any further decentralization was unlikely, because the upper-level civil servants also continued to resist decentralization, just as they had under de Gaulle. The interests of the civil servants of the many different corps of the state, according to Suleiman, ensured against any successful reform effort, especially given the entry of upper-level civil servants into the political arena, with their vested interest in maintaining the status quo in local administration.[95]

Another reason for the government's resistance to reform was that the left was winning increasingly in municipal and departmental elections. In 1977 the left had come to dominate the councils of eight out of the twenty-two regions, enjoyed a majority in the councils of forty-one of the ninety-six French metropolitan departments, and controlled four-fifths of the towns with more than thirty thousand inhabitants. Following the traditional pattern, the right became less interested in reform the more it saw that this would benefit the left. Giscard d'Estaing in particular, once he saw the success of the left in the local elections of 1977, resisted regional reform. He recognized that the left would have gained a majority in the regions had there been election by universal suffrage, thereby giving the left a platform from which to criticize the national government and thus "Italianizing," in Debré's word, the national political scene.[96]

The response to the government's initiatives

But there was more to the failure of reform than this, because the right itself had achieved no consensus on the need to reform. Whereas the left

[94]Tarrow, "Decentramento," p. 241.
[95]Ezra N. Suleiman, "Administrative Reform and the Problem of Decentralization in the Fifth Republic," in *The Impact of the Fifth Republic in France,* ed. William G. Andrews and Stanley Hoffman (Albany: State University of New York Press, 1981), pp. 70–4, 76, 78–9.
[96]Tarrow, "Decentramento," p. 248.

in opposition was becoming more and more convinced and convincing about the need for radical reform, especially as it was gaining increasing power in the periphery, the right was becoming less and less certain of the need for decentralization. Major questions involved the fate of the regions and their relative strength in relation to the departments and the reform of the communes. Although all parties were essentially agreed on leaving the communes as they were, while encouraging some form of increased cooperation among them, they were often very far apart indeed on what was to be done with the regions. This was especially true of the right, which was quite divided on the issue of decentralization.

The Gaullist party was split. Some, following de Gaulle's initiative, saw regionalization as a way of promoting economic modernization and sought only to reinforce this mission within the context of the regional reform of 1972. Others such as Michel Debré and his supporters adamantly opposed decentralization – Debré even referred to "interdepartmental" matters in order to avoid the use of the word "regional." Yet others such as Pompidou and Chirac were "political" in their approach to decentralization, considering it mainly as a way of rallying support.[97] All were agreed, however, that decentralization was not to jeopardize the unity of the nation – whether it was Jacques Monod in the RPR "proposals for France," who insisted that decentralization would only complete the democracy of the nation as a whole, not contradict it, or Pierre Racine, former Cabinet Director for Prime Minister Debré and director of the ENA (National School of Aministration), who agreed to decentralization "as long as one took care not to take apart the country administratively. To change life and society, the state needs to conserve responsible and strong structures in the provinces."[98] The reason the right in general supported the reform of Paris's local government was because it found that the dangers of the past that required the *tutelle* no longer existed.[99]

Although the Republican party was even more cautious on decentralization than the Gaullists, the Radical party, by contrast, was much more supportive of decentralization, as evidenced by the fact that in the late 1960s they appointed the regionalist Servan-Schreiber as their leader. But by the late 1970s, even they were much less favorably inclined toward decentralization, with Servan-Schreiber having reduced his own recommendations from the creation of a real regional power to the institution of regional administration. Only the Christian Democrats of the CDS in the center appeared to remain true to decentralization, linking it to a

[97]Machin, "All Jacobins," p. 142.
[98]Yves Mény, "Partis politiques et décentralisation," in *L'administration vue par les politiques,* ed. Institut français des sciences administratives (Paris: Cujas, 1978), pp. 98–9.
[99]See Mény, *Centralisation,* p. 279.

communitarianism based on increased local democracy. They proposed that the communes become equal partners with the state, that regions become a regular level of local government, that greater citizen participation be promoted through extramunicipal commissions and associations, and that communal autonomy be enhanced through a statute for elected officials and reform of the one for municipal civil servants.[100]

Whereas the bulk of the right became progressively less decentralizing while in power, with its ranks swelled by members of the administrative elite turned political, the left, while out of power became increasingly supportive of decentralization, albeit not of the government's decentralizing programs. The only governmental reform the left supported was giving Paris its freedom, on the grounds that it was a requirement of democracy. The left had opposed the 1971 law and the Guichard report in 1976 as attacks on the communes. It criticized the 1972 regional reform law as not going far enough at the same time that it protested the unrepresentative nature of the CES, claiming that it left the trade unions underrepresented and the government appointees and progovernment unions (for example, the CFT) overrepresented.[101] And the left became increasingly impatient with the successive governmental reform commissions. In 1977, Pierre Mauroy, president of the regional council of the Nord-Pas-de-Calais, criticized the Guichard Commission report for "rushing slowly," and argued for regional reform along with an increase in the powers of the communes and departments.[102] But the left as a whole had included decentralization in its platform before this, in 1972, as part of their Common Program. And they argued for a much more radical decentralization than any parties on the right.

The Socialists, beginning with their renewal in the 1970s, focused on *autogestion,* or self-management, for all aspects of society, including the political. The PSU was joined first by the clubs, which were part of the old FGDS, and finally by the PS itself. Of the Socialists, however, the PSU remained the most radical in its proposals, wanting *autogestion* for the regions and a real diminution of the state. But even the PSU did not go as far as the MRG (*Mouvement des radicaux de gauche*), which was much more in favor of regional autonomy than either the Communists or the Socialists, favoring the right of the regions to cultural differentiation. For the Socialists, regionalism was a useful element in the strategy to enlarge politically, as they sought to win over the ethnic regionalist movements. But they did not go nearly as far as the radical ethnic regionalists in their

[100]Mény, "Partis," p. 100.
[101]Wright and Machin, "French regional reforms," pp. 19–20.
[102]Speech for the plenary session of the regional council of the Nord-Pas-de-Calais, Jan. 24, 1977, extracted in "la genèse du projet," *La Décentralisation, Cahiers français,* no. 204 (Jan.–Feb. 1982), pp. 48–9.

vision of what the region was to be. For the majority of Socialists, the department was to remain the most important level of local government, whereas the state was to continue to play an important role.

In the "Le Pensec" bill of 1974, the Socialists proposed the direct election of the regional councils by universal suffrage and proportional representation, with their presidents elected by the councils. They sought to replace the economic and social committee with an economic, social, and cultural council with a larger worker representation than management representation. They demanded the abolition of the prefects, as they had at the end of World War II, with the executive power in the hands of the elected president of the regional assembly. The regions were to have their own budgets, enlarged by the transfer of taxes from the state along with a *fonds interrégional de péréquation*, or interregional equalization fund. They also recommended a separate charter for Corsica.

But the Socialists anticipated only a minimal expansion of the powers of the region beyond those contained in the law of 1972, by recommending "the creation and administration of regional establishments, enterprises, and public services."[103] The Socialists were as concerned about national unity as everyone else, after all. Their views were reflected in the words of Yves Durrieu of the national bureau of the UGSC (*Union de la Gauche et des Clubs Socialistes*), who remarked that "it is undesirable to adopt a federal formula that does not respond to French reality, which would artificially accentuate the divergences and unnecessarily favor centrifugal movements."[104] Moreover, the Socialists retained the departments, recommending their democratization and even defending them against the suggestion in a report by Edgar Pisani that they become the equivalent of super intercommunal syndicates on the grounds that: "If we want to decentralize quickly after March 1978, one must use what exists."[105] Their power base in the departmental councils made them unable to prefer the region over the department, even though the self-management idea favored the region.[106]

But if there was any ambivalence over the departments and regions, there was none over the communes. The Socialists, just as much as the majority, had no intention of altering their form or diminishing their number, since, as François Mitterrand himself declared, "Because the mayor is the best mediator, I favor his retention; and even the 36,000 communes and 500,000 benevolent municipal councilors are not enough. What would democracy gain in making them disappear?"[107]

[103] Mény, "Partis," p. 108.
[104] *Le Monde*, Jan. 6, 1971, cited in Mény, *Centralisation*, p. 67.
[105] A. Chandernagor, *Le Monde*, Oct. 13, 1977, quoted in Mény, "Partis," pp. 103–4.
[106] Mény, "Partis," pp. 107–8.
[107] *Le Monde*, Oct. 13, 1977, quoted in Mény, "Partis," p. 104.

Local democracy, in effect, was becoming more and more of an issue for the Socialists, who were responding to the demands for decentralization coming from outside the established parties of the left. In truth, it was here that could be found some of the most perceptive critiques of the existing state of affairs (that is, of the ungovernable state that was oversized, inefficient, and undemocratic) and some of the more progressive solutions (that is, *autogestion* and the creation of a new citizenry).[108] It was also here that most of the most innovative reform proposals appeared, pushed for by the GAMs (*Groupements d'action municipale*), or grass-roots, community action groups, intent on grappling with the "daily reality of alienation" and working on practical issues such as housing, schooling, and public transportation. The GAMs were intent on setting up *contre-pouvoirs,* or counter-powers to the established ones of local government. Where they succeeded, a new kind of local administration, open to community activists and the local population, emerged, such as in Grenoble under the leadership of its mayor, Hurbert Dubedout.

By the mid to late 1970s, the Socialists had become the standard-bearers for these new groups and the new kind of administration. In keeping with this, the Socialists had begun to elaborate better developed positions on decentralization. Now a decentralization capable of promoting economic development, as Jean-Pierre Worms argued in 1980, would be best accomplished by redistributing power equitably among local governmental units, allowing for real negotiation among them. At the same time, any threat of local "totalitarianism" occasioned by decentralization would be avoided by reinforcing the structures of civil society, for example, by giving local associations more power in order to create counter-powers to those of local governments.[109]

In their 1980 bill the Socialists proposed a "tranquil revolution" with regard to France's legal traditions, limiting the regulatory power of the state. They argued that instead of following the lead of the right, which put public power in the service of the development of capitalism, they would reinforce the power of local governments, making them less dependent on the national government in order to become "the efficacious instruments of the democratic administration" of the framework of daily life. The regions in particular were to gain enough power and responsibility in the areas of economic intervention, land-use planning, and cultural action to be able to hold their own against the state.[110] They again

[108]See, for example, Échange et Projets, *La Démocratie à portée de la main* (Paris: Albin Michel, 1977).
[109]Jean-Pierre Worms, "La décentralisation comme une stratégie de changement social," *Cahiers français,* no. 204 (Jan.–Feb. 1982), pp. 50–2.
[110]Justification for bill no. 1557, deposed at the National Assembly in January 1980, extracted in "Les presidents et la dècentralization," in *La Décentralisation, Cahiers français* (Jan.–Feb. 1982), pp. 45–6.

proposed the abolition of the prefect because now the prefectoral corps was "the instrument through which capitalism maintains its grip on the entire society."[111]

The Socialists thus became more and more radical in their views of decentralization over the course of the 1970s, focusing more and more on *autogestion* and local democracy, in part in response to the growing pressures from the groups outside the established left. Decentralization, however, was not an end in itself, but rather one part of a larger project implementable only once the Socialists had gained power. No matter how much the Socialists of the PSU and the PS promoted *autogestion,* they denounced the illusion of "self-managing islets," finding that the commune on its own could not be the lever for the radical transformation of the capitalist world nor the first stage in a socialist society in France.[112]

The Communist party, although less committed than the Socialists to *autogestion,* also favored decentralization.[113] Similarly, it certainly did not consider focusing exclusively on the conquest of the commune in order to create a socialist society. The Communist party insisted that "to really change life in the commune, one must change society."[114] And for that, again, the conquest of national power was a necessity. Thus, the Communist party sought to show themselves as the best *élus,* or local elected officials, of the communes and, with an "Italian" strategy, to show on a small scale and within the limits of the system that "a decisive advance of democracy is possible."[115]

For the Communists, decentralization was a way of breaking the oppressive, capitalist state apparatus, as well as the means for installing, in the context of an advanced democracy, a decentralized, but still unitary, state. Local government was to become the crucible of political democracy, as reflected in such slogans as: "From municipal management to communal self-management;" "Decentralize and debureaucratize;" "Break statism." For the Communists, much more so than for the Socialists, the departments remained unquestionably the important level of local government. They, too, defended the communes, especially against the ways in which the government had sought to consolidate them. The regions were to have a role in cultural matters and in the coordination of planning.[116] But

[111]Maurice Doublet, "La République et le préfet," *La Revue Administrative* 34 (Sept.–Oct. 1981): 459–92.

[112]Mény, "Partis," p. 112.

[113]See Georges Marchais, *Parlons franchement* (Paris: Grasset, 1977), pp. 56–70.

[114]"Le nouveau contrat communal," *L'Humanité,* June 8, 1976, cited by Mény, "Partis," p. 112.

[115]*L'Humanité,* Nov. 8, 1977, cited in Mény, "Partis," p. 112.

[116]For a full account of the Communist position on the regions, see Jean Giard and Jacques Scheibling, *L'Enjeu régional: Une démarche autogestionnaire* (Paris: Éditions sociales, 1981).

decentralization for the Communists, just as for most on the right, was not to threaten the overall centralization of the state. On the specifics of decentralization reform, the Communists introduced a number of safeguards against too much local autonomy, for example, by suggesting that next to the "horizontal" structures of local government there would be "vertical" administrations charged with executing the decisions of the elected assemblies, or that whereas the communes themselves could decide whether to be part of the national planning process, their decision not to do so would make them subject to normal state financing arrangements.[117] On the more general question of how decentralization would affect national unity, Georges Marchais declared in 1976 that the Communists would "make of liberty the cement of national unity"; a year later, Charles Fiterman, the secretary of the Central Committee of the PC, envisioned creating a "decentralized, unitary state" with their new bill on the regions, which was to establish the direct election of regional councils, but by proportional representation so as to ensure minority representation and a special statute for Corsica, which would not in any way threaten national unity.[118]

By 1981, then, the left had made a commitment to decentralization. But once in power would it continue to support decentralization? Most commentators had little hope that the Socialists and Communists would do any better than the right. They tended to find that the changes in the presidency, the influence of civil servants, the increasing power of centrist local notables, and the disillusionment of previous reform meant that reform seemed unlikely in the near future.[119] But they were wrong. For the first time in a century, and only the second time in two centuries, legislators passed significant decentralizing legislation.

[117] F. Damette "Une nécessité: la décentralisation," *Cahiers du communisme,* (July 1977), pp. 21–2, quoted in Mény, "Partis," p. 101.
[118] Mény "Partis," p. 98.
[119] See, for example, Machin, "All Jacobins," p. 149.

4

Legislating decentralization in the administration of local government: The reforms of the Socialist Fifth Republic

The beginning years of the Socialist Fifth Republic mark the end of the history of failed decentralizing reform efforts. In 1982 the government passed the *loi-cadre,* or framework law, which set the stage for the series of laws to follow that transferred executive powers, administrative functions, and financial resources from the central government to the different levels of local government. The process of decentralization, which took place primarily over the next three years, touched every branch of government at local and national levels – from elected officials' duties and number of elective offices to prefects' powers over local officials and judges' jurisdictions – as well as every aspect of public policy and administration, from the delivery of social services and the promotion of economic development to civil service reform. By the time the new neoliberal government in October 1986 declared a "pause" in decentralization to *mettre au point* certain technical aspects of the legislation, 48 laws and 269 decrees had been promulgated.[1]

The Socialists intended their decentralizing reforms as *la grande affaire du septennat,* or the main event of President Mitterrand's seven-year term, which would revitalize the periphery politically, administratively, and economically. Mitterrand himself termed it the "most important institutional reform since the beginning of the Third Republic."[2] Decentralization was to make local government more efficient and cost-effective. With decentralization, Mitterrand, like de Gaulle, sought to create more direct links between the center and the periphery, which in this case were to enable the government to "use the resulting social mobilization to accelerate the necessary changes in French society."[3] For

[1] The exact number actually depends on who is doing the counting. In other counts, the number is generally cited as 42 laws and over 300 decrees.
[2] Speech by President Mitterrand in Figeac, September 1982, cited by Bernard, *L'État,* p. 115.
[3] Caroux, "End of administrative centralization?" pp. 110–11.

the Socialists, specifically, decentralization was a way to break the vicious cycle of the *État-providence,* or welfare state, mentality by ensuring that industrial and urban development would have a "more dynamic base than centralization, which produces receivers of assistance and creditors towards a supposedly inexhaustible treasury."[4] Economic revitalization was to lead to an increased number of small as well as large industries and productive jobs in the periphery with fewer people on social assistance. And the concomitant political revitalization was to force local politicians to become as responsible for their decisions and as little dependent upon the state as individuals were to become economically.

The good of the polity and the health of the economy, however, were not the only motivating forces behind the Socialist push for decentralization. The Socialist conquest of local government through the 1970s, which culminated with the party's capture of national power in 1981, convinced most on the left that decentralization would further their own particular political aims, while promoting the public interest. Little did they know that in short order decentralization was to benefit the right. But by the time some members of the left began to have second thoughts about the reform, the process of decentralization had already become unstoppable – pushed through by Gaston Defferre, who was determined to make as much of a mark on the Fifth Republic with decentralization as he had on the Fourth with decolonization. It is Gaston Defferre who can take much of the credit or blame for the pragmatism that ensured that the reform, although less radical than the party program and electoral campaign had promised, was to be irreversible.

Pragmatism, or the politics of the possible, was very much at play here, and understandably so. The success of decentralization depended upon the Socialists' ability to pass quickly a framework law based on as wide a consensus as possible. Because this strategy meant waiting to work out the details until later, at the same time that the pressure to work them out quickly was intense, expediency often took the place of innovation. As could be expected, those areas of reform subject to the most organized or strongest pressures were the ones addressed first, and those areas subject to little pressure or much counter-pressure were considered last, if at all – in many cases the politics of the moment made certain reforms no longer attractive to many erstwhile reformers. The very logic that made decentralization unstoppable also made it more vulnerable to those organized groups with a vested interest in the new system.

Defferre's political strategy consisted of transferring power to local elected officials first and leaving until later the working out of the details of the transfer of local finances and of *compétences,* or administrative

---

[4]Ibid., p. 113.

functions, and duties. Although ensuring the irreversibility of decentralization, this strategy also left the reform vulnerable to rearguard action by civil servants concerned about their loss of power and local elected officials worried about the new responsibilities that came with the acquisition of power. In consequence, the plans for sweeping changes in the system of local finances were simply set aside as too complicated to implement given the press of time. The transfer of health and social services from the state to the department ended up following the traditional division of services, because the government judged that it would be unable to overcome the combined resistance of the central ministries to any wholesale reorganization. In addition, civil service reform, following delay upon delay resulting from resistance from national civil servants and local elected officials, was scuttled by the opposition. No attempt was even made to rationalize the structures of local government, either by reducing the unwieldy number of communes or by choosing between the departments and regions, thus leaving four levels of local government.

Decentralization, thus, was not as revolutionary as it might have been, because of the pragmatic way in which the Socialists proceeded with the reform. Nevertheless, had the Socialists not been so pragmatic, the reform would probably have suffered the ill-fated destiny of all previous such attempts. Although the Socialists may not have needed to make as many concessions as they did, the fact that they did meant the reforms were based on a wide consensus and thus were much less likely to suffer repeal. The proof of this is that, while the neoliberal government was in power from 1986 to 1988, it altered very few aspects of the reform.

THE PASSAGE OF THE FRAMEWORK LAW OF MARCH 1982

It was only by moving swiftly that the Socialists were able to pass the *loi-cadre*, or framework law, on decentralization of March 2, 1982, before those satisfied with the system as it was were able to consolidate their opposition to reform. And it was the timetable contained in that law that made the process of decentralization, once started, unstoppable. Gaston Defferre calculated that he could gain the necessary support for the reform only by immediately transferring the prefects' executive powers in the departments and regions to the presidents of those two levels of local government and by abolishing the prefects' *tutelle* over the mayors of the communes, before even beginning to work out the details of the subsequent transfers of administrative functions and financial resources. For only in this way, he felt, would the officials most likely to resist change (if the details of decentralization had been worked out in advance of the passage of the law) become instead its most ardent supporters. Once that first break with the old system was accomplished, Defferre was confident that the newly powerful local officials would be certain to press hard for the quickest transfer of the administrative functions without which their executive power would be meaningless and for the financial resources without which they would be unable to fulfill their obligations.[5] In fact, this worked as anticipated. Given, however, the inevitable delays in working out the details of the reform, it opened the government up to constant and politically damaging charges of foot-dragging. The main objection to decentralization from local elected officials, in fact, once the process had already begun, came from members of the opposition, accusing the government of bad faith because they were not implementing their reforms fast enough.[6]

Defferre's choice of strategy had a lot to do with his keen understanding of French legislative politics. As a politician since the Fourth Republic, he had seen decentralizing legislation fail countless times. And Defferre had learned the lessons of previous administrations. If any decentralizing reform was to succeed, it needed to be passed within the first months of the new government's arrival in power, and no later. Pompidou had decided to reform during his second term in office, but had died during the first. De Gaulle had proposed his referendum toward the middle of this term in office, and failed. As early as 1977, André Chandernagor, president of the regional council of Limousin on top of his other roles, had suggested: "A certain number of us have been saying that if decentralization is not done rapidly, within six months of the arrival of a new majority, it will never be done."[7] Once the Socialists came to power, Defferre seized the moment.

But why Defferre? Although it is true that Defferre had publicly supported decentralization as early as 1965, his support was not as strong, long-standing, or well articulated as that of Rocard and the PSU. Nonetheless, for Defferre, decentralization, as the "decolonization of the provinces," seemed to follow naturally from his central role in the "decolonization of the colonies" during the Fourth Republic. His determination was reinforced by his experience as a Socialist, big-city mayor, where he was generally free of the local complicity that paralyzed fellow politicians, very

---

[5]The late Gaston Defferre, former Minister of the Interior and Decentralization, interview with author, Paris, May 23, 1985. For further discussion of Defferre's strategy, see Philippe de Lara, "De nouvelles règles du jeu pour la démocratie," *Intervention* no. 3 (Mar.–Apr. 1983): 9; and Jean-Pierre Worms, "La décentralisation: Un processus, une chance à saisir," *Échange et Projets* no. 39 (Sept. 1984): 30–1.

[6]See, for example, *Le Monde*, Dec. 15, 1985; and *Le Figaro*, Dec., 22, 1985.

[7]André Chandernagor, *La Région en question? Cahiers de l'I.F.S.A*, no. 17 (Paris: Cujas, 1978), p. 100, cited in "Les présidents et la décentralisation," in *La Décentralisation, Cahiers français*, no. 204 (Jan.–Feb. 1982), p. 45.

sensitive to the new groups of *salariés* and associational groups at the periphery, and more likely to feel the frustrations of centralization, because he was more vulnerable to central government interference.

Determination is one thing, however, and success another. After all, Gambetta had been equally determined at the beginning of the Third Republic, but had only been able to bring about moderate reform, and legislators for the intervening century had similarly committed themselves to decentralization while out of power, but did little or nothing once in power. The difference for the Socialist Fifth Republic was that, unlike the left-leaning legislators at the beginning of the Third Republic, the Socialists had control of the government from the beginning, and did not have to weather a continuing crisis during which the legislation went back and forth between decentralizing laws and recentralizing laws and policies. Defferre's ability to translate his determination into action depended in great measure on the left's large parliamentary majority, along with its strong position in the periphery, which included holding a majority in thirteen out of the twenty-two regional councils as of 1981. Having gained national power through the conquest of the periphery, members of the left had no doubt that decentralization could only enhance their powers at the local level. By the time the left found that this was not to be the case, with the victory of the right in the municipal elections of 1983, it was already too late to stop the reform.

In other words, Defferre's success owes much to how fast he went about drafting and pushing the reform through Parliament. By using the same team in the Ministry of the Interior that had been in charge of recommending reform under the previous administration, Defferre was able to have a draft of the bill almost immediately. Within three weeks of the establishment of the Mauroy government, on July 5, 1981, the Council of Ministers adopted Defferre's decentralization bill. The parliamentary session opened on July 28, 1981, with the government's bill on decentralization, and the National Assembly discussed it until August 2, then again from September 8 to 11, and in second reading from December 14 to 20, 1981. The Senate took up its own version of the bill from October 28 to November 19 and in second reading from January 12 to 14, 1982. Once the joint parliamentary commission failed to reconcile the two versions, the National Assembly had its third reading of the bill on January 22, 1982, and the Senate had its reading on January 26, 1982. The National Assembly finally approved the fleshed-out bill during its fourth reading, on January 28, 1982. After much debate, then, but still in record time – within six months of its introduction as a bill – the framework law on decentralization was passed; it became law on March 2, 1982.

Defferre's success can be attributed not only to his strategy but also to

Table 4.1: *Number of units and levels of selected local governments in Europe*

Country	Size (in km²)	Population (in millions)	Levels and units of local government		Distribution of Communes (in percentage) by inhabitants (in thousands)		
1. France	549,000	55.6	26	regions	-.5	=	61.0 %
			100	departments	.5 to 1	=	18.0
			3	overseas territories	1 to 5	=	16.7
			2	special collectivities	5 to 10	=	2.2
			36,527	communes	10 to 50	=	1.8
					+50	=	0.3
2. Germany	249,000	61	11	lander	1	=	37.0
			237	kreise	1 to 2	=	57.0
			91	assimilated cities	2 to 100	=	5.3
			8,500	communes	+100	=	6.0
			(24,000	pre 1978)			
3. Italy	301,000	57.4	20	regions	-1	=	22
			94	provinces	1 to 10	=	62
			9,074	communes	10 to 50	=	8
					+50	=	8
4. Portugal	92,000	10.3	2	regions (islands)	-10	=	26.0
			275	communes	10 to 50	=	61.0
					50 to 100	=	7.5
					+100	=	5.5
5. Spain	505,000	39	50	provinces	-1	=	60
			8,027	communes	1 to 5	=	27
					5 to 10	=	6
					+10	=	7
6. UK (England)	255.000	56.8	47	counties	100 to 200	=	22.0
			36	districts	200 to 500	=	69.5
					+500	=	8.5

Source: Départements et communes (Sept. 1988), in *Cahiers français* no. 239 (Jan.-Feb. 1989).

his ability to build a consensus on the reform. The reform was "a sort of 'common minimal programme of the left and right.' "[8] It proposed little that was likely to be strongly opposed by local or national elected officials. Thus, it did little or nothing about one of the most pressing problems: the restructuring of the territory, in particular the reduction in the number of communes. It left France with by far the largest number of units of local government of any European country (Table 4.1). The institutions of the Revolution, the departments and the communes, were left untouched, along with the boundaries of the newer regions. Because the left at the local level had resisted most such reform efforts by previous governments, territorial restructuring was certainly not a top priority on Defferre's agenda.

[8]See Yves Mény, "The Socialist Decentralization." Paper presented at the conference, "Continuity and Change in Mitterrand's France" (Cambridge, Mass.: Dec. 5–8, 1985).

However necessary he recognized that it might be, Defferre had clearly determined that any forced rationalizing of the structures of local government would have elicited the very kind of immediate opposition to reform that the Socialists were the most intent upon avoiding.[9]

Only in rare instances did the Socialists resort to forcing the measures through in the face of major opposition. For the most part, the reform involved wide consultation and compromise with the many interested parties. The reform was certainly informed by Defferre's interests and perspectives as a big-city mayor (with his main advisors from big cities themselves, that is, M. Delebarre, general secretary of Lille, and P. Marnot, general secretary of Nantes). It also responded to a great variety of other interests, however, including those of the civil servants, who had been responsible for preparing the previous Bonnet bill and were charged with writing up this new bill at such a breakneck pace that they consulted with no one in the initial drafting of the law.[10] But Defferre made up for that, meeting with interested parties in the periphery to hear their concerns, such as the prefects and the departmental presidents, as well as with the major actors in the center, such as ministry officials and politicians.

Even in the parliamentary process, Defferre was intent on building consensus and eliciting the support of numerous members of the opposition, despite the Socialist majority, which meant that he could basically have had his way regardless of any opposition. There were many late night discussions and negotiations, with compromises and deals being struck. To give only one example, in the discussion of the first law Philippe Séguin, RPR deputy and mayor of Épinal, recounts that he was very active, spending many nights until the early morning hours in meetings with Defferre, with whom he got along well. His reward, he claims, was that the new regional accounting court was located in Épinal.[11]

Defferre's interest in building consensus was certainly part of the reason why the government allowed for full debates on the laws in the National Assembly and in the Senate (which had a majority on the right and considered its own bill rather than the Assembly version in reading after reading). Although the National Assembly returned each time to its own previous version of the bill in its second, third, and fourth readings, it accepted a large number of the amendments presented in the Senate, mainly because they served to clarify the laws and to make them more

[9]Pierre Sadran, "Les communes face aux autres collectivités locales," in *Les Pouvoirs locaux à l'épreuve de la décentralisation,* ed. Albert Mabileau (Paris: Pédone, 1983), pp. 44–7.
[10]One member of the team recounts coming back from vacation to find a note on his desk giving him three weeks to elaborate major portions of the bill.
[11]Philippe Séguin, interview with author, Épinal, June 18, 1985.

acceptable to local governmental officials generally, on the left or the right.[12]

In certain cases, Defferre backed off initiatives he held dear, mainly because his own majority's lack of enthusiasm came on top of the opposition's objections. Such measures as local elected officials being held personally responsible for their financial decisions before a Court of Budgetary Discipline and the right of general councils to overthrow their presidents were dropped, even though they had been central to Defferre's notion of increasing local elected officials' accountability along with their power.

Defferre, however, did not compromise on all of the more radical parts of his reform in the pursuit of consensus. There were certain instances in which consensus could not be achieved, for example, when the opposition appealed to the Constitutional Council to block the abrogation of certain aspects of the prefect's *tutelle,* and when it objected to the prefect's change in name from *préfet* to *commissaire de la République.* In the appeal to the Constitutional Council after the final reading of the bill in February 1982, the opposition charged that the modifications in the prefect's duties that eliminated the a priori review of mayors' decisions in favor of an a posteriori judicial system of review constituted a violation of Article 72 of the Constitution of 1958, which stipulated that "the delegate of the government is in charge of national interests, administrative control, and respect for the laws." The Socialists, needless to say, were relieved to find that the Constitutional Council, although declaring certain passages in the new law unacceptable, let the law stand, including the change from the prefect's a priori review to a posteriori review. This system was not touched when the opposition returned to power in 1986.

When the opposition returned to power, however, it did reverse the change in the prefect's title, turning it back from *commissaire de la République* to *préfet.* But this had only symbolic significance, despite the fact that it was one of the most hotly debated aspects of the change in the prefect's status. After all, even for the Socialists it had only been a symbol, albeit an important one, because it brought back the name used for three months during the Second Republic and in 1944 in Free France. Moreover, the Socialists had themselves compromised somewhat by dropping the title change out of the law, and by leaving to government decree the actual naming of the delegate of the state in the department as *commissaire.* The effect of this title change was minimal, in any event, especially because the prefects' civil service ranking system as prefects remained the same, and people generally continued to call the *commissaires* by their original name. Thus, although the neoliberal government's

---

[12]For a discussion of the parliamentary process, see Cathérine Grémion, "Decentralization."

proposal in June 1987 (established by a decree of March 1988) to get rid
of the title of *commissaire* altogether and to change back to the official
names of prefect and subprefect was symbolically charged, that is all it
was.[13] It had little significance for the decentralization reforms as a
whole.

The prefects' status and title were not the only issues to which the
opposition objected in the course of the parliamentary debates. Primary
among the substantive objections were also the impact of the reform on
rural communes; the new territorial civil service code; and local governments' new role in the promotion of local economic development. In the
Senate, especially, members of the opposition focused on the problems for
the smaller communes in dealing with the technical aspects of their new
duties, once deprived of the help of the prefect, and those problems
involving their role in economic development, in particular the provisions
allowing communes to bail out companies in trouble, because they felt
that this would make it increasingly difficult for mayors to resist local
pressures. In the National Assembly as much as the Senate, territorial
civil service reform was greeted with hostility especially by the members
of the opposition who were from the larger communes, on the grounds
that among other things this constituted a limitation on their administrative freedom.

These reforms, too, were passed, despite the failure to reach a consensus. Here, the lack of consensus decided their fate. Although some compromise was reached on the problems for the rural communes during the
passage of the framework law, with the provision that the departments
could set up technical services to help them out, this was not enough for
the opposition. Once it regained power, it passed legislation returning the
rural communes to the old system of budgetary review by the paymaster-
general in the place of the new system of regional accounting courts
(quasi-independent bodies set up to review the budgets of all local governments, see below). It also expanded the authority of communes to grant
building permits (initially, this could be done only if a land-use plan was
in place). In addition, it scuttled territorial civil service reform, while
strengthening local elected officials' authority over their administrative
subordinates, and it restricted the economic activities of the communes
with regard to aid to businesses in distress.

In addition to these substantive objections, the opposition was also
concerned about the process of reform. At the beginning of the debates in
particular, faced with the far-reaching nature of the reform and its implementation in stages, the right objected strenuously to the order and speed
of the reforms themselves, insisting that by dealing with structures before

[13]For details, see *Le Monde*, June 12, 1987.

administrative functions and finances the Socialists were putting the cart before the horse. This was when the right evoked the superiority of previous reform initiatives and raised the traditional fears for national unity. In the final analysis, though, most members of the right grudgingly acknowledged that only this kind of radical reform could have actually produced change, given the experience of the previous government. And even though some remained upset that Defferre did not seek to legislate at the same time on the transfer of powers, functions, and resources, as had the previous legislature, others recognized that the same fate would have befallen the law had this been done.[14]

In the end, the right voted against the decentralization law mainly on the basis of its opposition to the change in the role of the prefect, itself the primary cause of the failure of the joint parliamentary commission and the reason for its appeal to the Constitutional Council. This, along with the new economic activities of local governments, however, were the only remaining major bones of contention between the left and the right by the time of the third readings of the bill. Territorial civil service reform, the prefect's new title, and the new burdens of the rural communes, although also serious issues for the right, did not constitute major stumbling blocks to their support for the reform.

With the exception of the prefect's new role and the new economic activities of local governments, then, Defferre had managed to build a consensus on the reform. And this made it, unlike some of the Socialists' other initiatives, irreversible. The consensus, in fact, was such that, in a 1983 Expansion/Sofres poll asking the French which of the Socialists' measures they would want to see changed, no mention at all was made of decentralization, whereas all the other important initiatives such as privatization of the nationalized banks and industries, the Auroux laws on industrial democracy, the end of the fifth week of paid vacation, and the abolition of the tax on large fortunes were listed.[15] Part of the reason decentralization went unmentioned was certainly due to the fact that decentralization had not captured the public's attention the way numerous other Socialist pieces of legislation had, given the fast pace of the reform and the fact that the changes themselves had their greatest initial impact on local elected officials and local administrators, not the population at large. But one can be sure that, if the opposition had been truly opposed to these measures, they would have ended up on the Sofres list along with nationalization and industrial democracy. And they would have surely suffered the same fate as the nationalized industries, the other significant Socialist initiative, which were privatized as soon as the right

[14]See, for example, Jean Cluzel, *Les "Anti-Monarques" de la cinquième* (Paris: Librairie générale de droit et de jurisprudence, 1985), p. 53.
[15]Sofres, *Opinion public* (Paris: Gallimard, 1984).

gained a legislative majority in the elections of March 1986. As it is, the opposition left the vast majority of the left's decentralizing measures intact.

THE TRANSFER OF EXECUTIVE POWERS AND THE END OF THE *TUTELLE*

Although the framework law of March 1982 delayed a number of important issues, it implemented immediately one of the most symbolically significant aspects of the reforms. The transfer of executive power from the prefects to the presidents of the councils of the regions and departments, together with the abolition of the prefects' a priori *tutelle* over the administrative acts and budgets of mayors and its replacement with an a posteriori judicial system of review over the actions of local governments, signaled an end to the state's penetration of the periphery along with the consecration of the powers of local elected officials. With this, decentralization was able to place responsibility for local decisions more on the shoulders of local elected officials, while it left responsibility for representing state interests to the prefect.

The new powers of local elected officials and administrators

This first stage in the decentralization process had its greatest impact on the regions and the departments. It transformed local government at these two levels by transferring from the prefects to the presidents of departments and regions executive powers on a par with those traditionally exercised by the mayors of the communes. The regions and departments thus became local governments similar to the communes, with their own deliberative bodies, their own decision-making powers, and their own powers of execution. They were given much greater flexibility in the rules governing their meeting and work schedules as well as in those relating to the delegation of authority from assemblies to their executive councils and from president to vice presidents and territorial civil servants. And they gained complete freedom in elaborating the internal organization of their technical services and, for the first time in the case of the regions, the ability to recruit their own personnel for their technical services.

For the communes, the change from the previous system was more subtle than in the regions and departments, but no less important, for mayors now gained clear decision-making powers in carrying out their traditional duties. The three biggest cities, Paris, Lyon, and Marseilles, moreover, gained their own special provisions, including an organizational innovation providing for *conseils d'arrondissement,* or borough councils, each with its own mayor, in addition to the central, elected mayor and municipal council.

The change for the prefects, needless to say, was equally dramatic, because they lost their executive powers at the regional and departmental levels and their a priori *tutelle*, the very elements that gave the prefects the central position in their relationship of complicity with local elected officials. This loss of power came home to the prefects most forcefully with the transfer of executive offices, buildings, cars, and even furniture that accompanied the transfer of executive powers to the regions and departments. In the first few months after the framework law went into effect, each local collectivity had to sign an agreement over the division of goods. And decentralization was certainly in operation in the way in which this was carried out.[16] Some departments and regions chose to stay in the same building with the prefect; in others the prefecture became the *Hôtel du département,* and the prefect was forced to find other, often less lavish quarters; in yet others, especially the regions that shared quarters with the main department (given that the prefect of the region had also been in charge of the department), the newly powerful presidents chose to construct new buildings or to renovate old ones, mainly eighteenth-century *Hôtels particuliers.* One of the most tangible signs of decentralization, as well as one of the tangible costs, was this construction spree.[17]

The prefects, for all their loss of the trappings of power, were not left completely without powers or authority. They were made the state's sole representative in the periphery, meaning that all decisions made by the field services of the state had to pass through the prefects' hands. Moreover, the prefects' administrative, financial, and technical a priori *tutelle* over the actions of local collectives was replaced by an a posteriori legal control over all three levels of local government – regions, departments, and communes. This legal control enables the prefects to refer administrative matters, the legality of which they question, to administrative tribunals and budgetary matters to the *Chambres régionales des comptes,* or the twenty-two regional accounting courts created in 1983 and presided over by a magistrate from the *Cour des comptes,* the national accounting review court. There are restrictions on the prefects' powers of judicial intervention, however. With regard to budgetary matters,, the prefects can intervene only if the local collectivity fails to maintain a balanced budget, to meet its legally set deadlines, or to meet its financial obliga-

---

[16]For the details of the agreements, see Jean-Claude Thoenig and François Dupuy, "Les conventions entre l'État et le département: Le Début de la politique de décentralisation en France" in *Les Pouvoirs locaux à l'épreuve de la décentralisation,* ed. A. Malibeau, (Paris: Pédone, 1983), pp. 126–49.

[17]For the full costs of decentralization, see Part II, Chapter 10, under "The financial limitations and the 'transfer of unpopularity.' "

tions (for example, to pay its debts or social welfare); the prefects also follow more stringent procedures than before and, notably, must ask the advice of the regional accounting court. In such cases, a budget can be imposed on a region or a department, but only after a negative judgment of the regional accounting court. In technical matters, by contrast, aside from the norms and procedures to be codified by the state in regard to such things as sports arenas and other cultural and social facilities, the local authorities were left entirely free.[18]

The legislative debates on the transfer of powers

According to many legislators on the right, to say nothing for the moment of the prefects, the change in the powers and authority of the prefects went much too far, representing a threat to national unity and the proper functioning of the periphery; for others, especially on the left, it did not go far enough. The main issue for all concerned was the extent to which the state had removed itself from the periphery, with some arguing that it should have done so completely; others, that it had removed itself too much; and yet others maintaining that it had done so in the wrong way. For the prefects themselves, the change in their powers, along with the diminution of the role of the state in the periphery, was a serious threat to their own status and job security. They had to be assured by Defferre at a meeting called a few months after the beginning of decentralization that their positions would be secure.

The prefects found their greatest ally in the opposition, which was generally united in its resistance to the end of the a priori *tutelle* and the substitution of an a posteriori judicial review. In the National Assembly, members of the opposition during the debates of July 27 to August 3, 1981, argued that this judicial system constituted an a posteriori *tutelle*, which was "a repressive control, humiliating for the elected officials," as well as a politicizing one because it involved the replacement of the neutral administrative a priori *tutelle* with a partisan one of elected officials. Others protested that this would spell the end of the *concertation*, or collaborative relationship, between mayors and prefects and an end to their amicable dialogue. Similarly, in the Senate, often called the assembly of the small communes of France, most members of the right expressed the concerns of the rural communes in their desire for a continuation of the *tutelle* and in their fears that an a posteriori judicial review was in some ways a form of *tutelle* more redoubtable than the existing a priori *tutelle*.[19] The Socialist majority, by contrast, continued to insist that the

[18] *Le Monde*, Mar. 11, 1986.
[19] For a good summary of the arguments and counterarguments, see: "Communes et départements," *La Décentralisation, Cahiers français* (Jan.–Feb. 1982), pp. 58–62.

tutelle was "permanent, vexing, paralyzing."[20] Pierre Mauroy in particular demanded its elimination because it corresponded to an image of a "France centralized to an extreme degree, enclosed in the rigidity of its laws, its regulations, and its circulars."[21]

In the end, the Socialists simply went ahead with the vote for the end of the *tutelle*, leaving the opposition determined to appeal the proposed change in the *tutelle* to the Constitutional Council. And although the opposition, having substantially lost its appeal, did not reverse the a posteriori judicial review when it returned to power in 1986, it did modify a part of its application to the smaller communes. In early 1988 the new majority passed a law that exempted communes with fewer than two thousand inhabitants from budgetary review by the regional accounting courts, returning them to the old system of review by the treasurer paymaster-general.

The opposition was not as united in its views of the transfer of executive power as it was in its objection to the end of the *tutelle*. Among those most opposed were Oliver Guichard, who commented that the transfer of executive power to the departments would only bring disorder, and Michel Debré, who argued that the region would become politicized, creating local potentates and jeopardizing national unity.[22] (Debré's solution was his old project of dividing metropolitan France into forty-seven departments. Failing this, he suggested that the region remain a specialized local authority, which thus would not need to be elected by universal suffrage.)[23] Although some shared Guichard's resistance to the transfer of power to the departments and even more sympathized with Debré's concern about the region, numbers of others favored the transfer of power to one or the other level, although they often disagreed as to which level should be dominant. This division over whether the region or the department was to be favored held true as much for the Socialist majority as for the opposition. Whereas Mitterrand's followers preferred the departmental level over the regional, Rocard's preferred it the other way around. The RPR fought universal suffrage in regional elections, the UDF supported it.

The most extensive public debate about the reforms involved complaints about the lack of choice between regions and departments. Regionalists were especially concerned about the proposed transfer of important administrative functions and financial resources from the state to the departments. To them this suggested that the departments were indeed

[20]*Journal Officiel, Débats Assemblée Nationale*, July 28–Aug. 4, 1981.
[21]Pierre Mauroy, speech before the National Assembly on July 9, 1981.
[22]*Journal Officiel, Débats Assemblée Nationale*, Sept. 9–12, 1981.
[23]Ibid.

favored over the regions.[24] This, they felt, was to destroy the possibility of any truly progressive reform, for the departments have always been conservative forces in the periphery. The regionalists responded to departmentalists' discourses on the dangers of the regions with testimonials in the National Assembly as to the benefits of the reform and to its lack of impact on national unity because "a little regionalism can distance one from the nation, but a lot of regionalism brings one back."[25]

Departmentalists, needless to say, did not share these views. The departmentalist Paul Graziani (RPR), president of the general council of the department of Hauts-de-Seine, insisted that it was only appropriate to transfer to the department its new functions. He argued that the department was the key to ensuring everyday democracy, because it was neither too small, as were the communes, nor too big, as were the regions.[26] Thus, against those who complained that no choice was made between regions and departments, the departmentalists countered that a choice was indeed made, with the departments given what was rightfully theirs.

There were some departmentalists, however, who felt that the regions came out on top, to the detriment of the departments. Jean Cluzel, senator and president of the general council of Allier and regional councilor of Auvergne, vehemently opposed the creation of regional governments elected by universal suffrage, insisting that it only created yet another intermediate level between the locality and the center. Against the region, he argued in favor of the departments, communes, and the Senate as the only appropriate counter-powers to the state. He insisted that there was no regional interest in the way that there were communal and departmental interests; and he feared the results would be a recentralization at the level of the region.[27]

According to Defferre, however, the only possible choice was the one that was in fact made. And he insisted that the choice was not in favor of the departments. Although the departments received only the administrative functions they already had jurisdiction over through the prefects, the regions from the beginning were given much more power and stood to gain even more over time. According to Defferre, to abolish the departmental level altogether, which was what some regionalists might have wanted, was in any case a political impossibility, if the decentralizing laws were to be passed at all.[28] And he was right.

[24]Michel Crozier, for one, complained that decentralization had increased the powers of the departments and argued that instead it should have increased those of the region (in "Clochemerle ou la région, il faut choisir," *Projets* nos. 185–6 (May–June 1984).
[25]*Journal Official, Débats Assemblée Nationale,* Sept. 9, 1981.
[26]*La Croix,* Feb. 8, 1984.
[27]Cluzel, *Les "Anti-Monarques."*
[28]Defferre interview, May 23, 1985.

The departmentalists, after all, were a force to be reckoned with. In September 1984, slightly over half of the presidents of the general council were also members of Parliament, and the rest were former members or former ministers.[29] These departmentalists were certainly not willing to give up the fight. The regionalists, by comparison, were not nearly as strong, especially because the departmentalists were in many cases well-ensconced in the regional governments themselves.

The lack of a clear choice between the regions and departments, which was a concession to departmentalist pressures and led many to assume that the cause of the region was lost, has not led to the disastrous results many predicted. On the contrary, the regions have in fact gained an increasingly important new role in the promotion of local economic development as well as a legitimacy they did not have before decentralization. In fact, there has been no diluting of the reforms for the regions on the order of that of the rural communes; departments are cooperating with the regions; and the right has taken to the regions as readily as the left, with the most tangible proof of this the fact that regional governments have gone on a building spree to give physical evidence of their new presence. The local population itself has become increasingly aware of and supportive of the regions, with 59 percent of those interviewed in a 1986 survey stating that the region is the administrative unit of the future; 51 percent hoping for its continued development; and 44 percent even willing to pay higher taxes to allow it to do more to promote economic development.[30] The success of the regionalization has been such that, in the beginning of July 1987, Prime Minister Jacques Chirac summoned to Paris the presidents of the regional councils to complain that the regions were doing too much, were too dynamic, and were risking endangering the unity of the state.

THE TRANSFER OF ADMINISTRATIVE FUNCTIONS AND CIVIL SERVICE REFORM

Once the transfer of executive powers was complete, the order of the day for the director of local authorities in the Ministry of the Interior was to transfer administrative functions and authority as quickly as possible. The breakneck pace at which the details of these transfers had to be worked out, however, meant that the sweeping changes and reorganization of services originally planned were swept aside. Because the politi-

[29]René Dosière, "Les élections cantonales et le nouveau conseil général," *Correspondance municipale*, no. 255 (Feb. 1985).

[30] Beatrice Roy, "Images de la région." Paper presented for the conference, "La nouvelle région – An I," sponsored by the Observatoire interrégional du politique (Paris, Mar. 18, 1987), p. 3.

cians' pressure for quick reform was met by counter-pressures from the various ministries and *grand corps,* or elite corps, of civil servants, the transfer of administrative functions took the form that was likely to be the easiest to pass and to implement.

The new administrative functions

As a result of the transfer of administrative functions from the state to the locality, the regions now have charge of regional economic planning and policy, industrial development, and professional education. The departments are responsible for the delivery of health and social services, construction and maintenance of public thoroughfares, and school bus transportation. The communes have retained their traditional duties with regard to municipal services, whereas they have gained the freedom to set up their own *plan d'occupation du sol* (POS), or land-use plan, and to issue building permits (where they have a POS). Moreover, intercommunal administrative cooperation has been facilitated through the creation of intercommunal charters, the successors of the intercommunal syndicates of assistance. (See Table 4.2 for a basic list of those functions transferred and those retained by the state.)

In addition, every level of local government is charged with promoting local economic development despite the region's primary responsibility in this area; every level has some authority over some aspect of culture even though the state has retained major control in this field; every level including the state has authority over some ports and waterways, although the departments and communes are clearly the main beneficiaries of this part of decentralization; and every level has clear responsibility for construction and maintenance of preuniversity public education facilities with, in most instances, the regions taking the *lycées,* or high schools; the departments, the *collèges,* or junior high schools; and the communes, the *primaires,* or elementary schools.[31]

Finally, the prefects were not left completely without power or authority as a result of decentralization, for the new laws replaced the prefects' former executive powers and a priori control with continued responsibility for national interests (notably civil and economic defense), for respect for the laws, and for public order, as well as with increased "deconcentrated," or centrally delegated, powers over the field services of the state and over many matters of local concern previously handled directly by Paris ministries in the social services and economic spheres.[32] More specifically, the prefects were given authority in those aspects of local economic develop-

[31]For a brief review of the reforms, see "Trois ans de décentralisation," *Démocratie Locale* no. 38 (April 1985).
[32] For a full account of the prefects' new duties, see Bernard, *L'Etat.*

Table 4.2. *The transfer of administrative functions*

Function	Commune	Department
Social services	Sets up welfare case files through social welfare bureaus Can exercise functions of department by agreement	In charge of social welfare Medical assistance Social assistance to children, families, handicapped, elderly
Health	Organizes and finances municipal bureaus of hygiene and disinfection	Childhood and family health, vaccinations, fight vs. cancer, tuberculosis, venereal disease, leprosy
Housing	Action in favor of poorly housed Local program for the habitat	Advise on aid distribution for habitat Departmental commission on habitat
Education	Elementary & pre-elementary schools: location, financing, construction, equipment, and maintenance May modify school hours Extracurricular activities Create, organize, fund teaching of arts, dance, music, theater	Junior high schools: location, financing, construction, equipment, and maintenance Extracurricular activities Create, organize, fund teaching of arts, dance, music, theater
Professional education		Advice by departmental committees on professional education
Culture	Organize and fund municipal libraries and museums Conserve municipal archives libraries	Organize and fund departmental museums Responsible for central lending Conserve departmental archives

ment retained by the state and deemed necessary to national economic and social policies, that is regional planning, the promotion of innovation, unemployment policy, the fight against inflation, and the special programs in economically distressed regions such as the *pôles de conversion,* or enterprise zones. And they remained in charge of those departmental social services retained by the state.

In the transfer of administrative functions, the most pressure came from civil servants; and the groups most successful at resisting reform were the ones most centrally organized, generally those in which there had been little deconcentration, or decentralization, even before the Socialist reforms. Thus, whereas the tremendous lobbying efforts to resist the transfer of the already deconcentrated social services were only half successful, given the resulting division of responsibility between the state and the department, the resistance to decentralization of those supportive

Table 4.2 *(cont)* The transfer of administrative functions

Region	State
	Social security Protection of minors, elderly, women, handicapped, immigrants, aid to orphans
	Hospitals, public health, mental illness, drugs, alcohol
Define priorities for habitat Complementary aid to state Housing assistance	All other aspects Encourage energy quality, innovation, savings

High schools: Location, financing,
  construction, equipment, and
  maintenance
Extra curricular activities
Create, organize, fund teaching of
  arts, dance, music, theater
	All other aspects including:
	  curriculum, pedagogy, faculty pay
	  and appointments
	Higher education

Implement initiatives on professional
  education and apprenticeship,
  establish and fund regional programs,
  finance professional education
  organizations
	All other initiatives

Organize and fund regional museums
Conserve regional archives
Receive regional archives from state
  and private individuals
	Technical and scientific control of museums,
	  archives, libraries

Continued on pp. 124–5

of a completely centralized educational system was almost wholly successful, because only educational facilities were transferred to the different
levels of local government. Decentralization met a similar fate in the area
of culture, even though it did not have the same kind of active constituency opposing decentralization. In the area of culture as in education,
resistance to reform benefited from the French linkage of the concept of
national unity with the promotion of a national culture and the maintenance of a national education system. In the economic sphere, by contrast, decentralization worked very well indeed, in part because the central ministries affected were comparatively less powerful (for example,
Plan and DATAR) and, in any case, were more committed to decentralization itself and because many of the duties involved were themselves new
(for example, economic aid by communes) rather than transferred. The
deconcentration of the central ministries to the benefit of the prefect has

Table 4.2 *(cont)* *The transfer of administrative functions*

Function	Commune	Department
Planning	Elaborate and approve intercommunal charters	Advise on regional plan Aid for rural investment
Urbanism	Establish POS (Land-use plan) Elaborate intercommunal plan-EPCI Issue building permits (with POS)	Advise on perimeter Advise where there is departmental investment
Transport	Advise on regional transport schemata Advise on departmental transport plan Create and maintain communal and rural roads Exercise departments' school transport functions upon agreement	Advise on regional transport schemata Establish departmental transport plan Approve departmental plans of non-urban transportation services Maintain departmental roads Finance and organize school transportation system Advise on agreements with SNCF
Ports and waterways	Pleasure ports and port police	Maritime ports, commercial and fishing ports Aid for work preserving the marine culture
Environment & patrimony	Proposals or agreement on creation of zones (ZPPAU) for protection of architectural and urban patrimony Advise on departmental plans on itineraries of walking tours	Define and modify departmental plans on itineraries of walking tours
Economic aid	Complement regions' direct aid Indirect aid, e.g., loans, tax breaks, sale of land or buildings Aid for businesses in difficulty	Complement regions' direct aid Indirect aid, e.g., loans, tax breaks, sale of land or buildings Aid for businesses in difficulty

yet to be adequately implemented, again because of the resistance of powerful groups of civil servants at the center.

To begin with, the transfer of public health and social welfare services from the state to the department did not reorganize those services as originally planned – with the recipient of benefits in mind – because such a reorganization would have led to a drawn out battle with all the ministries together. The transfer of functions followed instead the traditional division of services, so that the different interests could be fought separately, one at a time. Defferre had calculated that the only way to get any reform through was to sacrifice the coherence of a masterplan to piecemeal, incremental change at a breakneck pace. But this set of pitched battles meant that the resulting system ended up being at least as complex, if not more so, than the previous one.[33]

[33] Jacques Rondin, *Le Sacre des notables* (Paris: Fayard, 1985), pp. 144–7.

Table 4.2 *(cont) The transfer of administrative functions*

Region	State
Participate in elaboration and implementation of national plan Regional plan Responsibilities in tourism	National plan
Approve POS, EPCI	
Establish regional transport schemata Create certain aerodromes Agreements with SNCF (railroad)	Maintain national roads
Creation of canals and river ports Aid to the fishing industry and to enterprises for marine culture	
College of patrimony and sites Lists preservation sites	All other aspects
Promotion of local business and job creation, expansion, innovation Direct aid to healthy enterprises All forms of indirect aid	Enterprise zones Promotion of innovation, fight against inflation, unemployment, etc.

In the social services area, the state retained the social security system as well as functions related to "national solidarity" such as the protection of minors, the elderly, women, the handicapped, and immigrant populations. The departments gained social welfare programs in such areas as medical assistance, aid to children (except orphans who remained under the aegis of the state) and to families, assistance to the elderly (such as help defraying the costs of lodging and meals), and some forms of assistance to the handicapped. In the health area, the state retained the hospitals, public health, and the fight against illness, drugs, and alcoholism, and the department took charge of childhood and family health, vaccinations, and the fight against cancer, tuberculosis, venereal disease, and leprosy.

This division of services produced continuing complication and sometimes duplication in the delivery of social services. Many individuals now have to deal with two levels of government, the state and the department, in addition to the different divisions within each level. In the case of the handicapped, for example, the department pays for their lodging, social security supplies their principal source of income, and the state arranges for their employment.[34] Furthermore, two government employees frequently now perform tasks formerly done by one. Retirement homes, for example, are now visited by departmental housing inspectors and state medical inspectors.[35]

The situation is all the more complicated by the fact that decentralization did not go as far as it should have in revamping the state services transferred to the localities. Because the transfer of health and social services from the state to the department followed the traditional division of services, it may have simply transferred the bureaucratic problems and financial burdens of the state to the locality – or even made them worse. The resulting system, moreover, may not be more cost-effective than the previous system, because Defferre made cost containment more difficult even for fiscally responsible, local elected officials by following the dictates of politics in transferring administrative functions.

Nevertheless, by giving local elected officials increased power and responsibility, decentralization will enable such officials to revamp their own services if they so desire. What this means is that local elected officials will have to start "rationalizing" expenditures that the state in the past simply "rationed."[36] Such rationalization, in fact, is already taking place in some local governments, exactly as Gaston Defferre had intended, although it is not as easy a task as it could have been, given the complicated interrelationships and the overlapping responsibilities between the state and the departments.[37] And in all, the transfer of health and social service functions was at least relatively successful: A goodly portion of these functions have been brought closer to the population by being put under the jurisdiction of local elected officials, who have the potential for streamlining the delivery of social services while trimming expenses.

By contrast, the decentralization of education predictably was one of the most limited aspects of reform. As a high-level servant in the Ministry of Education explained, the issue was always the transfer of only the physical plant and the *emploi du temps*, for example, but certainly not the pedagogical responsibilities. For one could not question, she insisted, the issue of equality in education. The attachment of the French to this idea – and

[34]Ibid., p. 21.
[35]*L'Express*, Mar. 8–14, 1985.
[36]Rondin, *Le Sacre*, p. 156.
[37]See Part II, Chapter 10, "The financial limitations and the 'transfer of unpopularity.'"

more importantly the attachment of the main, centrally organized teachers' groups – made any attack on pedagogy impossible. But even what was left to decentralize could itself be construed quite narrowly. After all, where does pedagogy stop and time management begin? For example, is the change from a Wednesday and Saturday half-day schedule to a full-day Wednesday and no Saturday schedule simply one of time management? Or is it pedagogical, relating to how students can learn? The resulting law only gave the different levels of local government responsibility for the construction, maintenance, and janitorial work, effectively transferring what were the greatest costs, given the generally terrible conditions of the buildings. The Socialist Minister of Education, Chevènement, turned out to be quite a centralizer in this area. His successor in the neoliberal government, Monory, however, appeared less so. In September 1986 he suggested that decentralization be extended to pedagogy, with the regional level gaining the responsibility of determining which *options,* or electives, would be taught in the *lycées,* leaving to the state only the organization of a *tronc commun,* or common core, of knowledge. It is a long way, however, from this to actual implementation, as it would require a complete rethinking of the national education system.[38]

The transfer of functions in the area of culture was equally limited. Many of the functions of the 1983 law were only transferred in 1986. And although the departments gained control of the central lending libraries and the communes, the municipal libraries, the state retained control over certain expenditures for libraries, as well as technical and scientific control over museums, archives, and libraries. With culture, as with education, decentralization was confronted with a centuries-old history of centralization based on the assumption that the pride of the nation, as well as its unity, depended upon the central direction – administratively and intellectually – of France's *patrimoine,* or heritage, so that all would have equal access to it.[39]

The transfer of functions related to the promotion of local economic development, although itself one of the more controversial and complicated areas of reform, was by contrast generally much easier than the transfer in the areas of culture and education, and much more extensive. This was because direct intervention in the economy by local governments was a commonplace even before the Socialist reforms, while the decentralization of economic activities had been a cornerstone of the DATAR's centrally directed policies throughout the Fifth Republic. Decentralization in this context was a natural next step. In this arena, even though economic development was clearly made the role of the region,

[38] *Le Monde,* Sept. 30, 1986.
[39] See Paul Mari, "Culture: Transfert de compétences ou transfert de tutelle?" *Correspondance municipale* (June 1986), pp. 33–5.

the other, lower levels of local government also gained certain functions and the state did not by any means abandon to the region all of its powers.

The region was given primary responsibility for promoting local business and job creation, expansion, and innovation; for providing job training and professional development; for overseeing and coordinating the regional planning process; and for determining, with the central government, the direction of local economic development. In addition, the region alone was allowed to provide direct assistance in the form of subsidies for healthy enterprises, although this could be complemented by departments and communes with, for example, *primes,* or credits, for business or job creation. Indirect assistance in the form of tax breaks, loan guarantees, sale of land or buildings, management consulting, promotion and distribution of local products were everyone's domain, however, as were direct and indirect assistance for enterprises in difficulty. This meant that, although decentralization made the regional government the main economic actor in the periphery, the departmental and communal levels of government were not to be excluded.

The central government, moreover, did not give up entirely its involvement in the promotion of smaller scale, local economic development. It reserved special areas of economic action for itself; and it required negotiation or consultation in other areas. For example, the state remained involved in promoting local development through its partnership with the region in the regional planning process, through its direct grant and subsidy programs for local business and job creation, and through its establishment of special reindustrialization or employment zones. An unprecedented number of actors thus came to be involved at the local level – including, in addition to the elected officials and administrators of local governments, traditional actors such as the prefects and field services of the state, the national ministries, the nationalized industries, the nationalized banks, and even the European Economic Community – along with a vast array of new incentive structures for local business and job creation, expansion, and innovation.

Needless to say, the involvement of so many different levels and units of government in the promotion of local economic development has, as in the social services arena, resulted in complication and sometimes duplication of efforts. Whereas such an outcome is necessarily a detriment to the delivery of social services, it need not be for economic development. On the contrary, decentralization in this arena has spurred a new economic activism in the periphery based on this new pluralism, which has promoted increased cooperation and competition among governmental actors in the periphery. The only major criticism of the reform has been the suggestion that there has been too much economic activism in some sectors. In response to its finding that communes were increasingly falling into debt as a result of the defaults of businesses for which they had guaranteed loans, the neoliberal government, with the law of January 5, 1988, effectively barred communes from giving direct aid to enterprises in difficulty by restricting such action to departments and regions.[40]

Of all the administrative functions transferred in this second phase of decentralization, those related to local economic development have probably been the most successful in terms of the changes they have brought about in the periphery. The least successful have been those involving the deconcentration of the central ministries to the benefit of the prefects, which have been very slow in coming. This was to have been a central part of the reform, with deconcentration accompanying decentralization as a way of bringing the state closer to the new loci of decision making in the periphery. But many central ministries have resisted deconcentrating authority even to their own field services, let alone to the prefect, and instead have been instituting recentralizing measures of control, and most of the field services of the state have in turn resisted being placed under the authority of the prefect.[41] The personnel of the field services of the state continue to prefer reporting to their own central ministries rather than to the prefects. The local elected officials, by contrast, prefer to deal with only one interlocutor, the prefect. So the best one can say about this area of concern is that there is likely to be some pressure to continue deconcentration and the centralization of deconcentrated authority under the prefect.[42]

For the moment, in any event, the transfer of executive power and administrative functions to the periphery has not as yet been accompanied by a concomitant, significant reduction in the size of Paris ministries. Defferre once remarked that the reform would be measured by the number of closed offices in the ministries. But those offices are not yet closed (as of March 1985, only 770 jobs had been transferred to the periphery), whereas many new ones have opened up in the departments and regions.[43] Deconcentration is occurring, but unevenly, in many cases at a snail's pace.[44] The administrative centralization of the state, therefore,

[40]J.-C. Bouzely, "Les nouvelles règles de l'interventionnisme local," *La Revue Administrative* no. 241 (Jan.–Feb. 1988): 66–7.
[41]See the discussion in Part II, Chapter 9, under "The new role of the state in the periphery."
[42]Marie-Françoise Bechtel, Marie-Christine Henry-Meininger, and Yves Jegouzo, "Chronique de l'administration française," *La Revue française d'administration publique* no. 41 (Jan.–Mar. 1987), p. 159.
[43]*L'Express,* Mar. 8–14, 1985.
[44]See discussion in Part II, Chapter 9, under "The new role of the state in the periphery."

although significantly diminished through the transfer of powers and functions to local governments, has not been reduced appreciably with regard to its primary representative in the periphery, the prefect.

Civil service reform and the transfer of personnel

Along with the transfer of new administrative duties, especially at the departmental and regional levels, came the temporary transfer of experienced personnel from the national civil service to the territorial civil service. In order to ensure the success of this transfer of personnel, the Socialists passed a civil service reform bill intended to make territorial service as attractive as national service. The new civil service code created a territorial civil service modeled on the national service, including employment protection and benefits, as well as professional standards for recruitment and performance.

Prior to decentralization, territorial civil servants had none of the employment protections and benefits of national civil servants and none of the career opportunities and incentives. On the whole, by comparison with the national civil servants, they were poorly paid, poorly trained, and more poorly treated, with little opportunity for upward or outward mobility, because they would have lost any seniority and pension benefits they might have had by moving from one department or municipality to another. The new code established by the law of January 26, 1984, was to remedy this situation by allowing mobility between the territorial and national civil service, as well as within the territorial service between different units of local government, without any loss of seniority, pension privileges, or other employment protections. In addition, it attempted to provide career opportunities and continuity in employment by establishing *centres de gestion*, or administrative centers, run by an elected council charged with (1) regrouping civil servants into corps, (2) ensuring the application of consistent standards to civil servants regardless of locality, (3) organizing competitions for the recruitment of territorial civil servants, (4) approving transfers and reclassifications of unemployed civil servants, and (5) overseeing appointments of and sanctions against civil servants generally.[45]

Civil service reform, in brief, was to provide local officials with the personnel necessary to enable them to exercise their new powers, perform their new functions, and distribute their new resources effectively. Without such a reform, the Socialists feared that the highly trained and well-qualified members of the national civil service on loan to the departments and regions would not stay and that the decentralization reforms would

[45]*Le Monde*, Mar. 11, 1986.

consequently founder from the lack of competent personnel.[46] Despite the Socialists' insistence on the importance of territorial civil service reform, however, the promulgation of the *statuts d'application,* or implementation rules, suffered delay after delay.

The delays themselves had two main sources: resistance from civil servants and resistance from local elected officials. The primary opposition to reform came from the *énarques* (civil servants trained at the *École nationale d'administration*) and other members of the upper-level, national civil service fearful of a rival territorial service. But they were not alone: Some members of local civil services were equally concerned that the reform would simply mean that members of the national civil service would be better able to take the best jobs for themselves, moving back and forth between the territorial and national services. For example, Pierre Costa, director-general of departmental services in the Alpes-Maritimes, although himself a member of the prefectoral corps, opposed the reform because he saw it as one intended to benefit members of the *grands corps,* who, given decentralization, had little of interest left to do and would welcome the change to take over the territorial services.[47]

Most territorial civil servants, however, were in favor of the reform, finding that it responded to a real need. Dominique Schmitt, secretary-general of the region of Lorraine and one of the few with so high a position who was not a member of a *grands corps,* echoing the sentiments of local civil servants generally, argued that it was important to make territorial service as attractive and prestigious as national service if one wanted equally good people to go there. The main question was how the law was to be elaborated: If it set up a monopolistic system with the only recruits allowed being graduates of the *grandes écoles,* and lawyers, paralysis would result. If instead people with varied backgrounds were allowed to enter, the result would be a better system than that of the state.[48]

Territorial civil servants, in short, recognized that they would stand to benefit greatly from such a reform, depending upon how it was elaborated. But they were no match for the *grands corps,* who enjoyed a high level of cohesiveness, organization, and easy access to central, decision-making organs in contrast with the territorial civil servants' fragmentation in the periphery and lack of cohesive organization to represent their interests.

National civil servants, moreover, were aided in their opposition by local elected officials, who were fearful that civil service reform of the

[46]Jean-Pierre Worms, Deputy from Saône-et-Loire, interview with author, Paris, May 9, 1985.
[47]Pierre Costa, director general of departmental services in the Alpes-Maritimes, interview with author, Nice, June 6, 1985.
[48]Dominique Schmitt, secretary-general of the region of the Lorraine, interview with author, Metz, June 18, 1985.

kind contemplated would represent a form of recentralization by the state that would limit their powers considerably in personnel matters by acting as a direct check on their freedom to choose whomever they considered best qualified for a given position. Christian Lalu, the director of the main lobbying group for the large cities, the Association of Big City Mayors, argued against the reform on the grounds not only that it restricted mayors' freedom but also that a national code for local civil servants modeled on the one for state civil servants was not appropriate for local governments, where a different kind of civil servant is required – one with greater political skills, for example.[49]

The combined opposition of local elected officials and national civil servants, then, helps explain the delay in implementing the reform. But this was not the only reason cited. Eric Giuily, director of the *Direction générale des collectivités locales* (DGCL), the local government department of the Ministry of the Interior and Decentralization, was charged with implementation. When questioned, he argued that the main reason for delay was the complexity of the task at hand.[50] Other civil servants intimately connected with the ministry agreed, but suggested that the problem may have been that the task was simply too complex for those charged with seeing it through. Whatever the reason for the delay, the fact remains that because it meant that the *statuts d'application* were promulgated only at the very last minute, on the very day of the Socialist defeat in the legislative elections of March 16, 1986, the territorial civil service reform had little chance of surviving in its original form. In July 1987, the government modified the reform by effectively giving local elected officials control over the territorial civil service. Although the statute that was passed did provide for a certain consistency in standards of treatment and employment guarantees, it did not allow for mobility and did not protect the professional independence of civil servants. Instead of creating national *corps* of territorial civil servants, it created *cadres d'emploi*, or employment categories, to which a civil servant could belong only as a result of being hired by a local elected official.

THE TRANSFER OF FINANCIAL RESOURCES

The transfer of financial resources suffered a fate similar to the transfer of administrative functions, in which political considerations worked against any radical change. The Socialists quickly saw that any major overhaul of

[49]Christian Lalu, director of the Association of Big City Mayors, interview with author, Paris, May 2, 1985.
[50]Eric Giuily, director of the local government department of the Ministry of the Interior and Decentralization, interviews with author, Paris, May 21 and June 26, 1985).

the system of local finances would be extremely complicated and politically hazardous. Thus, they took the most conservative path available, leaving intact a number of taxes they themselves had long criticized. And instead of providing local authorities with their own, wholly controlled sources of revenue, they gave them some resources directly through the transfer of state taxes and guaranteed others through a system of block grants. Even so, the Socialists encountered much opposition, mainly from the central ministries, which were led by Laurent Fabius in the Ministry of Finance and resisted any attempts to deprive them of the financial resources required to make policies. Many opposition members, moreover, objected to the complications and likely expense of the new system. Jean-Pierre Fourcade, senator and president of the committee on local finances, for example, protested: "If we combine the concept of four levels of administration with the mechanism of cross-financing, which the functionaries adore because this permits each one of them to put in his grain of salt and to retain his powers despite decentralization, it is clear that we have an absolutely marvelous system that is a formidable engine for producing additional expenditures."[51]

There is no question but that the resulting system ended up being even more complicated than the previous one, perhaps even less manageable, and no less expensive. Moreover, the resulting system, which combined block grants from the state with local taxes, still left local authorities dependent upon the state (although less so than before), if only because the state collected the taxes and set the amount of the transfer.

Local governments did quite well with this transfer of financial resources. After all, the last thing the Socialists wanted was to make local governments turn against decentralization because of finances. Every effort was therefore made to ensure that each transfer of function would be compensated by an equivalent transfer of financial resources. To make certain of this, a commission composed of elected officials and presided over by a magistrate from the national accounting court was established to oversee the process and to order rectification where necessary. Moreover, ministry officials were consistently working on remedies to some of the major problems that cropped up from the new laws.

To cover the costs of their new administrative duties in addition to their ongoing expenses, local governments received new financial resources from the state – half in the form of the transfer of regular state taxes to the locality and half in the form of revenue sharing through a variety of government grants based on different sharing formulas from different national taxes. The taxes over which local authorities now have total

[51]Cited in the first report of the commission on the implementation of decentralization by Christian Poncelet, Senate, no. 490, p. 79, annex to the proceedings of the July 7, 1983 session.

control – in most cases to raise or lower as they see fit – include automobile registration and licensing fees, property taxes, and the local business tax. Of the newly transferred taxes, the regions now have at their disposal the proceeds of the *cartes grises* (a one-time tax to register title of a new car), but the departments have the *vignette auto,* or automobile sticker (a yearly licensing fee based on the age and value of the automobile), and part of the *droit d'enregistrement* (various registration fees), the *droits de mutation* (a property transfer tax), and the *publicité foncière* (a tax on property advertising). As of 1987 both the departments and the regions gained the freedom to set the rate of local taxes.

In addition, the state provided many block grants along with a much smaller number of categorical grants and special subsidies for operating costs, for investment aid, and for the additional costs of decentralization. Although not a Socialist innovation, the extensive use of block grants, which enable local governments to spend their money as they see fit, was a key element in the Socialists' attempt to give local governments maximal financial autonomy without giving up total state control and, with it, the ability to equalize expenses and ensure in some measure distributive justice. In 1970 such grants represented only 50 percent of total state aid; in 1980 they had reached 60 percent; and by 1985 they constituted 80 percent.[52]

The Socialists created two new block grants: (1) *dotation globale d'équipement* (DGE), a block grant for capital investment created in 1983 to replace the categorical grants of the past and set to increase from one year to the next based on the rate of growth in the investments of all public administrations (that is, state, social security, and local governments, taken together); and (2) the *dotation générale de décentralisation* (DGD), a block grant created in 1984 to pay for the costs of decentralization where they exceed those covered by the revenue from local taxes and set to increase according to a formula based on the rate of increase of the revenue from the value-added tax (VAT) plus a certain added percentage. The Socialists also retained a third block grant, the *dotation globale de fonctionnement* (DGF), a grant for current operating expenses also aligned with the VAT created in 1979.

These were not the only sources of state funding for local governments, however. In addition to the DGF, state aid for operating expenses also came in the form of state reimbursement for certain property tax exemptions, the fund for the equalization of the business tax, and other specific subsidies. In addition to the DGF state aid for capital investment was complemented by the compens...ion fund for the value added tax (FCTVA) created in 1977 and other subsidies. Moreover, with the trans-

[52]*La Décentralisation en marche, Cahiers français,* no. 220 (Mar.–Apr. 1985), p. 60.

fer of new administrative duties in 1986 and beyond, came two new block grants in the area of education: the *dotation départementale d'équipement des collèges* (DDEC), to pay for the departments' expenses for the maintenance and construction of middle schools and the *dotation régionale d'équipement scolaire* (DRES), to pay for the regions' expenses for the maintenance and construction of high schools. With the transfer of duties in the area of culture, came an increase in the DGD (block grants in the form of the DGE and the DGF were ruled out for cultural activities by the decree of February 16, 1984) to pay the departments' operating costs and investment expenditures for central lending libraries and those of the communes for municipal libraries.

Taken as a whole, state transfers to local governments came to slightly over one-third of the total expenditures of local governmments in 1987, down from 41 percent in 1981.[53] But according to some, even this reduced amount from the state represented a danger to the independence as well as fiscal responsibility of local governments, because they depended for a significant portion of their revenues on grants based on automatic formulas having nothing to do with the health of the local economy or the soundness of local administration.[54]

The state's share of local financing, however, was not seen as a threat only to local governments. It was also a potential source of problems for the state. The system of block grants tends to be inflationary. It assumes an expanding economy and leaves the central government little power to reduce local spending in times of recession, because local authorities' funds are guaranteed to increase, whether they are aligned with the VAT or with the investments of all public administrations combined. Moreover, this system has led to numerous inequities in distribution that the central government sought to fix.[55]

Thus, in response to complaints by rural communes that they could no longer engage in capital investment projects because of the way finances were transferred, the DGE was revised with the creation at the end of 1985 of a special block grant for capital investment purposes to be disbursed by the prefect on the advice of a commission of local elected officials. (A similar revision for the benefit of the mid-sized communes, however, failed to get the necessary parliamentary approval, in part because of timing – it was closer to election time – and in part because its constituency was much less powerful than that of the rural communes.) Although many complained that this constituted a form of recentraliza-

[53]See the discussion of local finances in Part II, Chapter 10, "The financial limitations and the 'transfer of unpopularity.' "
[54]Jacques Bernot, "Les limites de la globalisation," *Cahiers français*, no. 220 (Mar.–Apr. 1985), pp. 62–5.
[55]Ibid.

tion by the state, at least it resolved this particular problem. But this was not the only problem for the rural communes. Subsequently under the neoliberal government in 1988, the DGE was again revised to ensure that rural communes and the poorest departments received at least 40 percent of the overall allotment (in 1986 and 1987, the rural communes had received only 34 percent, a reduction from before decentralization).[56]

The DGF, too, was revised in 1985 in an effort to respond to the needs of the poorest communes and the departments with fewer than two hundred thousand inhabitants. And this did have noticeable effects in reducing geographical inequalities between taxpayers in different communities.[57] Even before this, adjustments were made for those departments receiving more money than the costs of their transferred duties, by diminishing the amount of their state aid in favor of those departments receiving less money than the costs of their duties. Finally the business tax was reformed in 1986 in an effort to alleviate the burdens of local businesses' payroll taxes, by reducing the amount of local direct taxes and increasing to 25.6 percent the portion of the state's business tax receipts transferred to the locality. And even though local elected officials denounced this, too, as a form of recentralization, they accepted it politically because direct local taxes were diminishing, despite the fact that it also represented a reduction in local financial autonomy.[58]

All of these reforms to the system of block grants constitute an elaborate system of mechanisms to redress inequities in distribution. The problem with these reforms is that they could not help but lead to all sorts of distortions; and this could ultimately make the system collapse under the weight of all the readjustments and exceptions to the rule.[59] Perhaps only then will the system be completely overhauled, but only perhaps. Reform of public finances is always difficult, but especially so for France, given that the local taxation system interlocks in so many ways with the national system. Initiatives for reform in France as elsewhere have rarely been successful (for example, Great Britain, where after twenty years the only outcome was the poll tax); and when successful, they have taken a long time to come to fruition (for example, a full decade in West Germany in the 1970s).[60] Moreover, even when successful, there are always

[56]*Démocratie Locale* no. 52 (Feb. 1988): 2.
[57]See Alain Guengant, *Équité territoriale et inégalités. Le rôle de la DGF dans la réduction des inégalitiés financières entre communes* (Paris: Litec, 1983), p. 21.
[58]Bechtel et al., "Chroniques," p. 159.
[59]Bernot, "Les limites de la globalisation," pp. 62–5.
[60]See the sensible discussion of the problems for reforming the local taxation system in Douglas Ashford, "Decentralizing France: How the Socialists Discovered Pluralism," paper prepared for delivery at the conference, "A France of Pluralism and Consensus?" jointly sponsored by New York University and Columbia University (New York: Oct. 9–11, 1987).

unforeseen problems, as evidenced by those faced by the smaller communes and poorer departments with the Socialists' halfway reform. We should perhaps marvel that the Socialists were as successful as they were in this area. It is important to note that the neoliberal government, rather than producing any major overhaul of the local taxation system, only proceeded to continue to tinker with the system. Nevertheless, the Socialists did lose a golden opportunity to overhaul local finances, although what that overhaul might have looked like is open to speculation. Most of the suggestions, such as a single tax for each level of local government in place in the traditional taxes, raised as many problems as they would have solved.[61]

There is much, then, that the Socialists left undone. In their search for a consensus, the Socialists left some of the most pressing problems of French local government unresolved. By failing to rationalize the structures of local government, either by reducing the unwieldy number of communes or by choosing between the departments and regions, decentralization leaves four levels of local government (including the prefectoral) with different functions and often overlapping jurisdictions, thus complicating intergovernmental relations. By failing to reform the system of local finances, to reorganize health and social welfare, or to implement the originally passed civil service reform, decentralization risks compromising the efficient and cost-effective delivery of local services. Finally, as we shall see in the next chapter, by failing to include local democracy laws, decentralization increased the powers of the notables without establishing any formal counterbalance of increased direct citizen participation.

Despite these drawbacks, the Socialists did institute sweeping reforms, breaking the pattern of much talk and little action that had lasted a full century and fulfilling one of the last imperatives of the French Revolution. However incomplete these reforms may appear, they therefore nevertheless remain an amazing achievement.

[61]Jacques Blanc, "La réforme de la fiscalité directe locale," *Les Collectivités territoriales, Cahiers français*, no. 239 (Jan.–Feb. 1989), p. 78. See also Alain Guengant and Jean-Michel Uhaldeborde, *Crise et réforme des finances locales* (Paris: Presses universitaires de France, 1989).

5

Legislating decentralization in the politics of local government

The Socialists' reforms focused not only on the administrative aspects of local government but also on the political aspects. When Defferre proposed the decentralizing law of March 1982, he was as much concerned about the need for a political revitalization of the periphery as he was about the need for an end to the administrative inefficiency and the costliness of local government. Pierre Mauroy, in his investiture speech as prime minister, insisted that with decentralization "we will give back . . . to 500,000 elected officials the means for taking responsibility and initiative. We will give to citizens, *usagers,* consumers, the means of participating, truly, in the organization of their daily lives. . . . To build a new citizenry requires first of all to give the state back to its citizens."[1]

Once it became evident that the local elected officials who took responsibility and initiative were on the right, however, the left began questioning the political wisdom of decentralization, "stressing, with purely political logic, that it is becoming more and more paradoxical that the Socialists who have power at the center are redistributing it to the periphery."[2] These members of the left worked against some parts of the reform as vigorously as other groups did to defend their own interests. The result was that whereas electoral reform, especially in terms of the regions, was long overdue by the time it was brought forth, the limitation of the *cumul des mandats* was delivered only at the very last minute, and the local democracy laws were conceived but never developed.

In any event, these actual legislative changes in the politics of local government, however cautious, together with the reforms in local administration, have had far-reaching consequences for national and local politics. First, the Socialists have managed to open up local government to the more progressive urban groups traditionally left out of the local political

[1]National Assembly, July 10, 1981.
[2]Caroux, "End of administrative centralization?" p. 112.

equation by breaking up to a large extent the "conservative complicity" that for nearly a quarter of a century had been worked out between a right-wing center and the periphery. Second, and perhaps even more important, the current changes in local electoral politics may have helped bring about a critical realignment of the national electorate, thus paralleling the changes one hundred years ago, at the beginning of the Third Republic.

When Mitterrand, in his inaugural address, called upon the *couche nouvelle,* or new social stratum of *salariés,* the lower professional echelons of middle-level managers and the workers who brought him to power, to become the electoral mainstays of a new, more dynamic Fifth Republic, he quite deliberately evoked Gambetta's similar call to the new stratum of middle-income peasants and shopkeepers of the Third Republic. For Mitterrand, the *salariés* were the key to a realignment of the electorate behind a Socialist Fifth Republic, and from the early 1970s, the Socialists had targeted this group, even modifying their ideology and policy initiatives to appeal to it. The question today is, Will Mitterrand's strategy work for the Fifth Republic in a manner similar to the way in which Gambetta's did for the Third?

In other words, just as decentralization in the Third Republic resulted in the "revolution of mayors," which politicized the communes, will decentralization in the Socialist Fifth Republic similarly produce a "revolution of the presidents" and politicize the regions and departments? Will it enfranchise on the local level the new electorate of middle-level managers and workers at the expense of the Third Republic coalition? And, finally, will this new electorate serve on the national level to "recenter" and to democratize France; or will it be responsible for a further polarization in French politics as well as for a continuing inability to resolve France's current economic crisis?

In short, will the Socialists' brilliant political strategy to gain the allegiance of the new electorate work? Only time will tell, although for the moment at least the Socialists' strategy seems to have proven successful, helped not only by their ideological flexibility once in power, which included switching policies midstream and entertaining an opening to the center, but also by the failure of their rivals on the moderate and the extreme right to mount a lasting challenge with their own counter-ideologies: neoliberalism on the moderate right, racialism and nationalism on the extreme right. The recent Socialist electoral victories in the presidential and legislative elections of 1988 suggest that Mitterrand may have found the key to a new critical realignment of the electorate with a center-left *rapprochement* that, much like Gambetta's similar strategy one hundred years earlier, is predicated on a move toward more pragmatic politics and away from the polarizations of the past.

THE NEW LEGISLATION FOCUSED ON LOCAL POLITICS

The passage of the legislation focused on local politics, on the whole, was more difficult than that of legislation affecting local administration, in large measure because the Socialists themselves were divided on the issues involved. Political considerations interfered with the timing and configuration of the regional elections – which came very late and were designed to minimize their importance; with the passage of a law limiting the *cumul des mandats* – which occurred at the last minute; and with the promulgation of laws promoting local democracy and a statute for local elected officials – which were never even formally discussed subsequent to the framework law. Here, again, the fate of reform was dependent upon the relative strength of the constituency favoring or opposing it. And whereas pressure for the regularization of the regions through the election of their members by universal suffrage increased over time, there was no such pressure for the local democracy laws. In the case of local democracy in particular, little was left of the constituency that had initially pushed for it; instead, there was only resistance from the notables, who certainly did not wish to share their power with associations.

Electoral reform

Electoral reform affected the regions the most, with the institution of regional elections by universal suffrage and the election of the regional president. The departments experienced reform only to the extent that in certain cases cantons were subject to redistricting, but the elections themselves became much more important as a result of the transfer of executive power to their presidents. The municipalities, too, underwent some change, mainly because the system of proportional representation was extended to all communes with more than thirty-five hundred inhabitants and, thus, to 65 percent of the population. But this still left 33,849 communes with the more personalized, majoritarian, two-round system also in effect in the cantonal elections.

The Socialists' decentralizing reforms were meant to respond to the demands of the regionalists as well as to those of their urban-based electorate, primarily the *salariés*. By regularizing the status of the region and by turning it into another level of local government with its officials to be elected for the first time by universal suffrage, and by providing special statutes for Corsica and the overseas regions and territories (DOM-TOM), the Socialists intended to respond in some measure to the increasing demands for regional self-determination. By redrawing cantonal lines to reflect more accurately the population distribution for departmental elections and by providing for elections by proportional representation in the regions and in the communes with more than thirty-five hundred inhabitants, the Socialists sought to give more say to the urban agglomerations in which the *salariés* reside and to break, to some extent, the traditional rural domination of the periphery. Intentions are one thing, however, actions another, at least as regards the departments and the regions.

To begin with, despite their expressed intentions, the Socialists did not solve the electoral problems of the departments, mainly because they left intact the basic geographical outlines of the cantons, as established by the Revolution of 1789, and the electoral principles set by the law of 1871: Two-stage, majoritarian vote within each canton. Without massive re-drawing of cantonal lines or the introduction of proportional representa-tion for the cantonal elections of 1982 and 1985, the problems of repre-sentation in the departments necessarily remained to haunt the Socialists when they returned to power in 1988, with the departments continuing to be dominated by personalistic politics and the candidates of the rural communes.[3] Not atypical is the case in the Bouches-du-Rhônes where in 1988 one general councilor still represented two thousand inhabitants, whereas another represented sixty-five thousand. But in 1988, as before, urban-based general councilors pushed for redistricting or for propor-tional representation with cantonal lists according to party, whereas more rural councilors opposed redistricting for the obvious reason that they would lose their electoral base and party lists. They feared that introduc-ing party politics at the departmental level would erode their more person-alistic basis of electoral support. The Socialist government again did nothing to resolve the dispute, despite the fact that the party might have benefited from it, given the number of departments with a majority of voters on the left, based in the urban communes, but which had a presi-dent and departmental council on the right, supported by the predominat-ing rural communes. Significant electoral reform of the departments in 1988, just as earlier, died because the government was worried about alienating members of its own party hostile to any reform of the system.[4]

The Socialist government's sensitivity to its own party members' con-cerns about electoral reform also affected its actions with regard to the regional elections. According to the law of March 2, 1982, regional elections by universal suffrage were to be held within a year, at the latest at the same time as the municipal elections, and were to be based on proportional representation according to departmental party lists. Politi-cal considerations, though, interfered with the timing and extensiveness

[3]For a discussion of the redrawing of the cantonal lines specifically, see Sylvie Hubac and Jean-Eric Schoettl, "Découpage Cantonal," *Actualité Juridique. Droit Ad-ministratif* no. 2 (Feb. 1985); and *Le Monde*, Jan. 2, 1985.
[4]*Le Monde*, July 8, 1988.

of regional reform. Because the Socialists began losing election after election in the periphery, with the right winning control of fifty-eight departmental governments in the cantonal elections of March 1982 and then sweeping the communes in the municipal elections of March 1983, the government kept putting off the regional elections originally scheduled for 1983 or 1984.[5] The Corsican elections, moreover, brought back many of the fears of regional separatism. In the meantime, the power of the regional establishments was expanded, making them de facto another level of local government even though they were not to become another such level de jure until the regional elections. This left the regional president, who had already acquired executive power, in the awkward position of exercising power without the legitimacy gained only through election. The regional elections were finally held only at the last minute, in March 1986, at the same time as the national legislative elections. As a result, the regional elections themselves tell us very little, because they were overshadowed by the legislative elections.

The delay in the scheduling of the regional elections only added to the frustration of regionalists, who complained right from the start that the government should have made a clear choice between departments and regions. The regionalists of course were especially distressed to find that the party lists for regional elections would be drawn up by departments and elected on a departmental basis as opposed to being drawn up by regions and elected at large.[6] Their fear was that unless parties at the departmental level consciously chose to place proregion, economically progressive candidates on the lists, the regions would end up dominated by the traditional departmental officials, who represent more rural, less economically progressive interests. This should have been a matter of concern for the Socialist government itself, given that the members of its own targeted electorate, the mainly urban-based *salariés* consisting of middle-level managers and workers would be the ones to lose the most by not always finding their interests represented by the candidates for regional election. (Some Socialists did have a partial solution to this problem, which was to field candidates representative of the more progressive rural groups with an eye to gaining the departmental vote, for example, in the Saône-et-Loire.)[7]

The loudest complaints about the electoral arrangements and the timing of the elections at the same time as the legislative ones came from the

[5]See Gérard Gurnberg and Beatrice Roy, "Le choc des élections municipales françaises des 6 et 13 mars 1983," *Tocqueville Review* vol. 5, no. 1 (Spring-Summer 1983).
[6]For reactions to changes in the electoral process, see *Le Monde*, Feb. 2, 1985.
[7]Jean-Pierre Worms, Deputy from Saône-et-Loire, interview with author, Paris, May 9, 1985.

regionalists on the right, in particular the ANER, the national association of regional elected officials made up of the presidents of opposition regional councils (at the time sixteen out of twenty-two regions).[8] Michel Giraud (RPR), president of the regional council of the Île-de-France and president of ANER, argued that the new regional electoral arrangements would marginalize the region, making it less easily recognized by the population at large, whereas the timing meant that the regional elections would become the consolation prize for candidates who didn't make it onto the legislative lists, thus undermining the renewal of the political class.[9]

The departmentalists, of course, had a reaction quite different from that of the regionalists. The departmentalists generally feared the region, feeling that it was much less tied to local politics than the department and therefore uncontrollable. Moreover, with the regions elected by universal suffrage as of March 1986, departmental presidents worried that the regions would become a challenge if not a threat to their power and to their legitimacy as spokespeople for the periphery. Thus, they were relieved when the new electoral laws established a departmental basis to regional elections.

This decision, coming little more than a year before the elections were finally called, was clearly a response by the Socialists to political pressures from politicians within their own party as well as from others whose powers were departmentally based. Had the elections come earlier, it is unlikely that they would have been set up in exactly this way – either according to proportional representation or on departmentally-based lists. But by the time the Socialists decided to go ahead with the elections, they knew that they would necessarily end up in the minority of most regional councils. Proportional representation was the only way to safeguard their representation, however weakened. For this reason, proportional representation was extended even to the executive bureaus of the regional and departmental councils in the law of January 6, 1986. But this was to be quite short-lived. It was fought by the opposition in the Senate when it was brought up for discussion. When the neoliberals gained power, they did away with this system with the law of August 19, 1986, in the name of the autonomy of local collectivities and in affirmation of their powers to organize themselves as they see fit.[10]

Electoral reform in regional and departmental elections, in brief, did not go very far. Nevertheless, it went far enough to ensure an increasing

---

[8]*Le Monde*, Jan. 17, 1986.
[9]*Le Vie française*, Nov. 24, 1985.
[10]Yves Jegouzo and Christophe Sanson, "Décentralisation: La pause, pourquoi et comment?" *L'Année administrative 86* (Paris: Institut International d'Administration Publique, 1987), p. 38.

politicization of the periphery at both levels of local government. Party politics is there to stay, in particular at the regional level, where elections are by proportional representation and elected officials owe their place and position on the ballot to the party that puts them on its list. Moreover, even if the departmental officials' power remains primarily personalistic, due to their cantonal electoral basis, they as much as regional officials will be knee-deep in party politics, given the departments' role in establishing party lists for the regional elections. Equally important, as we will explore later, departmental and regional elections are now as clearly tied to national politics in the minds of the local electorate as the municipal elections had become in the years before the Socialists' arrival in power.[11]

The cumul des mandats

The law limiting the *cumul des mandats* passed at the end of December, 1985 was part and parcel of the Socialists' attempt to break the conservative complicity of prefects and notables and to encourage greater local democracy. By limiting the *cumul des mandats,* the Socialists sought to increase the size of the political class generally and to open up access to political positions formerly monopolized by a relatively small number of notables.[12] This *décumul,* or divestiture of mandates, was all the more important because it was the notables who were the first to profit from decentralization when their positions of prestige at the departmental and regional levels were turned overnight into ones of political and executive power. The *décumul,* though, was promoted for administrative as well as political reasons. Many Socialists worried that a continued *cumul* would either mean that the *cumulants* would not do a very thorough job in any of their positions or that, by leaving day-to-day decisions up to civil servants, they would promote a kind of recentralization via the bureaucracy.

The law finally passed on the *cumul des mandats* limits elected officials to only two major political mandates and sets up incompatibilities between certain positions such as mayor of a big city, departmental president, and regional president. It also allows legislators to take on only one more of the following mandates: representative to the European Economic Community, regional councilor, departmental councilor, councilor of Paris, mayor of a commune with twenty thousand or more inhabitants, vice-mayor of a commune of one hundred thousand or more. For the *cumulants* who hold large numbers of elected positions, the *décumul* has been gradual, with the elected official forced to abandon

[11]See Chapter 10, under "The politicization of local elected officials."
[12]Pierre Birnbaum, et al., *Réinventer le parlement,* p. 42.

only one major mandate per election and to decide only after the election which office to abandon. At the time it was passed, the law affected 117 members of Parliament.[13] After the spring 1988 legislative elections, the *décumul* affected 133 Deputies, one with 5 mandates, 12 with 4, 120 with 3.[14]

The law itself was considerably more modest than originally planned. Most importantly, it lacked a *statut des élus,* or statute of elected officials, which was to have regularized the status of local elected officials by providing them with training, civil service status (including a retirement program and employment protection for local elected officials regarding short- or long-term leaves of absence), and a rational pay scale.[15] On this last issue, all suggestions for a change in the system of remuneration for elected officials were simply ignored, whether it was the Socialist Senator Marcel Debarge's very generous proposal in a 1982 report to set a maximum salary of one and a half times the basic parliamentary salary, at 49,500 francs a month, or Jean-Pierre Worms's attempt to set a ceiling on salaries as a rider to another bill in 1985.

It is surprising that any law passed. For although there was no well-defined, powerful constituency pushing for reform, there was a powerful constituency resisting reform: the notables, some of whom were opposed for reasons of narrow self-interest, and others for the more general interests of their constituents. That such reform was even included in the original *loi-cadre* may have to do with the fact that big-city mayors had originally been involved with the reform, that is, Gaston Defferre and Pierre Mauroy. It was only big-city mayors who demonstrated in the 1970s an increasing repugnance for the *cumul.* Of fifteen big-city mayors surveyed, fourteen claimed to be against the accumulation of office. And even though many of them did hold a number of offices, they did not see them as very important.[16]

Some notables were sincere in their view that with decentralization, the *cumul* was all the more important because it would help counterbalance the newly powerful intermediate structures of government. For example, Philippe Séguin (RPR) – Deputy and mayor of Épinal, general councilor of the Vosges, regional councilor of the Lorraine, and Minister of Social Affairs and Employment in Chirac's government from 1986 to 1988 (at which time he did have to give up his Deputy's seat) – argued that a

[13]For further information, see Georges Gontcharoff, "La limitation du cumul des mandats," *Correspondance municipale,* no. 270 (1986); *Le Monde,* Dec. 26, 1985.
[14]Jean-Louis Villielm, "Les élus locaux," *Les Collectivités locales, Cahiers français,* no. 239 (Jan.–Feb. 1989), p. 60.
[15]For the details, see Renée Rousseau, "Le futur statut des élus locaux," in *Décentralisation en marche,* pp. 48–9.
[16]Michel Crozier and Jean-Claude Thoenig, "Le régulation des systémes organisés complexes," *Revue Française de Sociologie* vol. 16 (1975): 21 n.47.

cumul that allowed him to hold national as well as local office was essential because the department and the region were generally unresponsive to the needs of his constituency, a midsize city.[17] Other notables, by contrast, saw a continuing *cumul* as necessary in order to ensure greater coordination between the newly empowered intermediate levels. Raymond Marcellin, president of the general council of Morbihan, for one, was unhappy with the limitation of the *cumul* on the grounds that good coordination requires that the executive of the regional council have "perfect knowledge" of departmental realities and that it increased the risk of conflict between local governments.[18]

Finally, other notables saw the *cumul* as helpful in resisting central-governmental control. Thus, Jean-Marie Rausch (UDF) – at the time, Senator, mayor of Metz, regional president of the Lorraine, president of the Association of Big City Mayors, and more recently a minister in the new Socialist government of Rocard (1988) – was less concerned about the newly powerful intermediate structures (especially since he controls one) than about Paris, feeling that such a *cumul* was doubly necessary, given that everything in France is *rapports de force,* or power relations. Thus he insisted that the political benefits of the *cumul* outweighed its drawbacks and that he could easily accomplish the tasks attendant upon his *cumul* by spending in any one week four to five hours on the region, fifteen on the city, and ten going to Paris.[19]

Whereas political power was one of the most frequently cited reasons for opposing any extensive *décumul,* money was another compelling but essentially unmentioned factor. Although any one position may not pay very well, the accumulation of offices can pay handsomely indeed, depending upon the offices accumulated. As of the end of 1985, a *cumulant,* who was a Deputy or Senator with a base salary in the environs of 33,000 francs a month, received half of his or her legally set mayor's salary of about 10,100 francs for a city of eighty thousand to one hundred thousand inhabitants or about 1,530 francs for a village of fewer than five hundred inhabitants; half of the legally set regional councilor's salary of 560 francs per diem, ordinarily for no more than five days per month; and all of the departmental councilor's salary which varies according to department from a low of 873 francs a month on average for the Ariège to 13,340 francs for Val-de-Marne.[20] Since the March 1986 elections, moreover, the regional councilors' and presidents' salaries have been determined by the regions themselves, and have increased appreciably, with per diem amounts ranging

[17]Philippe Séguin, interivew with author, Épinal, June 18, 1985.
[18]*Le Figaro,* Jan. 8, 1986.
[19]Jean-Marie Rausch, interview with author, Metz, June 18, 1985.
[20]*Le Nouvel Observateur,* Oct. 25–31, 1985; and *Le Monde,* Nov. 7, 1985. For regional councilors' salaries as of 1987, see *Le Point,* Mar. 23, 1987.

from a low of 560 francs for the Poitou-Charentes to a high of 1,451 francs for the Île-de-France, with some regions also providing monthly salaries such as Provence-Alpes-Côtes d'Azur at 6,136 francs and Midi-Pyrénées at 9,000 francs (with no per diem).[21]

These figures, of course, do not include the higher salary of the presidents of a region or department, the extra compensation for regional and departmental vice presidents, heads of parliamentary commissions, presidents of an urban community, a *syndicat intercommunal,* and any of the large number of associations over which local elected officials ordinarily preside. In addition, they do not take into account the reimbursement of expenses for travel, for administrative assistants, and for secretarial services – let alone perks such as chauffeured cars, offices that double as overnight accommodations for legislators, and the tax breaks (whereas the salaries of Deputies and Senators are taxed, those for local elected positions are not). Jean-Marie Rausch, for example, earned a reported salary of 38,300 francs a months as of 1985, or at the time about $65,000 a year, for performing his many duties. Michel Giraud (RPR) earned a bit more that same year, 43,800 francs a month for his positions as Senator, mayor of Perreux, president of the regional council of the Île-de-France, and president of the Association of Mayors of France. But they came nowhere near Jean Lecanuet (UDF), who as Senator and as president of the Senatorial Commission of Foreign Affairs and Defense, mayor of Rouen, Deputy to the European Parliament, departmental president of the Seine-Maritime, and regional councilor of the Haute-Normandie earned an average of 61,500 francs monthly, or at the time about $104,000 a year.[22]

Money must explain a portion of politicians' resistance to the *décumul* – and understandably so, because without accumulating a substantial number of positions, elected officials who spend all of their time on their official duties may have a very hard time making ends meet. Among politicians, though, only Jacques Médecin (RPR) – Deputy, mayor of Nice, president of the general council of the Alpes-Maritimes – has been completely open about the fact that money was his main reason for becoming a Deputy on top of his other offices. On a mayor's salary alone, he explained, he would not even be able to afford his dry-cleaning expenses, which were high because his various official functions ordinarily required three changes of clothing during the day in addition to the requisite *smoking,* or tuxedo, in the evening. His account of his pecuniary motivation for serving as a Deputy would seem to be accurate because his attendance record at the National Assembly has been one of the lowest.[23]

[21]For regional councilors' salaries as of 1987, see *Le Point,* Mar. 23, 1987.
[22]*Le Nouvel Observateur,* Oct. 25–31, 1985; and *Le Monde,* Nov. 7, 1985.
[23]Jacques Médecin, interview with author, Nice, June 7, 1985.

It would be unfair to assume from the above that it was mostly members of the right who were opposed to the *décumul* and members of the left who were in favor. After all, the left could have pushed through the reform, but did not until the last minute. Moreover, many politicians on the left in the periphery were as clear about their opposition to the *décumul* as those on the right. Robert Capdeville (PS) – president of the general council of the Aude since 1973 and regional president beginning in 1983 (and ending in 1986 with the change in regional majority) – for example, was quite pleased with the lack of progress on passing the *décumul* and understood this to mean that legislators had recognized "the near umbilical cord that unites" the department and the region, "To deny it . . . would be to misunderstand completely the day-to-day reality of regional life."[24]

Not all politicians on the right opposed the reform. Michel Giraud saw the *cumul* as a danger to good administration because it did not leave one enough time to spend on any of one's mandates. But he was unhappy with the law that was passed because it didn't consider the statute of elected officials, which he felt was a necessity for local elected officials, given their need for training, for more time and money, and for insurance coverage (because they were held personally responsible for their actions). As evidence of his own opposition to the *cumul,* he explained that he himself had given up his seat on the general council after eighteen years (keeping, however, his Senate seat and the presidency of the region) and had pushed the youngest of his deputies to run in order to promote the renewal of the political class.[25] Giraud was not the only one to limit his *cumul* before a law to that effect was passed. François Poncet focused on his role as president of the general council of the department of the Aquitaine (as of 1978), even though he was also a Senator (as of 1983), because he found that the job became more onerous with decentralization.[26] Louis Philibert, president of the general council of the department of the Bouches-du-Rhône, similarly, deliberately limited himself to that one role; but in this case, the consensus among local politicians was that it was age alone that kept him from taking on any more responsibility.[27]

For the most part, the attachment of the notables to the *cumul* as a source of political power as well as a source of income combined to delay passage of the law limiting the *cumul*. Although the law was projected in the *loi-cadre,* it was shelved for most of the Socialists' term in office. The law only passed when the Socialists' countervailing, short-term, political interests supervened. The law was ultimately pushed through at the elev-

[24]*Le Monde,* June 23–4, 1985.
[25]*La Vie française,* Nov. 24, 1985.
[26]*Le Monde,* Jan. 24, 1985.
[27]Interviews of the author with local officials, Bouches-du-Rhône, June 1985.

enth hour only because it appeared to be a good way to limit the power of the conservatives, who were likely to gain a majority in the March 1986 elections. And the conservatives in the Senate, for their part, passed the law because they did not want to look bad, because they had been blaming the delay in passing the law on the Socialists' selfish political considerations.

Moreover, there has been no attempt by the neoliberals to rescind the law on the *décumul*. And it has already been at work as a result of the national as well as regional elections, with interesting results. As we shall see later, the *décumul* has helped increase the size of the political class and the amount of competition among personalities on the right and the left for the newly freed positions. This, in turn, has reinforced party politics: Local elected officials now have to rely, much more than in the past, on their political allies in positions of power at the other levels of local government because the *décumul* no longer allows the few to hold a monopoly on those positions.[28]

Local democracy

The Socialists were successful in pushing through the limitation of the *cumul* solely because of the narrowest of political considerations. But no such political considerations supervened in the case of laws related to citizen participation. Originally the limitation of the *cumul des mandats* was to have been only one of several ways in which the Socialists intended to encourage local democracy. However, the other reforms they had envisioned, such as tying associational movements to local governments by way of laws encouraging citizen participation and establishing referenda, never materialized, even though in the framework law of 1982 they were anticipated to be elaborated within a maximum of one year after the passage of that law. This was certainly a major source of disappointment for the *autogestionnaires*.[29] It is the absence of these other political reforms and the delay in passing the *décumul* that suggested to some scholars that decentralization was really a reform for the notables intended to increase their power and not, as claimed by the Socialists, a reform intended to promote local democracy.[30]

However, the fact that the Socialists did pass laws that increased the power of the notables and passed none (except the *décumul*) encouraging

[28]See Part II, Chapter 8, "New elites and new rules of the game?"
[29]See, for example, Jean-Michel Bellorgey, "De certains aspects du discours," *Échange et Projets* no. 39 (Sept. 1984): 19; Georges Gontcharoff, "La décentralisation peut-elle atteindre le citoyen de base?" *Échange et Projets* no. 39 (Sept. 1984); and Les Gracques, "La décentralisation peut-elle avoir un rapport avec l'autogestion?" *Correspondance municipale* no. 241 (Oct. 1983).
[30]Yves Mény, "Decentralization in Socialist France: The politics of pragmatism," *West European Politics* vol. 7, no. 1 (Jan. 1984).

local democracy, does not necessarily mean that the Socialists' actions were intended to promote the narrow self-interest of the notables. The assumptions of some *autogestionnaires* to the contrary notwithstanding, local democracy would probably not yet have begun even if the laws institutionalizing citizen participation had been passed. By the time the Socialists came to power, local political activism of the kind promoted by the *autogestionnaires* had already lost most of its momentum. The few surveys that exist on the subject suggest that the only stability or slight increase in associational activity was in the areas of sports and recreation (which remained steady according to a survey by the CCFD, the Catholic committee against hunger and for development) and culture (which, according to a Ministry of Culture survey, went up slightly from 28 percent in 1973 to 31.6 percent in 1981). The CCFD survey, however, found a significant overall decrease in associational activity, with the number of French claiming no associational ties going up from 47 percent in 1976 to 58 percent by 1983, and the highest decreases occurring in union membership, going from 14 percent in 1976 to 6.4 percent in 1983. A Sofres poll on local democracy found that, whereas in 1975, 51 percent of those interviewed agreed that they wish to have greater associational ties to their communes, only 47 percent felt this way in 1983.[31] Finally, local democracy has not penetrated much the inner workings of the associations themselves; because, of active members in 1983, an overwhelming majority of those in leadership positions were male, upper-level managers and professors.[32]

Nonetheless, in the past few years, there has been some evidence to suggest that the associational movement has revived, albeit not in the manner of the 1970s. For example, there has been a significant increase in the number of associations registered. It may be that the associational movement only appeared to have died because it is less directly tied to or focused on politics, and thus is less visible but no less active. At least, this is what Jacques Moreau, president of the cooperative bank, the *Caisse centrale de crédit coopératif,* suggests. Although he observed a decrease in political militancy, including union-related militancy, he has seen no concomitant decrease in associational militancy, especially where it corresponds to a specific need – in particular in business or professional cooperatives.[33] In other words, the economic crisis may have turned potential local activists' energies toward economic activity and away from political, while social activity continued as it had in the past. This has been true to some extent in the Lorraine, which doubled the rate of the creation of new

[31] Jacques Antoine and Véronique Camus, "Que disent les décentralisés?" *Projet* nos. 185–6 (May–June 1984): 526–8.
[32] INSEE, *Économie et Statistique* (Mar. 1988), reported in *Le Monde,* Apr. 1, 1988.
[33] *Le Monde Affaires,* Jan. 9, 1988.

associations from 75 new associations per month in 1982 to 150 per month by 1985, and where cultural and sport associations predominated; ecological associations, after their heyday in the 1970s, were on the decline; and associations promoting artisanry and, to a lesser extent, industrial development were on the rise.[34]

Whatever the future of the associational movement, it is clear that although its rise in the 1970s, along with the agitation of the *autogestionnaires,* provided an impetus for decentralization, they were not the major forces behind the decentralizing legislation. Those who fault decentralization for not encouraging local democracy, therefore, are in truth blaming it for not reviving an activism that had all but died. The fact that such activism was moribund probably explains better than anything else the failure of the Socialists to pass participatory laws. Without organized pressure for reform, given all the other issues demanding immediate attention, it was understandably let go. The lack of such a reform, in any case, does not deny the possibility of participation or increased local democracy in the future.

The fact is that the majority of those who could have pushed for such reform from the countryside, who might have organized and pressured, couldn't because they, too, were in Paris and had new administrative and political responsibilities. Thus, they had to believe that the electoral process had finally proven itself to promote local democracy. Therefore, although the main reason for the electoral emphasis in the decentralization reform was Defferre's own postwar Socialist experience, this was not the only reason. The socialists generally, including those most interested in local democracy, needed to see the electoral process as embodying such democracy; and they therefore were not opposed to the electoral bent of the reform. Even the associational movement, which had all but died by the time the Socialists gained power, had actually moved on to the electoral; one need only consider the large percentage of association-tied people elected in the municipal elections of 1983 to recognize this. Finally, by the time the Socialists who had moved to Paris had themselves recognized that they were wrong to have assumed that local democracy could somehow be assured, or at least not undermined, by decentralization with a decidedly electoral bent, many of them were already out of office. Those who remained saw little reason to give the right in the periphery even greater access to power than they already had.

The Socialists, in short, did even less to promote local democracy through legislation than they did to institute changes in local electoral constituencies or elites. But changes in all three of these areas have never-

[34]Anne Laurent, "Les créations d'associations dans la région: le sport et la culture d'abord," *Économie Lorraine* no. 43 (Feb. 1986): 8–12.

theless taken place on a large scale, mainly because the transfer of executive power, administrative duties, and financial resources has affected the political balance of power within each level of local government as well as between them, engendering, as we will see later, a new politics in the periphery based on changing elites and electorates.[35]

Just as decentralization in the Third Republic engendered a "revolution of the mayors" when they became the executive powers in the commune, so decentralization in the Socialist Fifth may very well have produced a "revolution of the presidents," bringing new groups into power in the periphery. But even without this, the periphery as a whole has become much more politicized. The introduction of party politics at the regional and the departmental levels has brought national politics more and more into play at the local level. The nationalization of local politics has in turn made what happens in the periphery of prime importance for the center. In the years since the Socialists took power, the conquest of local government by the moderate right and the extreme right has taken on national significance, often as a first step to national power or prominence. Decentralization has ensured that national politics can no longer be separated from the local, nor local politics from the national. And no where is this more the case than in the electoral changes that have affected national politics as much as local politics.

TOWARD A NEW ELECTORAL BALANCE?

Decentralization for the Socialists was part of a larger political strategy to gain the allegiance of a new emerging electorate in the country as a whole: the *salariés,* or wage earners made up of the left's traditional constituency of workers and its new targeted constituency of *cadres moyens,* or middle-level managers and employees. The Socialists' overwhelming victory in 1981 attests to the brilliance of their strategy, which included tailoring their policies and ideology to appeal to this electorate. Winning was one thing, governing another. The Socialists in subsequent elections have battled long and hard to retain the allegiance of this electorate, challenged by rivals on the right, abandoned by allies on the left.

In the interim, after all, the parties on the right have not been making the mistakes of their counterparts of a century ago. In addition to embracing decentralization wholeheartedly, they have also produced counter-ideologies meant to appeal to different portions of the Socialists' electorate. The center right's new ideology, neoliberalism, with its emphasis on "less state," deregulation, and denationalization, is intended to appeal to a large portion of the Socialists' own targeted electorate, the upper end of the *salariés* made up of the middle-level managers. The extreme right's

[35]See Part II, Chapter 8, "The new politics in the periphery."

racialist and nationalist ideology has sought to attract other portions of the left's constituency, disenchanted Communists as well as the lower end of the *salariés* made up of workers, along with portions of the moderate right's traditional constituency, such as farmers and shopkeepers. While the Gaullists have been searching for a new identity, flirting at times with the extreme right and at other times with the neoliberal center right, seeking to keep their traditional constituency and to gain portions of the new electorate, only the Communists have seemed content to stick with their old ideology and a diminishing portion of their traditional electorate, the workers, convinced that their ideological purity will ultimately redound to their benefit.

The Socialists' current success in retaining the allegiance of their targeted electorate in the face of these challenges owes much to their ideological flexibility, which has included changing their policies when these proved detrimental to their chosen electorate and has involved entertaining the possibility of a center-left coalition predicated on a move toward more pragmatic politics and away from the polarizations of the past. But the question remains as to whether the Socialists will be able to retain the loyalty of the new stratum of *salariés,* forging a new and lasting electoral coalition behind a new center-left Fifth Republic, and thereby engender a critical realignment of the electorate. Today, much as during the beginning years of the Third Republic, the loyalty of the new emerging electorate has been uncertain, as the right and left traded governmental power over a period of several years. The problem with the *salariés,* as Jacques Julliard explains, is that although they supported Mitterrand in 1981, "the wage-earning group has become so massive and tentacular that it has ceased to be a significant group. It covers such diverse social statuses and income levels that it has ended up including most of the contradictions in society."[36] The Socialists' ultimate success, therefore, rests on their ability to consolidate their support in the electorate over the next few years. This, in turn, will depend, more than ever before, on the Socialists' performance at the local level as much as at the national level.

Gaining the allegiance of the new electorate

Realignments are not inevitable; but in France one was long overdue, given the deterioration of the Fifth Republic alignment beginning in the late 1960s with de Gaulle's charismatic appeal waning and his subsequent departure from the political scene. But realignment does not simply occur when the time appears right, when the electorate has shifted in terms of age, sex, occupation, geography, or even values. Realignment demands a

[36]Jacques Julliard, "Mitterrand: Between Socialism and the Republic," *Telos* no. 55 (Spring 1983): 43.

Table 5.1. *Socioeconomic shifts according to occupation, 1962 to 1985 (in millions classified according to head of household)*

	1962	1975	1982	1985
Farmers	3.045	1.691	1.475	1.345
Artisans	1.039	0.865	0.904	0.931
Shopkeepers	0.941	0.792	0.797	0.824
Business heads	0.104	0.109	0.134	0.136
Upper-level managers/ intellectuals	0.892	1.551	1.985	2.095
Intermediate professions	2.114	3.480	3.971	4.108
Employees	3.535	5.093	6.247	6.407
Workers	7.488	8.118	7.749	7.339

Source: Adapted from INSEE *Données Sociales* (1987).

political party able to appeal to a changing electorate, with clear leadership as well as a new rhetoric, if not ideology, which speaks to the voters' economic interests as much as to their political interests and forges a coalition between different and often previously unaligned parts of the electorate. The Socialists' victory in 1981 owes much to their conscious political strategy, which involved moderating their ideology and campaign rhetoric to appeal to the middle-level managers and employees in an attempt to forge a new electoral coalition between them and the workers.

The Socialists first took advantage of changing demographics, which found the occupational groups that traditionally voted on the right declining while those on the left were rising (Table 5.1). Between 1962 and 1985, the Socialists' targeted occupational group of the *salariés* was the only one that actually experienced a significant increase in size, going from 13 million in 1962 to 17.8 million in 1985 for an overall increase of 37 percent with the *cadres moyens,* or middle-level managers (renamed "intermediate professions" by the INSEE in its recent statistical reports) and salaried employees nearly doubling in numbers, and the workers decreasing slightly. The occupational groups that traditionally voted for the right, by contrast, declined by 14 percent, going from 6.021 million in 1962 to 5.2 million in 1985, with the doubling of the numbers of upper-level managers and intellectuals unable to make up for the halving of the farmers' numbers.

All of this looks all the more impressive once one considers the changes in the distribution of these occupational categories in terms of their percentages in the potential electorate between 1968 and 1978 alone, the time during which the left made its most significant electoral gains (Table 5.2). The left's targeted electorate grew considerably on the whole, from

Table 5.2: *The potential electorate in 1968 and 1978 (in percentages)*

	1968	1978
Farmers, shopkeepers, artisans	12.1	8.2
Upper middle classes	3.2	4.2
Salaried middle classes	13.3	17.2
Salaried employees	4.8	5.5
Workers	18.8	18.6
Other	2.9	1.8
Inactive	44.7	44.5

Source: Gérard Grunberg and Etienne Shweisguth, "Profession et vote: La poussée de la gauche," in *France de Gauche: Vote à Droite,* eds. Jacques Capdevielle, Elisabeth Dupoirier, Gérard Grunberg, Etienne Shweisguth, Colette Ysmal (Paris: Presses de la Fondation Nationale des Sciences Politiques, 1981): 306.

36.9 percent to 41.3 percent, with the salaried middle classes up close to 4 points, the workers remaining almost steady, and salaried employees rising .7 points. The right's overall constituency, by contrast, declined appreciably, from 15.1 percent of the electorate in 1968 to 12.4 percent in 1978, with the growth in the upper middle classes, up by 1 point, unable to offset the close to 4-point reduction in the percentage of farmers, shopkeepers, and artisans.

In short, while the right's potential electorate, defined on the basis of occupation, was declining, that of the left was rising. This figure does not include the "inactives," that is, the retired and housewives, as well as the unemployed and students. Throughout these years, they represented a sizeable proportion of the electorate, and the majority of them, made up of the retired and housewives, tended to vote for the right in larger numbers. Even those retired whose previous occupations were traditionally linked with a preference for the left voted in greater numbers for the right. In the 1978 elections, for example, whereas 57 percent of retirees and housewives voted for the right and 43 percent for the left, the numbers were the exact reverse for those gainfully employed. The left did well only among the unemployed and students, with 62 percent of students and 73 percent of the unemployed voting for the left.[37] In sheer numbers, however, retirees far outweighed students and the unemployed.

[37]See Gérard Grunberg and Etienne Shweisguth, "Profession et vote: La poussée de la gauche," in *France de gauche: Vote à droite,* ed. Jacques Capdevielle, Elisabeth Dupoirier, Gérard Grunberg, et al. (Paris: Presses de le Fondation Nationale des Sciences Politiques, 1981), pp. 146–7, 309.

Only if all the inactives voted on the right would the conservatives have had a majority of the potential electorate defined on the basis of occupation. But "potential" is the key word here. The French often vote along occupational lines, especially if convinced that the policies of a given party are in their economic interest. There are, however, intervening factors, including the voting history of family and region, party loyalty, party program, party cohesiveness, the personalities of the candidates, the issues of the day in such areas as law and order, foreign policy, and immigration policies, as well as specific policies and problems such as levels of unemployment and inflation. Any explanation of the Socialists' victory in 1981 must take into account their ability to appeal to the changing electorate on the basis of these intervening factors. More specifically, the Socialists benefited from the electorate's growing dissatisfaction with the right and the deteriorating economic situation in which inflation had risen to close to 13 percent and unemployment had reached 7.4 percent; the unity of the left behind one individual, Mitterrand, and his force of personality versus the split on the right between Giscard and Chirac, and Giscard's lack of appeal; and the left's program, which offered hope for radical change through nationalization, an increase in the minimum wage, the creation of 210,000 jobs per year, and a series of social policies to benefit lower income groups.

There was more to the Socialists' victory than economic issues, party unity and programs, and the personalities of the moment, however. One also has to take into account the structural factors at work, including changes in education, with the number of secondary school students growing from 879,000 to 4.9 million between 1953 and 1976; in the labor market, in which the increasing number of women entering the work force only complemented the occupational changes noted above and ensured that the number of independent workers as opposed to salaried workers declined rapidly, going from 39 percent of the active population in 1954 to 18 percent in 1975; the urbanization of the population, with the number living in urban areas going from 59 percent to 70 percent between 1954 and 1968, an increase of 11 points, and continuing to grow, albeit less rapidly, between 1968 and 1975, when it grew by 3 points; and demographic shifts, with the coming of age of the large postwar generation and its overwhelming presence in the lower, left-leaning occupational categories.[38]

Shifts in values accompanied these structural and demographic changes. During the 1960s and 1970s, there was a sea change in terms of ideology, with a decline in religiosity and a rise in cultural liberalism, all of which were related to changes in the profile of the electorate and totally benefited

[38]Ibid., pp. 141–4.

the left.[39] The electorate itself also changed in terms of its approach to voting: Voters were becoming more sophisticated, more autonomous, and more likely to decide their vote on the basis of issues rather than on party allegiance or personality. The Socialists' success owes a great deal to their recognition of the structural, demographic, and value changes in the electorate, and to their long-term political strategy, which capitalized on these changes by identifying the groups that were to become part of "their" electorate, and then promoting policies designed to appeal specifically to them. This proved to be a brilliant political strategy, one not seen since Gambetta's similar strategy one hundred years before.

In a manner of speaking, the Socialists invented their new electorate. Recognizing that the working class was too small to provide them with an electoral victory, they devised a new electoral strategy, the *front de classe*, with which they sought to expand their appeal to what they defined as the new middle classes of the *salariés* consisting of professionals, people in the service industries, farm workers, teachers, civil servants, and middle-level managers. These *salariés*, they argued, had more in common with the blue-collar workers than the traditional bourgeoisie, because they were exploited by their employers and alienated from the oppressive bureaucratic organizations in which they worked.[40] The Socialists moreover made a special appeal to the *cadres moyens*, whose worsening economic and social situation they claimed they would remedy by mastering the economy through planning and a coordinated industrial policy; by reducing unemployment and ameliorating their working conditions through *autogestion* and new rights for workers; by lowering taxes and diminishing inequalities in wealth with the tax on large fortunes; by allowing them a more balanced life with the reduction in the work week and the lowering of the retirement age; and, finally, by giving them a new role in enterprises, by relying on their competence and ensuring them greater liberty.[41] With commitments such as these, the Socialists sought to demonstrate that their program would benefit more than just the left's traditional electorate of workers and that the interests of the *cadres moyens* would be much better represented by the left than by the right.

Decentralization was also an integral part of this strategy to gain the allegiance of the new electorate, because it promised the *salariés*, located mainly in the growing urban agglomerations, more of a say in a local decision-making process that was still dominated by conservative rural

[39]Ibid., pp. 155–65.
[40]For a good encapsulation of this, see Frank L. Wilson, "Socialism in France: A failure of politics not a failure of policy," *Parliamentary Affairs*, vol. 38 (Spring 1985): 167–9.
[41]*Cadres: L'Alternative socialiste*, preface by François Mitterrand (Paris: Club Socialiste du Livre, 1981).

Table 5.3. *Socialist penetration of the electorate, 1946 to 1981 (by occupation as a percentage of total in category)*

	1946	1962	1967	1968	1973	1978	1981
Workers	22	20	18	18	27	27.4	44
Salaried middle classes	21	19	22	15	29	29.8	45
Upper middle classes	27	28	12	11	21	21.6	36.5
Farmers	16	12	14	20	19	25.2	32
Inactive	29	15	14	19	20	24.3	29

Source: Adapted from Jacques Kergoat, *Le Parti socialiste: De la commune à nos jours* (Paris: Le Sycomore, 1983): 280

interests. The declining rural population, in fact, was predominantly made up of the right's traditional electorate, with farmers and the retired comprising the largest groups, with artisans and shopkeepers not far behind (54 percent in rural communes and towns with fewer than fifteen thousand inhabitants versus only 32 percent in major urban agglomerations in the provinces or in Paris). Of the right's traditional electorate, only the upper-levels managers and professionals lived for the most part in major urban agglomerations (58 percent versus only 12 percent in rural communes). The left's targeted electorate, by contrast, lived overwhelmingly in the cities, with only unskilled workers living primarily in rural villages or small towns (61 percent versus 32 percent in major urban agglomerations).[42]

Decentralization thus represented an effective element in the left's electoral strategy, because it would serve to emancipate the cities and the *salariés* residing in them, freeing them at the very least from conservative, central-governmental control in the person of the prefect and from conservative local control at the hands of the departmental council. In addition, the creation of a new regional level of local government was likely to give the *salariés* in the urban areas a new ally, in much the same way as the departmental level had always been the ally of the rural areas.

The success of the Socialists' electoral strategy can be seen quite clearly once we examine their penetration of the electorate from 1946 to 1981, when they finally gained national power (Table 5.3). After early postwar highs, the first big jump in support for the Socialists from what was to be their targeted constituency came only after they had formulated their new electoral strategy in 1973. Their proportion of the workers' votes jumped

[42]See Nicole Tabard, "Espace et classes sociales," *Données sociales INSEE* (1987), pp. 304–13.

almost 9 points from 1968 and that of the salaried middle classes (including employees, civil servants, and middle-level managers), over 14 points. Had there not been disarray on the left in the 1978 elections, the increases would undoubtedly have been equally impressive.[43] Instead, the electoral support of the workers and salaried middle classes remained steady, only to skyrocket in 1981, for an increase of 16.6 points over 1978 among workers, and for an increase of 15.2 points among salaried middle classes.

The story is somewhat different with support for the Socialists by the right's traditional electorate (Table 5.3). Whereas the upper middle classes consisting of industrialists, merchants, and professionals increased their support for the Socialists in 1973, up 10 points from 1968, not until the 1978 elections did the farmers and the inactives post an increase in support, up 6.2 points and 4.3 points, respectively. These differences continued between 1978 and 1981, when support from the upper middle classes went up 14.9 points, whereas from the farmers it went up only 6.8 points and from the inactives, only 5.7 points.[44] The Socialists' rhetoric, in short, was more appealing to the growing groups on the right than the declining ones.

The results of the presidential elections in 1981 show clearly that Mitterrand had captured the support of the new economically ascendant groups of *salariés* and Giscard d'Estaing had retained the support of the declining groups that had held power in the Third Republic and had traditionally been part of the center–periphery alliance. In the second ballot of the 1981 presidential elections, more specifically, Mitterrand received 72 percent of the workers' votes to Giscard's 28 percent and 62 percent of the lower managerial and white collar classes' votes to Giscard's 38 percent. By contrast, Giscard received 68 percent of the farming community's votes to Mitterrand's 32 percent and 64 percent of the votes of small shopkeepers and artisans to Mitterrand's 36 percent. (With other groups, the margins of difference were not as large, with the nonworking and retired as well as the upper managerial groups, professionals, and industrialists giving Giscard 55 percent of their votes to Mitterrand's 45 percent.)[45] The left, in short, appealed overwhelmingly to the new electorate, but not to the exclusion of the old Third Republic coalition.

[43]Jérôme Jaffré, "The French Electorate in March, 1978," and Georges Lavau and Janine Mossuz-Lavau, "The Union of the Left's Defeat: Suicide or Congenital Weakness?" in *The French National Assembly Elections of 1978*, ed. Howard R. Penniman (Washington, D.C.: American Enterprise Institute, 1980).

[44]Jacques Kergoat, *Le Parti Socialiste: De la commune à nos jours* (Paris: Sycomore, 1983), p. 280.

[45]Howard Machin and Vincent Wright, "Why Mitterrand won: The French presidential elections of April–May 1981," *West European Politics* vol. 5, no. 1 (Jan. 1982): 11.

Democratizing France

Retaining the allegiance of the new electorate

It is one thing to gain power, another to retain it. Unless a party manages to consolidate its support through the implementation of policies that favor the groups it has only recently managed to attract, its success will represent no more than an epiphenomenon or a short readjustment period in its rival's ongoing control of government. In this category, we could put the Boulangists in the 1880s, whose meteoric rise and equally rapid fall represented a period of readjustment for the young Third Republic; and the Poujadists in the 1950s, whose short-lived popularity suggested the decline in the already unstable third-force party alignment of the Fourth Republic, and a dealignment of the electorate in anticipation of the Gaullist realignment of the Fifth Republic.[46] Had the Socialists' loss of legislative power in 1986 not been reversed in 1988, and had Mitterrand or another Socialist not won the presidential election of 1988, instead of realignment, we might now be writing of a midsequence realignment for the conservative coalition, drawing parallels between Mitterrand's rule and that of Léon Blum and the ill-fated popular front of 1936, or even agreeing with those who argued that the 1981 election represented neither a realignment behind Mitterrand nor even a partisan dealignment, but rather a temporary dip in support for the conservatives as a result of economic dissatisfaction.[47]

The Socialists, however, did manage to retain the allegiance of the electorate after some very rough going. As it turned out, gaining the allegiance of the electorate was the easy part compared to retaining its allegiance in the face of economic crisis, of failed industrial policies, and of a renewed right, with its conquest first of the periphery and then of the center in 1986. The Socialists' success had a lot to do with their ability not only to implement their policies, thus providing representation of their targeted electorate, but also to change policies that proved to alienate that very electorate. A major reason for the Socialists' success, therefore, was their flexibility, that is, their quick recognition that their policies had only deepened the economic crisis. Although the turnabout represented by their policies of economic austerity begun in 1983 lost them the 1986 elections, it contributed to the return to health of the economy and the electorate's resounding vote of confidence in the series of 1988 elections.

[46]For a good, short electoral history see Roy Pierce, "French Legislative Elections: The Historical Background," in *The French National Assembly Elections of 1978*, ed. Howard R. Penniman (Washington, D.C.: American Enterprise Institute, 1980), pp. 1–37.
[47]See Michael Lewis-Beck, "France: The Stalled Electorate," in *Electoral Change in Advanced Industrial Democracies: Realignment or Dealignment?* ed. Russell J. Dalton, Scott C. Flanagan, and Paul Allen Beck, (Princeton, N.J.: Princeton University Press, 1984).

Decentralization in the politics of local government

In their first two-year period in office, the Socialists and their Communist coalition partner sought to continue to appeal to the new social stratum of *salariés* that had brought them to power by faithfully carrying out their electoral promises, including the decentralization of local government, the nationalization of major industries and banks, the reforms in the workplace to benefit the *salariés,* such as the democratization of labor–management relations with the *lois Auroux,* a fifth week of vacation, and a thirty-nine-hour work week.

In a very short time, however, the Socialists found that the policies that appealed to their constituency were also extremely expensive, and that the resulting inflation and deepening economic crisis jeopardized the well-being of the very electoral groups they sought to benefit. The Socialists' solution to this problem, which involved a switch from ideology to pragmatism in economic policy – or put more kindly, to do what had to be done – did not help them retain the support of their constituency. With their economic austerity measures, beginning in 1983, the Socialists lost Communist party collaboration as well as much of their working-class support, whereas their rhetoric of the first two years, although perhaps attractive to the workers, may have alienated many of the middle-level managers.

Moreover, although the Socialists kept the *salariés* happy at least for a time – that is, until rising unemployment and inflation became significant issues – the Socialists' actions with regard to the right's traditional electorate alienated many from the first. The very rich were certainly not pleased about the inheritance tax and the nationalizations made enemies of most of the industrialists. In addition, the Socialists did little to endear themselves to the members of the old Third Republic coalition. Although the Socialists did reasonably well with the artisans, using the *économie sociale,* or cooperative movement, in their efforts to have the artisans become part of a more progressive alliance in the countryside, they failed with the farmers, who remained generally opposed to the Socialists, in part because of their history of support for de Gaulle and in part because the Ministry of Agriculture under Edith Cresson had broken up the monopolistic corporatist relationship of the *Fédération nationale des syndicats d'exploitants agricoles* (FNSEA) with the state by opening up consultation with left-wing farming bodies.[48] Relations did ease somewhat when Michel Rocard, who was quite popular with the farmers, replaced Cresson and instituted policies quite similar to Giscard's. But the Socialists ultimately failed in their goal, which was "to bring farmers out of the 'ghetto' of a special relationship with the state, to make them feel equal to other citizens with no lesser or greater claims on the nation."[49]

[48]Sokoloff, "Socialism," pp. 252–3.
[49]Ibid., pp. 260–2.

The Socialists, however, were not losing support throughout the country only because of the impact of their social and economic policies. The demise of the *autogestionnaire* movement also had a significant impact, because it left the Socialists without the set of grass-roots organizers they had in the past. As ordinary citizens lost interest in local activism, only the intermediate layer of professionals and regular activists remained for the party to tap. As many of the professionals left the provinces for Paris, the Socialists left the field open to their rivals on the right in the periphery, who then proceeded to reproduce the left's similar conquest of local power in the 1970s, profiting from the local electorate's growing dissatisfaction with the Socialists' economic policies. The disappointing results of the departmental elections of 1982, in which the left fell below a majority for the first time since the beginning of the Fifth Republic; the disastrous returns in the municipal elections of 1983 in which the right won overwhelming victories; and the European elections of 1984, all speak for themselves.[50] And of course, these were only harbingers of the legislative elections of 1986, in which the Socialists' loss led to "*cohabitation*" with a right-wing government under a left-wing president. It was only in 1988 that the Socialists recaptured much of their targeted electorate as well as some of that of the right.

There are many explanations for the Socialists' victories in 1988. For the presidential elections in particular, the key was the presence of the very presidential Mitterrand himself, with his party unified behind him, in contrast to the disarray on the right. The right's two years in office, moreover, helped as much as anything, by giving voters a sense of what the other side would do. And the right, by appearing to be as radical on the opposite extreme as the Socialists were in their first two years – for example, denationalizing where the Socialists nationalized and abolishing the inheritance tax put in place by the Socialists – allowed the "new" Socialists to appear the souls of moderation and the new candidates of the center.

The Socialist triumph in 1988 owes much to the fact that the Socialists sought to appeal to their targeted electorate in new terms. Their new ideology, if one can call it that, which was encapsulated in their new rallying cry: "Modernization," bespoke their near about-face in economic matters since the institution of austerity in 1983. As of October 1985, at the Toulouse Congress, the Socialists had already effectively buried their old ideology, committing themselves to a market-oriented economy, and had even begun to define the conditions under which they

[50]See Alain Lancelot and Marie-Thérèse Lancelot, "The Evolution of the French Electorate," paper prepared for presentation at the conference, "Community and Change in Mitterrand's France," Harvard University, Cambridge, Mass., Dec. 5–8, 1985.

would be willing to participate in a coalition government with the groups of the center and the right after 1986. Of the program that had brought them to power, they retained only the policies promoting social justice, with in particular a continued emphasis on social welfare. This change in ideology had little impact on the 1986 elections. It did, however, on the 1988 elections, when the Socialists campaigned on their record, on the improvement in the economy and the fact that they had demonstrated themselves to be efficient managers, and on such vague slogans as "The Mitterrand Generation." Moreover, with their declared opening to the center, the Socialists continued to seek to widen their appeal, not only to those portions of their own targeted electorate that had turned to the right in recent years but also to the upper middle classes that traditionally vote on the right.

The wisdom of the Socialists' change in ideology, or at least in campaign rhetoric, is demonstrated most clearly when compared to the Communists, who alone among established parties appeared uninterested in finding a new ideology or program in the face of a diminishing share of its traditional electorate, the workers. Since 1981 the Communists have suffered their greatest losses in the postwar period. Although their percentage of the vote had declined already from a high of 28.6 percent in the 1946 legislative elections to 20.7 percent in the 1978 elections and then to 15.5 percent in the first round of the 1981 presidential elections, this was nothing when compared to their drop to 9.7 percent in the first round of the 1986 legislative elections and to their even more drastic fall to 6.9 percent in the first round of the 1988 presidential elections. Although they did redeem themselves somewhat with their 11.3 percent showing in the first round of the 1988 legislative elections, the Communist party remains in great trouble.[51] Because it has refused to try to develop new policies or to adapt its ideology to the new realities, it seems to have lost attraction for all but the most loyal of its supporters. In the meantime, its former electorate has voted in increasing numbers not only for the Socialists but also for the extreme right.

The Socialists' flexibility with regard to ideology and policy, by comparison with the Communists' rigidity, is in large measure what enabled the Socialists to regain a significant portion of their targeted electorate. A quick glance at the electoral results for the left from 1974 to 1988 in the first or second rounds of the presidential and legislative elections, as well as in the European elections, shows just much how the Socialists benefited from their own shifts in electoral strategy, in policy, and in ideology,

[51]F. Platone and J. Ranger, *Les Élections de l'alternance* (Paris: Fondation Nationale des Sciences Politiques, 1981), p. 71, cited in Gérard Le Gall, "Printemps 1988: Retour à une gauche majoritaire," *Revue Politique et Parlementaire* no. 936 (July–Aug. 1988): 15.

Table 5.4: *The pattern of support for the left in the electorate - 1974 to 1988*
(by occupation as a percentage of total in category)

Profession of head of household	National elections			European elections	National elections			
	Pres.[a]2d[b] 1974	Leg.[c]1st[d] 1978	Pres. 2d 1981	1984	Leg.1st 1986	Pres.1st 1988	Pres.2d 1988	Leg. 1st 1988
Farmer	28	27	32	22	25	26	35	16
Shopkeeper/ artisan	33	37	36	22	30	24	37	35
Upper level manager/ Professional	44	29	45	26	34	30	36	39
Middle-level manager/ employee	53	53	62	42	53	41	61	55
Worker	73	67	72	54	55	59	68	60
Retired	45	43	45	37	40	45	52	48

Source: Postelectoral polls--SOFRES, cited in Gérard Le Gall, "Printemps 1988: retour à une gauche majoritaire," *Revue Politique et Parlementaire* no. 936 (July-Aug. 1988): 21.
Notes: [a] Presidential elections
　　　[b] Second round
　　　[c] Legislative elections
　　　[d] First round

as well as from the right's stint in power (Table 5.4). From the right's traditional electorate, the Third Republic coalition increased its level of support for the left in the second round of the 1988 presidential election by comparison with the second round of the 1981 presidential election, with the left gaining among farmers by three points and shopkeepers and artisans by one point. Of these groups, however, the farmers remained the least enamored of the left, their displeasure clearly registered in the nineteen-point drop in the first round of the legislative elections from their all-time high of 35 percent in the second round of the 1988 presidential election. The difference in this last instance suggests that, whereas the farmers may have approved of Mitterrand as president, they were much more opposed to the Socialists' policies than others on the right, there having been no more than a four-point drop for any other sector of the right's traditional electorate. It also indicates, as discussed below, that this was one of the groups in which the National Front made its greatest inroads.

From the other groups on the right, the Socialists received the steadiest as well as the greatest number of votes over time from the inactives (see Table 5.4). Unlike any other part of the right, the inactives actually increased their support to over a majority (52 percent) in the second round of the 1988 presidential elections. Finally, among the upper-level managers and members of the liberal professions, unlike with all the other parts of the right's traditional electorate the left suffered its biggest sustained losses by failing to recapture their votes in the second round of the 1988 presidential election, remaining nine points below their score in 1981. Interestingly enough, this was the only group, on the left or the right, to have increased its support for the left in the first round of the legislative elections, up by three points, suggesting that the left's opening to the center and its economic policies since 1983 had had an effect.

Among the left's own targeted electorate, the pattern of voting has been equally uneven (Table 5.4). The most surprising change, perhaps, has been the steady erosion of the left's traditional electorate, the workers, whose support declined precipitously, with a decrease of seventeen points in the 1986 legislative elections from the second round of the 1981 presidential elections, which was a significantly larger decrease than for any other group on the left or the right. Add to this the drop in the workers' vote between the second round of the 1988 presidential election and the first round of the legislative elections, which at eight points is second only to that of the farmers, and it is clear that the Socialists have suffered their most significant losses with the workers. These losses, attributable to high abstention among the workers and the substantial inroads of the extreme right, can be explained by the fact that the workers are the ones who suffered most from the economic austerity policies and high unemployment during this period; were most disoriented by the split on the left resulting from the Communists' break with the Socialists; and most disturbed by the switch in Socialist ideology away from a class-based argument.

The left's greatest gains, by contrast, came with its targeted electorate of middle-level managers and employees, in which it charted its greatest increase of all groups – rising nine points between the second round of the 1974 presidental elections and that of 1988 (Table 5.4). The twenty-point difference between the first and second rounds of the 1988 presidential elections, the largest spread by far of all groups on the left or the right, suggests however that the allegiances of middle-level managers and employees are mostly toward the center, and that the vote for Mitterrand as opposed to Chirac represents support for the more centrist candidate. Thus, although the left managed to retain the allegiance of this group, registering only a one-point decline from its high in 1981 to the presidential election in 1988, by contrast with the five-point decline of the workers from 1974 to 1988, it must remain as concerned about the flight of this group to the centrist parties as it must about the flight of the workers to the extreme right.

With its opening to the center, however, the left may have found a way to retain the bulk of its electorate. A large majority of the electorate has generally tended to favor some kind of centrist arrangement, whether through the construction of a centrist coalition, through the creation of a party of the center, or through continued cohabitation.[52] The electorate has been very positive in its response to the Socialists' proposed opening in particular, with 48 percent of the electorate in favor of it according to an October 1988 Sofres poll as opposed to 30 percent against, and with a significant part of the Socialists' targeted electorate, the employees, overwhelmingly in favor at 61 percent. What is more, the left's electorate, at 59 percent, and the Socialists in particular, at 63 percent, were equally highly in favor. By contrast, the Communists, at 45 percent, were quite negative.[53] The Communists clearly feared a closing to the left with this opening to the center. They need not have worried too much, though, as the approach of the departmental and municipal elections along with certain legislative issues, for example, the vote on the new tax on large fortunes, encouraged the Socialists to look back to the Communists for alliances as early as September 1988.

The left–right dimension, in short, remains relevant, even with the Socialists' opening to the center. This has been confirmed by the fact that the trend toward a decrease in the left–right dimension noted between 1981 and 1988 seems to have been reversed following the 1988 presidential and legislative elections.[54] However, this reflects more the voters' acknowledgment of the reality of the continuing split between parties of the left and right than it does a rejection of any opening to the center.

In any event, from the overall results of the elections from 1974 to 1988, it should be eminently clear that the Socialists themselves, even sans ideology, have not lost their appeal. The reelection of Mitterrand to a second term as president in April, 1988, the new Socialist near majority in the Assembly after the elections of June 1988, and the opening to the center in the government established June 28, 1988, suggest that Mitterrand may have found the key to success, just as Gambetta did one hundred years ago, with a center-left coalition. The parallels go beyond this, though, because again it would appear that such a coalition is predicated, for the moment at least, on a more pragmatic approach to the solution to problems as well as a move away from the political polarizations of the past. Even if ideology remains, it becomes less of an impediment to

[52]See Alan Lancelot, "L'électorat français s'est-il recentré?" in *Élections législatives 1988*, ed. Philippe Habert and Colette Ysmal (Paris: Le Figaro – Études Politiques, 1988), pp. 40–2; and Sofres, *L'État de l'opinion* (Paris: Seuil, 1988), chap. 6.

[53]Sofres poll for *Le Monde* and RTL, *Le Monde*, Oct. 28, 1988.

[54]Sofres, *L'État de l'opinion: Clés pour 1989* (Paris: Seuil, 1989), p. 134; Habert and Ysmal, *Élections*, p. 43. See the discussion in Martin Schain, "Centrism and Party Realignment in France," paper prepared for delivery at the 1989 Annual Meeting of the American Political Science Association, Atlanta, Georgia (Aug. 31–Sept. 3, 1989).

concerted action as members of the center and the Socialist left focus more on the similarities than on the differences between their views.

The right's appeal to the new electorate

Realignment depends not only on the continuing appeal of the party in power but also on the inability of rival parties to challenge that power by appealing to an electorate that is necessarily in flux during periods of realignment. In France the main problem for the right was that it remained in disarray, despite the fact that the parties on both the moderate and the extreme right produced counter-ideologies in an effort to retain their own electorate as well as to appeal to portions of the Socialists' targeted electorate.

The Socialists' victory made amply clear to the parties of the moderate right that its electoral approach, which by the 1970s necessitated appealing to the Gaullist heritage while seeking to appease the various groups in the center and on the right was no longer working. They clearly needed a new ideology to counter that of the Socialists. And what better than "neoliberalism" which was in the air (and the bookstores) with the popularity of Reagan and all things American, not to mention Thatcher, who was making headlines with all of her privatization plans?[55] Whereas much of the Gaullist right behind Chirac adopted this for purely pragmatic reasons, one wing of the center was ideologically committed to a full-blown implementation of laissez-faire capitalism, which caused problems for the right when it was the governmental majority from 1986 to 1988.

This was not the only division on the right. A new actor on the extreme right, the National Front, had emerged and introduced a new racialist and nationalist ideology, one that was a much greater challenge to the unity of the more moderate right. What is more, it posed a threat to the left as well as to the right by winning over portions of both of their potential electorates. This in turn has led to a radicalization at the fringes that threatens the political stability of France, despite the recentering efforts of the Socialists and their attempts to reduce the left–right polarizations of the past.

The moderate right. Although the moderate right has always had a "liberal" wing in the UDF, loosely focused around Valéry Giscard d'Estaing

---

[55]See, for example, Laurent Cohen-Tanugi, *Le Droit sans l'état* (Paris: Presses universitaires de France, 1985); Florin Aftalion, E. Claasen, Pascal Salin, et al., *La Liberté à refaire* (Paris: Hachette, 1984); Guy Sorman, *L'État minimum* (Paris: Albin Michel, 1985); Henri Lepage, *Demain le capitalisme* (Paris: Librairie générale française, 1978).

and Raymond Barre (who, as Finance Minister under Giscard in the late 1970s, was responsible for the moderately liberal measures applied to the economy), this liberalism was nothing like that of the young "neoliberals" who sprang up after the Socialists came to power calling for more *liberté* and *moins d'État*. The neoliberals attacked the Socialists for greatly increasing the traditional state *dirigisme*, or interventionism in the economy. Often using arguments based on the experience of the United States or borrowed from Anglo-American proponents of laissez-faire capitalism, they advocated: (1) reducing the size of the state and the extent of its intervention in the economy; (2) allowing market mechanisms to operate as freely as possible; and (3) introducing as much flexibility as possible in the workplace. These young turks pulled all members of the moderate right further along in the direction of neoliberalism.

The result was that most politicians on the moderate right, who only a few years before when in power were themselves the staunchest supporters of state *dirigisme* and of a centralized industrial planning process, became "born-again" neoliberals who began calling for liberty in all things economic. This represented for them a radical departure from all past practice, including their own. The centrist and center-right parties grouped in the UDF were quick to rally to the new neoliberalism, although many politicians, including Barre and Giscard d'Estaing, remained more cautious in their policy proposals than the "ultra" neoliberals of the *"bande à Léo,"* the group led by François Léotard.[56] The Gaullists of the RPR also eagerly took up neoliberalism, despite the fact that they, too, were careful to differentiate themselves from the ultras, with Alain Juppé declaring himself for "liberalism not anarchy" in the RPR's social program of 1985.[57] But however moderate their neoliberalism, "less state" and more "liberty" became the moderate right's formula for the economic revitalization of France. And it promised in the 1986 electoral campaign to bring this about by making a radical break with Socialist policies and by implementing such "projects" as the denationalization of banking and industry and the deregulation of price controls, exchange rates, the financial markets, and the workplace.

With these policies, the moderate right sought to appeal to a large portion of the Socialists' own targeted electorate, the middle-level managers, and to forge a coalition between them and the upper-level managers. Once the right gained power in the 1986 legislative elections, the true neoliberals in government continued their appeals to this new electorate

[56]Compare Raymond Barre's moderate liberalism, as expounded in *Refléxions pour demain* (Paris: Hachette, 1984), or that of Valéry Giscard d'Estaing (see *Le Monde,* Oct. 31, 1985) with the ultra liberalism of Alain Madelin, for example, in his many articles in *Le Figaro,* as well as in *Libérer l'école* (Paris: Laffont, 1985).

[57]*Le Monde,* Nov. 6, 1985.

by pressing for more and more deregulation and privatization. The Gaullist right, on the other hand, although continuing with much of the neoliberal program, added its own appeal to the right's traditional electorate (the Third Republic coalition of peasants and shopkeepers as well as the retired), with a focus on law and order, with its antiterrorism and antipornography policies in particular, and with its willingness to entertain the possibility of an alliance with the National Front.

The Gaullists' appeals to the traditional right with antiliberal policies did not sit at all well with the neoliberals, which led to a growing rift in the government, as the ministers of the neoliberal right, led by François Léotard, Alain Madelin, and others of the Republican party, became increasingly disenchanted, in particular with the policies of the more authoritarian Minister of the Interior, Charles Pasqua. This split in the two parts of the moderate right came to a head in the presidential elections of 1988, with the candidacies of Barre and Chirac, in which much of the campaign involved fighting each other rather than Mitterrand, who remained for the most part regally above the fray.

The differences between the candidates and the parts of the moderate right they represented, moreover, were reflected in the profile of the electorates to which they appealed. Barre's electorate was much more "liberal" than that of Chirac. Hence, it was much less comfortable with the presence of Deputies of the National Front in the National Assembly (38 percent for Barre's supporters versus 48 percent for Chirac's), much less willing to see an alliance with the National Front at the national level (22 percent versus 40 percent), and only a bit more willing for such an alliance at the local level (25 percent versus 37 percent). Barre's electorate was also more liberal on law and order issues as well as immigration policy, being less in favor of harsher penalties for crime (39 percent versus 52 percent) and more willing to give French nationality to those children born in France of foreign parents who request it (36 percent versus 27 percent) and less willing to insist on a loyalty oath (27 percent versus 41 percent).[58] Finally Barre's electorate was much more open to the future, focusing consistently on such issues as the economy, Europe, and education, than Chirac's electorate, which was much more preoccupied with such issues as law and order and immigration.[59]

The split in the moderate right's electorate is reflected in their ages and occupations as much as their attitudes. Chirac's electorate is older, with more of the retired, fewer salaried employees, and less anchored in the

[58]Postelectoral survey by Louis Harris/*Le Figaro*, cited in Colette Ysmal, "Recul et divisions de la droite modérée," *Revue Politique et Parlementaire* no. 936 (July–Aug. 1988): 32.
[59]Exit poll by CSA/L'Événement, La Vie, le Parisien libéré, RFI, cited in: Ysmal, "Recul et divisions," p. 32.

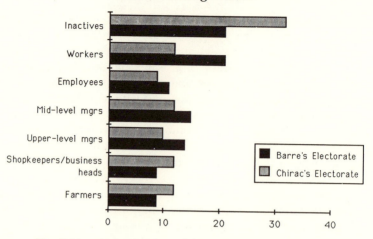

Figure 5.1: The divisions in the electorate of the moderate right – Barre versus Chirac in the first round of the 1988 presidential elections (in percentage of total in occupational category). Source: Colette Ysmal, "Recul et divisions de la droite modérée," *Revue Politique et Parlementaire* no. 936 (July–August 1988), p. 31.

lower classes than Barre's younger electorate, centered as it is on the *salariés* with a healthy portion of workers. Chirac, more specifically, has the loyalty of the Third Republic coalition, with four points more farmers and shopkeepers than Barre, as well as that of the inactives, with eleven points more (Fig. 5.1). By contrast, Barre has much greater support among the upper-level managers and liberal professions, at four points more; among middle-level managers, at three points more; among employees, at two points more; and, most significantly, among workers, at nine points more. Thus, whereas Chirac's electorate reflects all the characteristics of the traditional right, Barre's electorate tends to focus on the more progressive and "modernist" strata. As a result, the greatest challenge to Chirac's authoritarian right comes from the appeals of the extreme right to its more traditional electorate, but the greatest opportunity for Barre's liberal right comes from the left, as potential coalition partners with the Socialists' opening to the center. This opportunity rests on the fact that although the profile of Barre's electorate resembles that of the Socialists more than that of the traditional right, it has a long way to go in terms of reaching the same levels of support.

The Socialists, in short, are a natural ally for the Barrists. And Barre, by September 1988, recognized this as he agreed that the center should work with the Socialists. It is already clear that Barre's electorate of the 1988 presidential election favors an opening toward the center. In an October 1988 Sofres poll, 51 percent expressed their support for such an opening while 57 percent hoped, with Barre, that the center would reach a governmental accord with the Socialists. But other leaders in the UDF have not been so keen on such an accord, and it remains to be seen whether the liberal right will ultimately ally itself with the Socialists. Much of this depends upon how the various parties of the UDF see their future electoral chances, as strengthened by such an alliance or weakened, and if the UDF is scared off by the Socialists' continuing alliances in certain instances with the Communists. Whatever the outcome, it is clear that the UDF's electorate is more in favor of the opening toward the Socialists, divided 40 percent in favor, 40 percent against, than the RPR's electorate, which was 49 percent against.[60]

In the meantime, the Gaullists seem to be caught on the horns of a dilemma: If they ally themselves with the National Front, they diminish the possibility of continued alliances with the center as they push it more firmly into the arms of the Socialists. But if they shun the extreme right, they risk losing part of their potential electorate. Moreover, they can no longer so readily appeal to neoliberalism as an ideology, because the centrists in alliance with the Socialists are themselves clearly perceived as liberals, if not ultraneoliberal. Chirac himself should find it difficult to continue to make claim to such an ideology. Between the first and second rounds of the 1988 presidential elections, by contrast with the 1986 legislative elections, Chirac appealed more to the traditional ideological themes of the right, with a focus on "security," "nation," and "family," than he did to neoliberal ones with "social justice" and "liberty."

The moderate right, in short, has lost its cohesion and a clear ideology with which to oppose the left. The RPR in particular has been on a continuing, albeit unsuccessful, search for a new identity, appearing simply opportunistic as it at times flirts with the extreme right by emphasizing authoritarian themes and at other times with the neoliberal center by focusing on more liberal themes. The emergence of the *rénovateurs,* or renovators, clearly opposed to any alliance with the National Front and intent on internal party reforms has only complicated matters further for the RPR. The UDF, moreover, for all its greater unity on ideology, is even more split, with its more centrist members joining the Socialist government and others insisting that any such alliance is perfidy. The moderate right as a whole, in brief, feels squeezed on one side by the left and on the other by the extreme right. It is the extreme right, however, that has presented the most disturbing challenge to the right, even though the left has gained the allegiance of a larger portion of the right's pre-1981 electorate.

The extreme right. The moderate right has not been alone in seeking to challenge the Socialists' hold on the new constituencies. The extreme

---

[60]Sofres poll for *Le Monde* and RTL, *Le Monde,* Oct. 28, 1988.

right, with it new racialist and nationalist ideology, has attracted portions of the left's constituency (disenchanted Communists), and the lower end of the *salariés* (the workers), along with portions of the more moderate right's traditional constituency (farmers and shopkeepers). The National Front benefited from a variety of factors, including the electorate's declining political confidence in the government of the left, its continuing distrust for the established parties of the right, and the emergence of race as an issue, with immigration as its focus.[61] Decentralization also had much to do with the extreme right's success, because local politics became the stage from which it played to a national audience as of the 1982 cantonal elections and the 1983 municipal elections. The extreme right's political strategy, which involved ensconcing itself securely at the local level and from there moving toward the national, proved itself not only in the 1984 European elections, where it gained a number of seats, but in subsequent elections as well.

The National Front has appealed primarily to the groups most marginalized by the modernization of French society and to those most affected by its economic crisis. The extreme right's successes in 1984 at first appeared to represent a radicalization of the right's traditional electorate as a whole, with the upper-level managers and professionals joining the shopkeepers and artisans in its support. By 1986, however, Le Pen's support had narrowed to those occupational groups most threatened by modernization, the farmers and shopkeepers, as well as those most concerned about unemployment, the workers who entered the ranks of the extreme right's electorate at the same time as the upper-level managers and professionals were dropping out. In 1988 this new trend had established itself, with the extreme right chalking up substantial increases in these categories alone (Fig. 5.2). Thus, the National Front made major inroads into the Gaullist right's Third Republic coalition, with farmers rising to 20 percent in 1988, for a nine-point increase over 1986, whereas shopkeepers and heads of businesses rose even more dramatically, to 27 percent in 1988, for a thirteen-point rise over 1986. Upper-level managers and professionals, by contrast, who ended up the least favorable to the extreme right of any occupational groups, increased their support by only 2 percent, to 11 percent in 1988. Similarly, the middle-level managers of the left's electorate, although charting a 7 percent increase, came to only 14 percent of the electorate in this occupational category in 1988. Such moderation was not the case for the workers, who increased their support for the extreme right to 20 percent in 1988, for a nine-point increase over 1986.

[61]Martin Schain, "Racial Politics: The Rise of the National Front," in *The French Socialists in Power, 1981–1986*, ed. Patrick McCarthy (Westport, Conn.: Greenwood Press, 1987). See also idem, "The National Front in France and the Construction of Political Legitimacy," *West European Politics* vol. 10, no. 2 (April 1987).

Decentralization in the politics of local government

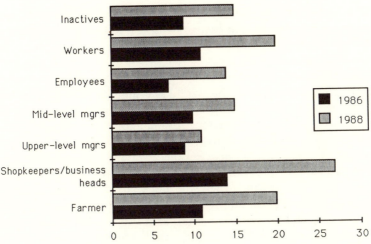

Figure 5.2: The growth in the extreme right's electorate (in percentage of total in occupational category). Source: Adapted from exit polls BVA, March 16, 1986, and CSA, April 24, 1988.

Le Pen's appeal had a variety of sources, depending upon the department, but tended to involve the same three major issues from 1984 through 1988: immigration, security, and unemployment. These three themes were to be seen most clearly in the more urbanized departments, which were also most affected by the economic crisis, such as the Bouches-du-Rhône, the pre-1986 Socialist stronghold that gave Le Pen 26.4 percent of its votes in the first round of the 1988 presidential elections; the Gard, 20.59 percent; the Moselle 19.91 percent; and Seine-Saint-Denis, the long-time Communist stronghold, 19.81 percent. In 1986, these same themes had already surfaced, differentiating clearly the extreme right from the moderate right. In a Sofres poll for *L'Express* in 1986, 60 percent of those voting for the FN cited immigration as their main concern, as opposed to only 16 percent of those voting for the UDF and RPR. The two electorates of the right were somewhat closer on security issues, with 50 percent of Le Pen's supporters citing it versus 31 percent of UDF and RPR supporters.[62] By 1988, at a time when immigration had slipped in the list of priorities of the electorate as a whole from seventh to eleventh place, it remained in second place for Le Pen's electorate, second only to unemployment, to which immigration was generally linked. Most striking, however, is the fact that whereas only 20 percent of the electorate as a whole saw the repatriation of immigrant workers as one of the ways of solving the problems of unemployment, 67 percent of Le Pen's electorate cited this, for an increase of forty-seven points above the national average. The unemployment–immigration linkage, more-

[62]*L'Express*, Mar. 21–7, 1986.

173

over, seems to have won out over the traditional immigration–security linkage, suggesting that the influx of workers to Le Pen's ranks has had a marked influence over the issues concerning his electorate as a whole.[63]

Most importantly, however, is that where immigration was a major local issue it was the main variable capable of explaining Le Pen's electoral gains. Before 1984 the size of the immigrant population of the departments made little difference in the voting patterns for left and right; but after, the heavy presence of immigrants in a department was a good predictor of high extreme right support. Although Mitterrand gained five points overall between the 1974 and 1988 presidential elections, his support declined significantly in departments with the largest immigrant presence and where the FN charted its greatest gains, for example, in the Bouches-du-Rhône (−5.8), the Alpes Maritimes (−5.3), the Var (−4.5), the Vaucluse (−3.8), Southern Corsica (−1.9), the Gard (−1.7), and others. In departments with the lowest immigrant presence, by contrast, Mitterrand gained upwards of fifteen points.[64]

Immigration, then, together with the issues of unemployment and, to a lesser extent, security, have been potent issues for the extreme right, giving it a way to make great inroads into the established parties of the left and the right. The result has been that in the first round of the 1988 presidential election, Mitterrand ended up with his weakest score since 1974: 45.3 percent as opposed to 47.2 percent in 1981 and 46.1 percent in 1974, suggesting that the extreme right had a significant impact on the left's electorate.[65] Still, there is no doubt that Le Pen, garnering 14.6 percent of the votes cast, hurt the moderate right the most, in particular Chirac, who with 20 percent of the votes came out only three points ahead of Barre at 16.6 percent.[66] After all, the FN has not only attracted a large part of the right's traditional electorate but also part of its new electorate, the young – where Le Pen's 17 percent equaled Barre's share and outdid Chirac's by five points – and the workers – where Le Pen's 20 percent outdistanced the 16 percent of Barre and Chirac together.[67]

The extreme right, in short, presents a serious challenge to the established parties. And this will remain the case despite its losses in the legislative elections of June 1988. The extreme right's decline to 9.8 percent in the legislative elections, in effect, showed less a diminution in its general appeal than it did the switch from a purely national election to one with a local basis, in which the electorate was more likely to vote for

[63]Jérome Jaffré, "Le Pen ou le vote éxutoire," *Le Monde*, Apr. 12. 1988,

[64]Le Gall, "Printemps 1988: Retour à une gauche majoritaire," *Revue Politique et Parlementaire* no. 936 (July–Aug. 1988): 20–2.

[65]Ibid.

[66]Ibid., pp. 22–3.

[67]Pascal Perrineau, "Le front national," *Revue politique et parlementaire* no. 936 (July–Aug. 1988): 39.

politicians with strong local ties, in particular the *cumulants*. This lack of loyalty to the extreme right on the part of its voters was already apparent immediately after the first round of the presidential election, in which only 57 percent of Le Pen's electorate expressed an intention to vote for the National Front in the event of legislative elections, with 20 percent moving instead to the moderate right, 7 percent to the left, and 2 percent to the ecologists.[68] The return in the legislative elections to a majoritarian system harmed the extreme right much more than it did the left, despite Minister of the Interior Pasqua's opposite intentions. Add this to the high level of abstention of the extreme right's electorate in the legislative elections, which was further evidence that the vote in the first round of the presidential election was a protest vote as much as anything else, and the losses of the extreme right in the legislative elections become perfectly understandable.

The national presidential elections, after all, reflected both the electorate's desire to have "a profound political change" (at 64 percent versus 25 percent) and its conviction that the results of the elections "would not change things very much" (at 63 percent versus 32 percent) according to a Sofres poll in early April 1988. A vote for Le Pen in the first round of the presidential elections was thus a safe vote because it wouldn't affect the outcome, but it would express the views of the voter. Le Pen's own electorate, in fact, was the only one in the 1988 presidential elections in which a significant percentage hoped to see a candidate other than Le Pen win, with 17 percent rooting for Mitterrand, 16 percent for Barre, 26 percent for Chirac, and only 28 percent for Le Pen. Moreover, only 17 percent of his electorate thought he was the candidate best able to fulfill the role of president of the Republic.[69] A vote for Le Pen in the first round of the presidential election, in short, was a safe way of expressing discontent and disquiet. But it could not be so in the legislative elections. The legislative elections would make a difference in who was elected, so protest simply for the sake of protest was much less in order there. The result is that the extreme right did well in the legislative elections only in areas in which it had already established a local base and had well-recognized local notables running for office, for example, in the Alpes-Maritimes, the Bouches-du-Rhône, and the Haut-Rhin, by contrast with areas in which it had obscure militants running against notables of the moderate right, for example, in the Moselle, in the Bas-Rhin, and in the Savoy.[70]

The decline of the extreme right in the 1988 legislative elections to close to 10 percent of the electorate, the same as its 1984 showing, does

[68]CSA exit poll, Apr, 24, 1988, cited in Perrineau, "Le front national," p. 36.
[69]Jaffré, "Le Pen."
[70]Perrineau, "Le front national," p. 37.

not necessarily suggest that the Le Pen phenomenon is ephemeral, although it could. What it does demonstrate, just as the rise of Boulanger did one hundred years ago, is that the electorate is in a time of transition, undergoing profound socio-economic changes with the rise in the middle-income strata and the continuing decline of the groups of the Third Republic coalition – the farmers, artisans, and shopkeepers – and, to some extent, of the products of the industrial revolution – the workers. These latter groups are more ready to turn to anyone willing to speak to their fears, especially because they feel to a large extent abandoned by the major governing parties with their modernist ideologies focused on the more progressive middle strata. But even the middle strata are unsure of the governing parties, as their constant shift in votes suggests. For the time being, at least, it is open to question whether the major parties can manage to rally their former supporters under a new or revised banner. As long as these parties remain in disarray, with the moderate right internally divided and the Socialists uncertain whether an opening to the center or a reopening to their left is better, those on the extreme left and extreme right will continue to be disaffected and a potential source of instability, whereas those more to the center will continue to switch their votes back and forth between left and right.

The realignment of the electorate behind the Socialists over the long haul is therefore not a foregone conclusion. Much depends upon the Socialists' ability to consolidate their support in the electorate over the next few years. Which party wins in the end, however, is less important than the question of whether the new stratum of *salariés* will itself become the foundation of a new, stable alignment of the electorate, free from the left–right polarizations of the past. And this remains unclear, because the Socialists' opening to the center, together with the cooperation of the centrist parties, has left room for a new and more radical politicization of those on the fringes. France at the moment is divided into three close to equal parts: the govermental right (UDF-RPR) representing approximately 36 percent of the votes, the governmental left (PS) with 34 percent, and the critics made up of the extreme left and the extreme right at 30 percent.[71] Whether these will be a destabilizing force or not remains a significant issue for the future of the Republic, as well as for the Socialists' tenure in power.

This disaffection and potential instability at the national level, however, may be offset by the changes in politics at the local level. After all, the linkages between national and local politics have never been clearer. Many of the problems in alliances and coalitions at the national level are

[71]See the discussion by Thierry Pfister, "Le nouveau paysage politique: Les trois France," *Revue Politique et Parlementaire* no. 935 (May–June 1988): 5–14.

finding experimental solutions at the local level. As the local electorate becomes more attuned to the new party politics in regions, departments, and the larger communes, it may not find the political situation nearly as disconcerting at the national level as it has been finding it.

Thus, our parallel with the Third Republic may still hold. Decentralization one hundred years ago produced the "revolution of the mayors," which politicized the communes and brought into politics a new electorate that served to stabilize the Republic. Decentralization today could have as much if not more of a "revolutionary" impact on French politics than that of the Third Republic. For this time the revolution has already politicized the departments, regions, and communes, not only promoting the rise of party politics in the periphery generally but increasing as well political competition among parties and personalities at all levels of local government. What is more, this has already to a great extent enfranchised the *salariés* at the expense of the Third Republic coalition. What remains to be seen is whether this new stratum will emerge as a powerful political force in the periphery, with new leaders capable of translating their aspirations into the solid, local underpinnings of a national coalition. Below, we will see the beginnings of an answer, through the extrapolation from current trends in local electoral politics and changes in local elites. What is already clear is that decentralization in the Socialist Fifth Republic, as part of a larger political strategy to enfranchise a new electorate of *salariés,* has largely succeeded, even if the allegiance of that electorate remains in doubt.

PART II

The impact of decentralization on local politics and administration

Introduction: *When informal rules become formal roles*

The French government's reputation as one of the most centralized in the world, although not undeserved, is nevertheless one that has traditionally been overstated. Long before the Socialist decentralization reforms of 1982 to 1986, which transferred executive powers, administrative functions, and financial resources from the state to local governments, local politicians and administrators had found effective ways of bypassing the formally centralized system to achieve a far greater measure of local autonomy and power than legally permitted or publicly acknowledged. And yet, it has only been in recent years that a majority of scholars have come to recognize the informal decentralization that had its beginnings in the early years of the Third Republic. It is almost as if, once convinced of the hidden power of the periphery, they could not envision its change. As a result, many scholars, although admitting that the reforms have produced formal changes in the local system of government, undervalue their long-term impact.

On average, the most positive accounts of decentralization have come from the administrative law scholars and experts on legislative politics, who have decried the complete lack of reform for nearly a century and today hail the new laws as revolutionary. By contrast, the most negative assessments continue to be made by political sociologists, who for the past decade or two have described the informal, decentralized circuits of power hidden behind the centralized, formal-legal system of local government and now tend to see only readjustments in an essentially unchanging local government system. In between, we find a wide variety of social scientists insisting that the reforms, although important, nonetheless have serious drawbacks. Some suggest that the reforms have succeeded in producing only small changes in administrative practices and processes, but others complain that they have failed to rationalize local governmental structures, to reorganize the delivery of social services, or to overhaul the local taxation system. And whereas a number decried the lack of

181

increase in local democratic participation, yet others insist that all the reforms have done is to give more power to the local notables and traditional elites.

There is, needless to say, a great deal of truth to these criticisms. But decentralization has nevertheless produced significant changes in the local governmental system. In the Socialist Fifth Republic, just as in the early years of the Third Republic, decentralization set the stage for a new local governmental system, one that now, even more than in the past, stands to revolutionize center–periphery relations, altering not only administrative roles and institutional arrangements but also the local balance of political power.

With decentralization in the Third Republic, the mayors, as the elected executive power in the communes, became members of a new elite, which accumulated offices rather than titles. It was more representative of, and responsive to, the new electorate of middle-income peasants and shopkeepers in the periphery and was more influential in terms of national politics. As such, these new notables gained the political power necessary to counterbalance the prefect's administrative control, thus establishing the relationship of mutual dependence in the Third Republic, which was to become the "modus vivendi" of the Fourth Republic and then the "complicity" of the Fifth, all of which ensured that local elected officials had a great deal more say in local administration than the law allowed or the rhetoric admitted.

These notables' relationship of complicity with the prefects, however, remained for the most part unrecognized until relatively recently. Scholars who focused on the formal and legal institutions saw a continuing pattern of centralization during the Third Republic, with the increases in the prewar years and the excesses under the Vichy regime not much attenuated by the return to the status quo ante during the Fourth Republic or by the failed reforms of the Fifth. On the other hand, scholars who focused on the formal and legal system of centralization embodied in the law and in local officials' rhetoric saw a blocked society incapable of responding to crises, with administrators and elected officials alike locked into their hierarchical roles and stalemated relationships. But although the rhetoric and the laws supported the view of a totally centralized, blocked system of local government, the reality was one in which local government systems were highly adaptable to change because local officials participated in informal circuits of power in the periphery, developing informal practices enabling them to get around most blockages thrown up by the formal-legal system.

Local officials, however, did everything they could to obscure the reality of an informally decentralized and politicized periphery, insisting that they were powerless next to the central and centralizing state, apolitical next to the political and politicizing national government. With the rhetoric of centralization, more specifically, local officials focused on the state's administrative overcentralization and its financial stranglehold in an attempt to escape responsibility for their actions as much as to express their frustration with the formal-legal system of centralization that contributed to the inefficiency and lack of cost-effectiveness of local government. With the rhetoric of nonpartisanship, they sought to dissemble their own political leanings in their efforts to allay the electorate's fears of patronage and political favoritism, to facilitate their relations with the prefect, as well as to protect themselves against central political interference. These two rhetorics combined to create a wall of words behind which local and national elected officials and administrators could work together productively – although not necessarily efficiently or cost-effectively – without fear of alienating the local electorate, the central government, or even one another.

The politico-administrative system before Socialist decentralization, in brief, was one that, although quite inefficient and overly expensive, worked reasonably well, despite the largely negative rhetoric that hid the reality from public view. But it was increasingly unable to meet the challenges of modern society, the demands for local democracy, and the requirements of a modern welfare state.

With their decentralization reforms, the Socialists intended to make local government generally more responsible and responsive to the needs of the local population, more efficient and effective in the delivery of services, and less costly. To accomplish this, they altered the formal roles of all major actors in the periphery, redefining their duties and widening the scope of their activities. The result was that they effectively formalized the informal powers of local elected officials, turning the reality of informal decentralization hidden behind the rhetoric into a new formal-legal reality and thereby transforming the local politico-administrative system.

Decentralization was not, however, a case of changing society by decree, typical of a blocked society. On the contrary, it was a case of "unblocking society by decree." By formalizing much of the informal system of local government, the Socialists did more than simply legitimate the existing practices of the many actors in the local system; they changed the system itself, introducing a new kind of transparency into local officials' practice and a new pluralism into the institutions and processes of local government.

In the political sphere, more specifically, this pluralism is evident in the new politics in the periphery, which is characterized by increased political competition among parties and personalities at every level of local government, although not yet by much of an increase in direct local democracy.

Representative democracy, however, has flourished with the increasing politicization of the periphery along national party lines and in terms of national political issues, as well as with the greater responsiveness of the local political elite to the needs and desires of the local electorate. This elite, moreover, has expanded as a result of the limitation of the numbers of offices local elected officials are allowed to accumulate. At the same time it has become increasingly differentiated according to the mandates of its members, with the younger, more urban-based, regional elite more responsive to the urban areas and the new electorate of *salariés* than to the more rurally focused, departmental elite and its declining electorate of peasants and shopkeepers – the old Third Republic coalition. Decentralization today, just as one hundred years ago, has brought in new notables, but ones who accumulate fewer offices, depend for power more on their formal roles and duties than on their informal influence, and represent to a much greater extent the new electorate of wage earners.

In the administrative sphere, the new pluralism is apparent in the increasing interdependence among the different, newly empowered levels of local government as well as in the diversity of policies local governments have developed in response to their new duties in such areas as social services, urban planning and rural development, and local economic development. In this last area, moreover, the regions have become the equivalent of local, industrial-development brokers. And here, the new administrative pluralism takes the form of a new decentralized *dirigisme,* in which the regions' new *dirigiste,* or interventionist, powers are exercised in a highly decentralized fashion, in coordination and cooperation – and sometimes in competition – with the other levels of local government, the state, and even the European Economic Community.

Decentralization, moreover, has engendered a change in the roles of local officials, in the administrative and political rules they follow, and in their interrelationships. The prefects have diminished in power, given that their new mediative role has not been accompanied by significant deconcentration. The presidents of the councils of the departments and regions, by contrast, have taken over as the new potentates in the periphery, given their new executive roles and responsibilities for the promotion of local economic development and the delivery of health and social services, respectively. The mayors of the big cities have had their informal powers officially consecrated, and the mayors of the rural communes have gained considerably more responsibility than they bargained for.

The interrelationships among the actors at these four different levels of local government have also changed as a result of their shifts in status. The prefect is no longer a threat to anyone but the rural mayors. Presidents of regions and departments see one another as the main challenges to their authority, whereas the big-city mayors have few worries about any of the other actors. The former concerns about the state's *tutelle*, however, have been replaced by concerns about the potential unofficial *tutelle* of one level of government over another, whether the regions over the departments and the big cities in economic development matters or the departments and the prefects over the rural communes in administrative matters.

The decentralization reform, in brief, has opened up local governments generally to new patterns of development, to new kinds of interrelationships among new and old actors in the system, and to new forms of political and administrative activity. Evidence of this opening can be found not only in what local elected officials have been doing but also in what they have been saying. In place of the old rhetoric, local officials have created a new rhetoric that represents as much an honest attempt to respond to the new reality as an effort to escape it.

The new rhetoric, which is focused on the limits of decentralization, reflects local elected officials' concerns about the real administrative and financial constraints of the reform and their attempts to remove them as much as it does their fear of being held responsible for their actions. It is this fear that fueled local elected officials' insistence, especially at first, that the financial limitations of decentralization involved a "transfer of unpopularity," and served to obscure the fact that the state actually provided adequate compensation for most of the newly transferred duties, even though the new resources neither grew as quickly as before nor were distributed as equitably as intended.

The new rhetoric of good management reflects local elected officials' recognition of the importance of their new duties and larger administrative roles and their fear of the electorate's response to the reality of their new, clearly political roles in an increasingly politicized periphery. Although local politicians' rhetoric has not succeeded in "depoliticizing" local government in the eyes of the public, it has served to facilitate their interactions with one another and with the prefects. What is more, it reflects a reality of better management, with local elected officials administering local governments more efficiently and cost-effectively, if not always more democratically.

Thus, even though decentralization has not been the democratizing force many had hoped, it has nevertheless set up the structures that can lend themselves to such democratization in the future. At the very least, it has been a revitalizing force for the political class in the periphery. Similarly, even though the way in which the Socialists transferred administrative functions and financial resources does little to set the groundwork for a more efficient local government, let alone a less costly one, decentralization itself has ensured that there is nothing to stop local governments from streamlining their own administrative services, redirecting resources to areas they consider most in need, and reducing expenses. And this, in fact, has already been taking place.

What is more, without the changes in laws, the very real changes in local government would have continued on the rather contorted course they had been following before the decentralization reform, with the proliferation of informal practices that contradicted the formal and legal system. And although in some areas the new, uniform laws may very well have forced local officials yet again into developing informal ways around the limitations imposed, in other areas they have created new opportunities for local elected officials, by legitimizing courses of action formerly observed only in the more progressive or more powerful regions, departments, and communes. Moreover, despite the fact that society may still be stalled in a number of areas, most notably as regards rural communes or local democracy, there is no longer a formal-legal system encouraging stagnation in these or other areas, even if the new formal-legal system hasn't exactly legislated change in these areas either.

Part II, in sum, considers the impact of the reforms of the Third Republic and the Socialist Fifth Republic on local politics and administration. And it employs three different approaches to do so. More specifically, it takes an historian's approach as it details the continuities and changes in the institutions and processes of local government over time; a political sociologist's approach as it analyzes the transformation from the old politico-administrative system along with actor's roles, rules, and interrelationships into the new; and a cultural anthropologist's or ordinary language analyst's approach when it considers the shifting uses of language in response to changes in practice from the old framework of local government to the new.

Chapter 6 examines local government before the Socialist reforms, with the informal, decentralized processes of local government hidden behind the formally centralized institutions, the informal, decentralized system behind the formal, centralized one. Chapter 7 considers the rhetorics of centralization and nonpartisanship that tended to mask the informal, decentralized reality. Chapter 8 discusses the impact of Socialist decentralization on local government institutions and processes, with the new electoral politics in the periphery and the new decentralized *dirigisme* in local economic development. Chapter 9 analyzes the new local politico-administrative system and the role changes for actors representative of the state, the regions and departments, as well as the urban and rural communes. Finally, Chapter 10 considers the new rhetorics of the limits of decentralization and of good management, and the new realities to which they respond, including the new system of local finances and the politicization of local officials' actions and interrelationships.

6

When informal rules counter formal roles: Local government before the Socialist reforms of the Fifth Republic

With decentralization in the Third Republic, the mayor gained a measure of political power in the local community that served as a counter to the prefect's administrative control. As a result of this, the mayor along with the other local political worthies over time developed a mutually beneficial relationship with the prefect, one in which the prefect tended to protect the locality from the incursions of the center and to allow the mayor and the other notables much behind-the-scenes influence in exchange for their cooperation. This "complicity" between prefects and notables in the periphery, however, went for the most part unnoticed by scholars – with a few notable exceptions – until quite recently. Scholars had a tendency to listen to the rhetoric of formal centralization, which often hid the reality of informal decentralization from view. And instead of considering the significance of the mayor's position as an elected official, most scholars focused on trends such as the continuing manifestations of state centralization in the powers of the prefect, the extension of the state's field services in the periphery, and the diminution of the powers of the mayor due to the professionalization of the civil service and to the increasing complexities of modern life. In short, although the series of decentralizing laws between 1871 and 1884 effectively ended the recurrent pattern of centralization of local governments, most scholars downplayed the importance of these reforms until recently.

Not until the mid- to late 1960s did scholars generally shift away from a focus on the formal and legal system of centralization to the informal system of decentralization hidden behind it. They came to recognize that, whereas the rhetoric and the laws supported the view of a single, totally centralized, hierarchical system and a blocked or stalemated society incapable of moving forward in response to crises, the reality was that local governmental systems were highly adaptable to change because local officials participated in informal circuits of power in the periphery. Instead of a relatively simple, apolitical, hierarchical system of center–

periphery relations weighted in favor of the administrative center, scholars found a complex politico-administrative system, or set of interlocking systems, operating in the interests of the periphery, with the interactions between prefect and notables characterized by flexibility and pragmatism, and with local government practice generally highly adaptable to change.

There is nothing surprising about this disjunction between the former view of a centralized, formal system of center–periphery relations and the more recent picture of a decentralized, informal one. A similar disjunction is equally apparent in the more traditional, historical approaches to center–periphery relations, and it primarily depends on where scholars focused their inquiry. Scholars who concentrated on the formal and legal institutions of local administration tended almost from the beginning to find a pattern of continuing or increasing centralization in local government due to the increasing size and weight of the state in the periphery. By contrast, scholars who considered the informal processes of local administration noted that, with decentralization at the beginning of the Third Republic, a new kind of mayor, whose power and prestige derived from the fact of his election, had emerged. Because this mayor gained political powers that offset the prefects' administrative authority, a new relationship of mutual dependence developed in the Third Republic, which became a "modus vivendi" in the Fourth. In the Fifth Republic a relationship of complicity developed, which ensured that informal, increasingly decentralized, processes existed, hidden behind the formal, increasingly centralized institutions of local government.

THE INSTITUTIONS AND PROCESSES OF LOCAL GOVERNMENT FROM THE THIRD REPUBLIC TO THE FIFTH REPUBLIC

Compelling arguments can be made for both the centralization and the decentralization of local government from the Third Republic up until the Socialist reforms. When one considers the formal and legal institutions of French local government, centralization does indeed appear as an unrelieved state of affairs – greatly increased in the prewar years and under the Vichy regime, needless to say, but not much attenuated thereafter with the return to the status quo ante during the Fourth Republic or with the string of failed reforms during the Fifth. Consider the increasing centralization of local government related to the expanding size and weight of the state reflected in the extensive powers of the prefect and the field services of the state; in the growing financial burdens imposed by the state on the localities, as well as the dependency of large and small communes on the state for financial help; in the increasing state *dirigisme,* or interventionism, in local economic development as a result of postwar planning and reconstruction; and in the continuing inefficiencies of local administration together with the extended time delays in getting projects approved through Paris.

An examination of the administrative processes, by contrast, suggests a quite different pattern of development in center–periphery relations. The growth of informal channels of local power and influence along with the increasing complexity in center–periphery relations served to render the centralized institutions and patterns of authority relations ineffective. Here, the focus is on the informal decentralization resulting from the relationship of complicity between local elected officials and administrators that originated in the decentralization reforms at the beginning of the Third Republic. The old aristocratic notables, whose powers depended upon money, class, and profession, were replaced then by new notables of election and position, who had gained political powers sufficient to serve as a counter to the formal administrative authority of the prefect. What this suggests is that the decentralization of the informal administrative processes existed alongside the centralization of the formal administrative institutions.

The formal centralization of local governmental institutions

The importance of the decentralization laws in the beginning years of the Third Republic was noted at the time by opponents and supporters alike, all of whom found that the laws promoted local autonomy and gave appreciable new powers to the periphery. But it was soon forgotten. By the 1890s, as we have previously seen, legislators in Parliament were already complaining about the deleterious effect of excessive centralization, as embodied in the powers of the prefect, on municipal liberty.[1] This view was only reinforced by administrative law scholars who, by concentrating on the formal powers of local officials as laid down in the legal texts, downplayed the significance of the reforms of the Third Republic.

Joseph Barthélemy, for example, made a point of describing the prefect as all-powerful and French government as irreversibly and unchangingly centralized since Napoleon I.[2] In much the same way, Maurice Hauriou, although convinced that the local election of the mayor ensured a certain modicum of political liberty, nevertheless echoed Barthélemy in his own emphasis on the overriding importance of the prefect's centralizing *tutelle administrative*.[3] Others such as J. Drouille and Gaston Jèze during this

[1] See Part I, Chapter 2.
[2] Barthélemy, *Le Gouvernement*, pp. 134–51, 164.
[3] Hauriou, *Précis élémentaire*, pp. 110, 176–7. Hauriou's views are significant, given the number of editions published: the ninth edition, for example, was published in 1919.

same time barely mentioned the issue of political liberty, finding that although mayors and municipal councilors had very little power, departmental councilors had even less because it was the prefect who, as the executive of the department, prepared the budget and administered all departmental services.[4] Jèze, more particularly, complained that France had "cold extremities."[5]

Through the 1930s this attitude remained prevalent, with scholars continuing to insist that the mayors' powers were negligible and the departmental councilors' powers nil next to those of the prefect. In their book the *Tutelle administrative,* to take only one example, the administrative law scholars R. Maspétiol and P. Laroque summarized the continuing preoccupation with the prefect's powers in edition after edition of administrative law texts.[6] This preoccupation was reiterated in studies of French politics such as that of Roger Soltau, who said: "There is not a village in France, however remote, in which the government in Paris does not have an agent to whom it can give orders. Elected bodies, municipal and departmental, exist indeed; but their powers are strictly limited."[7] Thus, he found that although there was "democracy of the central government," there was "the autocracy of the local administration."[8]

Administrative histories that underestimate the importance of the decentralizing legislation of the Third Republic have continued through to the present. Ernest Barker, for example, in commenting in the mid-1960s on France during the Third Republic, declared the *tutelle* to be all-important even though he admitted that local bodies did have a certain amount of autonomy in the area of "deliverative administration."[9] Ridley and Blondel, similarly, found that although the mayor was a strong executive, local government was subordinated to the central government, with the relationship going "back to the ancien régime, though its completion was the work of Napoleon." And they insisted that, after 1870, "no radical change took place in the principles underlying the system," although some democratization did occur.[10]

[4]J. Drouille, *Le Pouvoir disciplinaire sur les fonctionnaires publics* (Toulouse: V. Rivière, 1900), p. 108; and Gaston Jèze, *Les Principes généraux du droit administratif,* vol. 3 (Paris: Marcel Giand, 1926), p. 128. (The second edition was published in 1914.)
[5]Quoted in Charles Cadoux, "L'avenir de la décentralisation territoriale," *Actualité Juridique. Droit Administratif* (1963), p. 268.
[6]R. Maspétiol and P. Laroque, *La Tutelle administrative* (Paris: Sirey, 1931).
[7]Roger H. Soltau, *French Parties and Politics 1871–1921* (New York: Russell and Russell, 1965), p. 20. The book was written in 1930.
[8]Ibid.
[9]Ernest Barker, *The Development of Public Services in Western Europe. 1660–1930* (Hamden, Conn.: Archon Books, 1966), p. 17.
[10]F. Ridley and J. Blondel, *Public Administration in France* (New York: Barnes & Noble, 1964), pp. 85–7, 94.

More recently, scholars focusing on the formal and legal aspects of local government have revised their views to some extent. Instead of an increasingly centralized situation, they came to see decentralization at the beginning of the Third Republic as initially effective, with recentralization occurring progressively only after the turn of the century, and especially following World War I. They focused their attention primarily on the increasing size and weight of the state in the periphery and on such secondary developments as the professionalization of the civil service and the proliferation of the field services of the state in the periphery.[11]

Jean-Claude Thoenig in particular argued that from 1885 to 1910 the communes enjoyed a notable amount of autonomy in the recruitment of personnel. The political implications of this were significant; the resulting patronage system enabled the mayors to build the equivalent of local machines, with power centralized in the person of the mayor. But this relative freedom in personnel matters was not to last. In the first quarter of the twentieth century, the efforts of civil servants to form professional associations and officially recognized unions capable of protecting them from the arbitrariness and often corrupt patronage systems of (mainly big-city) mayors resulted in legislation that undermined the mayors' centralized powers, as the state became an arbiter between them and municipal employees.[12] Central ministries only added to these limitations by increasing their control over the appointments of a wide variety of different categories of governmental agents working in the municipalities. Moreover, the continued efforts by civil service unions to gain job protections, although understandable because the fragmentation of the local situation necessitated their turning to the central state for help, nonetheless set the stage for an increase in state centralization from the mid-1930s on.

During the early and mid years of the Third Republic, mayors benefited from an appreciable margin of administrative autonomy with regard to personnel matters, despite the rise of formal centralization. This was equally true in the economic sphere, even though the state became more *dirigiste* over time and less willing to allow local governments to participate in the promotion of local economic development except by paying for projects it alone planned. Thus, "municipal socialism" had its heyday in the early to mid years of the Third Republic, when local governments began to do a lot on their own, especially in the areas of transportation, washing facilities, and municipal food stores. The response by the *tutelle* authorities and by the *Conseil d'État,* or Council of State (the French equivalent of the U.S. Supreme Court), however, was to place considerable restrictions on this movement, denying any actions not directly re-

---

[11]Thoenig, "La Politique"; and Virieux, "Les tendances."
[12]Thoenig, "La Politique," pp. 60–72.

lated to municipal functions. Notably, they limited municipal police to such concerns as sobriety, proscribed any activities that might affect the principle of freedom of commerce and industry, and gave preference to the system of contracting out for goods and services.[13]

Local governments suffered a similar fate in terms of local finances; the state steadily imposed new financial burdens on the locality and, in so doing, limited their freedom to spend their money as they saw fit. During the Third Republic, first came the state-mandated expenses in such areas as education and public assistance. Then, after the law on the separation of Church and State of December 9, 1905, the communes had to pay for the maintenance of religious edifices. Finally, the state placed restrictions on what communes were allowed to pay for: they were forbidden to subsidize cults, free schools, commercial or industrial enterprises.[14]

Even though the early to middle years of the Third Republic allowed for a reasonable amount of local freedom, therefore, the state increasingly limited this, either inadvertently as with the professionalization of the local civil service and the increasing financial burdens on the locality or quite deliberately as in the case of the commune's powers in local economic development. The inefficiencies of local administration resulting simply from its mechanics also contributed to centralization. This remained constant across time, as even the most minor of decisions of the municipal council had to mount the hierarchical ladder to Paris. One of the best examples of this was the decree of January 6, 1898, by the president of the Republic, fixing the tax on dogs for the commune of Saint-Jean-des-Vignes, which took an entire year to be written into law. The initial decision by the municipal council on January 3, 1897, had to wait on the recommendation of the general council of the Saône-et-Loire in its session of August 19, 1897, the intervening recommendation of the prefect, and on the Ministry of the Interior before it was finally decided.[15] Although, over time efforts at deconcentration progressively diminished the number of minor decisions that had to go all the way to Paris for approval, this administrative centralization remained a problem. Only in 1968 was the prefect allowed to make decisions without the Minister's permission on such issues as appointing an assistant lockkeeper or naming a village street.[16]

After World War II, formal centralization increased much more rapidly than during the Third Republic, mainly as a result of the efforts to modernize the state through administrative rationalization, financial reform,

[13]Sautel, *Histoire*, pp. 522–3.
[14]Ibid.
[15]The text of the decree appears in Pierre Legendre, *L'Administration du XVIIIe siècle à nos jours* (Paris: Presses universitaires de France, 1969), pp. 71–2.
[16]Williams and Harrison, *Politics and Society*, p. 292.

and deconcentration, as well as in consequence of postwar planning and reconstruction policies that led to attempts to exert more control over the periphery in the areas of economic development and urban planning. In personnel matters during the Fourth Republic, for example, the deconcentrated service of government road engineers, half of whom had been attached to the communes, was integrated under central direction, and permanent local governmental employees gained the beginning of a common statute under which the Minister rather than the mayor or municipal council set salary scales and qualifications for positions.[17] In local economic development matters, communes increasingly had less say than before, but more responsibilities. In the 1960s, for example, as a result of the Fifth Plan, communes were required to contribute to the financing of state-run, capital-investment projects in their areas, paying the costs over and above the government commitment.[18] The response of the central government to the urban activism of the local governments of the 1970s, finally, was an attempt to regain control over urban development through the contracts with midsized cities, countryside, and suburban areas.[19]

In financial matters, too, communes felt the heavy hand of the state as they increasingly depended upon it for financial help. Even the biggest cities were in financial straits as they coped with the problems attendant upon urbanization; with the investment implications of the postwar baby-boom; and with the antiquated local taxation system, which had not been reformed since World War I and was traditionally expected only to top off the shortfall in subsidies from Paris.[20] Any reforms of the local taxation system, moreover, occasioned only increased centralization. The substitution in the late 1960s of the short-lived, national employers' tax on salaries for the traditional, local indirect taxes only further undermined the financial autonomy of the commune. Instead of going back to some local system of taxation when the national tax was abolished in 1969, the state continued to provide local governments with the amount they would have received had the tax not been eliminated. This ensured that, by 1974, close to half of local taxes came to the locality through the filter of the state.[21]

The formal centralization of the institutions of local administration was also reinforced by expansion of the field services of the state into the countryside. By 1958 every ministry had a regional network, whether the national education ministry with its nineteen educational academies, the agriculture ministry's forty "water and forest" regions, or the DDE

[17]Mawhood, "Melting an iceberg," p. 506.
[18]Ibid.
[19]Yves Mény, "Local Authorities and Economic Policy," in *Economic Policy and Policy-Making under the Mitterrand Presidency 1981–1984*, ed. Howard Machin and Vincent Wright (New York: St. Martin's Press, 1985), p. 195.
[20]Williams and Harrison, *Politics and Society*, p. 298.
[21]Mény, *Centralisation*, pp. 272–6.

(*Direction départementale d'équipement*) with its ten or so deconcentrated agents per department. And because these deconcentrated field services often resisted decentralization attempts by their own ministers, deconcentration simply meant that the hand of the center could be felt more heavily in the periphery.

Thus, the engineering corps of the *ponts et chaussées* (bridges and roads) of the DDE, in adapting to the change in its role from serving rural society to urban society, made certain to develop policies guaranteed to maintain its own power. As Thoenig explained: "If the engineers of the Ponts (et Chaussées) pushed for a more efficient state policy in the area of urban development, it was not, as the minister wanted, in order to redistribute the roles between the state and the local collectivities or to decentralize power from Paris to the provinces. On the contrary, it was in order to reinforce the hold of the State apparatus on local initiatives." In consequence, instead of coming up with solutions to the problems of urban development that would have encouraged greater independence on the part of local collectivities, they came up with ones that continued their dependence.[22] And the same was true for the other corps, such as the *Inspection des finances* and the *cours des comptes*. A case in point here is the *trésorier-payeur général*, or treasurer-paymaster general, who over the years moved from simply checking local accounts to passing judgment on the financial decisions as well.

In the public works arena in rural development, evidence of centralization was found in the role played by the *génie rural*, or the rural engineering corps, part of the Ministry of Agriculture, and by the *ponts et chaussées*. The level of deconcentration of both these field services was such that their reach into the periphery was extensive, generally giving them more day-to-day contact with rural mayors than even the subprefects had. It was a representative of the central government who took charge of local construction programs, advised on the suitability of local projects, and was paid a royalty for doing so. In some ways, the engineer had more power than anyone else in local construction projects. Mayors only had first signatory power on building permits, and not the last. Because the engineers of the DDE had to be consulted and could recommend on projects, including suggesting modifications if they deemed it necessary, they had tremendous control over whether a project would proceed and what it would look like.

The field services of the state, in brief, had the ability to exercise great influence, if not control, over local administration and development. Regional reform did little to alter this situation or to attenuate the formal

[22]Jean-Claude Thoenig, *L'Ère des technocrates: Le Cas des Ponts et Chaussées* (Paris: Les Éditions d'organisation, 1973), pp. 102–3.

centralization of government in the economic sphere. This was in large measure because the regions were regarded as a threat, not only by local elected officials in the departments and the communes, but also by the agents of the state in the periphery and civil servants in the central ministries. The reform also was implemented in such as way as to allay the fears of elected officials and administrators alike.

The regions, as they were originally set up in the beginning years of the Fifth Republic, were deconcentrating, not decentralizing, institutions. But they were extremely weak and thus posed little threat to the communes and departments. Even though the regions were set up as "federations of departments," they had neither the attributes nor the resources to enable them to impose on the departments or even on the larger urban districts and communities. By law they could not take the initiative on any project, having to wait for the state or local governments to propose some action in which they could then participate financially. And because they did not have their own personnel or sufficient financial resources, it was very difficult for them to make informed decisions that would have an impact on local governments, even after the consecration of the region as a public establishment as of 1972.[23]

Even so, they represented a threat to many in the central government. Although they were set up as semirepresentative institutions and only had limited functions, the government was so apprehensive about the COD-ERs, or regional economic development commissions, that it initially refused them funds and put their meetings in the hands of the regional prefects. For the prefects, however, the regions represented an intrusion on their already well-established control in the departments. They therefore resisted them, especially at first. Thus, the prefects dragged their feet when it came to setting up meetings of the regional administrative conferences with the departmental prefects and often rejected the results of studies intended to establish objective criteria for the determination of public investment policy carried out by the regional missions.[24] The result was that both the members of the CODER and the technocrats of the regional missions felt marginalized, with their advice ignored even when they had a chance to offer it.[25]

The regions were often left out of the central policy-making and implementation processes affecting them. Even after the official establishment of the regions in 1964, the interministerial commissions set up to solve regional problems generally had little to do with the regional administrations, including the regional prefect as well as the CODER (for example, in

[23]Mény, *Centralisation*, pp. 254–7.
[24]Howard Machin, *The Prefect in French Public Administration* (New York: St. Martin's Press, 1977), p. 98.
[25]Williams and Harrison, *Politics and Society*, p. 293.

the interministerial commissions on land-use planning and public works for Corsica in 1966, for Aquitaine in 1967, for the Paris basin in 1966).[26] Even when they were consulted, the regions and regional prefects found themselves marginalized by the increasing numbers of ministerial agents appointed to implement specific policies in such areas as reindustrialization (for example, the *commissaire* for industrial conversion in the Nord and the Lorraine as of 1967), rural development (for example the *commissaire* for rural renovation in Quest-France, Auvergne, and Limousin), and urban development (for example, the *missions d'aménagement,* or planning commissions, for the new towns of the Paris region).[27]

Finally, even central ministries with regional operations or responsibilities tended to make policies and plans without considering the newly established regions. For example, even though a number of central organizations deconcentrated an increasing number of decisions to the regional level, such as the *Caisse des dépôts et consignation,* they had little to do with the regional governments. Industrial development decisions continued to be made at the national level, often without consulting regional elites, such as the decision to locate an important steel center near Marseilles.[28] The DATAR, which is the land-use agency for regional development charged with promoting the "decentralization" (that is, deconcentration) of industrial expansion by encouraging industry to decentralize their operations and to locate in the provinces in an effort to relieve the congestion around Paris, tended to handle all its development decisions from the center, despite the fact that the CODERs were to serve it in an advisory capacity.

Moreover, despite the official delimiting of regional boundaries, certain ministries broke down French territory into other circumscriptions of different sizes and shapes for various purposes, thus threatening a proliferation of specialized regions challenging the importance of the officially consecrated regions. The Ministry of Construction, for example, broke the French territory down into only eight sectors for planning purposes in 1962 and 1967 and the INSEE into eight "zones of study" for similar purposes in 1967. The creation of the Paris basin and various other river basins in order to deal with their particular problems of development often ignored regional boundaries, as did newly created public financial establishments in the Basse Seine and the Lorraine.[29] The result was that the region was never the central, local organ for planning and economic de-

[26]Mény, *Centralisation,* p. 244.
[27]Ibid., pp. 244–50. See also Lucien Sfez, *L'Administration prospective* (Paris: A Colin, 1970).
[28]Sidney Tarrow, "Regional Policy, Ideology and Peripheral Defense: The Case of Fos-sur-Mer," in *Territorial Politics,* ed. Tarrow et al., pp. 97–122.
[29]Mény, *Centralisation,* pp. 250–4.

velopmnent anticipated by de Gaulle. And this only added to the already existing weakness of the regional institutions themselves.

Although the regional reform did little to attenuate the formal centralization of the central ministries and their field services in the periphery, the lack of reform of local government institutions, in particular of the communes, had similar consequences. In one sense, it was the very decentralization of the communes, and their division into so many small units, that contributed to the centralization of the prefect's powers. In 1968, with thirty-eight thousand communes, France had more units of local government than all five members of the European Economic Community plus Switzerland combined. Most were very small and rural, with only thirty-two communes having over one hundred thousand inhabitants, fifty having between fifty thousand and one hundred thousand, whereas thirty-five thousand had under two thousand inhabitants. This system did have its benefits, because close to half a million people sat on local councils, thus encouraging a high turnout in local elections and an important place for the *mairie*, or townhall, in citizens' hearts. But it also had tremendous weaknesses. In 1964 the Ministry of Industry found that nine out of ten communes, containing a third of the population, lacked the financial and administrative resources to do an adequate job of running programs of social investment, whereas twenty-four thousand communes with under five hundred inhabitants were incapable of providing even basic services satisfactorily.[30] These communes, in consequence, depended on the departmental prefects for administrative help and on general council members for political help. The overall result was that as the institutions of local government demonstrated themselves increasingly unable to manage the myriad problems confronting them, the institutions of the national government expanded to meet them.

We have thus what would appear to be overwhelming evidence for the formal centralization of the institutions of local government, given that the communes, without adequate administrative or financial means to handle their own affairs, seemed to be completely dominated by the prefects and dependent upon the field services of the state. (The departments certainly must have been so dominated, because the prefect was the executive power in the department.) Meanwhile, the regions, which could have been a decentralizing force, were bypassed by local governments as well as by the central ministries and their field services. Any reforms, whether of local personnel or finances, tended only to lead to further centralization. And any initiatives of local governments in the area of economic development and urban planning were proscribed by law as soon as the central government could manage it.

[30]Williams and Harrison, *Politics and Society*, pp. 296–7.

But this is not the whole story. Although the institutions of local government were indeed centralized, the interactions of local elected officials
and national and local administrators within the context of these institutions resulted in administrative processes that were actually quite decentralized, with local elected officials wielding a good deal more power
informally than was allowed formally.

The informal decentralization of local governmental processes

Although there was certainly a significant amount of centralization at all
levels of local government subsequent to the decentralizing legislation at
the beginning of the Third Republic, this did not completely deny local
freedom and autonomy, the above arguments to the contrary notwithstanding. The law of 1884 affected the balance of power in the periphery
by providing local elected officials with political powers to counter the
administrative authority of the prefect as well as of the other representatives of the state in the periphery. This in turn led to the development of a
new set of informal relationships, which allowed local elected officials a
greal deal of behind-the-scenes influence over the prefect's decisions,
thereby ensuring much more decentralization in the administration of the
periphery than the legal rules and formal institutions would suggest,
especially since the growing centralization resulting from the more and
more direct intrusions of the field services of the state in the periphery
was offset by their administrative atomization.

The passage of the municipal law of 1884 was a major political event
for the periphery, producing what Daniel Halévy hailed as *la fin des
notables,* the end of the rural aristocracy that had so long dominated
local government.[31] The end of the aristocratic notable, though, only
spelled the beginning of a new breed of notable, one whose power and
prestige were to come, not from aristocratic titles or ownership of lands
but rather from the *cumul des mandats,* the accumulation of the titles of
political office. And because the route to such power and prestige ordinarily started with municipal politics, local politics became and remained
tremendously important to national legislators. Moreover, even if mayors
did not accumulate too many offices, they had a significant influence on
national politics through their role in the election of members of the
Senate as well as on local politics, because the general councilors of
departments were almost invariably mayors. As a result, the mayor held a
position in the periphery that could not be ignored and had an important
effect on his relationship with the prefect.

[31]Halévy, *La République,* especially pp. 369–72.

The result was the beginning of the relationship of complicity between prefect and local notables, which later scholars were to focus on when discussing local government in the Fifth Republic. But in the Third Republic, it was primarily a relationship of mutual dependence. André Siegfried in the 1930s had already made note of this "most interesting of adaptations that has renovated the spirit of our departmental administration." In commenting on the increasingly close collaboration between the prefect and the general council, which resulted from the growing complexity of local affairs, Siegfried concluded: "Thus is born a local democracy, nearly Swiss in spirit and very serious in the administration of affairs, in which one finally perceives something constructive."[32]

Even before the Third Republic there were signs of a closer relationship between prefect and local notables than ordinarily assumed. As far back as the July monarchy, some of the power and authority retained by the state in local government was nonetheless mitigated by the beginnings of a system of mutual dependence between prefects and local notables, which was to come into its own as a result of the reforms in the Third Republic.[33] Even at this time, the influence of local elected officials was in actuality much greater than their legal powers allowed. The agents of the government were not only willing to collaborate, because they came from the same social classes and shared the same political opinions, but generally felt constrained to collaborate, because local elected officials (elected on the basis of *capacité,* or profession, as well as property) were often very powerful legislators, former ministers, journalists, and former, high-level civil servants. The prefect, working in the same department for years, tended to develop important ties with the local notables or, according to one commentator, "a sort of indissoluble marriage," and the subprefect already had such ties as a result of being from the department itself.[34] The mayors, however, were in no way key actors in this context. After all, the prefect appointed the mayors, and the job itself was often regarded more as a chore than an honor, as evidenced by the high turnover during that period. In the big cities, moreover, the central figures were the *grands notables,* who tended to be Deputies, not mayors, given that the *cumul des mandats* was relatively rare at the time.[35] According to

[32] André Siegfried, *Tableau des partis en France* (1930), p. 223.
[33] Burdeau, *Libertés,* p. 103.
[34] Ibid., p. 107. See also A. Jardin and André-Jean Tudesq, *La France des notables: La Vie de la nation 1818–1848* (Paris: Seuil, 1973), and idem, *La France des notables: L'Evolution générale 1815–1848* (Paris: Seuil, 1973).
[35] See André-Jean Tudesq, *Les Grands Notables en France 1840–1849,* vol. 1 (Paris: Presses universitaires de France, 1964), p. 324; and Maurice Agulhon, L. Girard, J. L. Robert, and W. Serman et al., *Les Maires en France du consulat à nos jours* (Paris: Sorbonne, 1986), p. 9.

one member of the republican left, Cormenin, the local power of the Deputy made him "the real master" of the department.[36]

Local notables, in brief, whether national politicians or local elected officials, did have considerable informal powers as a result of their positions, thus ensuring at least a modicum of informal decentralization behind the formal, centralized system. But it was still, of course, a decentralization to the benefit of the highly privileged, if no longer titled. Only with the Third Republic was there to be a decentralization to the benefit of the less privileged, with a new, more representative, elected elite replacing the old in its relations with the prefect and other representatives of the state in the periphery.

The old notables of the nineteenth century, in other words, were notables in consequence of their economic, social and political power. Their access to local office depended, for the most part, on their money, social status, or professional competence.[37] The new notables of the Third Republic, by contrast, were notables because of their election to local government as well as because of the functions they performed within that context. These notables were characterized by the network of interconnecting relationships that linked them, on the one hand, to the local population and to the local government they represented, and on the other, to the political and administrative structures.[38] Their focus, more specifically, was on power, which – in the context of the local governmental framework – meant the prefect first and foremost.[39] The result was that, although mayors now had their own independent power base in consequence of their election to their position, they continued to depend upon the prefect. And the prefect, of course, minus the power to appoint the mayors, was now all the more dependent upon the mayors for their cooperation.

Few administrative scholars, up until comparatively recently picked up on this relationship of mutual dependence. A notable exception was Walter Rice Sharp in the 1930s, who, although agreeing with administrative law scholars as to the tremendous centralizing powers of the state, argued that such centralization was not accompanied by administrative integration and that this devolved to the benefit of local elected officials, whose powers had increased markedly as a result of their national influence. Sharp found that the mayor had "acquired a prestige little short of remarkable" and a national as well as local importance, when considering

---

[36]Burdeau, *Libertés*, p. 107.

[37]See Jardin and Tudesq, *La France des notables: La Vie*; idem, *La France des notables: L'Evolution*; and Tudesq, *Les Grands Notables*.

[38]Mény, *Centralisation*, p. 302.

[39]Michel Longepierre, "Le système administratif départemental et la vie politique nationale," in *Les Facteurs locaux de la vie politique nationale* (Paris: Pedone, 1972), p. 83, cited in Mény, *Centralisation*, p. 302.

the *cumul des mandats*. He even quoted Maxime Leroy, who once re-marked that France was "really governed by thirty thousand mayors."[40] As a result of this national power, Sharp noted that "the prefect's depen-dence upon local members of Parliament for political good will and electoral activity reduces his scrutiny of the wisdom of local spending almost to a formality."[41]

Local elected officials, however, derived their powers not only from their relationship of mutual dependence with the prefect but also from the atomization of local administration. Sharp was convinced that al-though the centralization was excessive, it was also ineffective, because "despite the common notion abroad that the French governmental sys-tem is over-centralized, this centralization has not been accompanied by administrative integration . . . [not only in Paris] . . . but even more in the inter-relation of the field establishments of the central government."[42] The problem, he found, was that the prefect's "importance as a national administrative officer" was diminishing and the indirect hierarchical pro-cesses that put the prefect at the center of the center–periphery relations were being undermined as a result of the increasing size of the field services of state and their direct communication with Paris ministries, which served "to 'shortcircuit' hierarchical procedure by passing over and around the prefecture."[43] Such competition between the prefect and the field services of the state and the concomitant administrative atomiza-tion, in short, left local elected officials with more freedom than the formal laws would suggest.

In the mid-1950s, at a time when most administrative historians contin-ued to describe the all-powerful, centralizing prefect as a primary cause of the stagnation of local life, Brian Chapman echoed Sharp's view of the mayor's local importance and expanded on his view of the prefect's relationship with the mayor. Thus, he argued that the "vitality of French local government" is related to "the personalization of executive responsi-bility in the Prefect, the crystallization of local political activity round the Prefect and the Mayors, and the balance of forces between administrators and politicians at the local level."[44] At the same time that Chapman described the prefect's pivotal role in the periphery, he also pointed to the inherent weakness of the prefect's position that made him dependent on

---

[40]Walter Rice Sharp, "France," in *Local Government in Europe* (New York: Appleton-Century, 1939), pp. 147–8.
[41]Ibid., p. 192.
[42]Sharp, *French Civil Service*, p. 42.
[43]Walter Rice Sharp, *The Government of the French Republic* (New York: C. Van Nostrand Co, 1938), pp. 186–7, quoted in Alfred Diamant, "The department, the prefect, and dual supervision in French administration: A comparative study," *Journal of Politics* vol. 16 (1954): 475.
[44]Chapman, *Prefects*, p. 172.

local notables. The prefect's frequent mobility, in the first place, under-mined his ability to play the pivotal role effectively. And thus, Chapman noted:

In a world where other administrations are by no means content to accept with-out question the Prefect's supremacy in the Department, it is only if he can become firmly attached to a particular post, understand the profounder currents of local life, and act as a point of stability as well as of leadership, that he will be able to pursue a steady and purposeful policy.[45]

Interestingly enough, Chapman found the prefects to be relatively weak in the first part of the Third Republic, but with their powers increasing after 1919. In 1939 they were the unchallenged authority in the depart-ments. This changed, however, during the war years with the regions and the development of the field services of the various ministries, so much so that they only began to regain their former preeminence in 1949, and this only when the associations of mayors, general councils, and local authori-ties asked for a return to the traditional system.[46]

There was to be no full return to the traditional system, however, due to the increasing size and importance of the field services of the state. As Alfred Diamant noted, the lack of administrative integration discussed by Sharp in the 1930s was even more pronounced by the 1950s, with the prefects losing their battle to maintain control over the periphery to the field services of the Paris ministries. He found the most tangible sign of this to be the fact that the technical services were no longer physically housed in the prefecture and therefore were no longer quite literally under the prefect's eye or beholden to the prefect for even the normal housekeeping functions provided in the past. In addition, the prefect's functions related to authorizing expenditures were diminishing in rela-tion to those whose functions were related to accountability, whether the *Trésorier-payeur général,* who had to be consulted on certain types of authorizations, or the tax collector, whose powers of review over munici-pal expenditures gave him the kind of influence over decisions by the mayor and municipal council only the prefect should in theory have had.[47]

Most important, however, was the fact that, as a generalist, the prefect was unable to exert control over the increasingly specialized, professional staffs of the field services of Paris ministries. This, Diamant argued, meant that the *tutelle administratif* "becomes atomized, and the local units, which are accustomed to listening to the authoritative voice of the central authorities in the person of the prefect, are confronted with a

[45]Ibid., p. 148.
[46]Ibid., pp. 163–7.
[47]Diamant, "Department," pp. 484–5.

multiplicity of voices, often producing conflicting orders."[48] It is small wonder then that the prefect would rely more and more on his special relationship with local elected officials in order to retain as much local power and authority as possible or that local elected officials would continue to have a strong bargaining position with regard not only to the prefect but to the other local representatives of the national government as well.

Thus, at the same time that formal centralization appeared to be increasing as a result of the more and more direct intrusions of the field services of the state in the periphery, informal decentralization was enhanced by the administrative atomization resulting from that centralization. The situation, in effect, was increasingly complex, but no less decentralized than before, with the growing, formal centralization offset by the rising number of informal, semiclandestine means of getting around the formally centralized institutions.

In the meantime, prefects and notables in the Fourth Republic were returning to the relationship of mutual dependence of the Third Republic, against the backdrop of the unimplemented provisions of Title X (transferring the prefect's executive powers to the president of the general council) which led general councilors to seek to enhance their powers and prefects to resist any diminution in their own powers. By 1949 and 1950, though, prefects and the presidents of the general councils of the departments were being officially encouraged to reach a "modus vivendi;" and by 1951 the general councilors themselves were satisfied that harmony had returned.[49]

The equilibrium promoted by this modus vivendi was to continue, however, only until the mid-1960s, when de Gaulle's functional regionalization disturbed the tacit accord between prefects and general councilors by placing deconcentrated powers in the hands of a regional prefect whom no elected assembly could counterbalance. At the time, local elected officials were quite clear in their disapproval. René Pleven, for example, expressed his disappointment with the new regional organization in 1964, because it broke with "the close and trusting symbiosis in action between local elected officials and the representatives of the central power." And Abel-Durand complained that it pulled apart the modus vivendi established between prefects and general councils.[50]

The prefects, too, opposed regionalization, seeing it as an attack on the

---

[48]Ibid., p. 489.
[49]Mény, *Centralisation*, pp. 334–6.
[50]René Pleven, "La réforme régionale," *Départements et Communes* (May 1964): 13; and Abel-Durand, Speech at the XXXIIIrd Congress of the APCG (Association of presidents of general councils), *Départements et Communes* (May 1966): 19, cited in Mény, *Centralisation*, p. 338.

departments where they had their power base. At best, they were willing to allow the grouping together of departments through interdepartmental conferences or agreements; and from the first they were hostile to the IGAMEs. The principle of "first among equals" was instituted with the regional prefect, who was at the same time prefect in the department. This risked undermining the principle of equality, which ensured that prefects communicated very little among themselves about the results of their actions, and left them "monarchs" in their departments. More communication, necessitated by a regional prefect to whom departmental prefects would have to report, threatened their positions and the modus vivendi they had established with local notables.[51] In the end, however, the equilibrium of the modus vivendi returned, as local elected officials successfully conquered the regional establishments.

It was only after the mid- to late 1960s that large numbers of scholars began to recognize this modus vivendi and the fact that much more informal decentralization of local government existed than had been traditionally assumed, despite the lack of change in legislation. Many of these scholars, as discussed in the next section, explained this in terms of the complex, local politico-administrative system only as it appeared during the Fifth Republic. Others such as Jean-Jacques Chevallier noted the political impact of the decentralization of 1884, returning to Daniel Halévy's argument that the *révolution des maires* affected the very tissue of society, by bringing republican politics to the village.[52] And still others such as Frédéric Bon and Michel-Antoine Burnier saw the informal dencentralization starting with the beginning years of the Third Republic as a function of the power of the new social stratum of peasants and shopkeepers in the periphery, and as a result of the new political democracy that, together with the difficulties in communication, "left local powers with an appreciable margin of autonomy."[53]

But there were also those who took a more historical approach, arguing that continuing decentralization in the face of formal centralization was a function of the adaptability of the institutions of local government to change through time, especially since the Third Republic. Thoenig found that, despite the increasing centralization resulting from the professionalization of the civil service, communal autonomy was preserved at least until the end of the 1930s by the capacity of many mayors to play with the laws and by the goodwill of the prefects, who interpreted the law

[51]See the discussion in Mény, *Centralisation*, pp. 346–54. See also Pierre Gémion, "Résistance au changement de l'administration territoriale: Le cas des institutions régionales," *Sociologie du Travail* no. 3 (1966).
[52]Chevalier, *Histoire des Institutions*, p. 335.
[53]Frédéric Bon and Michel-Antoine Burnier, *Les Nouveaux Intellectuels* (Paris: Seuil, 1971), p. 42.

quite liberally, while attempting to avoid obvious abuses and political incidents. He suggested that the growth in central administrative control being imposed on local personnel practices, in the meantime, encouraged the increasing differentiation between practices in big cities (the mayors went to Paris to negotiate individually the rules and their applications) and in rural communes (mayors had no such central access).[54]

For scholars focused more specifically on the administrative processes of the Fifth Republic, this informal decentralization of the local framework persisted. Thus, Charles Roig found that the problem with French government was less centralization than maintenance of the status quo, and that in this context national and local powers managed either to neutralize one another or to achieve a tacit complicity.[55] Vincent Wright noted that the institutions themselves were informally decentralized as a result of the competition amongst the various field services of the state, divided as they were into different *grands corps,* with every new local program meaning competition for local clients and support.[56] Mény, in addition, saw state centralizing controls in the periphery decreasing in other areas, too. By the 1970s, for example, he found that the local control exercised by the prefects and the field services of the state was diminishing mainly in relation to the more activist local governments, especially in the growing towns.[57]

More recently, Douglas Ashford argued that a significant amount of decentralization, at least since the Third Republic, had been embodied in the pragmatic bargaining relationship maintained between the mayor and all other political and administrative officials of center and periphery. He noted that this, combined with the *cumul des mandats,* which allowed mayors to hold national office, meant that mayors had much more national influence and local governments a much greater ability to resist or moderate the directives of the national government than the legal histories or institutional studies would lead one to believe. Thus, Ashford insisted that "the French local system is more attuned to problem solving because it is more intimately linked to higher levels of political and administrative decision-making."[58] He concluded that the resulting bargaining relationship was characterized by flexibility and pragmatism, the very things that made center–periphery relations highly receptive to changing circumstances and needs.

[54]Thoenig, "La Politique," pp. 509–10.
[55]Charles Roig, "Théorie et réalité de la décentralisation," *Revue Française de Science Politique* vol. 126 (1966): 464.
[56]Vincent Wright, "Politics and Administration under the French Fifth Republic," *Political Studies* vol. 22 (1972): 44–65.
[57]Mény, "Local authorities," p. 195.
[58]Douglas Ashford, *British Dogmatism and French Pragmatism* (London: George Allen & Unwin, 1982), pp. 5, 8, 18.

Albert Mabileau and Pierre Sadran saw the flexibility Ashford described in the adaptability of the framework of local government in the Fifth Republic to the arrival of new actors and to the creations of new rules. They found, more specifically, a continuing openness in the local framework, as evidenced by the greater and greater differentiation between urban and rural areas in terms of their relations with the departments, regions, and central government; by the increasing number of special shortcuts available to mayors who held positions of national importance; and by the more direct interactions of the field services of the state with the services of local governmental units and with the new breed of local notable, whose political power was based more on competence as an administrator than on personalistic ties.[59]

To say that a decentralization that benefited local power and autonomy continued to thrive in the Fifth Republic, however, does not mean that citizen participation or local democracy was much of a reality beyond the polling place. Part of the problem for the Fifth Republic by the 1970s was that the increasing demands for participation of the *autogestion* variety were not being totally satisfied, even though mayors were increasingly responsive to new groups in the periphery and to local associations, especially in the big cities.

For the most part, local elected officials from the smaller towns and villages preferred to continue to operate as they always had with the prefects and other agents of the state in the periphery. Thus, in answer to a question about whether, when public officials had to negotiate with one another, conceive policies together, or generally work things out, the process should be subject to the control of public opinion or direct universal suffrage (for example, referenda) or whether it should be a more ad hoc process, without the direct pressures of public opinion, 64 percent of the responding mayors, general councilors, and members of Parliament from villages and towns of fewer than fifty thousand inhabitants (N = 62) chose the latter, less public process over the former, more democratic process. (It is important to note, however, that local elected officals were at least more responsive to issues of local democracy than the agents of the state, 80 percent of whom [N = 206] preferred the less public process.)[60] Moreover, when asked whether they felt that too many people already intervened in the administration of public affairs and that the number should therefore be reduced or that too few had a voice and that it was necessary to enlarge the circle, 78 percent of the members of Parliament, general councilors, and mayors in communes of fewer than

[59]Albert Mabileau and Pierre Sadran "Administration et politique au niveau local," in *Administration et politique sous le Cinquième République*, ed. F. de Baeque and J.L. Quermonne (Paris: Presses de la Fondation Nationale des Sciences Politiques, 1981).
[60]Crozier and Thoenig, "La régulation," p. 13 n. 28.

fifty thousand inhabitants (N = 50) and 76 percent of departmental and communal civil servants (N = 199) favored the former reduction in numbers.[61] In other words, although the framework in which local officials operated was becoming more responsive and adapting to the changes in the periphery, the framework itself in most instances did not expand to allow for increased citizen participation in the process of government. It was a framework that was, nevertheless, reasonably decentralized, despite the formal centralization of local government.

Scholars who considered the relationship of politics to administration in local government, then, from the very beginning, with the passage of the decentralizing legislation of 1884, saw a significant amount of decentralization in the informal practices of local officials, even if they didn't see much local democracy. Those who focused exclusively on the formal and legal aspects of local government, by contrast, saw only continuing or increasing centralization. It should not be surprising, therefore, that a similar split occurred between scholars who sought to discuss the system of local government.

THE LOCAL POLITICO-ADMINISTRATIVE SYSTEM

The view of a mayor powerful at the local level is something that surfaced only at infrequent intervals over the course of the century; and it was not to affect most scholars' views of the local government until the mid- to late 1960s. This was as true of systemic accounts of local government which considered the structures, functions, and goals of the local politico-administrative system as it was of administrative and political histories which focused on the characteristics and development of local governmental institutions, processes, and events. As long as scholars focused on the formal and legal aspects of local government, as well as on the public rhetoric of local officials, they remained convinced that the local politico-administrative system was highly centralized, and, in Michel Crozier's terms, a *société bloquée,* or blocked society, incapable of change. But once scholars turned to the informal aspects of local government, they discovered a highly decentralized local politico-administrative system hidden behind the formal-legal system.

The difference between the historical and systemic accounts of local government, then, is not so much in their views of centralization or decentralization but, rather, in how they explain it. Whereas the historical traces the continuities and changes over time in local governmental institutions, processes, and events, thus giving us insight into the intricacies of "what happened," the systemic focuses on the structures, func-

[61]Ibid., p. 18 n. 40.

tions, and goals of the politico-administrative system at one time, however long a period of time that may be, thus giving us a sense of how it all fits together. One significant difference, however, is that the historical stresses evolutionary change over time, either through increasing centralization or decentralization, whereas the systemic generally tends to be more radical in its treatment of change, either by seeing no change at all or revolutionary breaks. Interestingly, most of the systemic approaches to French center–periphery relations see little change at any time, whether they find a centralized or a decentralized system.

The formal, centralized system

The centralizing views of historical scholars who focus on the formal and legal aspects of center–periphery relations have their counterpart in the work of scholars who "systematize" the historical by describing an increasingly centralized, formal-legal system of center–periphery relations. Primary among these "systemic" scholars is Stanley Hoffmann who found that decentralization in the Third Republic did little more than put groups at its foundations which ensured that it would be a "stalemate society," remote from the "real country." Thus, he insisted that the Republic itself was "a façade behind which the bureaucracy made decisions" and the source of a bureaucratic centralization that continued unchecked into the Fifth Republic. He argued, moreover, that the governmental system as a whole was characterized by a fear of face-to-face relations, which left it incapable of resolving its recurrent crises.[62]

Perhaps the most prominent of such systematizers, however, is Michel Crozier, who elaborated on the above themes in *The Bureaucratic Phenomenon*, arguing that the stalemated French pattern of authority relations led to a cycle of decentralizing crisis followed by centralizing routine in which the ever-present, formal and legal system became ever more powerful. Crozier, more specifically, saw a stalemated pattern in which short periods of crisis, which often translated into greater decentralization and citizen participation, were always followed by long periods of routine when the governmental system, which was alone able to confront the crisis, reemerged stronger than ever to recentralize, to impede citizen participation, and to condemn the mayor to passivity in the face of an all-powerful prefect.[63]

Decentralization, in Crozier's systematization of de Tocqueville's analysis, is thus simply a mechanism contributing for a short time to the reequilibration of an increasingly centralized system. Because of the in-

[62]Hoffmann, "Paradoxes," pp. 8–9, 17, 115.
[63]Michel Crozier, *Le Phénomène bureaucratique* (Paris: Seuil, 1963), pp. 307–17.

creasingly greater distance of the impersonal, centralized authority from the base, this system leads that authority to make decisions increasingly less adapted to the needs of the base and ultimately, therefore, to create the very conditions that lead to a new crisis, which it must then resolve.[64] Crozier concludes that this stalemated pattern of crisis—routine was perhaps adapted to the delicately balanced equilibrium Hoffmann describes for the stalemated society of the Third Republic, but certainly not to the exigencies of a modern state.[65]

Both Hoffmann and Crozier, in brief, see nothing but an overly centralized state from the Third Republic on. By the mid- to late 1960s, however, their systemic accounts were already beginning to be challenged by Crozier's own colleagues and former students. Although not one denied that the formal and legal, centralized system Crozier described was real enough in its outward appearances and in its negative effect on administrative efficiency and cost, they all tended to agree that this could not deny the great amount of local autonomy and freedom involved in the decentralized exercise of power. Their view, to stand Hoffmann's observation on its head, was that bureaucratic centralization was the "facade" behind which local officials would proceed through hidden, face-to-face relations to make decisions in the interests of the locality. And their own systemic arguments suggested that Crozier's mistake stemmed from his failure to distinguish between the formal-legal system – in which the actors' formal roles, as laid out in state laws and decrees and in public rhetoric, suggested a stalemated set of interactions characterized by a fear of face-to-face relations – and the informal system – in which face-to-face relations were carried on behind closed doors (or systems).

Crozier, in other words, described a rigid system of centralization for the French state because he focused on the outward, formal-legal appearances of centralization and ignored the informal, inside relationships promoting decentralization that his own research also uncovered. Had he paid more attention to these informal aspects, instead of characterizing the mayor as a passive nonentity and the prefect as an all-powerful centralizing state agent, he might have seen both, rather, as power brokers and forgers of compromise, who together were engaged in a relationship of complicity that served local interests as much as, if not more than, the interests of the state.

To be fair, however, Crozier changed his views somewhat in response to criticism, even though others did not. In 1967 Crozier agreed that surface conflict did indeed hide underlying complicity; but he remained true to the main thesis of his original argument by insisting that the complicity itself

[64]Ibid., pp. 273–6.
[65]Ibid., p. 310.

resulted in a conservative blockage of the system in which responsibility was diluted, decisions put off indefinitely, and the resolution of difficult problems side-stepped.[66] In the mid- to late 1970s, however, Crozier contradicted his own argument about the recurring and thoroughgoing nature of centralization in the Third Republic and beyond. Thus, in 1979, he insisted that decentralization at the beginning of the Third Republic lasted well into the 1930s and not only provided the most amount of local democracy France had ever experienced, but also proved indisputably that centralization was not irreversible.[67] But even before this, Crozier seemed to find centralization not nearly as thoroughgoing as he had depicted it in the early 1960s. For example, in 1975, Crozier coauthored an article with Jean-Claude Thoenig that redefined centralization as a situation in which Paris was a prisoner of its own system, a system that was itself characterized more by interdependence and confusion than by hierarchy and that benefited the actors in the periphery as much as, if not more than, those in the center.[68] In another article coauthored with Thoenig in 1976, Crozier appeared to tip the scales decisively in favor of the periphery when he maintained that the prefect looked more to the local notables than to the center for guidance.[69]

The informal, decentralized system

Crozier, in short, appears to have taken to heart the critiques of his colleagues and former students; but this is quite understandable given that those critics tended to build on the less formal, more descriptive parts of Crozier's own approach, maintaining that hidden, face-to-face relations occurred alongside the formal denial of such relations. Thus, in 1966, Jean-Pierre Worms was one of the first to provide a theme that has dominated the literature ever since. He noted the complicity between the prefect (as the agent of the state) and "his" notables (as members of the local political elite, encompassing mayors as well as municipal and departmental councilors), who together developed a relationship of interdependence that ensured a measure of local autonomy and power denied by most centralizing theories including, of course, Crozier's.[70] Since Worms' original account of an informal system of center–periphery relations, there has been a proliferation of such "informal systems" theories. By the mid-1970s, Thoenig had found a more elaborate, informal interorganiza-

[66]Michel Crozier, *La Société bloquée* (Paris: Seuil, 1967), p. 101.
[67]Michel Crozier, *On ne change pas le société par décrêt* (Paris: Grasset, 1979).
[68]Crozier and Thoenig, "La régulation."
[69]Michel Crozier and Jean-Claude Thoenig, "L'importance du système politico-administratif territorial," in *Décentraliser les Responsabilitiés*, ed. A. Peyrefitte, p. 8.
[70]Jean-Pierre Worms, "Le préfet et ses notables," *Sociologie du Travail* 3 (July–Sept. 1966): 249–75.

tional system containing a honeycomb structure of interpersonal relations among local elected officials and administrators. In this system, the prefect nevertheless still played the key role by acting as the main conduit through which the periphery influenced the center and by which the center dominated the periphery.[71] And Pierre Grémion described a variety of systems of relations of complicity at the periphery, which in different ways and to differing degrees protected the locality from the incursions of the central authority.[72]

Decentralization in the service of the center. For Grémion, however, there was much less symmetry in the mayor–prefect relationship than for Worms and Thoenig. Where mayors held national office through the *cumul des mandats,* for example, the prefects were less likely to play the pivotal role Worms and Thoenig described for them because the *députémaire,* or mayor, who also held national office as a Deputy of the National Assembly, could always go around the local system and the prefects and straight to Paris for requests. These complicities between mayor and prefect or mayor and Paris were only two of many such relationships. According to Grémion, the complicated interrelationships of actors in the center and at the periphery made it increasingly difficult even to talk about systems of center–periphery relationships. When mayors or members of municipal councils could be presidents or members of departmental and regional councils as well as Deputies, Senators, or ministers, and when the technical field services of the ministries (especially the ministries of finance or public works – and within the latter particularly the DDE) could be strong enough to operate almost independently of the prefects even when the law states otherwise, then the interactions among those at the center and those at the periphery, as well as the distinctions between them, become so complex and numerous that it begins to seem pointless to speak of systems at all. This situation, which Grémion attributed to the many unsuccessful reforms of the Fifth Republic, is in essence why he saw an increasing disequilibration of the informal systems of the center–periphery relations and finally the breakdown of what he called the "Republican model of territorial administration" in favor of a rational corporatist state model that increased state power to the detriment of the locality.[73]

For Grémion, in short, the proliferation of informal systems of center–periphery relations was dysfunctional because it confused actors as to

[71]Jean-Claude Thoenig, "La relation entre le centre et la périphérie en France: Une analyse systématique," *Bulletin de l'Institut International d'Administration Publique* (Dec. 1975): pp. 77–123.
[72]Pierre Grémion, *Le Pouvoir périphérique* (Paris: Seuil, 1976).
[73]Ibid., pp. 423–8, 435–62.

their roles and undermined the structures and proper functioning of the informal systems, thereby returning power to the formal and legal system controlled by the state. The question is, Did this increasing confusion really return power to the state?

Grémion's suggestion that the state benefited from the breakdown of the "Republican model of territorial administration" could only be completely accurate if the state itself had remained a single, integrated system. And this remains to be proven, given that the state was "penetrated" by the periphery as much as the periphery was "penetrated" by the state. If the informal systems of local government were breaking down because of the increasing complexity of relations, the formal system of the central state also must have been breaking down, due to its own increasing size and complexity. (As we shall see below, this is the argument of Thoenig.) But Grémion did not see this. Instead of considering the fragmentation of the state as a result of its many competing ministries and their differing operations and field services in the periphery, he conceived of the state as unitary and thus bought the rhetoric of the state as one and indivisible. Grémion's unitary conception of the state is understandable, though, because Grémion was protesting against the repeated attempts by the government to impose a more rational, corporatist model on the periphery. But whether it succeeded or not is another issue, as is that of whether local government diminished in power as a result of its increasing complexity.

Sidney Tarrow, although agreeing with the basic outlines of Grémion's system, did not find that the increasing complexity of center–periphery relations had worked to the detriment of local elected officials' power, even though he, too, saw an increase in the power of the state. Tarrow argued that the increasing complexity of center–periphery relations had enhanced rather than diminished local elected officials' power, giving mayors a new role as policy broker and mediator between local groups and territorial administrators. But he argued that although this represented an increase in decentralization, because it put mayors at the center of the local system and altered the structure of their interactions with other participants in the informal systems of center–periphery relations, it did not bring with it a democratization of local systems of power. On the contrary, because of their special relationship with the prefects, mayors came to conceive of their role more in administrative than in political terms and to adopt the attitudes and ape the actions of the central administrative system. This decentralization to the benefit of the mayors, therefore, had a centralizing effect and, instead of promoting local democracy, turned out to be in the service of a corporatist, central power.

For Tarrow, more specifically, the local systems of center–periphery relations had changed dramatically as a result of the mayor's new incarnation as a policy broker and mediator. The change from traditional notable to policy broker, Tarrow explained, had to do with "a dramatic replacement of the old politics of personal acquaintance by a new politics of associational groupings, organization activities, and partisan conflict."[74] Especially in larger towns and cities, mayors' political ties were becoming more and more associational, less and less personalistic.[75] Mayors were now mediators between bureaucratic agencies, associations, and interest groups, as well as "administrative activists," who sought aggressively to bring their local projects to fruition.[76] And thus Tarrow maintained: "The basic network at the provincial French mayor's disposition is the informal one he enters by virtue of his complicity with the prefecture, that he reinforces with his involvement in an administrative subculture, and that he energizes by his own administrative activism."[77] That network, moreover, was one that Tarrow, along with Thoenig, found to be dominated by the mayor's special relationship with the prefect who helped protect local autonomy.[78]

For Tarrow, then, mayors had increased powers as a result of their new role, which brought them into contact with local groups as well as with the full range of territorial administrators. But this latter set of contacts, these "institutional and interpersonal linkages . . . become channels for central domination," in the same way as suggested by what Tarrow calls the bureaucratic-integration model of Crozier, Worms, and Thoenig.[79] Put another way, Tarrow argued that the mayors' close contacts with the territorial administration led them to see themselves primarily in an administrative role, especially if they thought of themselves as apolitical on top of that, for example, as in the case of peasant communities.[80] This, combined with the administrative integration of the *dirigiste* French state, drew the mayors into a dependent relationship in which they abandoned partisan politics, took on the technocratic policy preferences of state administrators, supported the status quo, and discouraged the representation of new groups or interests at the periphery.[81] Tarrow discovered, in effect, that the "policy values of higher administrators are passed on by local officials whose local 'game' of discouraging conflict supports their external one of seeking resources from the state."[82] This meant that, contrary to Worms' suggestion, informal complicity did not necessarily

[74]Sidney Tarrow, *Between Center and Periphery* (New Haven, Conn.: Yale University Press, 1977), p. 132.
[75]Ibid., pp. 131–2.
[76]Ibid., pp. 147, 150–1.
[77]Ibid., p. 156.
[78]Ibid., p. 155.
[79]Ibid., pp. 30–3.
[80]Ibid., p. 160.
[81]Ibid., pp. 171–2.
[82]Ibid., p. 230.

render the bureaucracy more flexible; political exchange occurred more within the bureaucracy and therefore made the whole system less vulnerable to partisan politics at the base and less open to local political and social groups seeking to influence policies.[83] Thus, although Tarrow did indeed find decentralization to exist in France, it was in the service of the central power.

Instead of Grémion's assumption that the increasing complexity of the informal systems of local government had directly devolved to the benefit of the central government by diminishing local power, in brief, Tarrow found that this had indirectly devolved to the benefit of the central government, by increasing the power of local officials, who in turn had fallen prey to the centralizing administrative culture of the integrated French administrative state. Tarrow, therefore, also saw the central state, now in the form of its representatives in the periphery, as unitary, and the periphery as multiple. And although he found, unlike Grémion, that the periphery had power, he insisted that it used that power for the most part in exactly the ways the state desired. But did it really? Here, the key question becomes, How sincerely did local elected officials buy the central administrative culture and implement it? In the next chapter, we shall see that the rhetorics of centralization and nonpartisanship were often used by local elected officials to gain and retain as much power for themselves as possible, while enabling them to appear to be powerless next to the central state in the eyes of the public, or to appear to do exactly what was expected of them in the eyes of the representatives of the central administration. Tarrow himself comments on this. So could there not then be a disjunction between what Tarrow's local elected officials did and what they said? Could the dynamic policy brokers who negotiated with everyone so effectively really have been so completely in the service of the central power? Couldn't some have been in the service of the locality, even if they made it appear as if they were not? And isn't it likely that a good number resisted democratization, not so much because they were tied into the central administrative culture, but because they were focused on keeping as much power as possible for themselves.

For Jeanne Becquart-Leclercq, these possibilities and others are encompassed by three different models, or ideal types, of relations at the municipal level between mayors, local administrators, and the local population. Becquart-Leclercq maintained that in only some local governments was decentralization completely in the service of the central power. And she took a much more optimistic view of the increasing complexity in the systems of center–periphery relations, suggesting that they were much more dynamic and capable of democratizing change than Grémion or

[83]Ibid., pp. 38–41.

Tarrow assumed, with the emergence of a third "cooperative-innovative" model of center–periphery relations that could offset the systemic immobility of both the traditional Crozerian model and the "circular-blocked" model of hidden complicity.

Only Becquart-Leclercq's Type I model contained a rigid immobile system characterized by hidden complicity and reflecting the traditional Crozerian view of the mayor as an "island of routine stuck on the past." Here the mayor appeared passive, ineffective, and subordinated to local administration and the *tutelle,* and there was no associational life. Whereas some of the communes Becquart-Leclercq studied took after this first model, the second circular-blocked model of Type II, which took after the Worms-Thoenig-Grémion approach, represented a majority of the communes. In this model the mayor, whose power was personalistic, was more of a paternalistic figure, who took care of particular problems (an *assistant sociale*) and gained legitimacy from his relations with the politico-administrative system rather than with the local electorate. Finally, a few of the communes studied contained the cooperative-innovative model, or Type III, which encouraged citizen cooperation and participation, and provided open access to power. Here the mayor had communal support, shared power with the municipal council, and allowed for evolutionary change.[84] (Tarrow's model, considered in terms of this typology, would include elements of Type III in what would still be essentially a Type II view. Although appearing to encourage citizen cooperation and participation, mayors in fact denied local groups any real access to power and looked more to the politico-administrative system than to their constituents for legitimacy.)

For Becquart-Leclercq, although most of the relations between the mayor and the local administration remained part of a closed system of complicity hidden from public view reflecting Types I and II, the presence of relations corresponding to Type III in even a few communes suggested that a new set of relations was developing in the periphery. Whereas traditional advice was ordinarily elicited on an individual and even clandestine basis, the new relationship gained its advice from groups in an open manner. Rather than having only informal channels of communication, through one-on-one interactions (if that), a new manner of circulation of information was occurring through meetings of commissions made up of all concerned, that is, mayors, civil servants, politicians. Instead of decisions made outside the mayor's purview, to be received as a verdict, they were made in the course of collective negotiations.[85] And this new set of relations in the third type of commune, Becquart-Leclercq

[84]Jeanne Becquart-Leclercq, *Paradoxes du pouvoir local* (Paris: Presses de la Fondation Nationale des Sciences Politiques, 1976), pp. 122–51.
[85]Ibid., p. 164.

argued, may even have been changing what happened in the first two types.[86]

According to Becquart-Leclercq, then, the changes apparent in the 1970s were not the cause for alarm that Grémion maintained. On the contrary, Becquart-Leclercq presented a more positive, dynamic view of a more open system of local government than did either Tarrow or Grémion, in which at least some mayors who benefited from an increase in power shared this power with the new groups they represented in the periphery, thus opening up, rather than blocking, access to decision-making processes. Her arguments were to some extent supported by others as well, most notably by François Dupuy and Thoenig who, although writing in 1985 after the advent of Socialist decentralization, summarized the results of research based primarily on the period before the reforms.[87]

Decentralization in the service of the periphery. Dupuy and Thoenig found a highly decentralized, politico-administrative system that actually managed to function reasonably well. Despite the fact that it was somewhat costlier and less efficient than it needed to be, it did in truth serve the interests of the local population. They contended that French administration was a universe in pieces, which gained its unity from the political world external to it and its legitimacy from the diversity of local agents' interpretations of national rules and regulations. The local politico-administrative system, in consequence, was much more open to local influence than the "circular-blocked" model would lead one to believe and much less integrated into the central administrative system than Tarrow suggested.

[86]To illustrate this, Becquart-Leclercq outlined a complex structure of the communal system in which each of several dimensions, or "zones" (for example, legitimacy, social integration and regulation, power and organization, social dynamics), contained a continuum between the two models of the traditional, closed, blocked system and the newer, open, cooperative system. In this complex structure, the zone of legitimacy went from, among other things, a delinquent and apathetic community to one of support and mobilization; the zone of social integration from traditional communities with pressures to conform, unconscious and confused rules of the game, and rejection of outsiders to differentiation of interest groups and clarification of cleavages; the zone of politics and organization from bureaucracy, hierarchy, blocked communication, rigid rules, and clandestine compromises to cooperation, decentralization and diffusion of power, clarity and suppleness, and instant feedback; and the zone of social dynamics from the status quo and defensive games designed to retain positions gained to one of change and innovation. And any commune could be at one end of the continuum or another on any zone. Ibid., pp. 169–73.

[87]François Dupuy and Jean-Claude Thoenig, *L'Administration en miettes* (Paris: Fayard, 1985). For a good summary in English of the basic outlines of the system described herein, see François Dupuy, "The Politico-Administrative System of the Département in France," in *Centre-Periphery Relations in Western Europe,* ed. Yves Mény and Vincent Wright (London: George Allen & Unwin, 1985), pp. 79–103.

When informal rules counter formal roles

French administration, Dupuy and Thoenig maintained, has its own rigidly stratified, hierarchical system of organization and a honeycomb structure of internal relations that together impede cooperation and communication among actors at different levels of hierarchy. In this system, the lower ranks of the administrative pyramid tend to be almost impervious to central control and more responsive to outside relations at the bottom than to inside directives from the top. This results in part from the fragmentation of a system in which administrators are differentiated into fifty or sixty different categories – as part of state, departmental, and auxiliary services and as part of different civil service grades and corps – and in which there is a clear sense that the lower levels can never move up into the higher levels of the hierarchy.[88] In brief, because the lower level agents generally find themselves isolated within the administration, they frequently turn to the external environment for support and end up more often than not representing the interests of the people they serve rather than those of the state.

Administrators in the system outlined by Dupuy and Thoenig have better communication with the outside than they do internally or interorganizationally. Although agents are protected from the public, and thus need not focus their attention on the outside, they themselves see great value in increasing their external contacts. And the more contacts they have, the more amenable they are to making special arrangements that do not exactly follow the letter of the law or, put another way, to being flexible in their interpretations of the rules or legal texts.

Ironically enough, this flexibility in interpretation of the law is facilitated by the elaborate sets of rules and regulations formulated by the center in order to control its agents in the periphery. Because such rules and regulations are generally abstract and often contradictory, they in fact allow local administrators great room for maneuver in finding innovative solutions to the problems they encounter. Many local administrators (but by no means all), already focused on the outside and interested in satisfying their clients, are quite happy to take advantage of this and to seek innovative solutions to problems not anticipated in the legal texts. But although such solutions create satisfied customers, they do not promote the better functioning of the system as a whole. Such solutions are all reached on a case-by-case basis and are never diffused throughout the organization. In part this is because it would require communication with the upper levels of the hierarchy and in part because such solutions are illegitimate to the extent that they contradict the civil servant's formal charge to apply the law equally and uniformly.[89]

[88]Dupuy and Thoenig, *L'Administration*, p. 41.
[89]Ibid., pp. 55–61.

The system, nevertheless, does allow for a great deal of public access, however inefficient it may be. And this access is itself organized hierarchically. At every level, administrators come to represent the interests of their clients, with the agent at the *guichet*, or counter, representing the public; the bureau chief acting as ambassador of those mayors whose dossiers he administers; the prefect identifying himself with the future of "his" department, especially when dealing with Paris. In certain cases, a local administrator may even do for the outside environment what he cannot do inside, by serving as an interlocutor for local mayors who do not communicate among themselves. Typical, according to Dupuy and Thoenig, is the case of "Jean," the head of the basic subdivision of the DDE, who performed an integrative function in the locality by engaging in face-to-face relations with the different mayors who did not communicate among themselves. He was acting as an entrepreneur in his attempts to satisfy his "clients" and come up with a satisfactory set of local land-use plans. But the more such functionaries focus on putting order on the outside and thus become part of local systems of interrelations, the less controllable they are by the hierarchy, and the more the administrative system falls apart.[90]

French administration, thus, is extremely fragmented, not only in its internal structure and organization but also in its external relations. And yet, Dupuy and Thoenig argued that the administrative system does not therefore fall apart. For, they insisted, it is held together from the outside by the political world, which is much less rigidly stratified and atomized and much more communicative and cooperative than the administrative world. It is the integrators of the political system, the *cumulants* who hold numerous elective offices at the national as well as local levels, who act as integrators of the administrative system, too.[91] Here, too, access is organized hierarchically, with each notable communicating with his or her respective level of administration. Thus, the prefectoral corps is in contact with the general councilors and other "personalities" of the department; the middle managers are in contact with mayors, communal agents, and other administrators; and the *agents d'éxécution*, or case workers, are in contact with the greater public.[92]

For Dupuy and Thoenig, in brief, the political world acts as the unifier of the administrative world. And the two worlds together form a complex politico-administrative system of interpersonal relationships that transcends formal structural boundaries to include *cumulants*, functionaries of the field services of the state and of the prefecture, as well as general councilors, mayors, and other local notables. Such a system, Dupuy and

[90] Ibid., pp. 121–7.
[91] Ibid., pp. 128–47.
[92] Ibid., pp. 45–51.

Thoenig concluded, makes France "not a democracy of election," but rather, "a democracy of access."[93] As such, this politico-administrative system, according to Dupuy and Thoenig, manages to function in a reasonably decentralized manner. It serves the interests of the local population despite the fact that its indirect system of communications makes it somewhat costlier and less efficient than it need be, because the political and administrative actors manage through their informal interrelationships to transcend the system's formal structural boundaries and even to turn its dysfunctions to their advantage.

By the 1970s, then, most scholars agreed that local elected officials had a good deal more power within the context of the informal systems or networks of relationships than suggested by the traditional, centralizing, systemic analyses that focused on the formal and legal system alone. But they disagreed as to how much power the central administration retained and how much substitution of open communication for hidden complicity had occurred. Grémion and Tarrow found that the proliferation of local circuits of power had devolved to the benefit of the central administration and had not much altered the hidden complicity, Dupuy and Thoenig argued the opposite, and Bequart-Leclercq found, at least in certain cases, with Dupuy and Thoenig.

One of the reasons for such differences in analysis, as Dupuy and Thoenig themselves explained, has to do with their focus on the interdependent relations of actors in systems consisting of the organization and its environment, by contrast with approaches that focus first and foremost on the structures of the organization and only secondarily, if at all, on its environment. Thus, Dupuy and Thoenig criticized organizational discussions that look at structures in order to understand how they function, maintaining that only a systems discussion is flexible enough to see beyond the formal structures to the actual problems, to what actors do to resolve them, and to the subsystems that may even operate autonomously.

Dupuy and Thoenig contrasted in particular Worms's account of the prefecture as an organization isolated from its environment with their own account of a politico-administrative system of interpersonal relations that transcends the particular organizational universe and the formal structural divisions, and in which the environment of the organization is as, if not more, important than the organization itself.[94] They illustrated this point with a lengthy discussion of the transport system. Instead of seeing the public sector and its agents in the center, with the public at the periphery in this system, they found that a centrifugal force is operative, which pushes local administrators themselves to the outside

---

[93]Ibid., p. 161.
[94]Ibid., pp. 180–4.

of the circle, and that the rules and regulations applied by administrators become part of the game played by the public. Here, regulation is only one small part of the system and does not have a central place except in the minds of administrators thinking of themselves as ensuring the public interest.[95]

In short, the main difference between Dupuy and Thoenig on the one hand and systemic scholars such as Worms, Grémion, and Tarrow, to say nothing of Crozier, on the other, is the weight the former give to the environment. In other words, so much depends on how the system itself is conceptualized, where its center is found, what its boundaries are, and which actors are seen as within its purview. Draw the boundaries of the system narrowly, with a focus on how the local political actors relate to the local representatives of the central administration (Worms), or draw them somewhat more broadly, with an emphasis on how the local political and administrative actors relate to one another within increasingly complex local systems (Grémion, Tarrow), and one is bound either to undervalue the importance of what is going on outside the system or to overestimate it, simply because it is outside the system. But draw the system as even more complex, bring in the environment that includes the larger public as well as the central administration as part of the many subsystems, and the weight of evidence swings the account in favor of local power and access. Here, the center becomes peripheral, the periphery central.

By considering all the actors in a system that includes the environment, Dupuy and Thoenig were in effect able to consider the real impact of the state, writ large, in the periphery. Their major contribution was to demonstrate that the state was not nearly the unitary and centrally controlling entity Grémion and Tarrow assumed. But Grémion and Tarrow, along with Becquart-Leclercq, with their closer focus on the ways in which mayors and prefects in particular operate, still provide important insights into this aspect of the informal systems of local government. If mayors do not act completely in the service of the central power, because the agents of the central power do not necessarily serve it completely, then it stands to reason that their administrative activism ensures even more real decentralization for the periphery than Tarrow suggested, even if not quite as democratic as Becquart-Leclercq expected.

Yet to be explained, however, are the glaring differences in analysis, not simply between those who differ over the nature of the informal systems, but also between those who see formal centralization in local governmental systems and institutions and those who see decentralization in the informal systems and processes of local government. This has

[95]Ibid., pp. 194–209.

something to do with confusions resulting from the great disjunction between the decentralizing practice and the centralizing laws and language. But to understand this, we must examine the role the rhetorics of centralization and nonpartisanship played in perpetuating the myth of formal centralization, while protecting the practical reality of informal decentralization.

7

Rhetoric versus reality in local government: Local politics and administration before the Socialist Fifth Republic

What people say is often as important as what people do. Saying is also a form of doing. Sometimes it adds understanding to what people do, other times it hides what people do from themselves as well as from others. How people say what they say, and to whom they say it, moreover, may very well alter the sense of their words, which may thus mean different things to different people. So it was with the rhetoric surrounding the issue of decentralization.

The reality of French local government, as we have already seen in the previous chapter, was that local elected officials had a great deal of hidden power and authority, both political and administrative. But these officials were the last to admit this, using a rhetoric that instead suggested they were essentially powerless next to the central and centralizing state, and apolitical next to the political and politicizing national government. With this rhetoric, in effect, they threw up a wall of words to obscure the reality of an informally decentralized and politicized periphery.

With the rhetoric of centralization, more specifically, local elected officials strove to hide their complicity with local administrators from public view. By complaining about the administrative centralization of the state and its financial stranglehold over local authorities, they sought to draw attention away from the reasonable amount of administrative freedom and financial resources their complicity afforded them. By blaming the prefect and the central government for unpopular decisions as well as for the inefficiencies or inequities of local government, they endeavored to escape responsibility for their own administrative actions and political decisions.

With the rhetoric of nonpartisanship, local elected officials also attempted to dissemble their own political leanings and actions. By proclaiming themselves apolitical, they sought to appeal to the electorate across party lines while allaying their fears of patronage and political favoritism. By claiming to be neutral, they endeavored to reconcile their political allegiances with their administrative functions and to mask any political cleavages that might interfere with their relationship with local administrators.

The use of the rhetorics of centralization and nonpartisanship should help explain why most administrative historians focused on the formal institutions of local government, seeing only centralization in center–periphery relations; and why early systems analysts have taken the formal and legal system at face value. By paying more attention to what local officials said than to what they did, they underestimated the impact of politics on the local balance of power and overlooked the informal practices that reinforced decentralization. It was the rhetoric of centralization – not reality – that made local elected officials appear completely powerless next to the central state; and it was the rhetoric of nonpartisanship – not reality – that made them look totally apolitical.

A wall of words, then, kept the actions of both local elected officials and administrators hidden from outside view. Words, nevertheless, can reflect a variety of underlying realities – as any good ordinary language analyst would tell us. And the words, or "language games," involving centralization and nonpartisanship, therefore, need not represent simply a protective cover for local officials. In fact, the rhetoric of centralization also reflected the day-to-day frustrations of local officials confronted with the formal and legal realities of centralization. First of all, these realities contributed to tremendous administrative inefficiences and costs. Secondly, they always left the door open to political interference from the center, something about which countless local elected officials, especially in the opposition, constantly complained. In partial response to this situation, the rhetoric of nonpartisanship served local elected officials as a way of minimizing the dangers of such central political interference and of facilitating their relations with local administrators.

The result of all this was a local governmental system that left local elected officials and administrators reasonably content. By the 1960s and 1970s, however, the situation was changing with the increasing politicization of the periphery and the breakdown of the rhetoric of nonpartisanship in the cities, in which the right's political use of the rhetoric, together with the left's political rejection of it, served to undermine the rhetoric. The bulk of local notables in the small towns and villages, however, still resisted change. And they continued to express themselves in one way while acting in another.

THE RHETORIC OF CENTRALIZATION

Because it served so well the interests of both local elected officials and administrators, the rhetoric of centralization, which constantly made ref-

erence to the formal and legal system, remained even though decentralization had been the informal rule since the Third Republic. With this rhetoric of centralization, mayors could always publicly blame the prefects for
unpopular decisions, which they themselves privately supported, and the
prefects could always play the same game by blaming the central government. Meanwhile, the mayors could be certain to influence the prefects'
decisions in matters of local interest in exchange for ensuring that the
prefects could count on the mayors' cooperation in matters of prefectoral
interest.

In engaging in this rhetoric, local elected officials focused their protests
on two main themes: the administrative overcentralization of the state
and the financial stranglehold the state had over the localities. Thus, they
made a point of complaining about the formal institutions of local administration without, however, publicly noting the satisfaction they received
from being able to work around those institutions to get their own way.
And similarly, they would decry the increasing financial burdens the state
imposed on the periphery and the many formal restrictions on their actions without mentioning the fact that they had the benefits of state
monies and a reasonable leeway in spending their funds.

As part of this rhetoric, local elected officials often used the arguments
developed in the legislature to protest the incursions of the central authority in the periphery and to demand greater local freedom and autonomy.
This was especially the case when they themselves were legislators as a
result of the *cumul*. And whereas big-city mayors depicted themselves as
constantly fighting the monolith of the state, the rural mayors claimed to
be the victims of central neglect or completely dominated by the subprefects who monitored their every move.

The rhetoric of centralization benefited local elected officials by enabling them to exercise much greater informal power and authority than
the law allowed. It threw up a wall of words that essentially protected the
informal systems of center–periphery relations discussed in the previous
chapter, making it possible for local elected officials and administrators
to use centralizing language in the context of their formal roles, while
engaging in decentralized practice in the fulfillment of their duties.

But although this disjunction between language and practice had certain advantages such as making the decentralized practice of local government practicable, it also had a number of disadvantages. Primarily, it
adversely affected the efficiency and effectiveness of local administration
at the same time that it left local governments subject to prefectoral
control and vulnerable to central political interference. Thus, the rhetoric
was not simply "rhetoric"; it also represented a protest against the realities of centralization.

Rhetoric versus reality in local government

The administrative overcentralization of the state

It is almost impossible to read any book about local government or to consult any survey of the attitudes of local elected officials without finding the overall focus to be on the negative effects of the administrative overcentralization of the state. Among national politicians as much as among local elected officials, administrative centralization was blamed for just about every problem facing local government. By the 1970s, it seemed as if everyone was demanding the democratization of everyday life, the decolonization of the provinces, and the debureaucratization of government. Much of this, however, was really empty rhetoric on the part of local elected officials who were quite satisfied with the hidden reality of a local governmental framework in which they got their way much of the time.[1]

The discourse in the center. For the past century, the administrative overcentralization of the state has been a major theme, as the legislative debate beginning in the 1890s clearly shows. By the 1970s, however, this theme had become the primary focus of discussion. The radical calls for "decolonizing the provinces" and "debureaucratizing the state" echoed in the society at large and in the legislature. But the very success of these views was also in some ways their failure, because they were taken up by all groups, including those opposed to reform, and in the end sounded like empty rhetoric. Even the most radical of recommendations had become, in the words of Yves Mény, "banalities consumed" by all sides, and adopted by the mass media.[2] In the meantime, the rhetoric of administrative overcentralization was generally used as a way of avoiding responsibility by all. The blame, however, was distributed differently depending upon the groups.

The left blamed the government, and in particular the political party in power for the overadministration. The conservative party in power, by contrast, as often as not blamed the "administration," writ large, meaning the technocrats of the central bureaucracy. But, as Mény pointed out, it was generally the very politicians who had come out of administration, graduates of the National School of Administration, the ENA, such as Jacques Chirac and Valéry Giscard d'Estaing, who were some of the

---

[1] In response to the question, Are you in favor of a real decentralization of the administration of public affairs? 52 percent of local elected officials from communes of fewer than fifty thousand inhabitants (N = 68) and 63 percent of departmental and local civil servants (N = 191) declared themselves unfavorable. (Crozier and Thoenig, "La régulation," p. 19 n. 41.)
[2] Mény, "Partis," p. 96.

strongest voicest in favor of diminishing the power of the central administration.[3] One wonders if this was not another part of the old game: Complain loudest about that about which you can, or will, do the least. After all, these were the same people who resisted decentralization reforms, despite the fact that decentralization was clearly the one sure way of diminishing the power of the administration.

Most illustrative, perhaps, is the exchange between Alain Peyrefitte and Michel Debré. Peyrefitte, in *Le Mal français*, complained that "political power is the prisoner of administrative power," and that the bureaucracy was in control.[4] The response from Debré, the proponent of centralization, was telling. He insisted that the administration was not in power because it prepared and executed decisions made by the politicians, but that, "if you talk to me about bureaucracy, technocracy, or *énarchie,* it is because the political authorities have been negligent in their duty."[5]

Debré was right, of course; the politicians were negligent in their duty. Because they were for the most part *cumulants,* their interest as local elected officials was to resist decentralizing reforms that, as legislators, they would be assumed to support. But in another sense, Peyrefitte was right, because the civil service was still very much in the center of opposition to reform. As Ezra Suleiman explained, the *grands corps* saw any decentralization as a threat to its autonomy, its elite status, and its power in the periphery. He concluded: "When one considers the *interests* involved in a continued centralization of the state apparatus, one understands why decentralization has been confined (and consigned) to political rhetoric."[6]

What one cannot understand is why the administrators turned politicians did not make common cause with local elected officials to decentralize and to diminish the power of the civil servants of the central bureaucracy, unless one recognizes the differing realities or interests underlying the rhetoric. As we have already seen with the legislative debates, the politicians were in fact ambivalent about decentralization. The ruling majority generally saw it as not in their political interest. Moreover, much of the time this majority could use the central administration to do their bidding. They railed against the bureaucrats, in other words, as often as not because they depended upon them so much to do their bidding. This was especially true in the Fifth Republic, because the ruling party didn't control a majority in the periphery.

[3]Mény, "Partis," pp. 114–15.
[4]Peyrefitte, *Le Mal,* pp. 3–5.
[5]Cited in Peyrefitte, *Le Mal,* p. 286. For an insightful discussion of the exaggerated rhetoric of Peyrefitte with regard to the centralization of the French state, see Ezra N. Suleiman, "Administrative Reform and the Problem of Decentralization in the Fifth Republic," in *The Impact of the Fifth Republic on France,* ed. William G. Andrews and Stanley Hoffmann (Albany: State University of New York Press, 1981), p. 78
[6]Suleiman, "Administrative Reform," pp. 70–4, 76.

The discourse in the periphery. By the same token, the local elected officials complained about overcentralization and the control exercised by local bureaucrats; they saw them in many ways as the emissaries of the central government in the periphery. And yet, these civil servants served as a buffer for the local elected officials against the central government. Because of the complicity that had grown up in the periphery, it was rarely one's own prefect who was the problem, it was the central ministries. The prefect, after all, was necessary for the local notables to be able "to take credit for what is done and to avoid blame for what is not done." But by the same token, the prefect needed the local notables, without whom he could not accomplish his own ends.[7]

Behind the public rhetoric of centralization, in short, was the cozy reality of a prefect, along with other representatives of the center in the periphery, who protected local elected officials' interests in exchange for their cooperation. This was illustrated by local officials' response to questions about their attitudes toward local administrators in survey after survey. For example, in a study that helped crystallize the informal systems approach to center–periphery relations, Crozier and Thoenig found that 91 percent of mayors accumulating one or more mandates and 60 percent of those with only one mandate agreed with the statement that "at every opportunity, they [departmental administrators] don't hesitate to defend local interests against Paris," by contrast with 9 percent of the former and 40 percent of the latter, who agreed that "they do what Paris tells them with little concern for local interests."[8] Although the vast majority of those mayors with a lot of clout saw local administrators as acting in their interests, a sizeable majority even of those with minimal clout did, too.

There was some difference in mayors' attitudes toward the prefectoral institution per se, however, as a result of the size of the commune; the mayors of the smaller communes were most content with the institution, and big-city mayors, the least. Thus, Tarrow found in his study of mayors in smaller communes that they saw the prefect concerned as much with protecting the rights of the community as with implementing national policy. A not atypical attitude was that of the mayor who declared: "If there were no prefect or subprefect, there would be no more local autonomy."[9] Similarly, Crozier and Thoenig noted that among local elected officials from communes with fewer than fifty thousand inhabitants (N = 62), 67 percent considered the existence of the prefectoral institution to be an advantage, whereas among big-city mayors (N = 15), 73 percent, or 11 out of the 15, found it an inconvenience.[10] This disjunction results

---

[7]Worms, "Le préfet," pp. 262–3.
[8]Crozier and Thoenig, "La régulation," p. 12 n. 26.
[9]Tarrow, *Between Center*, p. 155. See also idem, "Decentramento," p. 242.
[10]Crozier and Thoenig, "La régulation," pp. 17, 21.

from the fact that big-city mayors increasingly tended to go to Paris for their needs and had little to do with the prefect, by comparison with the mayors of the smaller cities, towns, and villages. With the exception of the big-city mayor, then, local elected officials had a very positive attitude toward the prefect.

This attitude was evident not only in local elected officials' responses in academic surveys but also in governmental surveys that sought their views on local governmental reform. Most telling, perhaps, is the response in the consultation over regional reform in the fall of 1968 to the question about who should be the executive power in the region. Of the local elected officials and others (including, for example, representatives of unions, chambers of commerce and agriculture, the professions, industry) responding to the question, 80 percent favored a new regional prefect and only 1 percent wanted the executive of the region elected by universal suffrage. (The only other solution to gain much support was the election of the regional executive by the Assembly. The workers' unions preferred this by a majority of 51 percent – but the overall support for this measure was only 11 percent.)[11] Most suggested that preference for a regional prefect went without saying, and no one even alluded to the unused possibility offered by the Constitution of 1946 for the departmental president to become the executive power. Thus, the general council of Yonne, reflecting the views of all respondents except the workers, declared that "the French solution, which consists in having the prefect execute the deliberations of the General Council and the preparation of the latter's work, has amply proven itself." And it argued against the executive's election by universal suffrage on the grounds that this would be dangerous because it would "taint the institution with federalism."[12]

The prefects, in short, retained a special place in the hearts and minds of local elected officials in the periphery, and understandably so, given the prefects' long-standing power, however much they sought to minimize it. Since the Third Republic, in effect, the prefect had been portrayed as "less of an arbitrary hierarch and more of an urbane mediator between central and local government" or "less an incarnation of central authority and more an architect of concerted action between all the

[11] Of the 80 percent, 72 percent agreed that the prefect should serve the region alone, with only 2 percent wanting the prefect to serve the department as well. Other responses were: 11 percent favored the election of the regional executive by the Assembly, 2 percent wanted state appointment of the executive on recommendation by the Assembly, 7 percent preferred two executives consisting of the prefect and an elected official, and 10 percent preferred two executives consisting of the prefect and a council. See Tables XLVII and XLVIII in Jean-Luc Bodiguel, "La consultation régionale," in *La Réforme régionale,* ed. J. L. Bodiguel et al., pp. 148–9.
[12] Ibid., pp. 191–2.

prevailing social and political forces who are willing to play the game." Increasingly through the 1960s and 1970s, the rhetoric of the prefects downplayed the powers they had over local elected officials through the *tutelle*, emphasizing instead their ability to mediate. But although the prefect in role sought more to cajole, consult, and persuade than to command, the prefect's ability to command remained, to be used whenever necessary.[13] The consultative or mediative posture taken by the prefect was essentially the mystification Jacques Chevallier described as part of the "participative state."[14] In the participative state, it was the prefect more than anyone else who determined who would participate and on what terms.

After all, the prefect still had the powers of the *tutelle* over local authorities. But it was used to varying degrees with differing effects. Whereas the *tutelle* over persons, that is, the ability to suspend or revoke mayors and municipal councilors, was so rarely used as to constitute no impingement on local democracy whatsoever, the *tutelle* over acts, which could take the form of a substitution for the decisions of the municipal council, their annulment or their prior approval, was used in the first two instances quite rarely, in the last on a regular basis. But in all three instances of the *tutelle* over acts, the *tutelle* itself served the purposes of local elected officials. In the first two cases – that is, the *tutelle* as substitution, ordinarily employed when a municipal council voted a budget in deficit (budgets by law have to be balanced) or refused to pay for the increasing number of state-mandated expenses, and the *tutelle* as annulment, allowable only when a decision was illegal because it was outside of a legal meeting of the municipal council, was beyond its jurisdiction, or in some other way was a violation of the law – the exercise of the *tutelle* was often deliberately elicited by municipal councils. When that occurred, it was vigorously protested by the municipal council, mainly to generate publicity against fiscal constraints in general or against the actions of the prefect in particular.[15]

By contrast, the *tutelle* as prior approval, which affected such actions as the conferring of building permits, went comparatively without comment. The smallest communes upon which this *tutelle* fell the heaviest tended to welcome it. Here the interaction was essentially one of "local coadministration by local authorities and the central power," given that the technical services of the state would prepare and implement the deci-

---

[13] Jack Hayward, *The One and Indivisible French Republic* (New York: Norton, 1973), pp. 23–4.
[14] Jacques Chevallier, "L'Intérêt général dans l'administration française," *Revue Internationale des Sciences Administratives* vol. 41, no. 4 (1975).
[15] For a full account of the different *tutelles*, see Mény, *Centralisation*, pp. 260–4.

sions of the mayors as well as judge them when rendering advice to the prefect in the context of the *tutelle.*[16]

The public rhetoric, however, was often different from what rural mayors would admit in private. For example, most rural mayors complained loudly about the fact that, because they only had first signatory power over building permits, building projects often changed drastically by the time they received final approval from the prefect, on advice from the technical services of the state. Every rural mayor had a story of the *direction départementale d'équipement* (DDE), or departmental services for infrastructure, coming in, six months behind schedule, to build an eyesore – for example, an ugly new concrete wall to replace the crumbling stone wall in the seventeenth-century cemetery. Despite this problem, rural mayors generally found that this system itself proved an opportune way to avoid responsibility for their actions in a particularly sensitive area. After all, who would want the responsibility of turning down a friend's application for a building permit? It was much easier and safer to arrange things with the prefect and the field services of the state, letting them take the heat for any negative decisions. Often such arrangements were worked out very well indeed, in particular with the prefect, as in the case of the mayor in the Lot who would write favorable (*oui*) with a small first letter if he were opposed to granting a building permit and with a capital letter (*Oui*) if he were truly in favor.[17] As one rural mayor put it: "The *tutelle* of the state, in the end, isn't as bad as all that. It allows me to be counseled and to be covered if I make a mistake. I don't have any desire to be free."[18]

The *tutelle,* in short, enabled rural mayors to blame the prefect and the field services of the state for any unpopular decisions regarding local development and to take credit for the popular ones, even when credit wasn't necessarily due. When it came to inaugurating the new swimming pool, it was always the mayor who was to be congratulated for his foresight, despite the fact that the central ministries were responsible for making available the monies for any locality that applied and for pushing so hard that the end result was an overabundance of swimming pools. The *tutelle* for rural communes clearly served the interests of all involved, from the members of central ministries on down to rural mayors.

The larger communes were little affected by this *tutelle.* Here, the *tutelle* could have been very heavy indeed, because these communes were

[16]F. P. Bénoît, *Le Droit administratif français* (Paris: Dalloz, 1968), p. 147, cited in Mény, *Centralisation,* p. 263. See also Paul Bernard, *Le Grand Tournant des communes de France* (Paris: A. Colin, 1969), p. 229, cited in Mény, *Centralisation,* p. 263.

[17]Jean-Pierre Requier, mayor of Martel, departmental councilor of the Lot, and regional councilor, interview with author, Martel, Aug. 3, 1989.

[18]Quoted by Crozier and Thoenig, "La régulation," p. 16 n. 35.

the ones experiencing the most urban development activity. Instead, they were essentially let alone because they were judged to have the technical capability to manage on their own. In reinforcement of this judgment, the legal requirements of this *tutelle* progressively diminished for the larger communes through reforms during the Fifth Republic.[19]

Even at the regional level, the *tutelle* was not as heavy-handed as some local elected officials argued, despite the fact that the central government itself was more wary of the regions than of the two regular levels of local government. Although the state did use its powers of *tutelle* to annul some of the decisions of regional councils, it closed its eyes to any number of legal actions that were equally doubtful. Thus, it annulled in January 1974 the Limousin regional council's institution of extraordinary sessions and its creation of regional services under the authority of the president and in December 1978 the Provence-Alpes-Côte d'Azur regional council's granting of subsidies to the regional unions of the CFTC and the FEN. It let stand, however, such questionable decisions (according to the *Cour des comptes* in its annual report of 1979) as using monies designated for public works projects for the financing of wine fairs (Bourgogne) or for subsidizing the cost of skiing equipment for regional ski committees (Franche-Comté).[20] The Limousin's action, moreover, was motivated by reasons similar to those at the municipal level: to gain public support for an end to certain constraints, in this case, those limiting the powers of the region and its ability to have technical services of its own attached to the regional council.

The one clear exception to the diminution in the *tutelle* was Paris, which had been under special statutes and the strict control of the state since the Third Republic, to say nothing of the period before that, stretching back to the Revolution. Paris, although itself the symbol of centralization, was the city most adversely affected by centralization. In addition to having more *tuteurs,* that is, the prefect of Paris, the prefect of police, along with one or more ministers, Paris was subject to a heavier *tutelle* and had an essentially powerless municipal council. Moreover, the state services could act with uncontrolled autonomy, creating such problems as the seemingly planned but in fact uncoordinated development of Paris, for example, the Montparnasse tower and the Défense area.[21]

The prefectoral *tutelle,* then, with the exception of Paris, was not overly constraining in most cases, especially because the prefect had

[19] Mény, *Centralisation*, pp. 260–4.
[20] Charles Vigoroux, "Quelques éléments pour un bilan des E.P.R., C.G.P.," *Service régional urbain* (Nov. 1979), discussed in Pierre Sadran, "Les accommodements avec la loi de 1972," in *La Décentralisation, Cahiers français*, no. 204 (Jan.–Feb. 1982), p. 33.
[21] See Mény, *Centralisation*, pp. 278–85. See also A. Grioterray, *L'État contre Paris* (Paris: Hachette, 1962), p. 284.

become "domesticated," entering into the local game or the informal system of relationships in the periphery, as discussed in the previous chapter. The technical *tutelles* of the field services of the state, by contrast, were heavier, especially because protests against them by local elected officials could not be used effectively to garner public support, given that the public couldn't see them and national politicians didn't really have much knowledge of them either. Such *tutelles*, moreover, involved not only substantive matters but also procedural ones: for example, the larger urban agglomerations were constrained by such a *tutelle* simply by having to follow the complex technical procedures for fulfilling the requirements of the planning contracts of urban districts with the state.[22]

Generally, local elected officials preferred to deal with the prefect over and above the agents of the field services of the state. Tarrow's mayors, for example, retained their special relationship with the prefect, despite their increasing interaction with the agents of the field services of the central ministries, with 75 percent of those gaining "special favors" receiving them from the prefects by contrast with 17 percent from the agents of the field services. In the view of one mayor, the generalist prefect was preferable to the technicians of the field services, who "impose a project on you and give you twenty-four hours to accept it."[23] The problem for this mayor, as for many others, was that the agents of the field services of the state were less "domesticated" than the prefect.

Grémion's lament about the breakdown of the republican model of administration due to the proliferation of the field services in the periphery very much reflects the views of those mayors who valued most their relationship with the prefect. It is important to remember, however, as Dupuy and Thoenig have pointed out, that the agents of the field services of the state were also very much in the business of serving local interests.[24] And the *tutelle* of the field services of the state, in consequence, was not as extreme as many made it out to be.

Over the course of the Fourth and Fifth Republics, local elected officials had been "domesticating" even the agents of the state in what was becoming increasingly a three-way game between local elected officials, prefect, and technical agents of the state. Although local elected officials did tend to prefer their relationship with the prefect over those with the agents of the field services of the state, they nonetheless cultivated a close relationship with the latter in an effort to counter the powers of the

[22]Mény, *Centralisation*, pp. 265–6.
[23]Tarrow, *Between Center*, pp. 136–7.
[24]See the discussion in Part II, Chapter 6, "Decentralization in the service of the periphery."

former and to ensure against any two-way, prefect–field services relationship that could cut out local elected officials. Thus, local elected officials protested vigorously against the technical *tutelles,* in particular that of the Ministry of Finance, as attacks on communal liberty. However, when it came to giving prefects more power, by creating a regional prefect and by giving departmental prefects more deconcentrated authority over the field services of the state, local elected officials were equally concerned about losing "this *tête-à-tête* with the heads of these services, this contact which is everyday life."[25]

Despite the rhetoric of overcentralization, then, the individuals who embodied that overcentralization in their very persons were held in high regard by the local actors most responsible for the rhetoric. And this was because those local actors had a highly satisfactory interaction with them – so much so that most had little wish to change the situation through decentralizing reforms. Crozier and Thoenig noted that, in response to the question, Are you favorable to a real decentralization of the administration of public affairs? 52 percent of local elected officials from communes of fewer than fifty thousand inhabitants (N = 68) and 63 percent of departmental and local civil servants (N = 191) declared themselves unfavorable.[26]

French mayors, in effect, took great satisfaction in their administrative roles, indicating that their interaction with the local administration was not nearly the nightmare the rhetoric suggested. Crozier and Thoenig found that, in response to a question about whether they found the situation in the administration of public affairs satisfying, 67 percent of local elected officials from communes of fewer than fifty thousand inhabitants (N = 86) and 75 percent of the functionaries of the state (N = 198) answered in the affirmative.[27] Similarly, Tarrow discovered that close to 50 percent of French mayors in his study mentioned administrative experiences as their most agreeable experiences in public life (next to only 29 percent for Italian mayors), whereas only 14 percent mentioned such experiences as their worst (compared to 27 percent of Italian mayors). And he found that 55 percent of French mayors felt the highest degree of administrative satisfaction with their job (by comparison with only 28 percent of Italian mayors). For Tarrow, this demonstrated the French mayors' integration into the administrative culture, with the most highly satisfied mayors being those who were the most activist administratively and who had the highest frequency of administrative contacts. For us, it

[25]Speech by Abel-Durand. XXXIII Congress of the Assembly of Presidents of General Councils. *Départements et Communes* (Sept.–Oct. 1963), p. 14, cited by Mény, *Centralisation,* p. 306. For the three-way relationship, see ibid., pp. 304–7.

[26]Crozier and Thoenig, "La régulation," p. 19 n. 41.

[27]Ibid., p. 20 n. 44.

also indicates that, despite their rhetoric about the unresponsiveness of the central administration, mayors themselves recognized that they had a good deal of power and ability to get things done. This was evidenced even by their comments; one mayor remarked that his job was rewarding, despite the tremendous amount of bureaucratic red tape he had to go through, because "it's you who are the boss."[28]

Mayors, in brief, felt a good deal more powerful and effective in their jobs than the rhetoric would suggest. This was also apparent from the fact that, in their efforts to get their own way, many felt they were able to pressure the prefects, by threatening to resign or to take legal action. Moreover, when this did not work, mayors looked outside the confines of the strict mayor–prefect relationship for support. Thus, whereas many conservative mayors looked to Paris for support, the Communists tended to count on the local population to back them up in their demands.[29]

Mayors were not the only ones whose powers were hidden behind the rhetoric of centralization. At the departmental level, too, there was a great deal of negative rhetoric hiding the reality of close relations and the powers of a local elected official who, in this arena, was not even the executive power. The relationship between the president of the general council and the prefect was similar to that between the prefect and the mayor, in which the president showed aggression toward the prefect but each nevertheless listened carefully to the other, acting and perceiving their roles in complementary ways, playing games that were complementary and reciprocal.[30] Power was in a real sense divided between the two; so much so that in the response to a question asking local notables from rural villages or small towns (N = 132) to list the five people who "counted most in the department," the prefect and the president were in the first two slots 83 percent of the time, with a larger percentage going to the prefect when functionaries answered (53 percent for the prefect to 38 percent for the president), and a larger one going to the president when those with political connections answered (37 percent for the prefect, 46 percent for the president).[31]

A similar phenomenon was evident even in the regions consecrated as public establishments in 1972. The regions followed the pattern of the departments in terms of center–periphery relations and financing, with its elected officials gaining important political weight and, with this, tipping the balance of power in favor of the periphery. In fact, the *Conseil économique et sociale* (CES), successor of the CODER, found itself marginalized, left out of the decision-making processes for the most part,

[28]Tarrow, *Between Center*, p. 145.
[29]Ibid., p. 147.
[30]Thoenig, "La relation."
[31]Crozier and Thoenig, "La régulation," p. 13 n. 27.

with no joint meetings with the executive bureaus or invitations for their representatives to participate in the meetings of the regional council.[32]

Local elected officials at every level of local government, in short, felt quite powerful and effective in the performance of their duties, despite the rhetoric of centralization. But this is not to say that local elected officials therefore had no good reasons for using the rhetoric, or that it was simply a way to take credit even where it was not necessarily due for the positive while avoiding responsibility for the negative consequences of their actions. Although French mayors were not dissatisfied with the local system as a whole, they were indeed impatient with bureaucratic delays and rigidities, and they justifiably complained about projects denied authorization, difficult functionaries, and the government's policies of financial stringency.[33]

The rhetoric of centralization, in effect, also reflected local elected officials' day-to-day frustrations with the formal and legal realities of centralization, which still left the prefect in a position of control and increased the administrative inefficiency of local government. For even when the prefects only mediated and barely exercised their *tutelle*, thus leaving local elected officials a great amount of local autonomy, the legal reality of centralization represented a continuing source of administrative inefficiency. The formal laws and decrees ensured that, even if administrative decisions and budgets were agreed upon at the local level, they still had to mount the hierarchical ladder to Paris for rubber-stamp approval before they could be implemented. And this meant that the formal and legal aspects of centralization, even though empty of much real content in terms of the exercise of power, nevertheless created administrative nightmares such as time-consuming paperwork, bureaucratic foul-ups, and start-up delays on projects at the local level. Even representatives of the central government in the periphery complained about this, using the rhetoric of centralization themselves to avoid responsibility for the bureaucratic foul-ups and excess paperwork.[34]

The discourse of local administration. The administrative inefficiencies resulting from the rhetoric of centralization, however, did not only have an impact on local projects, it also affected the very practice of local administration. Dupuy and Thoenig have argued that because local administrators generally accepted the assumption behind the centralizing rhetoric that a unified state, based on principles of uniformity and equal-

---

[32]Vigoroux, "Quelques éléments," p. 31.
[33]Tarrow, *Between Center*, p. 152.
[34]Dupuy and Thoenig, *L'Administration*, pp. 62–3. For further detail about these problems, see Part II, Chapter 6, "The formal centralization of local governmental institutions."

ity before the law, was necessary and legitimate, most saw their decentralizing actions as illegitimate, thus ensuring that such action would never lead to generalized rules of administrative behavior. The resulting inefficiencies, however, were not enough to spur reform, because they, too, could be part of the elaborate game of words designed to obscure local officials' cooperative action.

Dupuy and Thoenig, more specifically, contended that the traditional rhetoric, which referred to the unity of French administration and based the legitimacy of administrative action on principles of uniformity and equality in the local application of rules and regulations formulated by the central ministries, tended to increase the fragmentation of the French administrative system while denying it any possibility for regeneration. They maintained that the traditional rhetoric masked a tremendous amount of diversity as well as inequality in the application of the rules and regulations. Because rules formulated by the central administration to ensure uniformity and equality before the law were generally abstract and often contradictory, they in fact allowed local administrators great flexibility in finding innovative solutions to problems, which, in their very innovativeness, denied the principles of uniformity and equality contained in the rhetoric. But rhetoric is one thing, reality another. In a curious twist, Dupuy and Thoenig found that, because these solutions represented similar kinds of special arrangements, they actually provided for greater equality of treatment – despite surface inequalities – than would any strict adherence to the letter of the law.[35] The rhetoric, as a result, masked a reality in which administrators, in violating the principles embedded in the rhetoric, in fact promoted the very equality before the law that the principles called for. But administrators themselves could not see this, taken in as they were by their own rhetoric, which made them see their own actions as illegitimate.

Paradoxically, then, the legitimacy of the system, as determined by its satisfied customers, depended upon the diversity of interpretations of the law by local administrators who, because they were themselves steeped in the rhetoric of uniformity and equality, assumed their own actions were illegitimate. And this sense of illegitimacy, added to the lack of internal communication and cooperation in the administrative system, ensured that innovative administrative action responsive to local needs and interests would never lead to generalized rules of administrative behavior.

Dupuy and Thoenig, in short, offered something of a backhanded compliment to French administration. Although it was a failure, an administration in pieces when judged in terms of the rhetoric, it was nevertheless quite successful in reality. But that reality was one that left local

---

[35]Dupuy and Thoenig, *L'Administration*, p. 259

administrators in an unhealthy position, subject to feelings of contradiction and frustration because they could not operate efficiently. It was also one that would subject the administrative world to continuing problems, given the paradoxes that were unlikely to be resolved as long as civil servants conceived of their roles and structured their work in one way while acting in another.

By comparison the political world had few problems. The very problems that left local administrators frustrated and incapable of operating efficiently were the ones that left local elected officials in a position of strength, because they were the fixers of the system. Local elected officials, in brief, benefited from the weaknesses of the local politico-administrative system, because they acted as integrators of the administrative world from the outside, avoiding responsibility for any of its inefficiencies while taking the credit for solving any and all of their constituents' problems. But given this, it raises the question as to how much sincerity there was to local elected officials' protests against the formal and legal system of centralization.

The rhetoric of the administrative overcentralization of the state did in fact represent a protest against the realities of formal centralization, but a protest that did not demand significant change in the local governmental framework. Local elected officials clearly did feel empowered and powerful within the context of center–periphery relations. And they quite naturally bridled against any limitations on their power. Thus, they complained about the central state and its representatives in the periphery. But, for all that, they would not change the situation: they were quite satisfied with things as they were. This was equally true of their view of local finances, despite the rhetoric that suggested that the state had a financial stranglehold over local governments.

The state's financial stranglehold

Local elected officials' complaints about the financial stranglehold of the state over local government had two major components. First, they insisted that they did not receive sufficient resources from the state and, second, that the state itself exercised too much financial control over local government. Although there is much truth to the complaints, in both cases local governments nonetheless had a good deal more money and flexibility than their public rhetoric suggested.

In the first place local elected officials benefited from the fact that the central government was unable and, in some sense, unwilling to contain the costs of local government. The legal reality of centralization not only ensured the administrative inefficiency of the decision-making processes of local government; it also added indirectly to the costs of many of the resulting decisions. With the central government the ultimate authority in all financial matters, local officials generally had few incentives to be fiscally responsible. They could always take the credit when their inflated budgetary requests were approved, whereas they could always lay the blame on the central government when their budgets were cut or their special projects denied funding.

The prefects themselves, moreover, were as much to blame for the rapid rise in the cost of local government as anyone else. For they engaged in the practice of *saupoudrage,* or diluting the impact of public monies by giving a little bit to all askers, by approving or preparing budgets more with an eye to gaining the cooperation of local notables than to ensuring cost-effective local administration. The Paris ministries, in a politically rational but economically irresponsible move, were themselves guilty of a similar kind of *saupoudrage* when it came to the requests of big-city mayors or other nationally important notables, for whom they provided subsidies in exchange for votes.[36]

Even the technical field services of the state were guilty of such *saupoudrage,* with those technicians charged with recommending construction projects never failing to add extras to the project or to propose additional and often unnecessary work. In many departments, rural pathways and secondary roads were kept in perfect condition even when they were barely used, simply because the engineers of the state wanted to keep busy and prosper (given the percentage they received in royalties from any project of which they were in charge).[37] Sometimes the engineers of the state even went to the mayors in rural communes at the time of their budget deliberation and advised them on the public works the commune ought to fund for the following year.[38] All of this was very hard to stop, even had local governments wished to do so. Although since 1949 local governments could by law choose private architects or other public engineers to

[36]Hayward, *One and Indivisible,* pp. 20–1.

[37]The income can be substantial, legally up to double that of an engineer's base salary. See Michèle Champenois, "Les ingénieurs de l'État, mercenaires des communes," *Le Monde,* Apr. 16, 1977. Champenois explains that local government pays into a departmental treasury honoraria calculated on the basis of 4 percent for projects costing less than 20,000 francs; 3 percent between 20,000 and 200,000 francs; 2 percent between 200,000 and 1 million francs; and 1 percent for any amount above this. The money is then distributed based on a hierarchical scale ranging from an index of 4 for a foreman to 80 for the chief public works engineer. The result is that, for construction work completed in 1973 and paid for in 1975, the averages paid ranged from 51,000 francs for the head engineer, 37,000 francs for the regional public works engineer, 26,000 francs for the departmental public works engineer, 5,000 francs for technical assistants, and up to 3,000 francs for the foreman. For first-class general engineers, honoraria represent 28 percent of their income. At the higher ranks it is 41 percent, which nearly doubles the base salary.

[38]J. de Savigny, *L'État,* p. 57.

draw up and implement local projects, they had to receive the approval of the technical services of the state as a result of the *tutelle*.[39]

The regions followed the model of the departments in local finances, also engaging in the practice of *saupoudrage*. The regional council became a super general council, disbursing funds equally among the different departments. For example, in the Auvergne until 1979, all four departments received the same amounts for snow removal, regardless of need or size of department. In Languedoc-Rousillon regional funds for road work were divided as traditionally by departments, half across the board, half prorated on the basis of population.[40]

Local governments, in brief, benefited handsomely from the fact that the central government did not contain costs effectively. But this did not stop local elected officials from complaining that there was too little money to go around. And although their criticisms were justified in the sense that there was never enough money (there never is), local governments nonetheless did have significant amounts of money at their disposal.

Local budgets grew rapidly both in terms of administrative and investment expenditures from the 1960s on, even outdistancing the state in certain areas. From 1962 to 1981, the growth in expenditures by local governments was remarkable, going from 4.5 percent of the GNP in 1962 to 23 percent in 1981, with an average increase of 5.7 percent per year.[41] Moreover, although the overall growth in expenditures was only slightly more rapid than that of the state, at 32.9 percent for local authorities versus 30 percent for the state (in constant francs from 1973 to 1978), the 15.8 percent increase in investment expenditures for local authorities contrasts greatly with the 7.9 percent decrease in the state's capital expenditures (in constant francs from 1973 to 1978). Local administrative expenditures, in addition, rose by 42.7 percent (in constant francs from 1973 to 1978) by contrast with the 36 percent rise for those of the state. Finally, whereas in 1973 public investment by local authorities was only slightly higher than that of the state, at a little over half of the overall amount spent, by 1978 close to two-thirds of public investment was by the local authorities[42] (Table 7.1). By 1980, moreover, the amount spent by local authorities had increased to 75 percent of all public investment.[43]

[39]Mény, *Centralisation*, pp. 267–71.
[40]Vigoroux, "Quelques éléments," pp. 32–3.
[41]Jean-Christophe Donnellier and Janin Quettier, "Les comptes régionaux des administrations publiques locales de 1962 à 1981," *Archives et Documents* no. 179 (Sept. 1986): 12–13.
[42]Ministry of Economy and Finance, "Les comptes des collectivités et des établissements publics locaux," *Statistiques et Études Financières* no. 387 (Feb. 1982): 26. See also Robert Delorme and Christine André, *L'État et l'économie* (Paris: Seuil, 1983).
[43]Commission du Bilan, *La France en mai 1981*, vol. 5. *L'État et les citoyens* (Paris: La Documentation française, 1981), p. 270.

Table 7.1. *State and local government expenditures, 1973 and 1978*

	1973	1978	Overall variation (%) in constant francs 1973/1978
Expenditures of the state (civil)	183,744	397,002	+30.0
Administrative expenditures	158,657	358,567	+36.0
Capital expenditures	25,087	38,435	-7.9
Expenditures of local authorities	89,636	198,051	+32.9
Administrative expenditures	59,269	139,610	+42.7
Investment expenditures	30,367	58,441	+15.8

Source: Ministry of Economy and Finance, "Les comptes des collectivités et des établissements public locaux," *Statistiques & Études Financières* no. 387 (Feb. 1982): 26.

Among local authorities, the departments experienced the greatest percentage increase in expenditures, at 45.2 percent in constant francs between 1973 and 1978 by contrast with the communes' increase of 26.5 percent (including the urban communities but not counting Paris or the syndicates of communes or urban districts). Paris was the only local authority that actually experienced a decrease in expenditures, going down by 11.2 percent in constant francs between 1973 and 1978. The figures may be deceptive here, given the reorganization of the city as of 1977 into two administrative entities, a city and a department. Even before this, however, the budget of Paris grew quite slowly, rising on average 9.6 percent per year between 1973 and 1976 by contrast with an average growth rate of 18.3 percent for the other communes and 18.7 percent for the departments during this same time period. Most importantly, the communes had the largest amounts of money, at 50.5 percent of the total budget for local authorities in 1973 compared to the departments' 24.7 percent and at 48.1 percent of the total in 1978 compared to the departments' 26.9 percent. If one were to add in to the communes' budgets the expenditures of the syndicates of communes and the districts, at 8.1 percent in 1973 and 9.5 percent in 1978, the communes would come out even further ahead. The regions, by comparison even with Paris, let alone the communes and departments, gained and retained only a very small and relatively insignificant part of the total, with their 1.2 percent in 1974 reaching only 2.1 percent of the total in 1978.[44] (Fig. 7.1, and Table 7.2)

It is small wonder, therefore, that the strongest complaints about lack of resources came from the regions. With the regional reforms of 1972,

[44]Ministry of Economy and Finance, "Les comptes des collectivités," p. 27.

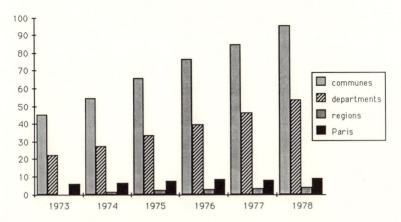

Figure 7.1: Local government expenditures (in billions of francs). Source: Ministry of Economics and Finance, "Les comptes des collectivités et des établissements public locaux," *Statistiques & Études Financieres* no. 387, (Feb. 1982): 27.

most local elected officials were rightly disappointed with the limited resources made available. Moreover, the fact that most of their monies were to be raised by additional local taxes rather than through the transfer of state resources, as anticipated in 1969, left many regional councilors unhappy. It led a number of regional councils to balk at raising taxes to the maximum allowed by the government, insisting that the government should itself pay for the projects it wanted. Even when the regions did take full advantage of the resources available to them, though, the amount they gained was extremely inadequate. Consider that in 1975 the projected budget of the department of the Nord was to exceed slightly that of all the regions put together.[45]

Despite the inadequacy of the regional reform in terms of the amount of money it provided, we should not forget that it represented a new source of funds for the regional authorities. Regional budgets for investment (leaving out the Paris region), quadrupled in a very short period, going from 575 million francs in 1974 to 2,370 million in 1978, reaching more than 3 billion in 1979; and they averaged a 25 percent increase per year after the initial 50 percent increase from 1974 to 1975.[46] The regions, however, were not the only ones to benefit financially from reforms. Every time local finances were reformed, the communes and departments benefited.

[45]Wright and Machin, "French regional reforms," pp. 16–18.
[46]Catherine Guillermet, "Les politiques et stratégies des établissements publics régionaux à travers leurs choix budgétaires," in *Centres et périphéries: Le Partage du pouvoir*, ed. Yves Mény (Paris: Economica, 1983), p. 48.

Table 7.2. *Expenditures of local authorities according to category, 1973 to 1978*

	1973			1974			1975		
	Fr.[a]	%[b]	Growth[c]	Fr.	%	Growth	Fr.	%	Growth
Communes[e]	45.2	50.5	16.7	54.3	50.0	20.1	65.5	49.4	20.6
Departments	22.1	24.7	11.2	27.1	24.9	22.6	33.3	25.1	22.8
Paris	6.0	6.7	2.5	6.4	5.9	7.3	7.3	5.5	13.7
Regions[f]	--	--	--	1.3	1.2	--	2.06	1.5	58.2
Régies[g]	1.5	1.7	12.5	1.8	1.7	22.3	2.3	1.7	22.7
Syndicates & districts[h]	7.3	8.1	22.6	9.6	8.8	31.5	12.1	9.1	26.1
Other	7.5	8.3	35.2	8.1	7.5	8.1	10.2	7.7	25.8
Total	89.6	100.0	16.7	109.0	100.0	21.4	133.0	100.0	22.2

Source: Ministry of Economics and Finance, "Les comptes des collectivités et des établisse-ments publics locaux," *Statistiques & Études Financières* no. 387 (February 1982): 27.
Notes: [a] Francs in billions. [b] Percentage of total budget for local authorities.
[c] Percentage increase over previous year. [d] In constant francs, 1973-8. [e] The figures include urban communities, but not syndicates of communes, districts, or Paris.

The communes and departments both made substantial gains as a result of particular local tax reforms. For example, the value-added tax (VAT) introduced in 1966 looked like a form of state recentralization because it replaced the local tax on commercial transactions with direct state payments of a given proportion of revenues (based on a complex formula of sharing and redistribution, VRTS). It was, however, more generous financially than the previous system because it increased at a faster rate than inflation. To this was added the 1979 VAT compensation fund (FCTVA), which was promoted by big-city mayors and local elected officials on the left and reimbursed local authorities for the VAT they paid two years before on capital expenditure. Thus we find "a genuine block grant for capital expenditure, given on an 'open-ended basis' and at a uniform rate, which tends to place a *prime à béton,* or premium on concrete (meaning construction), and therefore benefits the richest communes, because they are the ones that tend to invest the most."[47]

Moreover, the January 1979 consolidation of government subsidies into a single, overall operations appropriation (*dotation globale de fonctionnement*) for local governments was a significant resource for local governments, given that the appropriation grew more rapidly than government resources and represented more than 34 percent of the resources of the communes and departments. This situation was only en-

[47]Mény, "Local Authorities," pp. 192–4.

Table 7.2 *(cont)* *Expenditures of local authorities according to category, 1973 to 1978*

1976			1977			1978			Overall variation*d*
Fr.	%	Growth	Fr.	%	Growth	Fr.	%	Growth	
76.2	48.7	16.3	84.5	48.5	10.8	95.2	48.1	12.6	+26.5
39.4	25.1	18.2	46.4	26.6	17.9	53.4	26.9	15.0	+45.2
8.4	5.3	14.8	7.8	4.5	-6.4	8.8	4.4	12.4	-11.2
2.7	1.7	32.5	3.4	2	26.2	4.1	2.1	20.3	---
2.6	1.7	15.7	3.03	1.7	16.0	3.5	1.8	15.6	+40.1
15.4	9.8	27.1	16.2	9.3	5.0	18.7	9.5	15.9	+54.3
12.0	7.7	18.1	12.9	7.4	7.5	14.3	7.2	10.7	+14.9
157.0	100.0	18.2	174.3	100.0	10.2	198.1	100.0	13.6	+32.9

Notes (cont): *f* For the regional public establishments, the 1974 figure takes into account the first 15 months of operation. *g* Régies are autonomous public or semi-public organizations established by communes or departments. *h* The syndicates of communes numbered 11,487 in 1973, 15,491 in 1978. The districts numbered 131 in 1973, 162 in 1978.

hanced by the January 1980 measures adjusting local taxes and introducing the principle of progressive taxation, providing for the reimbursement of the VAT payable by local governments on investment expenditures, and easing the process of getting loans, particularly for communes with fewer than ten thousand inhabitants.[48]

The overall local taxation system, however, was never fully reformed. Therefore, however generous the central government was in its piecemeal changes, the overall system remained a serious problem, if only in its complexity. Over time, this system, with its *quatres vieilles*, or four main local taxes, (housing tax and land taxes on built and unbuilt property), had left the communes cash poor. They were also left in a weak borrowing position, because lending was controlled indirectly by the state, which, by denying grants to the *caisse des Dépôts*, forced it to create "waiting lists" for loans to the communes (thereby keeping state subsidies down to between 14.7 percent and 11.7 percent of total local investments).[49] At the same time, local taxes themselves increased; between 1975 and 1979, they went up 30 percent in constant francs, with local taxes going from 24 percent to 35 percent of all direct taxes.[50]

[48]Mény, "Central Control," p. 209.
[49]Mény, "Local Authorities," pp. 192–4.
[50]Max Querrier, "Collectivités libres ou corrois de transmission?," *Projet* no. 142 (Feb. 1980): 166; Odon Vallet, "D'abord, entrer dans la vie des communes," *Projet* no. 142 (Feb. 1980): 152.

Within these limitations and despite their public complaints, however, local elected officials were generally quite content with the financial resources at their disposal. At the same time that local elected officials protested against the weight of the *charges*, or state-mandated expenses, encumbering them, they showed great satisfaction in being indispensable to the state's action, often taking credit for the successful completion of local projects.[51] Tarrow's mayors, for example, although complaining about their lack of financial resources as much as their lack of administrative control, nonetheless tended to get a good deal of job satisfaction. Typical was the mayor who, although complaining that "the costs are insupportable," "there are no credits to be had . . . our possibilities are very limited . . . you have to cry for months for the 15 million old francs," nonetheless concluded that, in the end, "it's a good sort of job when there aren't the difficulties we have now."[52]

Although local elected officials were clearly more satisfied than they would publicly admit with the amount of money at their disposal, they were not at all happy about the amount of financial control exercised by the state over local authorities. The fact that the state collected local taxes and determined the formula for distribution to local governments was on its own enough, they felt, to demonstrate its influence on the direction of local spending. Add to this the system of subsidies, which according to J.–J. Servan-Schreiber was a source of "irresponsibility, waste, inefficiency" and which in the words of J. de Savigny "organizes mendacity" by making local governments go begging to the central government for funds, and the power of the central government over local governments becomes clearer.[53] Finally, put the prefect's a priori review powers over the communal budget on top of this, and how could anyone imagine that the commune was anything but under the iron thumb of Paris?

Local officials' complaints were in many respects on target. The system of subsidies did place the communes in some sense into the hands of the central power. Even the relatively modest participation of the state in communal public works allowed it tremendous influence, because any such participation gave the state the power to modify the technical characteristics of the project as well as to determine its completion date. And the commune could not blithely refuse such subsidies, because there was a close relationship between receipt of the subsidy and acquiring a loan from the public lending institutions (*caisse des dépôts et consignations, caisses de crédit agricole*) that were expected to extend most of their loans

[51]Mény, *Centralisation*, pp. 308–9.
[52]Tarrow, *Between Center*, p. 146.
[53]Servan-Schreiber, *Pouvoir régional*, p. 32; and J. de Savigny, *L'État*, p. 155.

to subsidized public works projects. What is more, accepting such loans subjected local governments to strict controls by agents of the Treasury.[54]

For departmental officials, too, the system of local financing through subsidies symbolized state centralization. This is basically why, in the consultation over regional reform in fall 1968, numbers of general councils especially opposed subsidies from the central government. They preferred instead a system that would have given the region the bulk of its resources by the transfer of state receipts. (At the same time, however, they were not enthusiastic about a regional tax either, recognizing that any such tax would cut into the revenues of the other levels of local government.)[55] As it turns out, the regions did not have to worry so much about state control through a system of subsidies, because their revenue was based on a regional tax. They faced another kind of indirect control, however, this time exercised by local governments.

A serious limitation for the regions was the fact that they had to act in concert with other public entities and couldn't take any initiatives in organizing projects and in funding them on their own. This meant there were tremendous delays in the spending of regional monies, because the regions were dependent upon the decisions as well as the administrative and technical means of the local authorities they were subsidizing, leaving some regions such as the Rhône-Alpes with more money unspent than in their annual budgets.[56] Moreover, although the regions found their hands tied by this and other restrictions on their financing of projects, the state did not honor the restrictions on its own actions, even when the law required that the regional council decide on a proposed action. Thus, the decrees of 1976 transforming certain regional consultative powers into decisional ones for particular state credits failed to make much difference, because most often the reports on state grants grouped advice and decisions in the same document.[57]

Clearly then, local elected officials were most concerned about the potential influence the state could have over the local policies and projects simply through the disbursement of funds. And this was, of course, one of the realities of the formal and legal system of centralization. The French policy elite could in fact guide the direction of local development simply through its choice of priorities in such areas as public works. Thoenig, for example, noted that when policy-makers pushed for swimming pools and industrial zones, the mayors all wanted to have them, leading to a situation in which there were too many industrial zones and

---

[54] Mény, *Centralisation*, pp. 271–2.
[55] Bodiguel, "Consultation," pp. 166–79.
[56] Vigoroux, "Quelques éléments," p. 30. See also Guillermet, "Les politiques," pp. 48–53.
[57] Ibid.

unmaintained swimming pools.[58] The kinds of projects Tarrow's mayors claimed as their highest achievements, moreover, were those encouraged by the French state. Those mayors who demonstrated the greatest administrative activism and complicity with administrators, those typically in the large, rapidly growing, middle-class communities most favored by the French state's policies toward the periphery, were the ones who succeeded in getting major capital building projects for their communes, as well as more in the way of social services and housing.[59]

The question here, of course, is whether all of this means that local elected officials were in fact led by the state, with the state imposing policies and disbursing or withholding funds from on high, or rather that they acted in conjunction with the state for the determination of what were the necessary local services and projects to be funded. Certainly, the swimming pools are an example of the former, with small, rural communes being especially dominated by state policies because they had few resources of their own. The proletarian and farming communes were indeed, as Tarrow argues, discriminated against by the state, with the rapidly growing, middle-class communes benefiting the most from the state's preference for growth, concentration, and services.[60] With all this said, what remains unclear is how the policy decisions favoring one or another kind of project were made. After all, the prefects in the periphery and the agents of the field services of the central ministries were often providing the information and assessments that were to become the data upon which later policy decisions were based. And these local civil servants, as already discussed, were very much part of the complicity in the periphery. They were therefore likely to couch local projects in terms that made them look like ones that fit into national priorities, even if they didn't quite fit. What is more, the mayors of the larger cities were in any case able to act outside this system, influencing policy and getting special projects funded, even if these were not ones on the preferred list.

Even the state control of local finances, then, looms less large when one considers how it may have been attenuated by the complicity in the periphery. But there is one area in which it remained a serious issue for local elected officials: the political. The state's financial control always left open the possibility that the central government would use its financial powers over local governments politically, to the detriment of local elected officials, especially when they were members of the opposition. This in particular goes a long way toward explaining Gaston Defferre's support for decentralization in 1982. For as a Socialist confronted with a conservative government for nearly a quarter of a century as well as a big-

[58]Thoenig, "La relation."
[59]Tarrow, *Between Center*, pp. 160–1.
[60]Ibid., p. 171.

city mayor left in large measure out of the center–periphery complicity, Defferre claimed to have good reasons for being concerned with political interference.[61] And such interference did occur, if not always in the ways anticipated, for example, when Giscard d'Estaing proposed a large-scale development project of 15 billion francs encompassing three regions in the southwest in 1979 that was calculated to woo voters away from the left.

With the decline of planning in the 1970s, moreover, the proliferating planning contracts with the cities, midsized towns, and suburbs were increasingly used politically, as vehicles for patronage if not for electoral purposes. They were a way of reinforcing the power of the prefects over and against the *cumulants,* as well as of controlling to which side governmental money went. When Michel Poniatowski was Minister of the Interior from 1974–6, prefects were even asked to indicate the political "color" of the municipalities. The Guichard commission, in commenting on this politicization of the planning contracts, stressed that "the contractual policy all in all gives good political results. The temptation to use the contractual procedure to give government action better impact is a very real one."[62]

The legal realities of the state's financial centralization, then, always left open the door to political interference from the central government. And the rhetoric of centralization, therefore, reflected not only politicians' frustrations with the formal-legal reality of centralization, which added to the administrative inefficiencies and costs of local government, but also their constant fears of political interference and their resentment of it when it did occur. Local elected officials, though, did find a way out of this latter dilemma by making recourse to another kind of rhetoric, that of nonpartisanship.

THE RHETORIC OF NONPARTISANSHIP

Local elected officials generally used the rhetoric of *apolitisme,* or nonpartisanship, to avoid central political interference as well as to appeal to the local electorate across party lines, allaying its fears of patronage and political favoritism. The rhetoric of nonpartisanship, however, was also a strategy designed to enable local elected officials to move more easily into the apolitical administrative culture and to mask the political cleavages that could undermine any relationship between them and state-appointed administrators. After all, what better way to get what you want, especially if you are in the opposition, than to cultivate an appearance of

---

[61]Gaston Defferre, interview with the author, Paris, May 23, 1985.
[62]Cited in Mény, "Central control," p. 213.

neutrality when dealing with the prefect? The prefects, in turn, were quite happy to play this game, to appear as impartial mediators, although it became increasingly difficult for them to maintain this fiction. All of this, by the way, was facilitated by the fact that local elected officials are even called *élus*, or "the elected," rather than politicians to encourage the appearance of nonpartisanship. Similarly, local citizens were for the longest time called *les administrés*, or the administered, and local government was always termed "local administration" to downplay the political aspects of local life.

The rhetoric of nonpartisanship, however, did not reflect a nonpartisan reality, because it served to mask both local political cleavages and national political allegiances. But it did serve as a convenient rhetorical tool, ensuring local elected officials' power and reinforcing their working relationship with the local administration. As a result, the rhetoric of nonpartisanship acted as one more building block in the wall of words, combining with the rhetoric of centralization in such a way as to allow local and national elected officials and administrators to work together effectively, without fear of alienating the local electorate, the central government, or even one another. But if this worked so well, why change? The problem, as Jacques Caroux explained it, was that the complicity at the periphery was one that "can function only by bypassing central state rule and local populations."[63] The local populations, in fact, were less and less willing by the 1970s to be bypassed, whereas the central state was more and more unhappy with the complicity that denied them control over local government while increasing its costs. The periphery itself, moreover, had been changing: its increasing urbanization and industrialization had brought a radicalization of the rapidly growing cities in which the left, winning election after election, was no longer willing to play the nonpartisan game.

The discourse of local elected officials

Local elected officials, especially in the smaller towns and villages, used the rhetoric of nonpartisanship as a political strategy to allay their constituents' fears of the problems attendant upon local politics, that is patronage and political favoritism, and as an administrative strategy to facilitate their relations with the prefects and other representatives of the state in the periphery. At the departmental level, the rhetoric of nonpartisanship was as much a political strategy similar to the mayors' as it was a legal requirement. But here, no one was fooled as to the politics of the locally elected officials, because national political allegiances normally

[63]Caroux, "End of administrative centralization?" p. 108.

were kept just below the surface, with decisions generally based on majoritarian politics. What is more, over time even the rhetoric of nonpartisanship of the mayors, especially in the cities, began to lose any credibility, as the national government increasingly sought to polarize local elections, all the while continuing to use the rhetoric of nonpartisanship. As the rhetoric of nonpartisanship began to lose its effectiveness, a new rhetoric began to appear, the rhetoric of good management, pioneered by the Communists, who used it for the same reasons that more conservative mayors had used the rhetoric of nonpartisanship: to allay their constituents' fears of the problems attendant upon local politics.

Nonpartisanship in the communes and departments. Over the course of the century, a large number of mayors presented themselves in increasingly nonpartisan terms in their electoral campaigns – especially in rural and midsize communes as well as in the more conservative urban communes. They tended to describe their jobs as essentially technical and administrative rather than political.[64] But this in no way meant that local government was not intimately tied to national partisan politics. The rhetoric of nonpartisanship certainly fooled no one as to the politics of the candidates and the national political implications of the process. National politics have in fact played a significant, albeit sometimes undocumented, role in local elections, despite the "rhetoric of nonpartisanship" that, as Kesselman puts it, "asserts that political principles are irrelevant to whatever activity local governments conduct."[65]

National political cleavages were ever present at the local level. Although nonpartisanship may have been used as a strategy to overcome such cleavages, therefore, it could not in fact deny their existence. In his 1967 electoral analysis of the Fourth Republic, Duncan MacCrae concluded that national political cleavages played themselves out on the local level to a significant degree and that "politically important ties are more likely to go beyond the town in France rather than to unite it," even though some consensus may be possible on local issues, as Kesselman has maintained.[66] Similarly, in his 1977 study of center–periphery relations, Sidney Tarrow used electoral data to show that the mayor's political allegiances, although traditionally left unstated in local elections, especially in rural communes, nevertheless reflected those of the community at large in national elections.[67]

[64]This is confirmed by numerous studies, including: Crozier and Thoenig, "La régulation," p. 9 n. 23.
[65]Mark Kesselman, *The Ambiguous Consensus* (New York: Knopf, 1967), p. 8.
[66]Duncan MacRae, *Parliament, Parties, and Society in France 1946–1958* (New York: St. Martin's Press, 1967), pp. 259, 261 n. 80.
[67]Sidney Tarrow, *Between Center,* p. 40.

In a 1976 study of midsize communes in the Nord, moreover, Jeanne Becquart-Leclercq, using the statistical results of a survey of attitudes of mayors in forty midsize communes in the Nord, made much the same point as Tarrow and MacRae. She showed that, despite nonpartisan labels in local elections, that the electorate was well aware of the political affiliations of the candidates and often voted accordingly, whereas nonpartisanship represented a façade used to mask real cleavages and to appeal to the community as a whole through its "service" ideology.[68] Jollivet and Mendras found a similar politicization in rural communes.[69] Even Lawrence Wylie, whose case study of a village in the Vaucluse described the apolitical nature of local election results and suggested that personality rather than party politics was at play, made clear in the course of his discussion not only that everyone was aware of the candidate's party affiliations but also that the elections themselves always produced a left-wing majority, in keeping with the traditional voting history of the Vaucluse.[70]

For some scholars, however, the rhetoric of nonpartisanship reflected a certain kind of reality at the communal level, giving mayors local power while denying them national political importance. Henry Ehrmann, for example, agreeing with those scholars who saw a significant amount of decentralization in center–periphery relations, insisted that the mayor, rather than being condemned to passivity by the prefect, "emerges as the powerful executive which law and custom permit him to be."[71] But for Ehrmann, the mayor's power came in large measure from the fact that he was a nonpartisan force accepted as such by the *tutelle* authorities as much as by the local population. And this was despite the fact that local elective office was generally the route to national power in a partisan role, and that the Deputy mayor often used his national position to gain advantages for the locality.[72] Mark Kesselman, similarly, in his study of small town mayors maintained that the mayor was a local autocrat "remarkably free of institutional constraints," who used "the rhetoric of *apolitisme* to avoid open conflict and engineer harmony in the commune."[73] With this, the mayor was able to create the "ambiguous consensus" based on a fictional view of the community that would help him to

[68] Jeanne Becquart-Leclercq, *Paradoxes*, pp. 39–44, 75.

[69] M. Jollivet and H. Mendras, *Les Collectivités rurales françaises* (Paris: Colin, 1971), pp. 148, 157.

[70] Lawrence Wylie, *Village in the Vaucluse* (Cambridge, Mass.: Harvard University Press, 1974).

[71] Henry Ehrmann, *Politics in France* (Boston: Little-Brown, 1968), p. 86. For other views of the strong mayor, see C. Schmitt, *Le Maire de la commune rurale* (Paris: Berger-Levrault, 1969); and de Savigny, *L'État.*

[72] Ehrmann, *Politics*, pp. 87–91.

[73] Kesselman, *The Ambiguous Consensus*, pp. 150, 13.

consolidate his local position and thereby to strengthen his bargaining position with the prefect.[74]

Whereas Kesselman and Ehrmann saw the use of the rhetoric of non-partisanship as centered primarily on the relationship between mayors and their constituencies, Sidney Tarrow, in his study of small town mayors, considered it mainly in the relationship between mayors and prefects. Tarrow found that the weakness of organized party penetration in the periphery, combined with the strength of state territorial administration – not only in its negative manifestations, for example, in the prefect's *tutelle,* but also in its positive ones, that is, in its provision of needed services and resources – meant that mayors quite naturally developed a close relationship with the prefecture. Hence, instead of political parties providing linkages between center and periphery or representing grass-roots interests, it was local government, together with territorial adminis-tration, that was mediating grassroots interests and implementing na-tional policies.[75]

In this context, the rhetoric of nonpartisanship represented a strategic decision of the mayor designed to facilitate his relations with the territorial administration. The rhetoric itself, however, tended to "enforce an admin-istrative and apolitical vision of the community upon the mayor."[76] And this, in turn, encouraged a certain conservatism grounded in an emphasis on maintaining the status quo, since the more administratively active the mayor, the less politically active. But even this, according to Tarrow, had its advantages, because the rhetoric of nonpartisanship was a way of convinc-ing the prefect that there were no real political problems in the commune that would interfere with its smooth administration.[77] This meant that mayors were basically let alone to do what they wished. For Tarrow, the rub here was that what the mayors wished was generally the same as what the local administration wished.

Sidney Tarrow thus found that what started as a rhetorical tool de-signed to serve local interests, by enabling local elected officials to move more easily into the apolitical administrative culture, actually ended up serving the interests of the central power, with the mayors becoming imbued with the technocratic policy preferences of state-appointed admin-istrators. Therefore, although Kesselman and Tarrow differed on the primary reasons for the rhetoric of nonpartisanship, they agreed on its effects: local elected officials do indeed exercise local power, but they are no challenge to the power of the central state, which retains its national political monopoly and its administrative hegemony.

[74]Ibid., pp. 14, 164.
[75]Ibid., p. 70.
[76]Tarrow, *Between Center,* p. 165.
[77]Ibid., p. 172.

Tarrow, in short, much as Kesselman and Ehrmann, concluded that the rhetoric of nonpartisanship minimized the political in the mayors' relationships in the locality. Becquart-Leclercq qualified this view somewhat in her study of midsize towns, by arguing that mayors successfully used the rhetoric of nonpartisanship to deny concerns about the problems that are often attendant upon politics, but not to deny or even minimize politics itself.

Jeanne Becquart-Leclercq found, first of all, that the harmonious vision of the commune presented by Kesselman's mayors contrasted greatly with the feeling of many of their constituents, who saw "violent conflicts," even "civil wars," which did not, however, result in any organized opposition. She suggested this may have been because opposition appeared to follow interest-group lines rather than partisan or ideological divisions, or even townspeople versus outlying, poorer rural population, or old versus young.[78] This nonideological, or nonpartisan, division had been noted by others, such as Edgar Morin for Plodémet or Lawrence Wylie for the village in the Vaucluse.[79] For Becquart-Leclercq, however, the separation between political ideology and practical problems did not mean that nonpartisanship was the rule in the commune. Rather, the mayor's nonpartisan rhetoric reflected an appeal to the community's views of what was legitimate mayoral practice rather than to any real community harmony. It was essentially a political strategy of the mayors designed to give themselves as much electoral support as possible.[80]

For Becquart-Leclercq, the mayors' legitimacy depended on their being "apolitical," but not necessarily "antipartisan"; and this meant that the voter rejected not the parties, but rather the political patronage that could often go along with party politics. In the context of the midsize commune, the legitimate mayor should not discriminate against anyone on the basis of party and should be the "mayor of everyone." The nonpartisan label in local elections, thus, became a symbol of the refusal of patronage and political favoritism, but did not represent an antipartisan stance. This was as true for voters and mayors on the left as it was for those on the right.[81]

Jeanne Becquart-Leclercq, in brief, argued that the effects of the rhetoric of nonpartisanship did not always lead to increased central power, whereas recourse to the rhetoric itself was primarily an electoral strategy that fooled no one as to the politics of the candidates or to the often deep,

[78]Becquart-Leclercq, *Paradoxes*, pp. 189–90.
[79]Edgar Morin, *Commune en France: La métamorphose de Plodémet* (Paris: Fayard, 1967); and Wylie, *Village*.
[80]Becquart-Leclercq, *Paradoxes*, p. 191.
[81]Ibid., pp. 40, 89.

political cleavages in the commune.[82] National politics and partisanship, in short, was ever present at the local level, even when it went unstated. And this was especially true of the big cities and departments.

In the general councils of the departments, just as in the municipal councils of the commune, the rhetoric of nonpartisanship was very much the rule throughout the century. But here, just as in the big cities, the political majority was generally clear, given that the *cumul des mandats* ensured that the president of the general council was almost always a nationally prominent politician. As a result, national political allegiances were always kept just below the surface. Thus, Michel Longepierre found in a study of the Isère in the Rhône-Alpes from 1945 to 1964 that the ritual of egalitarianism in the general council, in which members acted as if all cantons were the same in power, even though they weren't, meant that an effort was ordinarily made to ensure that each circumscription "received its due." This generally fell apart, however, whenever the president of the general council had to make a judgment. At this time, as Longepierre argued, the myth of the equality of all cantons, regardless of their relative size, weight, and political leanings, tended to give way to majoritarian politics.[83]

This is not to say, however, that national party politics necessarily played a key role in departmental affairs. Rather, it was that power was exercised by whatever national parties were involved in the majority coalition of the department, which in the 1960s often meant a moderate right–moderate left coalition and, increasingly in the 1970s, a Socialist–Communist coalition. The politics in the general council, at least as it worked in the Isère, often tended to be prudent, which consisted in not tying one's destiny to a given parliamentary majority, while receiving from it all the possible benefits that could accrue from the central administration, which it controlled by maintaining a well-meaning neutrality.[84]

Nonpartisanship at the departmental level, though, had a basis not only in the complicity or bargaining relationship between the prefect and "his" notables – the general councilors-mayors – but also in law. We should remember that from 1871 on, political debates as such were proscribed by law in the meetings of the general council of the department. Nonpartisan language thus was not only sensible politically, given that the prefect remained the executive power in the department, but also necessary legally. Most revealing, perhaps, about the emptiness of the rhetoric of nonpartisanship in the departments is that the minute executive power was transferred from the prefects to the presidents of departments and regions in

---

[82]Ibid., pp. 39–44, 75, 169–73.
[83]Michel Longepierre, *Les Conseillers généraux dans le système administratif français* (Paris: Cujas, 1968), pp. 141–53.
[84]Ibid., p. 143.

1982, and the proscription against political discussion removed, the councils of departments and regions almost immediately became forums for national political debate.

Nonpartisanship, in short, although an important part of local elected officials' discourse, helping them in their relations with the local population and the representatives of the central administration, could not disguise the fact that national politics and partisanship were ever present at the local level. By the 1960s and 1970s, however, in the cities generally, the rhetoric itself was becoming less and less useful to local elected officials.

The breakdown of the rhetoric. Most studies of the rhetoric of nonpartisanship focus on the smaller towns and villages, where the mayor did indeed use it for the most part as a political strategy to win elections by allaying the community's fears of political favoritism and patronage. In the cities generally by the 1960s and 1970s, however, where an ever-expanding proportion of the population was residing, given demographic shifts, the uses of this rhetoric were changing. It was increasingly exploited for political purposes by the right, as the national government attempted to polarize local elections in an effort to gain more power in the periphery, whereas it was consistently imprecated by the left. In this context, the left's clear rejection of nonpartisan rhetoric, together with the right's use of the rhetoric of nonpartisanship in a partisan fashion, only succeeded in undermining the rhetoric itself.

The national government can be blamed in large measure for the slow demise of the rhetoric of nonpartisanship, which, especially during the early years of the Fifth Republic under de Gaulle, it sought to use to its own advantage, although not very successfully. In addition to using the rhetoric as part of its campaign strategy, the government used the apolitical label applied to local elections to mask its failure to conquer local government. Even though the government could not win a significant number of seats in local government, the nonpartisan label that its actions encouraged local elected officials to take enabled it to downplay the number of opposition seats. Thus, in 1965 the winner of local elections was a nonexistent party: the *Action locale et intérêts municipaux* (ALIM), or local action and municipal interests, with the number of such councilors going from 125,160 to 200,523 between 1959 and 1965. This obscured the fact that the UNR, with 39,427 seats, had a relatively low number of councilors, especially because the Ministry of the Interior listed them next to 16,254 for the Communist party, 40,029 for the SFIO, 25,096 for the MRP, with a nebulous center-left gaining 61,256 seats.[85]

Most importantly, though, the government sought to minimize not

[85]Mény, "Partis," p. 114.

only the appearance but also the fact of left and center power in the periphery through the use of electoral laws.[86] The long tradition of French governing parties of altering electoral law in order to ensure their own stay in power affects local elections as much as national ones. In 1959, in an attempt to influence the outcome of the election, de Gaulle got rid of proportional representation in all towns between nine thousand and twelve thousand inhabitants, leaving only the largest cities with proportional representation. And he extended the majority system to the largest cities in 1965 (over thirty thousand), establishing that the successful list had to gain half the seats in the first ballot, a plurality in the second, and forbidding second ballot alliances between first ballot opponents. In both cases de Gaulle expected to polarize public opinion and shatter the center parties' coalition, forcing the Socialists into alliances with the Communists and everyone else, by reaction, into alliance with the UNR. Although this benefited the center and the right initially, given the division on the left in 1965 and 1971, it helped to unite the left in subsequent elections. The result was to introduce, in the words of Yves Mény, the logic of the center into the local political game, encouraging bipolarization and the politicization of the periphery along national political lines.[87] This came home to the right quite dramatically in the 1977 elections in particular, when many discovered that the rhetoric of nonpartisanship that they used in a partisan fashion as a way of differentiating themselves from the "partisan" left had itself become a liability in their campaigns. It had become all too apparent, as Mitterrand argued in the preface to a book in 1977 that municipal nonpartisanship was a "camouflage" for a conservative politics "that does not want to say its name."[88] None of this was lost on the local electorate.

The local electorate was becoming increasingly politicized and saw more and more clearly the importance of local politics for national elections. Whereas in 1965, 30 percent of the French noted that their attitude to de Gaulle would influence their choice in the municipal elections, by 1977, the proportion of those linking their choice of mayor with their attitude toward the president of the Republic came to 44 percent. Moreover, whereas in 1970 19 percent of those polled considered municipal elections to be political in character, 62 percent considered this to be the case in 1977.[89] In the local elections of March 1977, moreover, the

[86] For an excellent account of the many different ways in which the Gaullists sought to gain power and influence in the locality, see Mark Kesselman, "Overinstitutionalization and political constraint: The case of France," *Comparative Politics* vol. 3, no. 1 (Oct. 1970).

[87] Mény, "Partis," p. 114.

[88] François Mitterrand in the preface to: Franck Sérusclat, *Elections municipales, élections politiques* (Paris: Flammarion, 1977), p. 7.

[89] Jean-Luc Parodi, "Sondages et municipales," *Pouvoirs* no. 24 (1983): 167–8.

abstention rate – a reliable indication of nationally important elections – went down to 21.2 percent, outdoing not only the rates of 1971 and 1965, at 24.8 percent and 21.6 percent, respectively, but even the 1969 regionalization referendum, in which 21.6 percent abstained. Local elections, in short, were increasingly seen by politicians and the public alike as national contests and tests of government support.[90] And for good reason, because local elections were increasingly becoming the battleground for the Socialists and Communists in their attempt to gain national political power, just as it had been for their predecessors at the turn of the century.[91]

By the 1960s and 1970s, even if the rhetoric of nonpartisanship continued to be used as in the past in the small towns and villages, this was no longer true of the cities of any size. In the local elections of 1971, as much as in those of 1977 in small, middle-sized, and large cities alike, the left explicitly rejected the nonpartisan rhetoric of its opponents, insisting that local politics could not be disassociated from national politics. Thus, it made a point of arguing that voting for the left represented a political protest against the national conservative majority, and that local electoral success was only the first step in the process of transformation of society. This contrasted directly with the continued nonpartisan rhetoric of conservative candidates, who, as part of their political strategy, sought to minimize political factors in order to emphasize the neutrality and nonpartisan nature of their administration, arguing in essence that local administration was no place for party politics. But even the right, in the face of the left's accusations of partisanship and, as the campaign heated up, of fascism, could not help throwing it back at them, even evoking in certain cases the image of Soviet dictatorships if the left were to come to power.[92]

Even if nonpartisanship had worked as strategy in the past, then, it worked less and less well, even as a rhetorical tool, as cities and countryside alike were becoming increasingly politicized. In its place, however, was the beginning of a new rhetoric: the rhetoric of good management. Increasingly throughout the 1970s, the more progressive mayors, faced with the politicization of local politics along with the growing complexities of local administration, sought to project an additional image of

[90]Machin, "All Jacobins," p. 144. See also Jack Hayward and Vincent Wright, "Governing from the centre: The 1977 French local elections," *Government and Opposition* vol. 12, no. 4 (Autumn 1977): 433–54; and Michel Cotten, "Les réponses des maires au questionnaire sur l'administration locale," *Revue Administrative* no. 181 (Jan. 1978): 91–2.

[91]See Peter Gourevitch, *Paris and the Provinces* (Berkeley: University of California Press, 1980), pp. 28–9.

[92]Denis Lacorne, *Les Notables Rouges* (Paris: Presses de la Foundation Nationale des Sciences Politiques, 1980), pp. 72–81.

themselves as managers rationally organizing their administration.[93] Moreover, for the left in particular a necessarily politicized administration, as Denis Lacorne noted, did not of necessity bring with it political favoritism. Left-wing mayors all saw the need to act in the name of the general interest rather than to impose choices "dictated by the politics of parties," in particular in municipalities where no one party on the left was dominant, and they all saw the need to appear to be an "impartial administrator."[94]

The rhetoric of good management, however, was really to come into its own only with Socialist decentralization. Although mayors certainly talked of being good administrators long before 1982, this was more as a corollary to the rhetoric of nonpartisanship rather than a rhetoric in its own right.[95] Only the Communists resorted to the rhetoric of good management on a regular basis in the majority of the communes they controlled before this time.

Before 1982, in effect, the rhetoric of good management seemed to be primarily the domain of the Communist mayors. They were unable, as well as unwilling, to use the rhetoric of nonpartisanship and appealed to the electorate with the rhetoric, and even the reality, of good management. With this rhetoric, they were able not only to allay the electorate's fears of patronage and political favoritism almost as effectively as with the rhetoric of nonpartisanship, but at the same time they were also able to appeal more positively to the electorate's desires for the more efficient delivery of city services. What is more, the rhetoric facilitated their relations with the representatives of the central administration.

The Communists' use of the rhetoric of good management can be traced back at least as far as the early Fourth Republic. They were already expressing then their concerns about reconciling the requirements of good management and the need (as stated by Etienne Fajon in March 1953) to acquire "a certain number of administrative skills. . .to direct effectively and well municipal administration" with the desire to integrate municipal politics into an overall Communist political strategy.[96]

[93]See A. Mabileau and P. Sadran, "Administration et politique au niveau local," in *Administration et politiques sous la Ve République,* ed. F. de Baeque and J. L. Quermonne (Paris: Presses de la Foundation Nationale des Sciences Politiques, 1981); and J. Dumas and P. Sadran, "Le processus de réforme communale en France," *Revue Française D'Administration Publique* vol. 1 (1981).

[94]Lacorne, *Notables,* pp. 81–2.

[95]In his study, Tarrow found that when asked what they regarded as the most important quality for a mayor, 29 percent of mayors talked of administrative skills, as opposed to 24 percent for the norm of communal harmony. When compared to Italy, however, where 24 percent mentioned administrative skills but only 8 percent spoke of the importance of making nonsectarian or nonpolitical decisions, it becomes clear that the latter quality is the significant one. *Between Center,* p. 144.

[96]Paul Thibaud, "Le communisme municipal," *Esprit* (Oct. 1966), cited in Yves

Their success in living up to this rhetoric of good management is evident even from the attitudes of local administrators. There are many comments like that of the prefectoral official who found that in Nîmes, which had a left-wing administration since 1965, the Communists "are good administrators, we like them a lot."[97] The Communists themselves, in their relations with the prefects and other representatives of the central government, often tended to downplay the political in favor of the administrative in their efforts to get along with them. This was made possible by the Communist party itself, which during the 1960s established that their performance in local government was to demonstrate the responsibility of the PCF, not to build socialism in France.[98]

Even though the Communist mayor's discussions with the prefect continued to be carried out on apolitical terms, the mayor's political orientation was apparent to all, not only from the kinds of policies promoted, but also from the organization of municipal decision-making itself. Whereas in center-right cities, policy-making was a collaborative effort between the mayor and the heads of the municipal services, with the elected members of the municipal council peripheral, in Communist municipalities the work of the municipal services was subordinated to *commissions municipales,* or committees of the municipal council. Moreover, although center-right mayors had both informal and formal access to the center, whereas the Communists had only formal access, the Communists probably did as well as the center-right in gaining approval for their projects, mainly because right-wing prefects tended to go along with left-wing mayors' desires.[99] But does this mean that whereas local elected officials used the rhetoric of nonpartisanship to hide reality, the prefects' use of the same rhetoric actually reflected a nonpartisan reality? In other words, was the prefect truly apolitical?

The discourse of local administrators

Certainly, in the beginning years of the Third Republic, the prefect was no more apolitical than the mayor. Thus, in the early 1900s, even someone like Barthélemy, who downplayed the importance of decentralization for local government, nevertheless admitted that it did have a politicizing

Mény, *Centralisation et Décentralisation dans le Débat Politique Français* (Paris: Librairie générale de droit et de jurisprudence, 1974), p. 101.
[97]Jerome Milch, "Paris is not France: Policy Outputs and Political Values in Two French Cities" (Ph.D diss., M.I.T., 1973), quoted in Tarrow, *Between Center,* p. 168.
[98]Tarrow, *Between Center,* pp. 169–70. See also Thoenig, "La relation."
[99]Martin Schain, "Communist control of municipal councils," in *French Politics and Public Policy,* ed. P. Cerny and M. Schain (New York: St. Martin's Press, 1980). For a Communist mayor's account, see Fernand Dupuy, *Être maire communiste* (Paris: Calmann-Lévy, 1975).

effect on prefects and mayors alike. He found that the prefect, rather than being neutral, was a political agent, appointed by the central government to carry out its will, whereas the mayor, instead of being nonpartisan, was "a man of party from whom one cannot expect impartiality."[100] We should note, however, that the political use or abuse of the prefect had been much more pronounced between 1815 and 1879, when they were used more as electoral agents of the government in power and as chiefs of police than as administrators.[101] This tradition was slow to fade. But as of 1885, at least, orders for the neutrality of civil servants in elections had replaced circulars urging voting for governmental candidates. By the 1930s, the government's agents were no longer seen mainly as the political emissaries of the political majority in power. By this time, administrative historians such as Walter Rice Sharp were commenting on the increasing political neutrality of the prefects, which had begun in the 1920s as a result of the development of professional standards in the recruitment and promotion of prefects.[102]

While the prefect's role became increasingly apolitical during the Third Republic and beyond, the appointment of the prefect from the start remained relatively apolitical in times of stability and relatively political in times of crisis. Chapman, for example, did not see decentralization in the Third Republic as having politicized unduly the appointments of the prefect. Political appointments, he insisted, had always been the rule in "exceptional times, and when there is a real change in political direction," for example, during Vichy and at the time of the liberation. But he found that even in exceptional times, such as under Napoleon, the political ties of the prefect were less important than his willingness to serve the new government. The first appointed prefects consisted of anyone willing to follow Napoleon – including former Deputies of the Third Estate, clergymen, nobles, royalists, moderates, Jacobins from the Convention, émigrés, jurists, generals, and terrorists. And when Napoleon fell, many stayed on.[103] Émile Monnet, writing in 1885, remarked on this fact, finding that "at the time, it was believed that a prefect is only as good a prefect as he is administrator, and that a good administrator is not made in a day. Today, we have changed this theory: the prefect is born and dies with his minister, his competence is replaced by his inexperience of men and things, and his devotion to public affairs by his servility with respect to the caprices of politics."[104] For Monnet, between the first Empire and

[100]Barthélemy, *Le Gouvernement,* pp. 148, 165.
[101]Chapman, *Prefects,* pp. 31–2.
[102]Sharp, *Civil Service,* pp. 297–8.
[103]Chapman, *Prefects,* p. 24. For more detail, see Godechot, *Les Institutions,* pp. 586–9; and Pierre Henry, *Histoire des Préfets* (Paris: Nouvelles Editions Latines, 1950).
[104]Monnet, *Histoire,* p. 339.

the Second, politics had come to play a major role in the appointment and tenure of the prefect.

Nevertheless, although politics had always had an impact on the prefectoral corps, prefects had always had a way of surviving the political purges that now and again interrupted their careers. Thus, from Napoleon on, we see an increasing professionalization of the prefectoral corps: At the time of the coup d'état of December 2, 1851, 60 percent of the prefects had already been part of the prefectoral corps during the July monarchy and 70 percent had been subprefects.[105] And a similar pattern followed from the Second Empire through the Third Republic because, as Vincent Wright concluded, however pressing the political reasons for dismissing prefects – including their symbolic value, the pressure by adherents of the new regime, the need to have a politically trustworthy administration able and willing to carry out the government's orders, and the fear of sabotage – the dismissals were always incomplete. Among the reasons for this were the need for qualified individuals and for administrative continuity, the desire to win over some and to avoid creating enemies of others, and the concern about public opinion and the politics of the moment. This meant that adherents of previous regimes were able to imbue the next with their administrative traditions and mores, ensuring the basic continuity of the politico-administrative system behind a façade of instability.[106]

Even in times of crisis, then, the appointment of prefects was less affected by political considerations than one might have assumed, and the prefectoral culture, less unsettled. In times of political stability, by contrast, such appointments were hardly political at all for a variety of reasons. Blatant patronage, for one, tended to be avoided because it could be dangerous to the Deputy and problematic to the government. Such patronage was hard to carry through anyway, because in the Third and Fourth Republics parties in the coalition cabinets had to agree to nominations and the important Deputies of the department had to be consulted.[107] Appointments of the prefect, moreover, also involved other, equally important considerations, such as the fit of character and person with a given department. For example, as Chapman explained, "A politically difficult Department like the Var requires a prefect of strong character, acute political sense, and an unhesitating brusque manner." And this kind of "vulgar man" with "radical leanings and a contempt for social niceties" would never work in Nancy among other places.[108] The

[105]Bernard, *L'État*, p. 37.
[106]Vincent Wright, "Les épurations administratives de 1848 à 1885," in *Les Épurations administratives XIX et XX siècles* (Geneva: Droz, 1977), pp. 68–80.
[107]Chapman, *Prefects*, pp. 153–9.
[108]Ibid., p. 161.

appointment of the prefect, in brief, was often apolitical because of the politics of the allegedly nonpartisan mayors and other local elected officials of the department.

During the Fifth Republic, when a conservative government was in power for over twenty-three years, the political role of the prefect could be downplayed – especially because the prefects carrying out the orders of the government in most cases were careful not to appear too political. At least the appearance of neutrality was essential, because the government itself had to take care to treat fairly opposition mayors (even Communists), especially if they were Deputies, for fear of adverse national publicity. But the emphasis here must be placed on appearance and on the accompanying rhetoric that downplayed the political realities of a UDR-controlled national government and a civil service increasingly political in its career path.

The contemporary apolitical rhetoric has its origins in the ENA, which, when set up by Michel Debré after the war, was to imbue future civil servants with *le sens de l'État.* He insisted, "It is not one of the missions of the school to play politics or to impose a particular doctrine."[109] Thus, Ezra Suleiman found that one of the ironies of the entry of politics into administration and of administrators into politics is that it developed most rapidly during the Fifth Republic, under the Gaullists. He found that it was a consequence of the elitist system of training and all of the job securities and other privileges attached to their positions that allowed members of the *grands corps,* regardless of their political affiliation, to move easily into politics.[110]

First, the apolitical rhetoric came into conflict with the increasing numbers of civil servants entering political life, especially in the Fifth Republic. Whereas the percentage of civil servants who became Deputies hovered around 20 percent in the Fourth Republic, the number steadily grew during the Fifth Republic, reaching 38.8 percent in 1978 (Table 7.3).[111] The figures are even more impressive when considering the number of civil servants running for election. Whereas in 1956, 48 members of the *grands corps* stood for election, with 16 successfully elected Deputies, by 1967 the numbers standing for election had increased to 109, with 53 successfully elected.[112] In the 1978 elections, 125 of the 480 Deputies elected were civil servants (although not all *grands corps*), with the num-

[109]Michel Debré, *Réforme de la fonction publique* (Paris: Imprimerie Nationale, 1946), pp. 24–5, cited in Suleiman, "Administrative Reform," p. 73

[110]Suleiman, "Administrative Reform," pp. 73–4. See also Jeanne Siwek-Pouydesseau, "La politisation des hauts fonctionnaires en France," *Res Publica* vol. 16, no. 2 (1974).

[111]"Les fonctionnaires au gouvernement et à l'Assemblée," *La Fonction publique 2, Cahiers français* no. 197 (July-Sept. 1980): 40.

[112]Debbasch, *L'Administration,* p. 58.

Table 7.3. *Civil servants in the national assembly in the Fourth and Fifth Republics (in percentages of total Deputies)*

	1946	1951	1956	1958	1962	1967	1968	1973	1978
Upper-level civil servants	4.36	2.5	2.7	6.5	9.2	11.5	12.5	11.0	13.2
Other civil servants	2.5	2.6	3.6	2.5	2.5	1.5	3.0	6.5	4.2
Teachers	14.65	14.3	15.0	9.0	9.0	15.0	9.5	15.0	20.4
Military	2.0	0.6	0.7	1.5	2.0	1.0	1.0	0.5	1.0
Total	23.5	20.0	22.0	19.5	22.7	29.0	26.0	33.0	38.8

Source: "Les fonctionnaires au gouvernement et à l'Assemblée," *La Fonction Publique 2, Cahiers français,* no. 197 (July-Sept. 1980): 40.

ber of civil servants who were candidates representing 10 percent of the candidates in the Republican party, 7.2 percent in the RPR, 6.9 percent in the M.R.G., 5.2 percent in the PS, and 1.6 percent in the PC.[113]

This move into a political career was facilitated by the fact that civil servants were just about the only ones who could easily take a *détachement,* or leave of absence, from their positions and be certain of a place when they returned, despite some guarantees established for other professions by the law of January 2, 1978. And although, as Alain di Stefano commented, the entrance of functionaries into political life had led to its renewal, it also makes it harder to maintain that the civil service is apolitical.[114]

Secondly, at the national level, from the beginning years of the Fifth Republic, the upper reaches of the civil service could not help but be identified with the party in power and be more responsive to the requests of its members. After all, a majority of members of the eight governments of the Fifth Republic were members of the upper levels of the civil service; at 55 percent or 145 of its members in the government, it far outdistanced the 11.4 percent or 30 heads of industry, the 9.9 percent or 26 lawyers, and the 6.8 percent or 18 journalists.[115] Moreover, within the central ministries themselves, although Suleiman found that ministers did indeed

[113]A. Guède and G. Fabre-Rosane, "Une Sociologie des candidats des grandes formations," *Le Monde,* Mar. 17, 1987; and idem, "Sociologie des candidats aux élections législatives de mars 1978," *Revue française de Science Politique* vol. 28, no. 5 (Oct. 1978): 852–5.

[114]Alain de Stefano, *La Participation des fonctionnaires civils à la vie politique* (Paris: Librairie générale de droit et de jurisprudence, 1979), pp. 263–4.

[115]"Les fonctionnaires," *Cahiers français,* p. 40.

seek to "purify" the administration in order to avoid its contamination by "politics," he argued that this meant nothing more than contamination by the political opposition. Opposition Deputies had much less access to central ministry officials than their mainstream colleagues; and even where they had access, they had much less influence.[116]

This same phenomenon was quite apparent at the local level. The prefects were increasingly identified with the party in power, active in its support, and likely to pursue political careers subsequent to their stint in the countryside.[117] But although prefects became increasingly political in their careers, they simultaneously cultivated the appearance of being apolitical in the performance of their duties when in the prefectoral role. Thus, as Jean-Pierre Worms has noted, the prefects generally employed the "rhetoric of the general interest" in the effort to negate any conflict.[118] But conflict there was, because opposition mayors had much less access to prefects or to central ministries than their mainstream colleagues. One of the responses to this, on the part of the mayors, was to take up the apolitical rhetoric themselves and to distance themselves in this way from the appearance of being partisan in terms of national politics.

In any event, by the 1970s the rhetoric of nonpartisanship, which had been successfully used as a way of downplaying the importance of politics in the periphery, was beginning to lose its appeal as well as its effectiveness with the increasing politicization of the periphery and the growing willingness of local elected officials to acknowledge their own political ties and to respond to the new groups in the periphery. The old complicity, however, had not disappeared, nor had the rhetoric of centralization, which continued to enable local elected officials to avoid responsibility for their decisions. Any thoroughgoing change in the local politico-administrative system in which informal decentralized processes underlay formal, centralized institutions was to wait until the Socialists' decentralizing legislation during 1982 to 1985.

[116]Ezra Suleiman, "L'Administrateur et le Député en France," *Revue Française de Science Politique* vol. 23, nos. 4–6 (1973): 756–7.
[117]Williams and Harrison, *Politics and Society,* pp. 282–3.
[118]Worms, "Le préfet," p. 258.

8

When informal rules become formal roles: The new pluralism in the institutions and processes of local government

The Socialists' decentralization reforms of 1982 to 1986 significantly altered the traditional institutional framework of centralization. By formalizing the informal, decentralized rules followed by local administrators and elected officials in the periphery, the new laws have produced great changes in the processes and institutions of local government. They have introduced a new kind of transparency into local officials' practices and opened up local politics and administration to new patterns of development, to new forms of administrative activity, and to increased political activity.

Many scholars, however, disappointed that the reforms did not go as far as the Socialists had anticipated, have tended to be quite conservative in their assessments of the impact of decentralization on local institutions and processes. For obvious reasons, only those focused on administrative law saw radical change in the Socialist reform – and this followed years of describing a pattern of continuing centralization attenuated at best by minor modifications in the law. Administrative law scholars produced countless new texts outlining the new laws and they carefully revised all the old primers.[1] In addition, whereas many experts published tomes examining the impact of the new laws on local administration in general,[2] others edited volumes that detailed the effects of decentralization on all aspects of local government,[3] and still others wrote books and articles concentrating on the impact of decentralization on one or another level of

[1] François Luchaire and Yves Luchaire, *Le Droit de la décentralisation* (Paris: Presses universitaires de France, 1983); and Jacques Moreau, *Administration régionale, départementale et municipale*, 6th ed. (Paris: Mémentos Dalloz, 1983).
[2] Jean Ravanel, *La Réforme;* Gérard Bélorgey, *La France décentralisée* (Paris: Berger Levrault, 1984); and Georges Gontcharoff and Serge Milano, *La Décentralisation*, vols. 1–3 (Paris: Syros, 1983–4).
[3] Franck Moderne, ed., *La Nouvelle Décentralisation* (Paris: Sirey, 1983); and Albert Mabileau, *Les Pouvoirs locaux à l'épreuve de la décentralisation* (Paris: Pédone, 1983).

local government. Here, we find accounts of the transformation of the prefect into the *commissaire de la République;* the impact of the transfer of power from the prefect to the presidents of the regional and departmental bodies; the importance of the regions' and departments' new or enhanced functions, powers, and responsibilities; and the effects of the new laws on the municipalities.[4]

Scholars who focused on political and administrative processes, by contrast, tended to see much less of a break with the past and generally couched the reform in terms of its continuity with previous history. Those concerned with the political process in particular argued that although the transfer of executive power did indeed change the political institutions, it had little immediate impact on political processes: its initial effect was only to increase the political powers of the notables.[5] And they suggested that although it had increased the politicization of local government generally, it had yet to bring about the flowering of local democracy the Socialists had expected.[6]

Of those focused on the administrative process, moreover, some insisted that the very real changes in administrative institutions complicated the underlying administrative processes but did not transform them except in minor ways, in part because the institutional changes were themselves not extensive enough in such areas as the transfer of social services and in the reform of the local taxation system.[7] Others, although less willing to take the Socialists to task for what might have been, nevertheless seemed to find little change in the local balance of power, with many features of the pragmatic bargaining relationship of the past remaining much the same.[8] There is no doubt that some of the major

[4] Bernard, *L'État;* Dominique Schmitt, *La Région à l'heure de la décentralisation* (Paris: Documentation française, 1985); Jacques Chevalier, François Rangeon, and Michèle Sellier, *Le Pouvoir régionale* (Paris: Presses universitaires de France, 1982); René Dosière, Jean-Claude Fortier, and Jean Mastias, *Le Nouveau Conseil Général* (Paris: Editions ouvrières, 1985); and the countless articles about municipalities in journals such as *Correspondance municipale.*

[5] Yves Mény, "La Politique de décentralisation: Réforme de société ou réforme pour les élites?" Paper prepared for delivery at the conference, "Administration et Société," sponsored by the Institut Français des Sciences Administratives (Paris, Jan. 27–8, 1983).

[6] Mark Kesselman, "Restructuring the French State: An End to French Exceptionalism?" Paper prepared for delivery at the Sixth International Conference of Europeanists (Washington, D.C., Oct. 30–Nov. 1, 1987).

[7] Mark Kesselman, "Representation without participation: Decentralization and the Crisis of the Welfare State in France." Paper prepared for delivery at the World Congress, International Political Science Association (Paris, July 15–20, 1985).

[8] Ashford, "Decentralizing France." Ashford is one of the scholars who is more positive about the Socialist reform when concentrating on its impact, potential as well as actual, on political and administrative institutions. See "Reconstructing the French 'État': Progress of the *loi Defferre," West European Politics* vol. 6, no. 3 (July 1983).

institutional problems of local government remain, such as the unwieldy number of communes and the presence of four levels of local government with different functions and often overlapping jurisdictions, thus complicating intergovernmental relations and the efficient delivery of services.

Admittedly then, moderation in the assessment of the impact of the Socialists' decentralization laws is indeed in order here. Nonetheless, we should not underestimate the importance of the changes that are in the process of taking place in both the political and administrative spheres. Although the Socialists sacrificed much that would have ensured the democratization of local government based on the increased influence of the local population, they did not give up on legislating pluralism in either sphere. On the contrary, they simply instituted it at a different level by introducing a greater pluralism in the institutions and processes of local government. Instead of finding the *pouvoirs* (powers) and *contre-pouvoirs* (counterpowers) created at the level of the local population and their interaction with local government, as the *autogestionnaires* had intended, we find pluralism instead at the level of local government itself and its interaction with the state in all areas of its activity. Decentralization, more specifically, brought with it a structural pluralism based on the complementarity among different levels and units of government representing different interests and sectors of activity rather than a popular pluralism based on the direct competition of interest groups, on referenda, and on greater direct citizen participation.

In the political sphere, the new pluralism is evident in the new politics in the periphery. Local elections are now clearly politicized along national party lines and focused, for the most part, on national political issues, with the local population seeing local elections as opportunities to register its views of the national government's performance. But although this nationalization of local elections has enabled political parties to extend their influence over the elections themselves, local politics remains reasonably separate from the national. Local parties play by their own rules of the game and enter into coalitions and alliances that stem from specifically local needs and situations. With the limitation of the accumulation of office, moreover, competition among the notables has grown, along with the size of a political class that has become increasingly differentiated according to electoral mandate, albeit not occupational profile. The regions, in effect, are gaining new, more intermediate, urban-based notables as the national notables have tended to retain their departmental mandates and their rural ties. The result is that natural alliances seem to be forming between the regions and urban areas on the one hand and the departments and rural areas on the other, thus further extending the pluralism in the periphery.

In the administrative sphere, the new pluralism is apparent in the increasing interdependence among the different levels of local government as well as in the more cooperative relations between regions, departments, and communes. And it is also evident in the diversity of policies local governments have developed in response to their new duties, whether the departments in the delivery of social services, the communes in urban planning and rural development, or the regions in local economic development.

The most dramatic changes have occurred in this last area, because regional economic development has been a sector of activity traditionally reserved for the central state. With the reforms, the regions gained significant interventionist powers, essentially becoming local industrial development brokers and the *dirigiste,* or interventionist, equivalents of the national government at the local level. The departments and communes, however, also gained powers in this area. And the state, in the meantime, did not give up all of its own powers, by any means. The result has been a set of local administrative processes with regard to the promotion of economic development best characterized by the term "decentralized *dirigisme.*" For although local *dirigisme* was made possible by the new interventionist powers and resources of local elected officials, its decentralized implementation was made inevitable by the number of acts – local, national, and even supranational – involved in every aspect of the promotion of local economic development.

THE NEW POLITICS IN THE PERIPHERY

The decentralization reform abandoned the project to legislate pluralism at the level of the local population in order to introduce a greater pluralism in the political institutions and processes of local government. Local democracy, rather than taking the form of referenda and direct citizen participation, appears in the legally mandated consultation procedures, in the local governmental commissions, and in the increased support for, and interaction with, local associations. Instead of direct democracy, in brief, we find a more representative one, in which local elected officials seek to be more responsive to their constituencies through formal, local governmental channels and in which the test of their power occurs in local electoral battles. Given the nationalization of local elections, however, such a test is no longer primarily local in character.

Local elections, in effect, now tend to be fought along national party lines and, with the exception of the municipal elections of 1989, to be concerned with national political issues. The emergence of the extreme right as a political force, the new vigor of the moderate right, and its successful conquest of local office in the early 1980s in response to the left's sweep of national office in 1981, all attest to the influence of na-

Democratizing France

tional debates, policies, and economic performance on the local electorate. Party politics, along with a greater emphasis on party discipline, has become the order of the day in all but the smaller communes. At every level of local government, new coalitions and alliances, both official and tacit, have sprung up. In addition, with the limitation of the number of offices local notables can occupy, political competition among personalities within the left and the right has grown, along with the size of the political class. But this is not all, because the increasing competition among parties and personalities in the periphery, added to the differing electoral bases of the regions and departments, increases the likelihood of greater differentiation between regions and departments, with partisans of different parties or at least policies (for example, rural versus urban) elected to the different levels. The regions, in fact, look as if they will become the natural domain of the urban communes, whereas the departments will stay that of the rural communes.

A new politics, in short, has taken over the periphery. The political class is becoming larger, increasingly differentiated according to the mandates of its members, and more concerned with the demands of local democracy and with the requirements of national party politics. In this context, the local notables best able to survive are those who are more responsive to their constituencies, more attuned to the national dimensions of local elections, and better equipped to manage the political and the administrative intricacies of local government effectively.

The politicization of local elections

Since decentralization, local elections have become much more politicized than ever before, with national issues the major focus of candidates in all but the smaller communes in all elections except the most recent municipal one. Even in the municipal elections, national party politics played as significant a role as it has in all other elections, defining the issues and anointing the candidates. National parties, in effect, have managed to impose much greater discipline on their members, to achieve greater control over local parties and their alliances, and to provide greater coordination in campaign strategy and rhetoric than in the past. Gone, for the most part, are the lists without a readily identifiable national party affiliation, in which purely local coalitions with unrecognizable names focus on local issues. Moreover, the local population's views of the performance of the national government have been increasingly reflected in the results of local elections. As the national opinion polls registered a slide in the popularity of Mitterrand and his government, so went the local elections. The municipal elections of 1983, the departmental elections of 1982 and 1985, and the regional elections of 1986 reflected the Socialists' losses in the polls, the

268

departmental elections of 1988 and the municipal elections of 1989 even more indicated their recovery.

This politicization, however, owes as much to the decentralization reforms as it does to the economic policies and ideological fights that put national issues at the center of local contests. The new powers of the presidents of the regions and the departments have made contests at this level crucial to the local balance of political power, and therefore local tests of national party strength. The regional elections by proportional representation, the role of the departments in drawing up regional lists, and the extension of the election by proportional representation to all communes with over thirty-five hundred inhabitants have increased politicization along national party lines at every level of local government.

The politicization of the local population. At the municipal level, the politicization of local elections became fully apparent in 1983. Although municipal elections, especially in urban areas, had become increasingly politicized over the course of the 1970s, it was not until the elections of 1983 that an overwhelming majority of the local population saw them as primarily political along national lines. The percentage of people able to identify the political party affiliation of the mayor had increased dramatically over the past, from 65 percent (as against 30 percent unable to do so) in 1975, to 81 percent (as against 11 percent) in January 1983 – a 16 percent increase in only eight years.[9] Even more importantly, perhaps, close to three out of four interviewed (73 percent as against 17 percent) agreed that the municipal elections of 1983 were, for France as a whole, above all political elections rather than local elections. Moreover, even when focused specifically on the elections in their own commune, a majority – albeit a much smaller one (51 percent as against 38 percent) – saw the municipal elections as above all political ones.[10]

This did not mean, however, that the French had completely abandoned their traditional focus on personality for party affiliation in municipal elections. Among the respondents, 50 percent agreed that, at the moment of voting, the personality of the candidate would above all determine their choice, whereas only 43 percent agreed that the political orientation of the list would. In the cities with more than thirty thousand inhabitants, however, the numbers were reversed, with 54 percent agreeing that political orientation was the main determinant of their vote as against only 40 percent for personality. This contrasts quite sharply with communes of fewer than two thousand inhabitants, in which 64 percent

[9]Sofres poll for La Croix, Jan. 6–12, 1983, Sofres, *Opinion public* (Paris: Gallimard, 1984), p. 119.
[10]Sofres polls for *Le Parisien Libéré*, Dec. 21–9, 1982 and for *Le Figaro*, Feb. 4–9, 1983, Sofres, *Opinion public.*

went for personality as against 30 percent for political orientation.[11] The smaller communes, in other words, tend to remain dominated by personalistic politics, and this has only been reinforced by the fact that communes of under thirty-five hundred inhabitants retained the traditional two-round majoritarian system of election of the mayor. In the 1983 municipal elections, in short, party politics and national political issues were ever present in the larger cities and towns, less pronounced, but still significant, factors in the smaller towns and villages.

Interestingly enough, in the cantonal elections in the departments that renew half of the general councils every three years, the politicization along national lines has been even more pronounced than that of the municipal elections, despite the departments' heavily rural domination and the elections' two-round, majoritarian format that favors personalistic politics. On the eve of the cantonal elections 1985, just as in 1982, close to three-quarters of those questioned felt that the elections would be political by contrast with only 19 percent who felt they would be local – about the same level as the municipal elections. Moreover, in a 1985 exit poll, 52 percent claimed to have voted for national reasons as opposed to 37 percent for local reasons. An even larger percentage than in the 1983 municipal elections insisted that they would vote according to the party affiliation of the candidates as opposed to their personality, at 46 percent in 1985, 49 percent in 1982 (as opposed to only 38 percent in 1976).[12]

The greater politicization of the cantonal elections is due in part to the fact that the local electorate tends to be much less familiar with the personalities involved in the department than in the municipality or the national assembly. In a 1985 poll, only 58 percent could name their general councilor as opposed to 94 percent who could name their mayor and 63 percent who could name their Deputy.[13] There remains, however, a certain amount of personalization of departmental contests despite its politicization: the majority party tends to be identified in terms of the president of the general council, for example, as Monorist or anti-Monorist in Vienne, Médecinist or anti-Médicinist in the Alpes-Maritimes, Poncétist or anti-Poncétist in the Lot-et-Garonne. But however much the personalization, the elections certainly continued to be seen as tests of the national government, as they had ever since the 1976 and 1979 elections anticipating the left's victory in 1981, with the left's losses in 1982 and 1985 seen to presage the right's victories in the European elections of 1984 and in the legislative elections of 1986.[14]

[11]Pre-Electoral Sofres poll for *Le Figaro*, Feb. 4–9, 1983 ibid., p. 120.
[12]Jean-Luc Parodi, "Cantonales 1985: La répétition des Européenes," *Revue Politique et Parlementaire* no. 918 (July–Aug. 1985): 7.
[13]Sofres poll, February 15–20, 1985, cited in Parodi, "Cantonales 1985," p. 7.
[14]*Le Monde*, Sept. 14, 1988.

The new pluralism in local government

Of all the elections in the periphery in the 1980s, the regional elections of March 1986 have been the most clearly politicized. These were national contests much more than local ones, because they were overshadowed by the legislative elections that took place on the same day. The format of the elections – proportional representation according to departmental lists – also contributed to their politicization along national party lines. Their use as a consolation prize by Parliamentarians likely to lose in the legislative elections, in particular on the left, also contributed to their more national character. The results mirrored those of the legislative election with the rout of the left.

By the 1989 municipal elections, things had changed somewhat. The politicization of the elections, as measured by whether the local population saw them as "political," had hit a record low. Fifty-five percent of those questioned saw the elections in their commune as purely local, up by seventeen points from 1983, by contrast with only 35 percent who agreed that the municipal elections were, for France as a whole, above all political elections rather than local elections, down by an impressive thirty-eight points from 1983. Moreover, the personalization of the elections had increased appreciably, with 58 percent intending to vote on the basis of the personality of the candidates, up eight points from 1983, whereas only 35 percent were determined to vote according to political affiliation, down eight points from 1983.[15]

Does this mean that France is going back to the less politicized local elections of the past? No, only that voters in 1989 saw much less need than in 1983 to express their views on national politics, given that they had had so many opportunities in the previous year, between the two rounds of the presidential elections in March – April 1988, the two rounds of the legislative elections in June 1988, and the two rounds of the cantonal elections in September – October 1988. The record-breaking abstention rate of 30.38 percent in the first round of the municipal elections, the highest since the liberation, attests to how tired the local electorate was with trooping to the polls to register its opinions. The population in general, moreover, was much more satisfied with the performance of the national government in 1989 than in 1983, as judged by the popularity ratings of Mitterrand and his prime minister. Whereas just before the municipal elections in March 1983, 48 percent of those interviewed expressed confidence in Mitterrand (versus 46 percent who did not) and only 39 percent had confidence in Pierre Mauroy (versus 53 percent who did not), in Sofres polls carried out in February and March 1989, 58 percent of those interviewed were confident that Mitterrand could solve the problems facing France (versus 39 percent who did not), whereas 55

[15]*Le Monde,* March 2, 1989.

percent expressed confidence in Michel Rocard (versus 39 percent who did not).[16] These differences are also reflected in the fact that only 39 percent of those interviewed in another Sofres poll in February 1989 intended to express their dissatisfaction with the national government through their vote, by contrast with 49 percent in February 1983.[17] The 1989 electoral results speak for themselves: the Socialists regained many of the cities they lost in 1983 and hailed the results as a vote of confidence in their government.

The cantonal elections of 1988 held only a few months before the municipal elections confirm this positive relationship between governmental satisfaction and the results of the vote, even if they tell us little on their own, squeezed as they were between the previous national elections and the referendum on New Caledonia. In these elections, too, the population had registered both its weariness with its constant trips to the polls by an extremely low turnout (50.87 percent) – especially by comparison with the record-breaking turnouts of 1982 (68.9 percent) and of 1985 (66.7 percent) – as well as its general satisfaction with the national government. The fact that Mitterrand's popularity was at 54 percent just before the elections is a good predictor of the fact that the Socialists had returned to their 1982 level of support (at close to 30 percent of the vote in the first round of the elections).[18]

It is quite natural, then, given the general satisfaction with the national government and the weariness with elections centered on national issues, that the local population would see the municipal elections as less political, and that local elected officials would focus primarily on local issues. This in no way means that the 1989 municipal elections themselves were less politicized along national party lines than any other such elections or that the local electorate was any less aware of the party affiliation of the candidates. In this election, as in previous ones in the 1980s, in contradistinction to the past, very few local campaigns were not identifiable according to national party. In fact, all local elections were much more partisan than ever before, with the national parties involved to a much greater extent in the composition of local electoral lists and in local campaign strategies.

Party politics in the periphery. In all elections since the Socialists came to power in 1981, the parties of the moderate right, in a break with the past, came to firm national agreements, which ensured that they had united lists in most local constituencies. The left, on the contrary, after coming to a national agreement in the 1982 cantonal and 1983 municipal elections,

[16]Lancelot and Lancelot, "Evolution," p. 11, and *Le Monde*, Mar. 4, 1989.
[17]Sofres poll, Feb. 18–22, 1989, *Le Monde*, Mar. 2, 1989.
[18]*Le Monde*, Sept. 28, 1988.

failed to do so in subsequent elections, mainly because the 1983 rift between the Communist and Socialist parties at the national level had not been mended. Local agreements were nevertheless entered into, but on a case-by-case basis. In the 1989 municipal elections, for example, the left was unable to arrive at common lists in 39 percent of cities with over twenty thousand inhabitants, by contrast with the right's agreements in 95 percent of such cities.[19]

Regardless of whether the national parties managed to reach agreement on combined lists, they were all heavily involved in the selection process for candidates for local election, although local parties and notables were the primary actors here. In the regional elections, for example, the national parties greatly influenced the choice of candidates by generally outlining the selection principles to be followed, by ratifying the lists, and, on the right, by negotiating the agreements between the two major allied parties. For the most part, only the more powerful notables were able to constitute their lists with little interference from Paris or from local parties, for that matter.[20]

In all such elections, local parties on both the left and the right were subject to national party discipline – or censure as in the case of the 1989 municipal elections in Marseilles, where the dissident Socialist incumbent mayor Robert Vigoroux ran against Michel Pezet, the official Socialist candidate, or in Sainte-Geneviève-des-Bois (Essone) and in Orly (Val-de-Marne), where dissident Communists and Socialists ran against the official united lists. These cases were exceptions on the left, however, as were those on the right that took advantage of the Socialists' opening to the center, most notably in Metz (Moselle), where the incumbent mayor Jean-Marie Rausch, also minister of foreign trade in the Rocard government, led a centrist list in which the Socialists participated; and in Auxerre (Yonne), where another incumbent mayor and minister of labor in the Rocard government, Jean-Pierre Soisson, led a centrist list in which Socialists also participated. The only other exceptions came from reformist members of the RPR, such as Alain Carignon in Grenoble, who sought to adapt de Gaulle's notion of *rassemblement* (rallying) to include centrists and Socialists on his ticket; or Philippe Séguin, who was at the head of a list "enlarged" beyond the traditional political cleavages and received support from Socialists at the national level while facing a Socialist list at the local level.[21] The censure had little, if any, effect in these cases, however, because all proved victorious in the municipal elections.

[19]For the cities, see *Le Monde*, Mar. 8, 1989.
[20]Albert Mabileau, "La nationalisation des candidatures par la médiation des notables," in *Régions: Le baptême des urnes,* ed. Pascal Perrineau (Paris: Pédone, 1987), pp. 36–8.
[21]*London Financial Times*, Mar. 8, 1989; *Le Monde*, Mar. 6, 1989.

The only other cases of national party disapproval, less exceptional but no less objectionable even though they did not involve censure, were where the moderate right and the extreme right ran common lists, in particular in the south of France in the smaller communes of the Bouches-du-Rhône, the Var, and the Alpes-Maritimes.

The power of the national parties was evident not only in their ability to impose party discipline on their own members in all but the above cases but also to diminish the impact of other smaller parties in local elections. In the regional elections, for example, the smaller parties for the most part did not field candidates either because of lack of interest or a lack of money, given the legislative elections held at the same time. And the two groups one would assume to have had the greatest stake in the elections were marginalized: the regionalists did very poorly, having managed to put together only a few lists in regions where there had traditionally been a strong movement for regional autonomy, as did the "socioprofessionals," who claimed to be apolitical and focused on the economic mission of the regions alone.[22] In the 1989 municipal elections, although the ecologists did well in a number of cities in the first round, they lost out in the second as the Socialists managed to rally voters to their own cause.

The campaigns themselves also attest to the central influence of the national parties. The moderate right, having learned the lessons of the left in the 1970s, had clearly stated, local party programs that followed the national program. In the municipal elections of 1983, the cantonal elections of 1982 and 1985, and the regional elections of 1986, the same neoliberal line heard at the national level was increasingly trumpeted at the local level. The moderate right as a whole, moreover, despite the fact that it had traditionally been less inclined to bring national issues into local contests, consistently underlined the national as much as the local character of the elections. It made it clear that the population was voting not only for officials to administer local government but also to make a statement about the policies of the Socialist government.

In the cantonal elections of 1988 and the municipal elections in 1989, however, with the neoliberal ideology in question (given the poor performance of the right in the national elections of the previous year) there was less focus on the ideology. Dispirited as a result of its losses in the presidential and legislative elections, the right did little to politicize the cantonal elections. By the time of the municipal elections, however, the RPR had regained its aplomb sufficiently to politicize the campaign by insisting that it was the first chance to get a judgment on Rocard's performance as prime minister.[23] Interestingly enough, having found that the

[22]Mabileau, "Nationalisation," pp. 29–35.
[23]*Le Monde*, Mar. 8, 1989.

first round of these elections suggested a positive judgment for Rocard, the RPR backed off from its politicizing rhetoric for the second round.

The partisan use of the rhetoric of nonpartisanship, so prevalent on the right in previous decades, had not been totally abandoned, though, despite the fact that this rhetoric was altered somewhat by the conjunction of a new rhetoric – that of good management – in particular among UDF and some centrist candidates. For example, the UDF denounced the Socialists for seeking to politicize the 1989 municipal debate, but insisted, in partisan fashion, that the choice was between their own liberal and social management and their opponents' Socialist one.[24] In the few contests that pitted the UDF against the RPR, moreover, the same kinds of denunciations were heard. The UDF's Raymond Barre in Lyon objected to the political campaign of the RPR's Michel Noir on the grounds that "Lyon should not become a partisan city," whereas Noir, the winner, made certain to present himself in apolitical terms by not even having an RPR insignia on his campaign posters.[25] Although most nonpartisan candidates lost, as in Châlons-sur-Marne, where the centrist candidate focused his campaign on his ability to manage the city better than the Communists, even accusing the Communist mayor of introducing politics into the management of the city,[26] one socioprofessional who waged a completely apolitical campaign did win in an upset victory against the incumbent Socialist mayor in Boulogne (Pas-de-Calais).

Such rhetoric of nonpartisanship and good management, of course, was not limited to the municipal elections. In the regional elections, the "socioprofessionals" situated on the liberal right, who had been active on the regional economic and social councils, also sought to depoliticize the elections. Many were the campaigns such as those of the three socioprofessional lists in the Franche-Comté (attaining together over 10 percent of the vote) that condemned political demagogy, arguing that only "new men" or "different men" (read antipolitical) were capable of properly managing the region, by running it like a business enterprise. For the socioprofessionals, the politicization of the elections would ensure only incompetence, waste, and inefficiency by contrast with the competence, efficiency, and optimum use of resources inherent in the focus on nonpolitical management alone.[27]

This rhetoric of "good management" was not in any way exclusive to the right in the campaigns.[28] On the contrary, the Socialists, after their

[24]*Le Monde*, Feb. 17, 1989.
[25]*Le Monde*, Mar. 7, 1989.
[26]*Le Monde*, Feb. 23, 1989.
[27]Philippe Plas, "Une volonté en quête d'objet: Discours politique et région en Franche-Comté," in *Régions*, ed. Perrineau, pp. 125–7.
[28]See the full discussion of this rhetoric and its use as a way of depoliticizing local government in Part II, Chapter 10, "The rhetoric of good management."

own politicization of local elections around national issues in the 1970s, shied away from such issues in the municipal elections of 1983, and understandably so, given their slide in the polls. Taking a lesson from the results of the cantonal elections, they emphasized the local character of the municipal elections and argued that local electors should consider primarily the quality of the management of the municipality during the previous seven years.[29] By contrast, the Socialists sought to politicize the 1989 municipal elections more along national lines (even though Rocard himself maintained that they were primarily local in character), presumably because they were confident that positive views of the national government would devolve to their benefit in the local election.[30] The Communists, instead, decided to play down the national political ramifications of the municipal elections, thus making a break with their own politicized rhetoric of 1983 as well as that of the Socialists in 1989.[31] Only the National Front focused almost exclusively on national issues; but the local population was much less attentive to this discussion than they had been in the past. And the FN, undergoing internal strife and having lost much of its national strength as well as its appeal based on its newness, had trouble even attracting candidates to run in many elections, even though it did end up doing well in some big cities in the South.[32]

Despite intermittent attempts by national as well as local parties to depoliticize local elections for political reasons, in sum, the increasing importance of national parties in local electoral campaigns, as much as the intrusion of national issues into the local debate, has ensured the politicization of the periphery along national lines. Although this, in turn, has meant that the major parties have managed to exert a certain centralizing influence on local elections, it has not gone much beyond this to impinge on local politics.

New elites and new rules of the game?

Since decentralization, the local rules of the game have remained reasonably separate from the national, just as they had before, but the rules themselves have been changing. For the most part, national parties have not been able to extend their control over local parties in anything other than elections, despite the fact that the politicization of local councils along national party lines has become a fact of life. Local parties, however, have become much more powerful, in particular in municipal and

[29]Stéphane Dion, *La Politisation des mairies* (Paris: Economica, 1986), p. 206.
[30]*Le Monde*, Mar. 8, 1989.
[31]*Le Monde*, Oct. 28, 1988.
[32]*Le Monde*, Feb. 10, 1989.

regional elections, where the introduction of proportional representation tended to reduce the size of the mayoral or presidential majority, thereby requiring coalition governments. Local parties also have generally followed their own course in making alliances and forming coalitions, often without the blessing of the national parties.

Moreover, whereas local party politics are differentiating themselves from national ones, local political elites are likewise increasingly differentiating themselves from the national elite. This has only been accelerated by the limitation of the *cumul des mandats*, which, by opening up major local positions, has led to an expansion of the political elite as well as an increase in competition among its members. The greatest change in elites, however, has occurred at the regional level, where new intermediate elites are taking over from the national notables who for the most part have chosen to retain their departmental presidencies. The regional elites tend to be younger, more urban-based, and more progressive than their more rural-focused counterparts in the departments. Although the elite is changing, it is no more representative in its occupational profile than it ever was. Members of departmental and regional elites in large measure tend to be managers, professionals, and teachers. Only mayors, the largest percentage of whom are in agricultural occupations, differ from the general profile; and most of them, in any event, would not qualify as notables.

The new rules of local politics. The new rules of the game are clearest at the regional level, in particular with the new coalitions of the moderate right and the extreme right and with the tacit alliances between the Socialists and the moderate right. They have resulted in large measure from the fact that the electoral laws requiring proportional representation have ensured that a number of regional councils do not have clear majorities and therefore have to ally themselves with other parties in order to win the presidency of the region. Of greatest concern to the national parties have been the understandings between the moderate right and the extreme right. In four regions – the Franche-Comté, Languedoc-Roussillon, Haute-Normandie, and Picardie – the extreme right was actively pursued to make up the necessary majority in the regional elections of March 1986. Moreover, in a number of elections for regional president, such as those of Jean-Claude Gaudin (UDF) in Provence-Alpes-Côte d'Azur in 1986 and Jean Tavernier in the Aquitaine in 1988, the moderate right made deals with the extreme right, for example, by promising them political favors or vice presidencies in return for their support.[33]

[33] *Le Monde*, July 13, 1988.

Not all members of the moderate right were willing to accept support by the extreme right, however. Although elected by a relative majority only at the third round, Michel Giraud in the Ile-de-France remained adamantly opposed to any alliance with the extreme right and he allowed them to be part of the executive bureaus of the regional assembly only because the law (subsequently rescinded) required it at the time. Bernard Stasi in the Champagne-Ardenne, also unwilling to accept the support of the extreme right despite his only relative majority from 1986 to 1988, benefited from a tacit alliance with the Socialists, who allowed the budget to pass by abstaining rather than by voting against, as the national executive bureaus of the PS had asked them to do.[34]

This kind of tacit alliance was not the only way in which local left-wing parties struck out on their own. In the Nord-Pas-de-Calais, for example, Communists collaborated quite amicably with the Socialists, unlike at the national level, voting with them on the budget. In return the president Noël Josèphe, allowed them to preside over three out of the eleven commissions (research, transport, and youth and sports).[35]

The regions, in short, are quite clearly developing their own rules of the game and thus separating themselves to some extent from the national rules even as national politics is penetrating the periphery. This has been equally true at the other levels of local government, mainly because in the departments and communes as much as in the regions, the national parties have exercised relatively little control over their local elected officials. This has been particularly the case on the right, in large measure because their elected officials, recruited on the basis of socioeconomic status rather than of party militancy or associational ties, see the party primarily as an outside point of support for local notables, who rely for power on their network of clientelistic relationships.[36] For the left, by contrast, the national parties have been much more important. Only the Communists, however, have been able to keep their local elected members very much under the thumb of the party. The party's system of control keeps reasonably tight reins on these members in the performance of their local mandate and relegates them to minor roles in the party structure in order to ensure that they do not gain an independent power base or challenge the party's central authority. For the Socialists, the party has served primarily as a system of selection and apprenticeship.[37] And generally, Socialist

[34]For accounts of the crisis as it unfolded, see *Le Monde*, Dec. 10–12, 16–25, 29, 30–1, 1987.
[35]*La Croix*, Mar. 5, 1986.
[36]Dion, *Politisation*, pp. 2, 3, 6.
[37]Ibid., pp. 3–6. See also Raymond Pronier, *Les Municipalités communistes* (Paris: Balland, 1983).

mayors control the local party, whether they start out with such control or not.[38]

With the exception of the Communists, then, the local political elites jealously guard their powers, seeking to maintain their independence from the national parties and, in certain cases, even from the local parties. As time passes, however, and local notables find themselves forced to give up their third and fourth mandates as a result of the limitation of the *cumul des mandats,* they are likely to find themselves more dependent on national party members to further their interests in Paris (especially if they hold only local office) and on local party members to support their interests in the level or levels of local government from which they are excluded. Party discipline at the national as well as at the local level is likely to benefit, therefore, as local elected officials are forced to put more faith in their fellow party members. But such discipline will be complicated by the increased competition among personalities on the left and the right resulting from the limitation of the *cumul.* A case in point has been the contest for mayor of Marseilles between Michel Pezet, former president of the regional council, and Defferre's chosen successor, Robert Vigoroux, who was unwilling to give up his position even in the face of being expelled from the Socialist federation and despite the promise of a Senate seat. Conflict between personalities within parties, in brief, will become an increasing problem at the local level, together with party discipline as a result of the *décumul.*

The changing elites. Most importantly, the limitation of the *cumul* is helping to open up the local political system. As it stood, the system was weighted in favor of the small number of elected officials who held two or three offices, holding local as well as national mandates. In 1983, 93 percent of Senators and 82 percent of Deputies benefited from this. Of the 640,000 municipal elected officials, not more than 5,312 can attain departmental office, whereas not more than approximately 1,000 can aspire to national office. Of those who do accumulate, a large majority are mayors of cities with more than thirty thousand inhabitants (in 1978, 36 percent held parliamentary office versus 0.5 percent for mayors of cities with fewer than thirty thousand).[39] There has been little difference

[38]For example, in the case of Alternance, a city of seventy-five thousand in the red belt surrounding Paris, the new Mitterrandist mayor who had been the national party's selection was unable to exert any control over the municipal councilors from rival Socialist groups for his first two years in office. He was ultimately able to consolidate his power with the help of two militants lent to him from the national party. Dion, *Politisation,* pp. 69–74.
[39]Jeanne Becquart-Leclercq, "Cumul des mandats et culture politique," in *Les Pouvoirs,* ed. Mabileau, p. 214.

in this regard between the right and the left. Whereas the pattern in the 1960s was for the right to accumulate more offices than the left, this had reversed itself by 1981, when the Socialists accumulated more offices than the right. By 1983, however, with the right's victories in the cantonal elections, the right and the left had close to equal rates of accumulation, (at between 82 percent and 83 percent for all Deputies but the Communists, at 77.3 percent), suggesting that the *cumul* had less to do with party policies than with electoral majority.[40]

Although the *décumul* will not alter the normal, primarily generational process of change in the political class as older politicians die or leave office, it will at least speed it up a bit by opening up positions formerly monopolized by a small handful of *cumulants*. The political system itself, moreover, may become more fragmented, with more problems in communication between levels of government by virtue of the fact that the integration accomplished by the *cumulants* in their very persons will diminish. But this in turn may ensure that the system as a whole will become more responsive to pressures from interests that in the past had much less influence.[41] Although the new notables are likely to become more responsive to the local electorate, they are not likely to become more representative of it in terms of their socioeconomic backgrounds. The local notables have always represented a social as well as a political elite, and this is not likely to change much.[42] The right's elected officials will continue to be members of the traditional local elites, who are from the liberal professions, farming, industry, and commerce and are generally chosen primarily because of their socioeconomic status; the left's will remain civil servants – primarily teachers (as of the municipal elections of 1977, over 45 percent of socialist mayors were teachers) – recruited for their union or associational ties.[43]

Decentralization, in brief, has not affected the overall, elite occupational profile of elected officials. It has served, however, to differentiate elected officials by occupation as well as by residence at the various levels of local government. The municipalities are dominated by those in agricultural occupations living in rural areas; the departments are dominated by those in management, the liberal professions, and teaching, representing, if not always living in, rural areas; and the regions are dominated by managers, professionals, and teachers, representing, as well as residing in, urban areas.

The communes, more specifically, tend to be most heavily dominated

[40]Ibid., pp. 217–220.
[41]Ibid., pp. 225–8.
[42]See Agulhon et al., *Les Maires.*
[43]Philippe Garaud, "Le personnel politique local français: Permanence ou changements?" in *Les Pouvoirs*, ed. A. Mabileau, pp. 179–81.

by those in agricultural professions, which, at 36.7 percent in 1987, constituted the single largest occupational group among mayors, and least heavily by members of the liberal professions at a surprisingly low 5.4 percent. The rest are reasonably evenly divided among the other occupational groups. The other part of the Third Republic coalition, the artisans and shopkeepers, along with the heads of enterprises, are at 11.8 percent; private sector employees, including engineers, managers, employees, and workers, at 14.1 percent; teachers at 7.8 percent; and civil servants and other public sector employees together, at 4.8 percent.[44] The predominance of mayors who are farmers is understandable once we remember that the large majority of the thirty-six thousand communes are rural, with twenty-eight thousand of them holding fewer than five hundred inhabitants. This predominance has not changed much over time: the average percentage of mayors in agricultural occupations was 46 percent from 1882 to 1966, although there has been some decline in very recent years, from an all time high of 51 percent in 1954 down to the average level of 45 percent in 1966, and then to 36.7 percent in 1987, paralleling the all time low of 37 percent in 1866.[45] The percentage change in the number of mayors in agricultural professions has, nevertheless, been pronounced in recent years, especially when compared with other categories, whether they went up or down. Mayors in agricultural professions decreased by close to 9 points between 1971 and 1987, whereas the shopkeepers and artisans along with heads of business fell by less than 3 points and the liberal professions by 0.4 at the same time that private sector employees gained 3.7 points, teachers 3.3, and civil servants 0.6 (Fig. 8.1).

This distribution of occupational categories at the municipal level contrasts markedly with that at the departmental level (Fig. 8.2). In 1985, the percentage of general councilors in agricultural occupations (10.15 percent) was 26.6 points lower than that of mayors in 1987; the percentage of those in liberal professions (24 percent) was 18.6 points higher than that of mayors; of those in the teaching profession (16.4 percent), 8.6 points higher than that of mayors; and of those in other public sector occupations (8.4 percent), slightly under double that of mayors. The other categories remain quite close in their distribution, with artisans, shopkeepers, and heads of enterprises at 12.4 percent, and with private sector employees (including engineers, managers, employees, and workers) at 13.4 percent. There have been changes over a short period of time even here, however, mirroring those at the communal level. General councilors in agricultural occupations declined from 21.9 percent in 1955 to

[44]Ministry of the Interior, cited in *Le Monde,* July 4, 1987.
[45]Agulhon et al., *Les Maires,* p. 83.

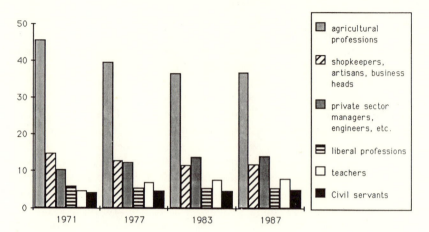

Figure 8.1: Percentages of mayors by occupational category. Source: *Actualités juridique-droit administratif* (Mar. 20, 1987); and *Le Monde,* July 4, 1987.

18.3 percent in 1964, then more rapidly, to 13.6 percent in 1974, and subsequently down to 10.8 percent in 1982, whereas those in intermediate professions (including middle-level managers and teachers) increased appreciably from 5.7 percent in 1955 and 7 percent in 1964 to 20.5 percent in 1978 and 21.5 percent in 1982.[46]

The occupational differences between local elected officials in the communes and the departments suggest that, although the rural remains dominant in the departments, those who promote the interests of its population are generally those who can afford to, both in time and money, given that departmental councilors are for the most part unremunerated (except for daily expenses and indemnities, which can add up, however). And these fit predominantly into the category of upper-level management and liberal professions, at over 35 percent.[47] It is at the departmental and regional levels, in short, that the "notables" are most clearly in evidence. But there are nevertheless important differences between the regions and departments in terms of their representation.

Those elected at the regional level tend to differentiate themselves quite markedly by occupation from mayors and, to a lesser extent, from general councilors (Fig. 8.2). Farmers at 6.3 percent in 1986 tend to be underrepresented in the regions, at 30.4 percentage points lower than among mayors in 1987 and 3.9 percentage points lower than among general councilors in 1985. By comparison, the rest of the Third Republic coalition of artisans and shopkeepers, along with heads of enterprises, at

[46]Dosière, Foretier, and Mastias, *Le Nouveau Conseil,* pp. 52–7.
[47]Ibid., p. 55.

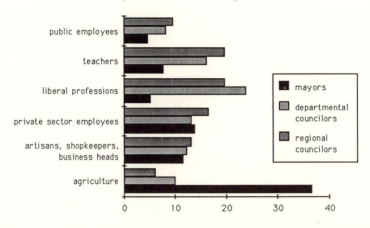

Figure 8.2: Comparison of mayors, departmental councilors, and regional councilors by occupational category (in percentages). Source: *Actualités juridique-droit administratif* (Mar. 20, 1987); and *Le Monde,* July 4, 1987. Notes: The figures on mayors are from 1987, those on departmental councilors from 1985, those on regional councilors from 1986.

13.3 percent in the regions, came very close to the percentages among mayors (within 1.5 points) and general councilors (within 1 point). But this is the only category in which the three levels of local government have come so close to each other. There were over 3 percent more private sector employees in the regions (at 16.8 percent) than in the departments (at 13.4 percent) and over 2 percent more in the communes (at 14.1 percent). At the regional and departmental levels, the number of teachers came within 3.5 points of each other (at 19.9 percent to 16.4 percent, respectively) and the number of civil servants within 1.5 points of each other (at 9.9 percent to 8.4 percent, respectively). There was a more than 10-point difference, however, between these levels and the mayoral for teachers, and close to a 4-point difference for civil servants. Finally, only in the case of the liberal professions did the departments outdistance the regions (by 4.1 points); but the regions still came out far ahead of the communes (by 14.5 points). The result is that the regions contain many more of the Socialists' targeted constituency of *salariés,* at 46.6 percent wage earners to 39.5 percent independents (there is a negligible number of salaried agricultural workers included in those in agricultural professions), than either the departments, at 38.2 percent wage earners to 46.6 percent independents, or the communes, at 26.7 percent wage earners to 53.9 percent independents.

There is more to differentiate regional councilors from departmental and municipal ones, however, than the relative absence of those in agricultural occupations and the greater number of wage earners, and that is the prevalence of more urban-based notables. Even though the rural-dominated departments were responsible for drawing up the lists, the candidates for regional election tended to be from urban areas, with those at the top of the list primarily mayors of the major cities of the region. In some cases, mayors of the most important cities in the departments chose to run for the regional elections rather than the legislative ones, for example, in the Franche-Comté and in the Loire. Even lists with a balance between rural and urban forces tended to be exceptions to the rule of urban-led lists.[48]

Moreover, although more rural, departmentally based councilors remain on the regional council, they are a small minority. In a study carried out in 1986, these departmentalists represented only 10 percent of members of regional councils versus 42 percent who were convinced regionalists. And they are clearly distinguishable from the new breed of regional councilors not only in their preference for the departments but also in their profile: they tend to accumulate at least three elective offices and, for the most part, are general councilors or mayors of small communes with fewer than five thousand inhabitants. By contrast, the new regional councilors are convinced regionalists, who tend to be younger than the departmentalists (under forty years of age versus over fifty for the departmentalists), to accumulate fewer mandates (two-thirds have only one or two), often as a mayor or vice-mayor in a large or medium-sized city; and to base their status as notables on their technical understanding of political power or on their activities as party militants.[49]

What is more, the limitation of the *cumul des mandats* has only intensified the differentiation of the regional from the departmental elite. Where the *décumul* demands a choice between region and department, a large majority of the older, more nationally prominent notables have chosen the department, leaving the younger, more intermediate notables to take charge at the regional level. In the regional elections of 1986, in effect, only those elections crucial to the regional balance of power had a national notable heading the regional as well as the legislative list, for example, Jacques Chaban-Delmas in Aquitaine, Jean-Pierre Chevènement in Franche-Comté, Olivier Guichard in the Loire, and Laurent Fabius in Haute-Normandie.[50] And as of fall 1988, either in preparation for the cantonal elections or in anticipation of the municipal elections, even more national notables abandoned regional presidencies in favor of their departmental or communal mandates, to be re-

[48]Mabileau, "La nationalisation," pp. 39–40, 43.
[49]Annick Percheron, "Jeunes loups et vieux lions," *Le Monde,* July 5–6, 1987; and idem, "Quelle région pour les Nouveaux élus?" Paper presented for the conference, La nouvelle région – An I (Paris, March 18, 1987); and the study of Béatrice Roy, "Images de la région," carried out by the Observatoire interrégional du politique (Paris, 1986), pp. 6–7.
[50]Mabileau, "La nationalisation," p. 43.

placed by much less well-known, intermediate notables, for example, Dominique Baudis in Midi-Pyrénées – replaced by Marc Censi; Bernard Stasi in Champagne-Ardenne – replaced by Jean Kaltenbach; and Michel Giraud in Île-de-France – replaced by Pierre-Charles Krieg.

This differentiation in departmental and regional elites is even reflected in its electorate. The regional elite is geared to a younger, more urban electorate made up of the *salariés* than the departmental elite, which tends to appeal to an older population conforming in many ways to the old Third Republic coalition of farmers, shopkeepers, and artisans. Thus, a survey of the local electorate's views of the region uncovered that the most convinced regionalists, as found in the Rhône-Alpes, are managers and members of the intermediate professions who are urban and mobile, are confident in the future of the region, identify with the region, and defend its policies and its projects. By contrast, the departmentalists are for the most part farmers, artisans, or shopkeepers, who tend either to be old, rural, and sedentary, focused primarily on their commune, confident only in the future of the department, and opposed to what they see as a waste of resources at the regional level, as in the Loire, Poitou-Charente, and Picardie or, as in Limousin or Midi-Pyrénées, interested only in what the region can do for them.[51]

This differentiation between regions and departments in chosen electorates as much as in elites can only be intensified by the fact that the departments and the regions are mandated to perform very different functions for generally very different clienteles. Because the departments have primary responsibility over health and social services, they will probably remain the creatures of the rural communes and the declining social stratum of peasants and shopkeepers. The department's health and social services functions will necessarily tilt it toward the rural communes, given the aging of the population in those areas. In the area of economic development, too, its new functions ensure that its focus will be on the rural, having been charged with the coordination of communal policy and encouraged to set up a technical agency to counsel communes on the different aspects of public economic intervention. Even its mandate to aid enterprises in difficulty, although not necessarily located in rural areas, suggests that the department, even when it is not focusing on declining populations, is nonetheless focused on decline, albeit industrial.

The whole set of functions of the departments, in brief, suggests that they will remain traditional, in support of the traditional groups that dominate the countryside. By contrast, because the newly legitimated regions have control over local economic development, they are more

[51] Roy, "Images de la région." Paper presented for the conference, La Nouvelle Région – An I, pp. 9–11.

likely to become dominated by those having the most interest in such development: the urban agglomerations in which the *salariés* reside. Even their mode of election, which approximates much more closely the actual population distribution in the regions than the departments ever could, given their cantonal basis, favors urban populations. The regions, therefore, may give the *salariés* a political base they formerly had only in the large cities (which, because of their size, their own administrative resources, and the deputy mayors enabled them to go around departments and prefects directly to Paris).

Local elites, thus, have been changing as a result of their different mandates and their differing electorates. Moreover, they have been playing by new rules of the game, with increased competition coming not only from the growth in local party politics but also from the expansion in the political class resulting from the limitation in the accumulation of offices.

Toward a new local democracy?

The new politics in the periphery, however, has so far remained limited to the political class. And the democracy it has encouraged is primarily representative in nature, as opposed to the direct democracy hoped for by the *autogestionnaires,* in which citizens would express their opinions through direct participation in local government or as counter-powers to it. The local population, in effect, has generally appeared unaware of, or uninterested in, decentralization. The powers of local notables have increased not only because of the laws themselves but also because of the quiescence of the local population.

It is not really fair, however, to condemn decentralization as a whole because it has increased the powers of the notables but has not yet encouraged local democracy. Jean-Pierre Worms, Deputy of Saône-et-Loire, even agreed that in the beginning decentralization would produce bosses, but that these are "infantile sicknesses" that will go away, especially because the people themselves will begin to respond with "counter-powers to the new powers of local officials."[52] In a similar vein, former Prime Minister Pierre Mauroy suggested that, although for the moment we may indeed have decentralized Jacobinism, all reform is like good wine – it takes time for it to give its all.[53] It took some time before people, as individuals or as part of associations, realized that they had to go to the *Hôtel du département* or the *Hôtel de région* instead of the *Préfecture* for their needs. But there is evidence to suggest that decentralization has improved the

[52]Worms, "La décentralisation," pp. 31–2.
[53]Quoted in Antonio Martins, "Pluie et Bourrasque pour un ex-premier," *L'Alsace,* June 15, 1985.

relationship between the local population and its political representatives. In a recent survey, a majority of local leaders noted at least some improvement in the relations between citizens and local elected officials (8 percent saw a lot, 24 percent saw enough, and 29 percent saw a little, as opposed to 28 percent who saw no improvement). And a smaller majority (53 percent) also agreed that decentralization increased the influence of citizens over the decisions of local elected officials (versus 39 percent who disagreed).[54]

In any event, even if the local population remains uninterested in exercising its new powers, it is clear that local elected officials are all too aware of the potential impact of those new powers and are therefore doing everything they can to make certain that they are responsive to the needs and desires of the local population in anticipation of the awakening of the periphery. In consequence, the notables in the periphery are changing their policies and their modus operandi. According to Jean-Marie Rausch, the only local elected officials likely to survive in the new political context were those capable of changing from the old politics to the new, meaning that they had to become good managers of local administration as well as good democrats, attuned to the new needs and desires of the local population.[55] This is in fact what has happened. Even the old notables on the left who retained their seats or those on the right who regained theirs are looking increasingly like the new notables on both sides. Most are engaging in a new kind of politics: one involved in encouraging the participation of associational and socioprofessional groups in decision-making processes, one more focused on managing local government more efficiently and effectively, and one more responsive to the needs of the local population.[56]

New channels of communication have been opening up, with local governmental agencies seeking to be more responsive to their clients and to the associations concerned with urban life, for example, with urban renewal, pollution, traffic, and public transportation. Thus, they provide greater opportunities for citizen participation through more regular meetings with citizens' groups, enlarged municipal commissions, coordination committees for cultural affairs and sports, as well as increased support for the associations providing services to the city's population through subsidies, free office space, and technical assistance. Finally, municipal governments have been stepping up their efforts to reach the local population not only through the traditional means, that is through electoral campaigns, mailings, posters, and personal contacts, but also by turning

[54]*Le Monde*, Dec. 4–5, 1988.
[55]Jean-Marie Rausch (UDF), regional president of the Lorraine, Senator and mayor of Metz, interview with author, Metz, June 18, 1985.
[56]See the discussion in Part II, Chapter 10, "The rhetoric of good management."

to surveys, audiovisual montages, telephone answering services, exposi-
tions, and public access to municipal council sessions.[57]

Although part of this new politics is dictated by the new laws, for
example, the consultation required by the regional planning process,
most of it is a result of a new attitude on the part of local politicians who
are intent on responding to the needs and desires of the local population.
How to determine what the needs and desires of the local population are,
however, is the question. There have been many different answers to this,
as is suggested by the variety of ways in which consultation in the first
regional planning process took place, ranging from corporatist arrangements to direct democracy. In the Nord-Pas-de-Calais, for example, local
governments and the local population were only minimally involved as
the region set up corporatist committees consisting of members representing industry, administration, civil service, unions, and associations, in
addition to some experts on the subject of regional development and
some elected officials, who were not however participating in an official
capacity.[58] In regions such as the Lorraine and Burgundy, by contrast, the
region remained much more in control of the entire process, sending out
questionnaires to local governments. Because of the low response rate,
the region was left to set its priorities without significant input from most
of the presumably interested parties.

Although most regions focused on socioprofessional groups and associations, some used more democratic procedures. In Languedoc-Roussillon,
the region allowed for democratic participation in the planning process by
the citizenry at large by holding public debates in town meetings in the
major cities. Democratic sentiment, however, was not the main reason the
region chose public meetings. Rather, it was a way to exclude the hostile
departmental councils completely from the consultation process.[59]

In the second regional planning process, though, there were many more
instances of democratic participation in the formal consultation phase.
For example, the new initiatives of the Nord-Pas-de-Calais in the area of
education were generated by a highly democratic process in which regional and educational authorities consulted with such a wide range of
the interested parties (by the end, the region had consulted with over
twenty-five hundred individuals), that even a member of the UDF opposition had to admit that the regional majority had taken into account all of

[57]Dion, *Politisation*, pp. 30–2.
[58]Christophe Masse, Leonard I. Koni, François-David Hennion, "La participation
du département au Plan de la région." Paper presented at a conference sponsored by
the Nord-Pas-de-Calais regional section of the Institut français des sciences administratives (Lille, Mar. 12, 1984).
[59]L. H. Schlenker, "Local Industrial Strategies: A Key to French Economic Planning
in the Eighties?" *Comparative Politics*, vol. 19, no. 3 (Apr. 1987): 271.

the views *de base* as to what was to be done.[60] Such an increase in local democracy has actually characterized the whole area of education, with parents' groups getting more involved in such issues as the need to build more lycées as well as the maintenance of the physical plant in general. Local elected officials have been feeling public pressure quite directly. And feeling the pressure, they immediately set to work to repair the worst of the dilapidation in the schools.

This sensitivity to the demands of democracy, in brief, has affected most notables. But it is a democracy that is controlled by the local notables and carried out through formal governmental channels. Thus, although decentralization has indeed produced a greater local democracy, it is one characterized by pluralism in the structures of local government and in contests for local office; it has yet to reach the populace directly.

THE NEW DECENTRALIZED *DIRIGISME* IN LOCAL ECONOMIC DEVELOPMENT

At the same time that the decentralization of local government has enhanced a political pluralism based on political competition among parties, personalities, and political elites, it has also promoted greater administrative pluralism through increased administrative cooperation and competition among units within each level of local government as well as between levels. Nowhere is this increased administrative pluralism more apparent than in the sphere of local economic development, where the increase in newly empowered actors and the vast new array of incentive structures and programs has made a new pluralism inescapable.

Economic development in France at the national level is characterized by something I call "decentralized *dirigisme*," in which the *dirigisme*, or highly centralized, directive approach to economic development of the state, is decentralized in practice because it is implemented in a highly pluralistic and uncoordinated way.[61] By decentralizing responsibility for the public promotion of local economic development, the Socialists extended this decentralized *dirigisme* to the local level by giving local governments the powers and resources to become *dirigiste*, or interventionist, in their own right. This new *dirigisme* is contained in the local governments' new mandate to promote economic development, business expansion and innovation, and job creation, as well as in the new regional planning process, which has democratized as it decentralized

[60]*Le Monde*, Jan. 14, 1988.
[61]See Vivien Schmidt, "Industrial Management under the Socialists in France: Decentralized *dirigisme* at the National and Local Levels," *Comparative Politics* vol. 21, no. 1 (Oct. 1988).

national planning. This *dirigisme,* however, has itself been highly decentralized in consequence of the number of actors – national and even supranational, as well as local – involved in local economic development. The fact that national level *dirigisme* has not disappeared with official decentralization has only increased the decentralized implementation of local *dirigisme,* as local governments cooperate or compete with one another, with regional representatives of the field services of the state, and with the prefects, while they negotiate with national ministries (for example, Plan and DATAR), with the nationalized industries and banks, and even with the EEC for the large amount of different kinds of aid available for local economic development.

Thus, even though the decentralization laws gave the regions primary responsibility in the area of local economic development, all local elected officials – whether mayors, departmental presidents, or regional presidents, on the right or the left – came to see one of their major roles as that of fostering the "enterprise spirit" and of encouraging the growth of business in their constituencies.[62] Despite the fact that the economic crisis severely limited the amount of investment funds made available to every level of local government, thereby curtailing many efforts to encourage local economic development, it did not in any way cripple the decentralization project as a whole. On the contrary, it acted as a spur to innovation and experimentation in the promotion of local development as it brought home the urgency of attending to such questions as how to reduce unemployment, retrain workers, encourage job and business creation, and attract industry to depressed areas.

The decentralized dirigisme *in regional planning*

Although the decentralized *dirigisme* in local economic development involves a pluralism of interests, it has its focus at the regional level. The Socialists' decentralization reforms in the economic planning area in particular have turned regional governments into the equivalent of local industrial development brokers and, thus, the lower level *dirigiste* equivalent to the state for small and medium-sized businesses. As such, their power extends far beyond the financial means at their disposal or the particular arenas of action that are their strict, legal responsibility. Through their central role in the regional planning process, the regions

[62]For the many different ways in which the growth of business was encouraged, see, for example, Patrick Mollis and Jacques Rondin, "Les interventions économiques des collectivités locales," *Sociologie du Travail* no. 27 (Mar. 1985): 244–53; André Lefebvre and Jean-Claude Meyer, *Planification et amènagement* (Paris: Berger-Levrault, 1985); and Commissariat Général du Plan, *Interventions économiques des collectivités locales* (Paris: Documentation française, 1985).

can plot the direction of local economic development as well as influence the nature and extent of major local investment projects. They consult with local governments in drawing up regional plans, negotiate with the state on regional planning contracts, work with the nationalized industries and banks as well as with the DATAR and other central ministries in local development schemes, and even request aid from the EEC's various regional development programs (much to the consternation of national officials, intent on keeping control of the process themselves).

The regions' new "decentralized *dirigisme*" in the planning arena represents a significant improvement over the "deconcentrated *dirigisme*" of the past, in which national plans did little to promote small business enterprise and national planners focused on the large organization as the vehicle of economic development.[63] The Socialists, by contrast with the Gaullist planners, were convinced that local governmental promotion of small and midsize businesses and industries (the PME-PMI) was the route to economic recovery in the periphery because small firms have greater flexibility and more creativity than the larger ones (and the larger ones, in any case, are involved at the national level). Thus, they saw the creation of a dense network of small and medium-sized enterprises on the regional level, in the words of Jacques Caroux, as "the tool for recapturing the internal market and creating productive jobs."[64]

In the new regional planning process, the national plan is linked to regional planning contracts and elaborated on the basis of a reasonably democratic consultation process. The central state outlines the priority programs of the national plan after regional input and then negotiates planning contracts with the regions once the regions have outlined their own preliminary plans following input from the departments, communes, and the CES (regional economic and social committees). Decentralization is actually built into the mechanisms of the regional planning process itself, with the regions' mandate to consult with departments, the communes which are departmental seats as well as those with more than 100,00 inhabitants, and the CES. The plans themselves were generally drawn up by tripartite commissions made up of members from business, labor, and local government, and negotiated by the subprefect for re-

[63]In 1979, for example, out of the 8 billion francs in aid to industry, only 1.5 billion francs or 19 percent went to small business, with the bulk going to nationalized industries and large-scale firms with over twenty thousand employees. This might not seem a low figure until one considers the fact that agriculture received 17 billion francs, or that out of the total aid budget, which also included 33 billion frances for public services, the share for small business was only 3 percent. For the French planners' approach, see Stephen S. Cohen, "Informed bewilderment: French economic strategy and the crisis," in *France in the Troubled World Economy*, ed. Stephen S. Cohen and Peter A. Gourevitch (London: Butterworth, 1982), pp. 28–9.
[64]Caroux, "End of Administrative Centralization?" p. 113.

gional development.[65] The regions themselves were to decide on who the members of these commissions would be, as well as what their particular mechanism for consultation would be. Therefore, the kind as well as the amount of *dirigisme,* or central direction, exercised by the region varied somewhat from one region to the next and encompassed differences in who was consulted and whose advice was taken. The result, in the first regional planning effort, was a good deal more *dirigisme* than decentralization. But this has already been in large measure remedied in the second planning effort.

To begin with, the CES, or regional economic and social committees, were much less influential in the first regional planning process than might have been expected, given the importance of their role prior to decentralization. In some regions, the CES were asked for advice only after a regional plan had been elaborated, whereas in others there was no direct consultation at all. Only in a few regions did the CES play a central role in the planning process, for example in Franche-Comté and in the Midi-Pyrénées. The CES explained its marginalization in relation to regional identity and politics, suggesting that the least satisfied CES were found in regions with little regional identity such as Bourgogne, the Centre, and Basse-Normandie, whereas the most satisfied were in regions with an identity strong enough to enable them to overcome political cleavages such as Bretagne, Aquitaine, and Franche-Comté.[66] With the new regional planning initiatives for the Tenth Plan, however, the problem appears to have been resolved, with the CES having been consulted in the preliminary stages.

The experience of many local governments was similar to that of the CES with the first regional plan, although with much less deliberate marginalization. In some regions, the department–region planning relationship was quite well developed and formalized: the general councils of the departments elaborated their own plans, which were then incorporated into the regional plan, for example, in the Charente in Poitou-Charente and the Hautes-Pyrénées in Midi-Pyrénées.[67] In other regions, by contrast, the cities were the primary focus and the departments were left out almost entirely, as in the Languedoc-Roussillon.[68] In yet other regions, neither the departments nor the communes had much official input. Sometimes this was out of a seeming lack of interest, as in the case of Bourgogne (which received only 200 responses from rural communes out of the total of 2,040 questionnaires it sent out)[69] and the Lorraine

[65]For a discussion of the planning process, see Xavier Greffe, *Territoires en France* (Paris: Economica, 1984), pp. 238–9.

[66]Commissariat Général du Plan, *Evaluation de la planification décentralisée* (Paris: Documentation française, 1986), pp. 76–7.

[67]Ibid., p. 17.

[68]Schlenker, "Strategies," p. 271.

[69]Plan, *Planification*, p. 16.

(which did not fare much better).[70] Other times, however, this lack of input was quite deliberate, as in the case of the departments in the Nord-Pas-de-Calais, which in this way sought to avoid any possibility of regional encroachment over their domain.[71]

In some cases, moreover, the lack of participation of departments in the regional planning process had to do with differences within regions involving such factors as political cleavages, historical rivalries, and kinds and levels of industrialization. For example, in the region Provence-Alpes-Côte d'Azur, Jacques Médecin, president of the department of the Alpes-Maritimes as well as mayor of Nice, insisted that his department's poor showing in the regional plan had less to do with the region's left-wing majority at that time than with its preoccupation with heavy industry in the areas around Marseilles as opposed to his own department's focus on high technology and tourism.[72] In the Lorraine, Philippe Séguin, RPR Deputy and mayor of Épinal, complained that the Vosges was generally neglected by the region because of political and industrial differences (even though the regional council, like the general council of the department, was on the right), with regional resources focused on revitalizing heavy industry and divided between the more politically powerful departments containing the historically rival cities of Metz, whose mayor was Jean-Marie Rausch, a UDF Senator and regional president, and Nancy, whose mayor was André Rossinot, at that time the last nationally elected member of the *Parti radical*.[73]

Political cleavages, historical rivalries, and differences in levels and kinds of industrialization are only part of the story, however. Much of the lack of participation or regional *dirigisme* sans decentralization can be explained equally well by the fact that the regional planning process was itself so new and came at a time when local elected officials were preoccupied with their own new duties as a result of decentralization. In the Lorraine, for instance, upper-level, regional civil servants described the situation quite differently from Séguin, insisting that the problem was more administrative than political, and that neither the departments nor the communes realized how important the plans would be. The departments, already overburdened with their newly transferred responsibilities in social services, simply didn't do what they were charged to do by law in the area of rural land-use planning and consultation with the rural communes. Few cities, moreover, had done any real planning or had anything other than interim programs. Some mayors were even openly

[70]Upper-level regional civil servants in the Lorraine, interviews with the author, Metz, June 1985.
[71]See Part II, Chapter 9, "The regions" and "The Departments."
[72]Jacques Médecin, interview with author, Nice, June 7, 1985.
[73]Philippe Séguin, interview with author, Épinal, June 18, 1985.

hostile to the effort. One civil servant recounts that when Séguin, in his capacity as mayor of Épinal, was asked to contribute to the planning effort, he responded that planning was for technocrats and that his own job was "to manage everyday affairs." Although he subsequently complained greatly about the lack of funds for his city, he actually did nothing in the planning process to secure such funds. Séguin was not alone in this, however. The departments and cities generally were marginalized as a result of their lack of participation in the planning process, finding themselves without the necessary resources for development. Every time they sought new resources from the state, they were referred back to the planning contract in which they didn't figure.[74]

Local governments, however, have learned from their experience. With the Tenth Plan begun in 1989 the *dirigisme* of the regional governments has become more decentralized with the greater participation of the local governments and the CES in the planning process.

The decentralization in the regions' *dirigisme* resulted not only from the role other levels of local government played in the regional planning process but also from that of the state, which exerted its own *dirigiste* pressures on the regions. State-level *dirigisme*, after all, did not disappear with the regional planning process, because regions had to draw up their plans with national priorities in mind or else face losing their credits. The regions, in consequence, risked allowing the state not only to mobilize their resources in the service of national objectives but also to frame their development strategies for the years to come.[75] This danger was reduced appreciably, however, by the fact that the state–region negotiation process was quite decentralized, both in terms of the amount of regional input into the process and the differing degrees of central direction exercised by the different central ministries.

To begin with, the fact that the regional plans accorded with the priority programs set out in the national plan does not indicate nearly as much central direction as one might assume. Intent on getting as much money as possible, the regions generally wrote up their plans to look as if they were in conformity with national priorities. There was, after all, a very long list of possible actions. The resulting contracts ended up being quite diverse, reflecting the different needs of the regions, for example, agriculture in the South and professional training in the North and East; the state's attempt to right the balance among regions in terms of industrial activity, that is, by particular efforts in favor of Poitou-Charente, Limousin, Auvergne, Aquitaine, Midi-Pyrénées, and Languedoc-Rousillon; and the state's interest in

---

[74]Upper-level regional civil servants in the Lorraine, interviews with the author.
[75]Jacques Chevallier, "La région dans le système politico-administratif français," in *L'Institution régionale,* ed. Centre universitaire de Recherche sur l'Administration et la Politique de Picardie (CURAPP) (Paris: Presses universitaires de Paris, 1984).

aiding local governments with special needs, for example, in cleaning up the seacoast or rural tourism.

Moreover, the actual state–region negotiation process suggests that the regions had a good deal of input, not only on their own authority during the negotiation process, but also prior to negotiation, through the prefects. The prefects, we should not forget, have traditionally kept the interests of the locality closer to heart than those of the state. And although decentralization returned the prefect to a role clearly representative of the central state, such a change is surely one slowly learned. When the regional prefects were asked at the end of 1982 to identify for the center (DATAR, in this case) the probable demands of the regions, they were more likely than not reflecting the desires of the regional councils.

This is not to say that the regions always got what they wanted. After all, however much input the regions have, whether directly or indirectly, the state retains the upper hand in financial terms. If in no other way, state control is guaranteed simply by the fact that the state loses nothing by holding out on signing the planning contract, whereas the region can lose a great deal.[76] And the state did not hesitate to exercise this power. In the case of Corsica, for example, which balked at certain provisions in the planning contract for political reasons, the state delayed the signing of the contract until Corsica agreed to certain state requirements. But Corsica, in the end, came out ahead, with the highest state share of financing by comparison to the region (at a ratio of 3.7 francs to 1 franc).

The state, in fact, often exerted pressure to get its way; but by giving in to some of the state's demands, the regions generally benefited handsomely. The Nord-Pas-de-Calais, by agreeing to go along with the state's rejection of a number of regional proposals and to put half of its budget into areas recommended by the Ninth Plan, ended up with an extremely advantageous planning contract (for every franc it put in, the state was to give the region 1.67 francs). Although the Nord-Pas-de-Calais did well, neighboring Lorraine – confronting very similar economic problems but controlled by the political opposition – did even better, getting its way in terms of substantive proposals and in terms of money (for every franc the region provided, the state was to contribute 3.2 francs).[77] In short, even though the state had a distinct advantage over the region in the negotiation process, given that its refusal to sign would leave the region without funds, it chose to exercise that advantage only in certain cases. And even when it did, it remains open to question who the real winner was in the end.

[76]See Jacques Chevallier, "Administration et développement local en France," *Revue Française d'Administration Publique* no. 34 (Apr.–June, 1985): 170–80.
[77]For a full discussion of the financing of the regional plans, see Part II, Chapter 10, "The regions' new resources and the promotion of local economic development."

It is misleading, however, to talk of the state as a single entity, even when considering the regional planning process, because the different ministries engaged in differing degrees of *dirigisme* in the negotiation as well as in the implementation of the state–region planning contracts. Of the ministries involved, the least amount of central direction came from those concerned with the modernization of productive activities, that is, the adaptation of business, service industries, and artisanry to technological change, support for investment in production, and so forth. The greatest amount of central direction quite predictably came from the ministries of education, research, and culture. Whereas the ministries of education and research generally seemed to ignore regional preferences in the placement of high schools or research institutes, the ministry of culture, although presenting no difficulties in the negotiating process or in the granting of funds, insisted after the signing of the regional contract on further specific contracts enabling it to exercise qualitative control.[78]

The amount of *dirigisme* exercised by even these most centralizing ministries, however, has been diminishing. The ministry of education, to take one example, has been much more receptive to regions' desires in the second regional planning initiatives, in partial response to the increasing pressures the regions have brought to bear in their efforts to gain greater influence in the areas of pedagogy, programs, and schedules. By 1986 it was clear that, although the ministry retains the last word, each region determines the order of priority in educational investments, depending on local needs, regional policies, or electoral interests.[79] By 1988 there was general agreement that the regions influence the direction of education, if not the "pedagogy," or content, of particular subjects of study, if only because their powers in adult education link up with high school construction and the creation of places for certain kinds of baccalaureates. Most importantly, perhaps, such influence has been welcomed by regional educational administrations such as that of the Nord-Pas-de-Calais (the *rectorat* of the Academy of Lille), which noted that the regional planning initiatives seeking the overall improvement of education and new high school construction involved doing more and doing it "faster than the State."[80]

The regions have not been successful in all areas, however. In professional development, there have been signs of recentralization, in large measure because this became an area of central governmental initiative under the neoliberal government.[81] For the most part, however, as the regional governments have become more confident – especially since

---

[78]Plan, *Planification*, pp. 29–30, 40.
[79]*Le Monde*, Nov. 13, 1986.
[80]*Le Monde*, Jan. 14, 1988.
[81]Bechtel, Henry-Meininger, and Jegouzo, "Chronique," pp. 157–8.

their legitimation through the election of their officials by universal suffrage in March 1986 – they have become more assertive in their own *dirigisme* with regard to the state, thus ensuring greater decentralization in the state's *dirigisme*. At the same time, they have also promoted greater decentralization in their own *dirigisme* through their encouragement of the increased participation of the departments, the communes, and the CES in the regional planning process.

The decentralization in the state's continued dirigisme

For all this, the state by no means gave up its own interest in promoting local economic development. On the contrary, it has continued to use its own resources to promote particular initiatives as well as to influence the overall direction of local development. Examples of this are the *bassins d'emploi,* or geographical areas centered around a depressed urban area in which employment is to be promoted, and the fifteen *pôles de conversion,* or reindustrialization zones established in 1984 in economic disaster areas, which were to receive special grants and subsidies in every possible kind of aid (for example, professional education, worker retraining, subsidies for industrial restructuring, funds for roads, housing, and public works) and which are administered by the prefect in consultation with the local governments concerned.[82]

The Socialists also passed a variety of measures intended to facilitate local business creation and innovation that went beyond those controlled by the regions. These included such provisions as: (1) eliminating taxes on the profits of industrial firms for their first three years in operation; (2) permitting employees with three years of seniority or more to take a sabbatical for one year (and in some cases two) in order to start a new business, with their jobs guaranteed upon return; (3) allowing laid-off employees to use six months of their unemployment benefits as investment or collateral for a newly created company; (4) requiring the clerk of

[82]In the *pôles* alone between the beginning of 1984 and mid-1986, for example, five hundred applicants received land-use planning credits, at an average of 47,000 francs per job, in order to create 27,500 jobs over a three-year period and to realize 7.65 billion francs in investment (the national average is 35,000 francs per job). In addition, industries in the *pôles* had available to them 2 billion francs from the FIM, an industrial modernization fund; 1.5 billion francs from the *Fonds spécial des grands travaux* (FSGT), a special public works fund; 460 million francs from the *Fonds d'intervention d'aménagement du territoire* (FIAT), a land-use planning intervention fund – mainly to restore abandoned industrial buildings; and the 640 million francs from the *Fonds européen de développement régionale* (FEDER), the European regional development fund. There were also special funds for the Lorraine and the Nord, where employers didn't have to pay payroll taxes and, for all communes in the *pôles,* there was the possibility of benefiting from the business tax equalization fund for a period of five years. *Le Monde,* Oct. 5–6, 1986.

the Commerce Court to respond within fifteen days to any demand to register a new business; and (5) giving grants to new businesses of twenty thousand francs per job created over three years. In addition, the Socialists sought to ease the way for venture capital companies by exempting such firms from paying corporate tax on the income and net capital gains on the shares of their holdings in nonquoted companies; by allowing the *Sociétés financières d'innovation* (SFI), which promote research and new inventions, a special depreciation allowance of 50 percent; and by passing the law of January 1985 mandating the formation of local public–private, venture-capital corporations to fund start-up firms in the hi-tech industry.[83] The Socialist government even created a division of the ministry of employment charged solely with encouraging local business initiative and job creation related to the *économie sociale,* that is cooperatives, associations, and worker-owned businesses.

What is more, the state involvement in the promotion of local economic development did not at all diminish with the accession to power in March, 1986 of the neoliberals who pledged themselves to "less state." Differences in political orientation may have affected the nature of government intervention in certain instances, but not the fact of government intervention. Whereas the left generally provided direct subsidies to business, the right tended to emphasize indirect subsidies; and the socialist *pôles de conversion,* which provided direct subsidies for firms locating in the designated, economically depressed areas, were succeeded by the neoliberal *zones d'entreprises,* or enterprise zones, which offer indirect subsidies in the form of a ten-year freedom from certain taxes. In addition, after cutting funding for small business creation and innovation in 1986 and 1987 by abolishing the FIM, a fund for industrial modernization, in 1986, and by reducing the budget of ANVAR, the national agency for applied research, which provides management consulting and financing through interest-free loans for up to 50 percent of a project, the neoliberal government increased such funding significantly for 1988. The ANVAR's budget this year jumped to 950 million francs (it was reduced to 699 million francs in 1986 from 706 million francs in 1985, and fell even lower in 1987). The agency took on new initiatives, including attempts to promote smaller companies' use of available technical information by meeting up to 75 percent (with a maximum of Fr. 7,500) of the costs of market research; to encourage research institute–industry cooperation by meeting up to 75 percent of the cost of collaborative re-

[83]Thirty-four of these *fonds communs de placement à risque,* or venture capital funds, were created by deposit banks with a total of 1.7 billion francs – a great change from the past, when the *Sociétés financières d'innovation* (SFI) in ten years only managed to get 150 million francs. *Le Monde,* Jan. 13–14, 1985.

search; and to back projects with a European dimension, given the opening of the EEC member countries' frontiers as of 1992.[84]

A national ministry such as the DATAR and the nationalized industries, which have always contributed to the promotion local economic development, have not stopped.[85] Since decentralization, the DATAR continued to influence regional development through its responsibility for overseeing the regional planning process and for distributing the larger regional development subsidies that fall under its jurisdiction, facilitating this latter task by further deconcentrating its operations with the creation of local representatives, the regional commissioners for industrialization. The nationalized industries, moreover, have promoted regional development by helping to distribute regional products internationally and by setting up development funds to provide low-coast loans to new firms and subcontractors, in particular in the *pôles de conversion*.[86]

The state, in short, contributed a great deal to regional economic development, above and beyond the regional planning process. But even in these areas, where the state's intentions could be seen as ones of recentralization and *dirigisme*, it could not exercise the *dirigiste* control it intended. In the *pôles de conversion*, for example, although the prefects officially have responsibility for the entire operation, their ability to coordinate is severely undermined by the great variety of other interested parties that play a role in the *pôles*. These include the DATAR and its commissioners for industrialization, the ministry of industrial redeployment and the delegated prefect for reindustrialization, reindustrialization companies created by the nationalized industries, to say nothing of the ministries with a mandate to implement various social policy measures, for example, the reimbursement of workers whose salaries have diminished in the new jobs they have.

Moreover, even the DATAR has become less *dirigiste* in its industrial decentralization plans. It let go of the brakes on expansion in the Ile-de-France region in 1985 because the policy was doing little to help either the region or the nation. Often a company unable to install itself close to

---

[84]*Financial Times*, Jan. 12, 1988.
[85]From very early on, the DATAR had its own regional grant and subsidy programs that complemented those of the other ministries. Financial assistance to industry formally began in 1955 with the *zones critiques*, the precursors to the *pôles de conversion*, as well as the *Fonds de développement économique et sociale* (DES), long-term, low-interest loans for industrial projects, whereas regional development grants (*primes de développement régionale*) were introduced in 1971 (and revised in 1976). For a full account of the DATAR's regional industrial policy, see John Tuppen, *France* (Boulder, Colo.: Westview Press, 1980), pp. 95–108.
[86]"Les restructurations industrielles," *Le Monde, dossiers et documents*, no. 118, Jan. 1985.

Paris would leave for another country rather than for the Lorraine, as the DATAR had intended. And it has often been less forceful (or at the very least less successful) in its attempts to get the nationalized industries to locate in depressed regions, for example, Thomson, which ended up building one plant in Nancy rather than the requested two plants in Longwy in the Lorraine (the other went to Germany); and Renault, which in partnership with the private enterprise Merlin-Gerin, set up an electronics plant in Grenoble and not in Longwy.[87]

The multinationals, needless to say, have never been under the same constraints as the nationalized industries and in consequence have generally simply shopped around for the best subsidy packages. Although some found them in depressed areas, for example, Rank-Xerox, which decided to retool a plant in the Nord rather than leave the country because of generous subsidies, including one from the prime minister's office, others have found them in growing areas, for example, Hewlett-Packard, which chose to build a new factory in Lyon, a growing center for services and high technology, rather than in St. Etienne, which had sizable subsidies to offer as a reindustrialization zone.[88]

State *dirigisme*, in brief, has not gone away; but it has been significantly diminished at the local level, in some cases deliberately, in others inadvertently. The state's *dirigiste* efforts, moreover, have been further undermined by the existence of yet another level of government: the European Economic Community, which also has a hand in regional industrial development through trilateral, multiyear contracts between itself, the French national government, and the regions, with funds coming from the regions, the state budget, and the FEDER (European Regional Development Funds). Because this involves a great deal of money – for example, from one previously negotiated contract, France is due to receive approximately 1 billion francs per year over a seven-year period for programs affecting the five regions of the Midi plus two departments (Drôme and Ardèche) – the French government decided to name a special delegate to the EEC not only to coordinate all their efforts but also to make certain that "each region does not carry out, behind the back of the state," its own European policy.[89] This, more than anything else, suggests that the regional governments are clearly becoming industrial development forces to be reckoned with.

[87]Sharon Zukin, "Markets and Politics and France's Declining Regions," *Journal of Policy Analysis and Management* vol. 5, no. 1 (1985): 52.
[88]For examples, see ibid., pp. 52–3.
[89]Even prior to this, in the period from 1981–5, France received from the EEC approximately 1,790 million francs per year for regional development, with 1985 a banner year, in which France received 14 percent more than in 1984, for a total of over 2 billion francs. Of this, over 400 million went directly to the participating local governments. *Le Monde,* Jan. 16, 1986.

Thus, local economic development would appear to be highly decentralized, given the number of *dirigiste* bodies from the regional level on up all vying for control. As a result, the region, sitting at the epicenter of all of this activity, cannot help but become ever more important as the primary local industrial development broker. But however *dirigiste* it may become, its local interventions will themselves be necessarily decentralized, given not only the diversity of the actions of the national ministries, the nationalized industries, the multinationals, and the EEC, but also those of the different levels of local government.

The decentralization in local government interventions

Although direct intervention in the local economy on the part of local governments was actually commonplace before Socialist decentralization, especially since 1974, it was legalized by the Socialists, as well as defined and delimited. There is no doubt that the regions saw the biggest increases in their ability to promote local economic development, even though this had been their mission since their inception. The departments, by comparison, experienced a modest expansion in their own capabilities in this area. At the communal level, economic decentralization produced the least dramatic change, because the big cities had been involved in the promotion of local economic development for a number of years, whereas the rural communes have had, and continue to have, comparatively little involvement in this area.[90]

The rural communes, to begin with, have always had minimal means at their disposal for the promotion of local economic development, and decentralization did little to change that situation. In interviews for a study commissioned by the Planning Commission, local officials from the small communes complained that they lacked the money, contacts, and technical expertise to attract new businesses.[91] The midsize towns similarly have been traditionally poorly endowed in this area, and for many mayors the situation has not improved much with decentralization. They argue that they have neither the resources of the big cities nor their favorable bargaining position with regard to the regions at the same time

[90]There are ways in which decentralization in this area has had an impact on the rural communes, for example, with the mayors' new final approval powers with regard to the granting of building permits and land-use planning and with the relaxed standards for setting up intercommunal syndicates of assistance. Although these powers give rural communes greater control over the direction of local economic development, they are a long way from providing rural communes with the means to promote such development.

[91]Pierre Kukawka and Sylvie Biarez, *Les Actions économiques des collectivités territoriales*, report prepared for the Commissariat Général du Plan (Grenoble: CERAT, 1985).

that they have greater problems in weathering plant closings and fewer means at their disposal for attracting new industries to their area.[92] The big cities, by contrast, have for a very long time had the means at their disposal, as well as a good deal of freedom, to promote local economic development, mainly because big city mayors were for the most part also national politicians benefiting from the *cumul des mandats* and therefore had direct access to Paris ministries. Thus, although the new situation has somewhat complicated the process of gaining funds, because the big cities now have to go to the regions for smaller grants but still to Paris for the larger ones, the tasks remained essentially the same.

For all the communes, however, regardless of the limits of their resources, the freedom to determine the nature, direction, and means of local economic development was increased significantly and with it therefore, the *dirigiste* powers of their local elected officials. This has proved to be no small thing, for it has been a major spur to an unprecedented amount of local economic activism.

Most mayors in even the smallest towns on both sides of the political spectrum have sought to promote local economic development in the traditional *dirigiste* ways open to them, for example, by bailing out companies in distress by buying their facilities, by attracting new businesses or supporting old ones through tax advantages, low-cost leasing or sale of municipally owned facilities. Loan guarantees have been especially popular, actually too popular: In 1985, although the communes provided 900 million francs of new loan guarantees, they were saddled with 97 million francs in loan defaults by companies in bankruptcy or in difficulty.[93] The response by the neoliberal government was a law limiting the communes' ability to help enterprises in difficulty, leaving this only to the departments and regions.

Despite this limitation, mayors on the left as much as on the right have continued to seek to promote local economic development with all the means at their disposal. They have therefore tended to welcome any added support made available by the other levels of local government as well as by the state. It is in this context that we must understand Philippe Séguin's remark, in lamenting the fact that the Vosges did not have a *pôle de conversion,* that not having a *pôle* is always a minus, even if having one is not always a plus.[94]

Most local elected officials on the right and the left at all levels of local government were quite close in the ways in which they sought to promote

[92]At one point the Ministry of the Interior sought to ameliorate the situation somewhat by providing for a special grant for the midsize cities, just as they had done for the rural communes; but this was vetoed by the Senate.
[93]*Le Monde,* June 27, 1987.
[94]Séguin interview.

local economic development. A recent study suggests that political differences in the promotion of local economic development are more evident on issues such as the relations with the unions and support for local workers' struggles than in the management of institutional and financial resources.[95] But there were, nevertheless, differences even in these latter areas. Whereas some local elected officials on the left focused on promoting mainly nontraditional local enterprise directly, certain local elected officials on the right insisted on promoting traditional local enterprise only indirectly, through privatization and contracting out for services.

On the left, more specifically, a number of local elected officials sought to find new "economic partners" on the local level – new entrepreneurs capable of inventing new activities and developing new technologies as well as new forms of economic organization related to the *économie sociale* involving cooperatives, associations, and worker-owned businesses.[96] There is some evidence to suggest, however, that differences in terms of the *économie sociale* are fading; current divisions are more ones of age, with younger elected officials generally more interested, than ones of right or left.[97] And although the *économie sociale* is continuing to expand, with artisans, shopkeepers, pharmacists, veterinarians, information specialists, and movers forming cooperatives in order to meet competition, the cooperatives themselves are no longer necessarily Socialist.[98]

On the right, by contrast, some neoliberal politicians saw decentralization as an opportunity to engage in neoliberal experiments. Jacques Chirac, for instance, in his role as mayor of Paris, took advantage of decentralization to undertake a privatization program in which he contracted out for a number of municipal services in such areas as street-cleaning, garbage collection, and water distribution (increasing the average Parisian's water bill by 20 percent), at the same time that he found ways to raise money outside of local taxes such as through advertisements on bus-stop shelters.[99] The money saved through the above neoliberal policies, however, actually only helped defray the costs of some rather expensive, new municipal services such as the 120 electronic information boards and the 78 motorcycles called *ramassecrotte*, which clean

[95] Dominique Lorrain and Pierre Kukawka, "Quinze villes et l'économie" (forthcoming), cited in Edmond Preteceille, "Decentralisation in France: New citizenship or restructuring hegemony?" *European Journal of Political Research* no. 16 (1988): 420.

[96] See Chevallier, "Administration," pp. 165–6. For a discussion of the great variety of ways in which this was implemented, see *Cahiers français, L'Économie Sociale*, no. 221 (May–June 1985).

[97] *Le Monde*, Oct. 15, 1986.

[98] *Le Monde Affaires*, Jan. 9, 1988.

[99] Note that at the time Chirac took over the city from the prefect of Paris in 1977, as the first elective mayor of Paris, he did not seem to mind the incredibly large and expensive bureaucratic machine (with more than forty thousand employees) he had inherited. It was only in 1981 that Chirac began his neoliberal initiatives.

the sidewalks. And although they do a rather poor job of removing dog droppings, they have nevertheless spared Chirac the necessity of fining Parisians for not picking up after their dogs themselves – dog owners, after all, are voters.[100] Chirac, in brief, moderated his neoliberalism with a healthy dose of traditional *dirigisme* and a good deal of attention to political considerations.

The right as much as the left, in any event, took advantage of the Socialists' decentralization reform to promote local economic development, even though there were differences between left and right in how that promotion took place. This was equally true of the other levels of local government.[101] But whatever the differences between left and right in the promotion of local economic development, there were none in terms of the acceptance of economic decentralization, which was wholehearted on both sides of the political spectrum at all levels, departmental, regional, and communal.

At the departmental level, where departmental councils have been more limited in what they could do to promote local economic development, they have nevertheless sought to do whatever they could with whatever means they found at their disposal. This has often meant duplicating the efforts of the region. Even when the department sought to complement the actions of the region, the projects of the two levels were in competition because generally no formal channels of consultation were established. Frequently, the department has not only created a development fund that parallels that of the region – for example, in the department of the Pas-de-Calais and its region – but has also had, and continues to have, an administrative unit attached to the general council that parallels in function the regional development agency – for example, in the Pas-de-Calais such a unit is headed by the departmental president and in the Nord it is headed by the first vice president.[102]

Usually, however, there has been at least a modicum of coordination because departmental agencies generally receive a large amount of their funding from the region, often as a result of the state–region planning contracts. In the Rhône-Alpes, the region has been financing, in the context of the state–region planning contract and along with DATAR and ANCE, the national agency to promote the creation of business enterprises, seven departmental agencies set up to promote business creation by shepherding businesses through the initial start-up process and by

[100]*Le Monde*, Oct. 29, 1985.
[101]For differences at the regional level, see Zukin, "Markets," p. 53.
[102]Deplanque, Canton, Betremieux, and Soileux, "Le développement local: Action économique des départements et de la région." Paper presented at a conference sponsored by the Nord-Pas-de-Calais regional section of the French Institute of Administrative Sciences (Lille, Mar. 12, 1984).

providing them with training.[103] But because of the number of agencies and groups involved in any one of these agencies (for example, in the department of the Drôme alone the agency is sponsored by the general council, the Chamber of Commerce and Industry of Valence, the cities of Valence, Romans, and Montélimar, various other business and professional groups, the field services of the state for labor, and the local banking committee), the *dirigisme* in operation is likely to be highly decentralized.

There is one domain of local economic action reserved primarily for the departments: rural *amènagement,* or land-use planning, which can be seen either as focused on infrastructure (*équipement*) or on economic development. Interestingly enough, different departments even within a single region conceive of it in different ways. For example, in the Nord-Pas-de-Calais region, the Nord has differentiated its activities from those of the region by limiting itself to infrastructural aid for such projects as water-purification and irrigation systems, sanitation programs for breeding and raising animals, and programs focused on promoting tourism, whereas the Pas-de-Calais, the more rural of the two departments, funds these sorts of activities as well as economic development projects related to the promotion of agriculture and the agro-alimentary industry.[104]

Decentralized *dirigisme* at the departmental level, then, is evident not only in the initiatives taken by the departments in competition and in cooperation with the regional and communal levels of local government, but also in their diversity. This diversity is even more apparent at the regional level. It is at the level of the regions where the greatest innovations in local economic development have occurred. In their efforts to help invigorate the local economy, regional governments have been involved in the creation of regional development corporations that provide investment capital or development grants to local businesses, in issuing capital grants for plant modernization, in subsidizing bank interest-rate loans and arranging low-cost loans through regional banks, in setting up regional centers for research and technological development as well as professional training centers, and in negotiating international accords, export agreements, and so forth. In most of these activities, moreover, they seek the cooperation of the departments and the participation of the communes.

In the Nord-Pas-de-Calais, for example, in addition to all sorts of new internal development projects focused on professional development and

---

[103]*Les Echos,* June 27, 1985.
[104]Christine Blondel, Marie-Thérèse Kaluzny, and Régis Richard, "Amènagement rural: Les compétences régionales et départementales." Paper presented at a conference sponsored by the Nord-Pas-de-Calais regional section of the French Institute of Administrative Sciences (Lille, Mar. 12, 1984).

subsidies for industry and job creation, the regional council has also turned to external relations, with elected officials traveling all over the world to "sell" the Nord.[105] In the second regional planning contracts of 1988, the regional council proposed expanding its initiatives in the area of education, not only by improving the overall educational level of the students but also by linking education to the economic revival of the region—in both cases by creating more professional high schools and reinforcing the ties of all high schools with industry.[106]

In Languedoc-Rousillon, moreover, the region has an internal development policy focused on the *arrière-pays,* or less-developed parts of the region, through which it seeks to introduce new technologies, computer links, and cable, to fight geographical inequalities and make the territory less isolated. At the same time, it also has an external-relations policy with China, Japan, Tunisia, Tuscany, and Catalonia, in addition to a *société d'économie mixte régionale d'exportation,* which "pilots and orchestrates the projects of the PMI-PME" in the international market.[107] In the Lorraine, by contrast, the focus has been mainly on internal problems related to the need for reindustrialization and has involved concentrating on professional development and on developing links between university research groups and industry, as well as on encouraging business creation and innovation with, for example, the regional development agency *Institut Lorrain de participation* (ILP).[108]

More recently, with the neoliberals in control of regional governments as of 1986, there has been some change in regional development policies. Although regional councils continue to spend the bulk of their resources on the same activities as did the Socialists, for example, travel, linkages with foreign governments and businesses, and so forth, they have altered the form of their support for business, preferring subsidizing bank interest-rate loans over providing development grants. Bretagne, for one, has concentrated on subsidizing interest rates, with 90 percent of its budget going for such activity. And Languedoc-Rousillon decided to drop its development grants in favor of subsidizing interest rates, setting up a 400-million-franc fund for that purpose.[109]

The above diversity in regional initiatives in local economic development suggests that the *dirigisme* of regional governments is, and will remain, quite decentralized. The products of such decentralized *dirigisme,* however, meaning the particular projects funded, are not always ideal examples of decentralization. On the regional level especially, the

[105]*Le Monde,* May 16, 1985.
[106]*Le Monde,* Jan. 14, 1988.
[107]*Le Monde,* June 23–4, 1985.
[108]"Lorraine," *Le Monde,* dossiers et documents, no. 118 (Jan. 1985).
[109]Schlenker, "Industrial Strategies," p. 272.

local development process tends to encourage close, symbiotic relationships between local bankers, regional planners, and members of industry, because they all depend on one another for loans to private companies and investment in public projects. Although this relationship is likely to have positive effects, in facilitating the financing and development of projects that the decentralized nature of much local intervention could tend to complicate and delay, it can also have certain less progressive effects. It has a tendency to increase the power of traditional industries, which often are less open to business creation and innovation. For example, regional development was not helped in either right-wing Lorraine or left-wing Nord by resistance from established employers to projects favoring new businesses.[110] In this context, moreover, it is important to note that the new law limiting the ability of communes to aid businesses in distress risks eliminating an important advocate for the smaller, often newer and less well-established enterprises, which often suffer from the fact that they cannot depend on the traditional circuits of power for help.

In the final analysis, it is the highly decentralized nature of local *dirigisme* – which includes the possibility of gaining support from communes, departments, regions, the DATAR, the nationalized industries, the state, and even the EEC – that has been extremely helpful to local industry, or at least to those firms that have been able to take advantage of this. And many have. One new firm in the Lorraine, for example, has benefited from just about all of the various kinds of promotional efforts mentioned above, receiving workers' unemployment benefits and new business grants from the state, low-cost loans from a nationalized industry (Sacilor), as well as loans from regional banks and venture capital from the *Institut Lorrain de participation*.[111] This pattern of multiple governmental sources of support for small businesses continued with the right in power since March 1986, despite their neoliberal rhetoric.

There is a negative side to the proliferation of programs and actors in the promotion of local economic development, though. In a 1985 report, an investigative committee for the Planning Commission found problems resulting from the new laws. In some cases problems arose because the new laws were too restrictive, for example, in limiting the ability of communes and departments to intervene except in complementary fashion in domains reserved for the regions (that is, in direct aid and in areas covered by the planning contracts) and in certain financing arrangements; in other cases because they were so vague, for example, in the definition of indirect aid, or so liberal, for example, with loan guarantees, as to allow local governments too much freedom. They discovered that

---

[110]Zukin, "Markets," pp. 54–5.
[111]See *Financial Times*, Nov. 19, 1985.

the very complexity of the system of seeking aid, given the proliferation of the procedures and the parties involved, was not only disconcerting to the recipients of aid, it also caused confusion and delays. Finally, they saw the lack of coordination in economic policies expensive, duplicative, contradictory, and inefficient.[112] These views were echoed in a 1987 report by the *Cour des comptes,* or National Accounting Court, which was concerned that the multiplication in the forms of intervention and intervenors would harm the coherence of efforts involved in the promotion of local economic development.[113]

It is true that it is easier to risk resources, whether through the duplication of efforts or the mistakes of prefects or local elected officials, who are in most cases just learning how to carry out their new functions, in a time of prosperity than in a time of crisis. But whatever the costs, pluralism is here to stay. Although the neoliberal government, in the words of Balladur, claimed to be unwilling to have "less State" result in more local government in this as in other areas, that is exactly what has occurred under the neoliberals themselves as much as under the Socialists.[114] But this is not at all likely to have the dire consequences some on the right predicted.

The highly pluralistic nature of the promotion of local economic development, resulting from the number of government bodies – local, national, and supranational – involved and the diversity of policies, programs, and incentives offered, cannot but help local development. Although the *dirigisme* of all these governmental bodies affords them the power to direct local development in the ways they see fit, its decentralization, ensured by the number of bodies involved, makes it highly likely that just about every way possible will be tried. This may lead to some duplication of services, waste of resources, and expenditure of time, especially where there is competition rather than cooperation between different levels of local government. It also may lead, however, to the distribution of grants and loans to a larger number of local firms with greater potential for job and business creation, expansion, and innovation than in the past.

As it is, local business leaders as much as local elected officials appear overwhelmingly positive about the role of local governments in the promotion of local economic development. In a recent survey for the *Caisse des dépôts,* a large majority of local leaders agreed that decentralization was a factor in the development of economic activity at the local level (81 percent as opposed to 17 percent who disagreed) and that decentralization has contributed to a greater *rapprochement* between local governments and local businesses (75 percent as opposed to 18 percent). More-

[112]Plan, *Interventions économiques,* pp. 33–44.
[113]*Le Monde,* June 27, 1987.
[114]Bechtel, Henry-Meininger, and Jegouzo, "Chronique," pp. 157–8.

over, with the new Europe-wide market of 1992 in mind, a large majority of the respondents (73 percent) thought that decentralization would favor direct economic and financial relations between local leaders and the European community (as opposed to 15 percent who thought it would not). A slightly smaller majority were willing to say that decentralization would represent a trump card in the new European market (65 percent versus 7 percent who thought it a handicap and 22 percent who saw it as neither the one nor the other).[115]

Decentralization, in conclusion, has been a success in the economic arena by introducing a new pluralism into local administrative arrangements with regard to the promotion of local economic development, thereby instituting a new "decentralized *dirigisme*" at the local level. This has only added to the pluralism accompanying the new kind of politics in the periphery that has increased the size of the political class, strengthened party politics, and introduced national cleavages and concerns at every level of local government. But the questions still to be answered are: Has this new pluralism significantly altered the local politico-administrative system, helping to change the roles, rules, and interrelationships of the various actors in the periphery, or has it only further complicated the system?

[115]*Le Monde*, Dec. 4–5, 1988.

9

Unblocking society by decree: The transformation of the politico-administrative system

Can radical reforms ever produce lasting change in the French local governmental system? Or must France, as the adage goes, always remain the same? In the case of Socialist decentralization, the answers of systemic scholars have been unequivocal. As we have seen in the previous chapter, scholars who focus on local governmental institutions and processes suggest that the very real transformation of the formal institutions has led only to moderate changes in the informal processes, whereas scholars concerned with the local politico-administrative system insist that the system may have undergone some internal readjustment, but it has not changed. In the view of systemic scholars, the new pluralism evident in the new politics in the periphery or in the "decentralized *dirigisme*" in local economic development may have complicated the system, but it has not altered its basic structures or modes of functioning. For these scholars, decentralization appears at best, to borrow Michel Crozier's terms, an attempt to "change society by decree," typical of the "blocked society."[1] But is this really the case?

In fact, we could argue, with apologies to Crozier, that Socialist decentralization is a case of *la société débloquée par décret,* or "unblocking society by decree." By changing the laws the way they did, the Socialists formalized much of the informal system. But in so doing, they did more than simply legalize the informal practices of the many actors in the local politico-administrative system. They eliminated elements contributing to some of the major blockages in the old politico-administrative system, by breaking the hidden complicity between prefects and notables that had for so long allowed both groups to avoid taking full responsibility for their actions and had contributed to the unresponsiveness, inefficiency, and increasing costliness of local government. This in turn has set the

---

[1] The titles of Michel Crozier's books are: *On ne change pas la société par décrêt* (Paris: Grasset, 1979), and *La Société bloquée* (Paris: Seuil, 1967).

stage for a transformation of the local politico-administrative system itself, by altering the nature of the roles, rules, and interrelationships among actors in the system.

By giving communes, departments, and regions each their own special administrative duties and functions, as well as the financial means to carry them out, the reforms ensure that each level of local government has become a separate, independent system in its own right. At the same time the particular division of labor has nevertheless increased the complementarity among the different levels of local government. This means not only that more actors at different levels and in different units are involved in decision-making processes but also that their interrelationships take on new significance as a result of their new powers. In this context, the issue of the *tutelle* has reemerged and taken on a wider meaning. Local governments are worried about potential threats to their freedom of action not only from the state but also from other local bodies, in particular the regions' ability to exercise control over the departments and big cities in certain economic matters and the departments' control over the communes in some administrative and financial areas.

The roles played by the actors in this new set of interrelated systems have changed, along with the rules they follow. The prefects are the great losers here. With the transfer of executive power to the presidents of the regions and departments, they have been left with a primarily mediative role; and although they now have clear responsibility as representatives of the state, they still have difficulty asserting their powers over the field services of the state. Deconcentration, which was to have enhanced the prefects' powers by devolving greater responsibilities from the center, has yet to be implemented fully, whereas the central ministries and the field services of the state continue to act as independently as they always have.

The presidents of regions and departments, by contrast, are the big winners in decentralization, having become the new intermediate level between the state and the communes for the promotion of local economic development and the delivery of health and social services. Each tends to see the other level as the primary challenge to its authority: the departmental president because of the region's larger electoral base, the regional president because of the department's larger budget. As for the dangers of the *tutelle*, whereas the regions are concerned about the encroachments of the state in its domain, the departments tend to be more wary of the regions in the area of local economic development than they are of the state in the area of social services.

The mayors saw the least amount of change: Big-city mayors exercise their former powers somewhat more freely and the rural mayors feel the limitations of their powers somewhat more keenly. Although in principle decentralization was to have applied equally to all communes, in practice it consecrated the differences that had already been evident in the periphery prior to the reform. Thus, it did little more than formalize the relatively independent powers the urban communes had already exercised informally before decentralization at the same time that it ended up leaving the rural communes in much the same position of dependence as before. Decentralization did, however, alter the relationships of the communes with the other levels of local government: the urban communes are now concerned about the possibility of a *tutelle* by the regions, albeit only minimally, whereas the rural communes have been extremely worried about the departments as well as the prefects, and rightly so.

CHANGING THE POLITICO-ADMINISTRATIVE SYSTEM

Systemic scholars have a tendency to see little change in the French local politico-administrative system, whether they describe it as centralized, stalemated, and an impediment to the development of a modern state or as decentralized, with informal systems that, even if they function well, are somehow illegitimate. In both contexts, systemic actors are completely bound by their roles, caught in the circuits of power and the rules of the game of the system itself. In the view of most systemic scholars, decentralization has done little to alter this situation.

Perhaps the clearest expression of the view of unchanging systems is that of Michel Crozier and Jean-Claude Thoenig. In an article coauthored in 1975, they argued that the "extreme vigor of the homeostatic properties of the local politico-administrative system" ensures that, instead of adaptation resulting from a system open to change, there are only internal readjustments of a system closed in on itself. It is a system independent of the individual actors, which imposes on even the most powerful the general rules and norms of its "collective game."[2] As Crozier indicates by the very titles of his books, because the system remains a "blocked society" and "one cannot change society by decree," it follows that the politico-administrative system cannot be altered by Socialist decentralization. This, at least, is the attitude of Thoenig, who, together with François Dupuy, was one of the first systemic scholars to publish a book considering center–periphery relations since the Socialist reforms.

Dupuy and Thoenig, in *L'Administration en miettes*, suggest the Socialist reforms left the French administrative system basically unchanged, with the Socialist decentralizing measures doing little de jure to alter the long-standing de facto decentralization of the system.[3] Even though the two authors do mention in passing that decentralization ultimately could

[2]Crozier and Thoenig, "La régulation," pp. 15–18.
[3]Dupuy and Thoenig, *L'Administration*.

radically alter the system they have elaborated, they offer little hope, and even less evidence, that any such change will come about. They appear to suggest that the new situation is not significantly different from the old, with the old blockages simply dressed up in new language.

For Dupuy and Thoenig, Socialist decentralization represents little more than a measure that further complicates the politico-administrative system by reinforcing the political aspects of the system, that is, the political world that serves to unify the administrative world, while allowing the administrative aspects of the system to remain a "universe in pieces."[4] The administrative world, according to Dupuy and Thoenig, continues to have a rigidly stratified, hierarchical system of organization and a honeycomb structure of internal relations that together impede communication or cooperation among actors at different levels of the hierarchy. In this world, innovative administrative action that is responsive to local needs and interests never leads to generalized rules of administrative behavior, because civil servants, steeped in the rhetoric of uniformity and equality before the law, conceive of all such action, including their own, as illegitimate. Dupuy and Thoenig, in brief, see no end in sight to the age-old problems of French administration, that is, the paradoxes that are unlikely to be resolved as long as civil servants conceive of their roles and structure their work in one way while acting in another.

Although Dupuy and Thoenig argue that the local politico-administrative system essentially remains the same, they do mention certain readjustments that suggest that a change in bureaucratic practices is in the offing.[5] They don't really specify which practices are to change, though, or whether they are for the better. On a positive note, Dupuy and Thoenig remark that changes in the system force the newly responsible actors to manage differently, by no longer transferring the costs toward the exterior or toward on high. But this, they maintain, results from the fact that decentralization represents the transfer of the administration of penury to the periphery with a situation characterized no longer by "small is beautiful," but rather by "small is efficient." They insist that this, in turn, has broken the solidarity in the politico-administrative system and turned it into a system in which relations are no longer an equal give and take because one of the partners absorbs the costs.[6] For Dupuy and Thoenig, decentralization has, if anything, produced disequi-

[4]Ibid., pp. 270–2.

[5]Please note that in an article written by Dupuy and Thoenig two years before this book, in 1983, they were much more positive about the possibility for systemic change. They argued that the rules of the game had already altered somewhat as a result of the transfer of executive power from prefects to local elected officials and of the increased politicization of local government. "La loi du 2 mars 1982 sur la décentralisation," *Revue Française de Science Politique* vol. 33, no. 6 (Dec. 1983).

[6]Dupuy and Thoenig, *L'Administration*, pp. 272–9.

librium in the system, increasing its confusions and accelerating its administrative fragmentation.

One need not, however, take such a negative view of the reform. Decentralization has replaced the informal decentralization of the past with a formal decentralization that clearly differentiates the powers and responsibilities of the various actors in the periphery, while redefining and redelimiting the structures and functions of the many different institutions of local government. In doing so, it has in fact changed the internal workings of the politico-administrative system. According to Jacques Rondin, even though the major actors and basic practices of the politico-administrative system described by Dupuy and Thoenig remain the same, the *sacre des notables,* or formal consecration of the power of the local political worthies, has dramatically altered the interrelationships among all actors in the system, breaking the former complicity between prefects and notables. There are new rules of the game through the redistribution of old roles among the same actors.[7] The former blurred lines of responsibility and authority have been clarified by making local elected officials solely responsible for representing local interests and the prefect, for representing state interests. At the same time, however, the interdependence of the different levels of local government has increased, given that they all compete with one another in one forum or another as providers or receivers of economic aid and technical assistance. The politicization of the periphery has only further complicated such competition.

Although Dupuy and Thoenig certainly can argue justifiably that much remains the same, therefore, this is not the whole story. In fact, we can even use the logic of their own arguments to suggest that the French local politico-administrative system, if not already a thing of the past, is at least in the process of transformation. For one thing, it has become much more difficult to talk about a single politico-administrative system, however complex, in which the political world serves to integrate from outside the administrative. With the abolition of the *tutelle,* the transfer of executive power, administrative functions, and the civil servants needed to carry out those functions, along with the limitation of the *cumul des mandats,* the political world is no longer completely external to the administrative, and the overall system itself is no longer as unitary.

Each level of local government now forms its own, clearly differentiated subsystem, with its own special set of functions, and with the political and administrative worlds formally integrated. Because the local administrative world today is formally responsible to the local political world to which it was formerly most responsive, innovative administrative action may now actually lead to more generalized rules of administra-

[7]Rondin, *Le Sacre,* p. 249.

tive behavior that are, nevertheless, specific to different levels of local government or different geographical locations. (We are already seeing signs of this in the departments, where social services are being delivered in a more efficient and cost-effective manner.)[8]

Socialist decentralization, then, contrary to the views of Dupuy and Thoenig, may very well have already transformed the administrative system by causing civil servants to conceive of their roles and structure their work in ways more compatible with their actions. And it may have similarly transformed the local political system by now making the powers local elected officials formerly exercised in the informal systems of center–periphery relations part of their formal roles. At the very least, center–periphery relations are no longer as Worms or Grémion described them, nor can they remain as Tarrow found them to be. Maybe the most progressive of the three models Becquart-Leclercq identified will become the standard rather than the exceptional model, given the changes in the laws.

The decentralization reform, more specifically, has certainly broken Worms' hidden complicity of prefects and notables. The prefect can no longer be seen as being at the center of the web of local relations by virtue of his formal role. Instead, local elected officials are formally at the center, thus bringing the real balance of power into the open and creating a new transparency in center–periphery relations. The reform has also brought some order into the confusing array of interactions of Grémion's system. It has clarified actors' roles and structured their interrelationships in a more functional manner, thereby ensuring that any loss of local power to the state would be returned.

The clarification of roles along with the new transparency, in turn, is likely to ensure that Tarrow's mayors can no longer see their role primarily in administrative terms, given that the political is ever present. Now, mayors necessarily see their constituents as their primary constituency. The central administrative power is much less of a threat, because mayors no longer depend on it as much as in the past. Mayors are therefore less quick to put themselves in the service of the central power, however fragmented it may be. This does not mean, of course, that mayors can ignore the central government entirely, or that they have abandoned the technocratic completely. On the contrary, the rhetoric of good management (as we shall see in the next chapter) suggests that the technocratic remains an important factor. But it is less in the service of the central power than in the service of the periphery. And the periphery itself is changing, with the first signs of this being the new politics evident in the attention local elected officials are paying to the electorate, to associations, and to the new groups in the periphery.

[8]See the discussion in Part II, Chapter 10, "The rhetoric of good management."

With the new politics in the periphery, moreover, the reforms could represent a consecration of Becquart-Leclercq's cooperative–innovative model. By writing into law many of the rules followed in the most progressive communes, making them the formal basis for new structural relationships, the reforms are likely to have pushed communes following Types I and II even further than Type III had pushed them informally. Another way of looking at this is to suggest that Becquart-Leclercq's Type III model was legitimated by the Socialists, becoming the foundations for the new set of laws and the beginning of a new set of practices.

At the very least, Crozier's distant, impersonal, and centralized authority is no longer as much of a player in the local politico-administrative system, the mayor can no longer remain passive, and the prefect is no longer even formally all-powerful. Bureaucratic centralization can no longer serve as a façade behind which local officials interact undisturbed, because now their hidden, face-to-face relations have been brought out into the open and formalized. Paris, one could say in response to Crozier and Thoenig, is no longer a prisoner of its own system, because the confusion of roles and relationships has diminished significantly, while the interdependence has been functionally restructured to a great extent.

We can argue effectively, in short, that the Socialist reform truly is a case of "unblocking society by decree." It has eliminated elements contributing to some of the major blockages in the old politico-administrative system, creating a new system in which the informal aspects of the previous system, which alone made that system functional, have become the basic structures of the new, multivariate system. By picking up on the most progressive elements of the informal relationships, the new laws have changed local officials' roles for the better, leaving them more ready to develop new kinds of local governmental rules and interrelationships. The evidence for all of this is contained in the new roles, rules, and relationships already in operation in the periphery.

CHANGING THE ROLES, RULES, AND RELATIONSHIPS

The new politico-administrative system, although different from the old, is no less complex in its setup and has altered the political and administrative roles, rules, and relationships of all major actors in the periphery. Primary among the changes produced by the Socialists' decentralization reforms was the redefinition of the role of the prefect as the main representative of the state in the periphery and the differentiation of this role from the new roles of regional and departmental presidents as well as from the traditional role of the mayor as the main representatives of local governments in the eyes of the state. With this new role differentiation, the Socialists intended to make all local officials fully accountable to the local population for their decisions and the prefects more accountable to the state. Moreover, by transferring from the state to the regional, departmental, and communal levels of local government different administrative *compétences,* or functions and duties, along with the necessary financial resources and authority, they sought to place administrative and budgetary responsibility squarely on the shoulders of local officials.

The effect of the role change on local actors is still working itself out. Although the formal roles set by law make clear the range of local officials' duties and their formal relationships, the law cannot, needless to say, establish how local officials will perform in their duties or what informal rules and interrelationships will develop among the various actors in the periphery. Interestingly enough, the actors themselves disagree as to the nature and significance of one another's role changes and how it has affected their power and position in the local politico-administrative system. What is clear is that, as Rondin notes, although the old actors are performing new roles and following new rules, it did not take the players in the new roles long to find the old ways of obtaining satisfaction without losing face.[9]

The new role of the state in the periphery: Retreat or renewal?

To begin with, the prefects' new role as representative of the state in the periphery is one that the prefects admit has significantly altered their position in the periphery. The prefects often characterize their new role as a switch from executor of the wishes of the general or regional councils and controller of the actions of municipal councils to a neutral and impartial mediator among the various decentralized bodies, as well as an overseer of their actions.[10] Although they argue that their powers are different, they insist that they are not diminished, given their new deconcentrated responsibilities.

The field services of the state, along with the central ministries, feel otherwise. Many have resisted deconcentration to the benefit of the prefect and, while paying lip service to the new powers of the prefect, essentially continue to function as they always have. Some central ministries, moreover, have sought to expand their influence in the periphery not only through recentralizing measures but even through the use of decentralization as a way of avoiding deconcentration, by dealing directly with local elected officials; and some field services have used their own deconcentrated structures to do the same, thus circumventing prefectoral

---

[9]Rondin, *Le Sacre,* p. 316.
[10]In numerous interviews with members of the prefectoral corps and with officials in the Ministry of the Interior in 1985 and 1986, this was the usual characterization.

Table 9.1. *The number of regional employees in the prefecture*

Regions	1980	1981	1982	1983	1984
Alsace	232	213	228	237	250
Aquitaine	364	356	361	381	392
Auvergne	183	179	168	166	186
Bourgogne	201	193	184	182	191
Bretagne	312	300	294	283	307
Centre	144	139	131	142	153
Champagne-Ardennes	155	156	156	163	175
Corse	95	85	78	94	93
Franche-Comté	147	148	137	141	149
Ile-de-France	128	137	132	142	136
Languedoc-Roussillon	203	205	195	194	200
Limousin	140	138	132	131	137
Lorraine	366	368	364	371	381
Midi-Pyrénées	299	284	294	276	294
Nord-Pas-de-Calais	578	580	558	562	581
Basse-Normandie	168	167	163	164	170
Haute-Normandie	257	255	252	263	273
Loire	225	214	215	218	227
Picardie	167	165	171	170	172
Poitou-Charentes	135	131	136	133	137
Provence-Alpes-Côte d'Azur	519	498	502	488	499
Rhône-Alpes	421	408	416	408	410
France total (metropolitan)	5,439	5,319	5,267	5,309	5,513

Source: Journal Officiel (Apr. 25, 1985), cited in Jean Cluzel, *Les "Anti-Monarques" de la cinquième* (Paris: Librairie générale de droit et de jurisprudence, 1985), p.28

control. The result has been little retreat of the state from the periphery except in the prefectoral realm, and little renewal except in the latter case as well.

The prefects. The prefects are quite clear about the fact that, today, the rules of the game of local government are determined by the full range of actors in the periphery and no longer by themselves. Now the prefects themselves recognize that they can no longer command, and the consultative or mediative posture taken before decentralization has become a major part of the way in which they conceive of their new role. The prefects' demeanor and the way they play their role has changed accordingly. The prefects now see themselves, and are seen by others, as mediators more than anything else.

By and large, the prefects argue that their powers are different but not diminished. Most importantly, the prefects cite their formal control over all the field services of the state, their central position in regional planning and economic development to represent the interests of the state in the periphery, and their a posteriori powers of review and referral to judicial authorities. They do admit, however, that along with the transfer of their executive powers, they have lost some of the trappings of power: Although they have retained their uniforms, they generally have fewer chauffeured cars available to them, smaller expense accounts, and less plush surroundings. But they have kept their staffs. It is important to note that the number of prefectoral employees did not diminish significantly (Table 9.1). The number was reduced by 20 in Provence-Alpes-Côte-d'Azur, from 519 in 1980 to 499 in 1984, and it was increased by 15 in the Lorraine, going from 366 in 1980 to 381 in 1984. In France as a whole, although the total number of prefectoral employees dipped by 172 in 1982, when employees were transferred to local governments, it was up by 246 by 1984, thus charting an overall gain of 74 from 1980, when there were 5,439 regional prefectoral employees, to 1984, when there were 5,513.

Initially, although the prefects generally put a good face on things, they were quite disturbed by their change in status and role. Many had a difficult adjustment period. Some left the prefectoral corps for the departmental services, whereas others spent their time seeking to reimpose their *tutelle* over the regions, departments, and communes, as well as trying to expand their deconcentrated powers. The discontent was highlighted by the former prefects who moved into the territorial civil service, such as Pierre Costa, director general of the departmental services of the Alpes-Maritimes, and were convinced that there was no job left for the prefects.[11] But this loss of prefectoral power was felt most keenly at the level of the subprefects and was most clearly demonstrated in the generally recognized difficulty the Ministry of Interior had in recruiting subprefects in the first few years of decentralization.

For all the dire predictions, however, the prefectoral corps was not destroyed and few prefects retired. Rather, they switched places: something perfectly understandable given their change in role and the difficulty of engaging in their new functions with the same people as before.[12] Attitudes toward their new role have changed, moreover. Since 1985, top-ranking graduates from the ENA (National School of Administration) have again been choosing to be subprefects. But they see the job differently from before. They see themselves as the technical consultants of the mayors, instead of as their financial overseers. And rather than managers of large bureaucracies, they are the "deconcentrated" animators of government policy, explaining the implementation of industrial policy, employment assistance, social measures, and so forth.[13]

[11] Pierre Costa, director-general of departmental services, Alpes-Maritimes, interview with author, Nice, June 7, 1985.
[12] Rondin, *Le Sacre*, pp. 262–3.
[13] *Le Monde*, Sept. 17, 1988.

319

Democratizing France

For most of those who remained in prefectoral service, the change in role has been beneficial, bespeaking much more a renewal of the prefectoral corps than a retreat from a major position in the periphery. For Michel Besse, secretary-general of the prefecture of the Bouches-du-Rhône, the change was a welcome one because it gave the less interesting tasks to the departments, leaving the prefecture with the more challenging problems in planning, conceptualizing, and mediating.[14] For Gilbert Carrère, the regional prefect in Rhône-Alpes, the change brought the regional services of the state back to their true level, which was that of *conception,* or conceptualization, rather than *gestion,* or management.[15]

It is in the area of economic development where the planning and conceptualizing is at the forefront and where prefects, playing their newest role, have a good deal of leverage over local governments. In the case of regional planning, for example, the prefects negotiate the plans for the state with the regions, and they have the option not to sign for the state if they are not satisfied, thus leaving the region without state economic development funds. In addition, they have control over a large number of decisions regarding local economic development, for example, in approving tourist developments, in supporting cultural projects, and so forth. And they are in charge of disbursing many state subsidies, in particular for businesses in difficulty, as well as of coordinating efforts to solve the financing problems of such businesses in their capacity as chairpersons of departmental committees (the CODEFI – *Comité départemental d'examen des problèmes de financement des entreprises*) and regional committees (the CORRI – *Comité régional de restructuration industrielle*).

In their role as mediators, the prefects may intervene in any of the areas where the different levels of local government must interact. They play such a role officially in the regional planning process, for example, in smoothing relations between the regions and the departments or the bigger cities, and unofficially in any of the interrelationships between the levels of local government where they play no official part, such as when departments offer financial or administrative assistance to rural communes. The prefect has a particularly useful role to play when there are political differences between the two levels, intervening as a nonpartisan force to right the balance. Sometimes, however, the prefect may provide an alternative source of support, for example, when mayors turn to the prefect rather than to the departmental president for help when the latter is perceived as a political or administrative threat to the mayor's powers.

For all this, however, the prefects find their freedom of action reasonably circumscribed by the state on the one side and by the departmental

[14]Michel Besse, secretary-general of the prefecture of the Bouches-du-Rhône, interview with author, Marseilles, June 5, 1985.
[15]*Le Monde,* dossiers et documents, no. 145 (June 1987), p. 1.

and regional presidents on the other. The process of negotiating the first regional plan provides a very good illustration of the prefects' problems with their new mediative role. Here, although the prefects had an official role as negotiator, the state gave them little room to maneuver. The *Comité interministériel d'amènagement du territore* (CIAT), or interministerial commission on land-use planning, provided specific instructions as to the particulars of the negotiations, allowing the prefects no possibility of exercising any independent judgment. The prefects themselves complained that this handicapped them terribly, and the regional presidents agreed, arguing that they would like to be able to negotiate with a strong interlocutor able to ensure the coherence of the local actions of the state.[16] However, as the planning commission's evaluation report on the first regional planning process suggests, to leave negotiation completely up to the prefects would have left regional actors with "a veritable autonomy."[17] And clearly, the CIAT was not about to do this.

What is more, even though departmental and regional presidents were quite willing to make common cause with the prefects in contexts such as these, in which greater prefectoral autonomy devolved to their benefit, they have otherwise sought to shut them out of departmental or regional business. In the regions, Jean-Marie Rausch, president of the regional council of the Lorraine and mayor of Metz, was typical in his concern over what he saw as attempts by the prefect to expand his powers over the region not only through the *contrôle de légalité* but even through the *contrôle d'opportunité*. Nevertheless, he had no real fear of a prefectoral *tutelle*, given his stated view: "I'm not afraid of my prefect. If I agree with him, fine; if I don't, fine."[18] He was even less concerned about the specially delegated prefect sent by the central government to deal with the economic problems of the Lorraine (in addition to the prefect and the subprefect for reindustrialization), remarking that "the delegated prefect is for amusement, to calm down the unions, to entertain the peanut gallery."[19]

In the departments, similarly, the president of the general council calls the shots, keeping the former executive of the department as far removed as possible, and even having the prefect dismissed in cases of conflict, as has been the case twice in the Lot-et-Garonne.[20] Often, the prefect has become essentially persona non grata in the general council, as in the case

---

[16]Commissariat Général du Plan, *Evaluation de la planification décentralisée* (Paris: Documentation française, 1986), p. 47.
[17]Plan, *Planification*, pp. 23–5.
[18]Rausch interview.
[19]Ibid.
[20]*Le Monde*, Sept. 17, 1988.

of the prefect in the Val-d'Oise who had been invited to appear before that group only three times in the previous three years and whose personal contacts remained limited to the president of the general council.[21] The prefects no longer appear at every local ceremony as the guest of honor, having been replaced by the regional and departmental presidents. At least according to departmental and regional elected officials, the prefects' role is much more restricted to security matters, to employment, and to the promotion of governmental industrial policies, so much so that instead of finding their antechambers filled with elected officials, one finds them filled with the heads of enterprises.[22]

For regional and departmental presidents, in short, the prefects have gone almost overnight from an authority with tremendous power over all local officials and matters to one with comparatively little, who must nevertheless be watched because they seek to increase their limited powers at every reprise. Interestingly enough, this has also been the view of the central ministries and the field services of the state in the periphery. Only the rural mayors, as we shall see below, have found the prefects any real threat to their independence.

The field services and the central ministries. Along with decentralization to the benefit of the presidents of the regions and departments was to come deconcentration to the benefit of the prefects. But this was the least successful aspect of the reform. The important field services of the state remain quite independent of the prefects, even though all correspondence must pass through the prefecture first. Moreover, despite the prefect's formal authority, the central ministries retain direct oversight over the directors of their field services. And because they often simply "forget" to consult the prefectoral level, there are daily conflicts, in particular with those services in which the directors wish to make themselves known to their ministers. Only for civil servants in the areas of infrastructure, agriculture, and the Treasury have relations been generally better, due to the long-standing relationships they have had with the prefecture and the help prefects can offer in facilitating their relations with local elected officials or in providing political solutions to problems.[23] But even here, the prefect's deconcentrated authority remains merely a formality. The level of deconcentration of these technical services is such that the prefects, located solely in the department seat, tend to be bypassed entirely by agents of the agricultural or infrastructural services located in close proximity to the mayors who consult with them directly. Even if the prefect did take up an issue, more likely than not it would be referred to

[21]Ibid.
[22]Ibid.
[23]Ibid.

the technical services for a recommendation, thus reinforcing the independent operation of such services.

Only in relatively unimportant ministries such as the *Économie sociale* and the *Délégation à l'emploi,* charged to encourage job creation and to promote local enterprise and business start-ups, was care normally taken to ensure that local entrepreneurs consulted with the prefecture first. In the DDE (infrastructure), by contrast, no such care was taken or was required. In the view of those in the DDE, only the unimportant or reasonably new ministries such as the *Économie Sociale* had to operate that way, at the pleasure of the prefects and dependent on their cooperation.[24]

There are a variety of reasons why deconcentration to the benefit of the prefects has not taken hold except in some of the less powerful ministries. In the periphery, most importantly, perhaps, it has not been in the interest of most field civil servants, whose careers, in terms of the civil service *corps,* promotions, and so forth, are determined by their own ministries alone and have nothing to do with the prefectoral, which has its own *corps* and system of promotions. In the center, most obviously, however, the ministries have dragged their feet, unwilling to lose any of these powers either to their own field services or to the prefect. A report of the *Mission relative à l'organisation des administration centrales* (MODAC) to the prime minister in October 1986 shows very little progress with deconcentration. Of the three hundred proposed deconcentration measures, although 75 percent had been accepted by the ministries concerned, only 12 percent of these had actually been implemented. The report itself proposed reinforcing the role of the prefect as the sole representative of the state, making him a much more powerful interlocutor with the departmental and regional presidents. In addition it recommended reorganizing and streamlining the central ministries, defining clearly which tasks were to be deconcentrated, and designating one level, preferably the regional, as the primary one for state deconcentration.[25]

The central ministries' resistance to deconcentration to the benefit of the prefects has come in a variety of forms. The central ministries, to begin with, have put into practice certain recentralizing measures, for example, by concentrating financial decisions concerning funding for public works, culture, and land-use planning at the ministerial or interministerial levels; by constituting national commissions or delegations (labor and employment, culture); and by creating public establishments close to the central level (energy policy). In addition, they have added mechanisms that increase the need to refer matters from the deconcen-

[24]These views came out time and again in interviews with civil servants in these ministries in 1985 and 1986.
[25]Christian Serradji, official report to the prime minister of the Mission relative à l'organisation des administration centrales (MODAC), Oct. 2, 1986.

trated authorities to the center, for example, with clauses requiring prior consultation before taking action on a given delegated responsibility; by reclassifying deconcentrated credits in order to expand central problems (health or sports infrastructure); and with the proliferation of circulars specifying the ways to implement the deconcentrated responsibilities.[26]

Another way the center has sought to conserve its power has been by using decentralization against deconcentration, creating a direct dialogue between central ministries and elected officials. Putting the departmental president on a state commission, for example, could result in obtaining more local money for state projects as well as in getting local governments to accept more readily state policies in such areas as housing, consumption, road safety, and telecommunications. Moreover, by requiring very large numbers of actors in a particular consultation process – for example, the *Comité departementale des personnes agés* (CODERPA), a commission for the elderly – or by making the procedures so complex (credits for land-use planning), the central authorities guaranteed that they alone would be able to take the lead.[27]

Simply through their funding mechanisms, the central ministries retain the upper hand. In economic development, for example, regional prefects generally don't know how much of the money under their control they will be receiving at the beginning of the fiscal year, especially because funding in this area is provided through traditional subsidy programs, which are subject to budgetary cuts and internal ministerial reallocations. Often, they don't know how much money not under their control, that is national and departmental monies, has been received in their region by the end of the fiscal year.[28]

Of course, not all ministries have resisted deconcentration in the same ways or to the same extent. Different ministries had deconcentrated their finances to different degrees as of 1986. Almost complete decentralization to the benefit of the prefect has occurred in the areas of artisanry, tourism, professional development, and culture. About half of the agricultural credits have also been deconcentrated. In education, deconcentration has occurred in a number of areas such as school construction, but not in modern school equipment or in the construction of higher education facilities. Almost no deconcentration at all is evident in the areas of environment or infrastructure.[29]

A similar pattern of mixed resistance to deconcentration and decentralization is also evident in the transfer of personnel from the state to local

[26]Bernard, *L'État*, p. 210.
[27]Ibid., pp. 210–11.
[28]Plan, *Planification*, pp. 42–7.
[29]Ibid.

governmental services. By August 1986, the division of personnel from the *Direction départmentale de l'action sanitaire et sociale* (Health and Social Services) between the state and the department was for the most part accomplished, with 29 percent of the 56,500 civil servants involved staying with the state and 71 percent going to the departments. But things did not move nearly as swiftly with the other field services of the state. As of the end of 1986, nothing at all had happened with the departmental services of agriculture and forestry, the departmental services of youth and sports, the school inspection service, and the regional services of the state. The division of the departmental services for infrastructure was only very slowly being put into practice, with only eighteen *conventions* for the transfer of civil servants having been approved, affecting a mere 4.7 percent of civil servants concerned. Technical problems are clearly one of the main reasons for this. Another good explanation is the resistance of the personnel, who exhibit a high degree of organization and esprit de corps, by comparison with the personnel of the social services agencies.[30]

The transfer of personnel itself raises another set of questions about decentralization, given that recentralization is a risk simply because local governments end up employing civil servants trained by the state and imbued with its principles and prejudices. The national administrative culture, in other words, may very well have a detrimental effect on the development of differentiated, local administrative cultures or of innovative, local organizational structures, or policy-making processes. This is especially a danger when the heads of regional or departmental services are national civil servants *en détachement* from their corps.[31] The problem here is that even if they faithfully serve the elected officials who are their employers and follow their *politique* without question, they may very well implement such policy in a manner similar to that of their colleagues in the prefecture and technical field services, thus informally reintroducing the administrative practices of the center into the formally decentralized periphery. Such recentralization could be offset, however, if such civil servants were to see the departments and regions as local governmental systems in their own right, requiring different practices and working relationships from those of the state. There is at least anecdotal evidence to suggest such a change in approach is already taking place, as in the case of the head of departmental economics, educational, and cultural services in the Haute-Loire, formerly of the state's DDE, who noted that "before, questioned by a mayor, I responded as a functionary: I cited a regulation. Today, I speak in the

[30]Bechtel, Henry-Meininger, and Jegouzo, "Chronique," p. 158.
[31]See Mény, "Socialist Decentralization," pp. 18–20.

325

name of the elected officials. I must provide a political response."[32] But whether this political response translates into different kinds of administrative action remains to be seen.

The decentralization reform, in short, has had mixed results with regard to the state's presence in the periphery. The central ministries and the field services of the state continue to operate as they always have, despite the prefect's new formal powers. There has been little retreat or renewal here. The prefects' role, however, has indeed changed, suggesting retreat with regard to the powers they exercised in the past, renewal with regard to their role as power brokers much more than as power holders. Although the power holders who have taken their place have undoubtedly gained the more important roles in the periphery as the presidents of the councils of the regions and departments, the nationalization of the local civil service may serve as a form of recentralization of these otherwise decentralized bodies.

The intermediate levels of local government: New tutelles or new complementarities?

The most significant changes have occurred at the level of the regions and departments. Because of their new functions and powers, the regions and departments have become systems in their own right, with their own particular structures, functions, and goals. Departmental presidents have become the executives of large-scale bureaucracies already in operation, whereas the regional presidents, having taken over much smaller operations, have expanded them greatly. At both levels, the presidents have organized their operations and delegated responsibility in a variety of different ways, for example, in terms of political cabinets appointed by the chief executive alone, especially attractive to the *cumulants,* or in terms of regional or general council committees, following the example of Communist municipal councils.

Their interrelationships with one another, with the state, and with the communes have changed accordingly. Regional and departmental presidents tend to see one another as the main challenge to their new authority. Regional presidents envy the large budgets and bureaucracies of the departmental presidents and the latter worry about the new legitimacy of the former, given the department-wide basis of the regional councilor's mandate as opposed to the narrow cantonal basis of the general councilor's mandate. For all this, interaction between the departments and regions remains quite satisfactory, more complementary than competi-

[32]*Le Monde,* May 15, 1985.

tive. There is increased contact and continued dialogue between elected officials as well as civil servants from the departments and regions, given the multiplicity of jointly financed ventures. But such complementarity, in which one level of government has the upper hand, can also lead to a relationship of *tutelle* in those areas of overlapping responsibilities, a great fear of both the regions and the departments with regard to the state and of the departments with regard to the regions.

The regions. As the newest level of local government, the regions have had not only the greatest challenge in getting their operations up and running but also the greatest opportunity to shape the regional administration as they considered necessary, because they took over relatively small operations. The amount of organizational change, however, depended upon the region, because some regional presidents had set up effective regional agencies even before decentralization, for example, Defferre in Provence-Alpes-Côte d'Azur and Mauroy in the Nord-Pas de Calais.[33] Even so, their ability to recruit new personnel meant that they had to reshape, if not create anew, their organization in keeping with their new duties, which involved administrative tasks (for example, professional training, high schools) as well as policy-oriented ones (for example, planning, economic development, research transfer, land-use planning).[34]

Most regional officials have preferred their policy-oriented tasks over their administrative ones for an obvious reason: the former place them at the center of the promotion of local economic development, as local industrial development brokers, as we have already seen.[35] After all, the promotion of economic development is much more exciting than overseeing the maintenance of high schools, especially because the money is readily available in the former case, not so much in the latter.[36] With this in mind, the constant refrain of members of the right since 1986 that the region should not become bogged down by administrative tasks becomes more understandable, as does Bernard Stasi's insistence that the future of the region was in innovation and imagination, and that its greatest strength was that it had great flexibility and was able to take swift action.[37] What he neglected to mention is that the region's most appealing functions – both for the political capital they provided as well as for the

[33]Ashford, *British Dogmatism*, p. 228.
[34]Dominique Schmitt, "Les nouvelles administrations régionales," *La Décentralisation en marche – Cahiers français*, no. 220 (Mar.–Apr. 1985), pp 11–14.
[35]See the discussion in Part II, Chapter 8, "The new decentralized *dirigisme* in local economic development."
[36]See the discussion in Part II, Chapter 10, "The financial limitations and the 'transfer of unpopularity.' "
[37]*Démocratie Moderne*, May 8, 1986.

amount of power they gave its officials – were in its policy-oriented tasks in economic development.

The new regional planning process in particular ensured that the departments and communes would recognize the region's existence and its capabilities in its new sphere of competence – economic intervention.[38] It is in this process that the region, regardless of the government's intentions, cannot avoid exercising some *tutelle,* if only inadvertently, over the lower levels of government. The region, after all, has become the local industrial development broker and a *dirigiste* power in its own right. As such, it is charged to take the lead in all areas of local economic development under its jurisdiction, including in those areas where there is overlap with the lower levels of government. Among other things, this entails that the departments and the communes can only complement regional actions with regard to direct aid, which means that when regions do not act, they cannot either – including in sectors of activity traditionally those of the departments alone such as agriculture, artisanry, and commerce. Instead of seeing this particular limitation as another form of *tutelle,* however, the departments have seen it only as a serious inconvenience, to be solved informally simply by mislabeling aid (as indirect rather than direct) or by setting up *organismes-écran,* or dummy organizations.[39]

Although the region can thus exercise some *tutelle* over the departments and communes, the state has not completely given up its *tutelle* over the region in practice, even if it has in theory. The question is, What constitutes this *tutelle* and how serious is it? And about this, there is little agreement. Some scholars, focusing on the state's financial powers, insist that, in the regional planning process, the regions risk falling under the *tutelle* of the state simply because the state can not only mobilize regional resources in the service of national objectives but can also frame the regions' development strategies for the years to come.[40] Others, however, see more of a relationship of compromise between the state and the region, in which each seeks to accommodate the other to a certain extent.[41] In fact, although the state does indeed have the capability to exercise a substantive *tutelle* over the region as a result of its financial powers, it has not done so, as the decentralized *dirigisme* involved in the elaboration of the regional planning contracts suggests. The regions have a great deal of leeway in defining their priorities and demonstrating their

[38]Plan, *Planification,* p. 53.
[39]Plan, *Interventions économiques,* pp. 36–7.
[40]Chevallier, "La région."
[41]Michel Ozenda and Dominique Strauss-Kahn, "French planning: Decline or renewal?" in *Economic Policy and Policy-Making under the Mitterrand Presidency 1981–1984,* ed. H. Machin and V. Wright (New York: St. Martin's Press, 1985), p. 109.

fit with those of the state.[42] The substantive relationship is one of interdependence and mutual accommodation rather than one of *tutelle*.

The state, nevertheless, can exercise a purely financial *tutelle*, affecting the regions' ability to carry out their plans after the fact, through its financing of the regional plans, simply by not funding the contracts up to the amount pledged. It is this problem that led a Senate commission to report in 1984 that "regionalization appears to be the means for the government to master and to orient the actions of the decentralized collectivities."[43] For whereas the region is bound by the plan to put its money where it has promised, the state is not – or, at least, that is what the state assumed when it reneged on its commitment in its state–region planning contract to have a European x-ray cyclotron center built in Strasbourg and located it in Grenoble instead.

But even when the state does not renege on its promises, it manages to exercise further control, if only in the inevitable delays in financing the plans. Because the state's funds are often slow in coming, the region either has to get an advance from the Treasury to cover the whole amount of the expenditure or delay implementation as it waits for the money to be cleared. Moreover, because the contracts are treated like traditional subsidies, subject to reductions and cuts, the region has to wait until the end of the ministry's reallocation process to see its money as well as to find out whether it will receive the full amount – this has been especially a problem in the areas of environment, social assistance, and research.[44] The delays and uncertainties involved in the financing of the plans by the central ministries, however, are nothing compared to those when cofinancing by the different ministries and local governments is involved.

There are other areas in which something of a financial *tutelle* has resulted, however inadvertently, from decentralization. In certain cases, a measure intended to protect the regions from the encroachments of the state actually worked the opposite way. Because of the change to block grants, which in principle forbids the state to intervene in the areas of transferred functions, the state could not respond to specific requests from the regions. At the same time, the regions were asked to contribute matching funds in areas of competence reserved exclusively by the state. Some elected officials complained that such asymmetry in the state–region relationship constituted a transfer of *charges,* or costs, by the state to the regions.[45] If nothing else, it put the regions at a disadvantage with regard to the state.

[42]See Part II, Chapt. 8, "The new decentralized *dirigisme* in local economic development."
[43]Senate, no. 177. Annex to the *procès-verbal* proceedings of the Oct. 19, 1984 session.
[44]Plan, *Planification*, pp. 42–7.
[45]Ibid., p. 32.

The state, in short, does indeed have a good deal of power over local governments in the financing of local economic development. But this power is mitigated somewhat by the ability of the region to influence the state's decisions as well as to direct the departments' and communes' initiatives. The state has less influence over the departments in the area of social services, mainly because the functions have been separated to a much larger degree. For the departments, the regions remain the main threat to their independence, but only, needless to say, in the economic development area.

The departments. The departments essentially inherited their structure and organization from the prefectoral system. By and large they have followed a "presidential" model of organization, with a political cabinet that ranges from a simple secretariat to a veritable "cabinet" with individuals charged to elaborate and implement the president's policies as well as an executive bureau that tends to wield significant powers, often exceeding the authority granted it in the laws. Finally, the departmental services now have a director general, the president's appointee, and a hierarchical organization very similar to the previous prefectoral organization.[46]

For the departments, the main challenge has been much less organizational than it has been managerial, because the transfer of administrative functions in the area of social services left the departments facing greatly increased responsibilities and a much more complex situation because the state retained a certain number of social service functions for itself in areas of "national solidarity." Because of this overlap in functions between the state and the departments, the state continues to represent a threat to the departments' independence and a continuing source of confusion.

The relationship between the state and the departments, though, is more one of uneasy coexistence in its main areas of operation than one of potential *tutelle,* with the departments as much as the prefects and field services continually seeking to increase their own powers while limiting the other's. Because of the division of services, new entitlement programs have continued to be subjects of controversy, with battles between the state and the departments as to which should be in charge. For example, with the new *revenu minimal d'insertion,* announced in June 1988, which was to give individuals without any income a minimal monthly income, local elected officials kicked up a ruckus arguing that giving the prefects responsibility here went against decentralization as well as the dictates of administrative efficiency, given that mayors had the best knowledge of

[46]Jacques Gasnier, "Les nouvelles administrations départementales," *La Décentralisation en marche – Cahiers français,* no 220 (Mar.–Apr. 1985), p. 7.

the local situation since they were closest to it, whereas the departments, with their responsibility for social aid and their army of social workers, had the best manpower to administer the program effectively. The state's response, however, was that this was a question of national solidarity and that, because the money for this program was to come from the national solidarity tax on fortunes, it was appropriate for the state to administer the program.[47]

Although the departments have worked basically as coequals with the state in the delivery of social services, they worry about state *tutelles* in the context of public health and welfare policy-making. The Assembly of the presidents of the general councils of France in particular was concerned that, because of the overlap in responsibilities of the state and departments in such areas as the elderly and aging handicapped individuals, departmental policies would be dictated by the policy options chosen by the state. Moreover, they were concerned that, because it would be impossible to achieve any reasonable level of coordination in the policies of the prefect and the departmental president, despite this being required legally, all they could do was rely on the goodwill of the state to take into consideration the consequences of its policies for local governments.[48]

All in all, however, the state represents a minor problem as a potential source of *tutelle* over the departments in the social services area, especially by comparison with the area of local economic development, in which both the state and the regions represent a more serious problem. But here, different departments have responded differently, sometimes even playing off one level against the other.

The relationship of the departments to the region and the state in the Nord-Pas-de-Calais provides a good illustration of the complexities involved. In this region, the department of the Nord has a great deal of power resulting primarily from its weight both in demographic terms (it is the largest department in France) and in financial terms (its budget in 1985, at 5 billion francs, was 2.5 times that of the region at 2 billion francs). With this came its interest in maintaining its autonomy with regard to the region and to the field services of the state. This manifested itself in its tardiness in signing the agreements for the transfer of personnel from the state to the department as well as in its interest in breaking with the old administrative traditions of the general council. The department of the Pas-de-Calais, by contrast, has maintained a close cooperative relationship with the field services of the state, demonstrated by its

[47]J.-C. Bouzely, "La gestion du revenu minimal d'insertion," *La Revue Administrative* no. 244 (July–Aug. 1988): 360–1.

[48]Assemblée des Présidents des Conseils Généraux de France, "La décentralisation dans le domaine sanitaire et social depuis le 1er janvier 1984," *Action sanitaire et sociale*, dossier no. 3 (June 1984), pp. 13–16.

rapidity in signing the agreements for the transfer of personnel from the state to the department as well as in its creation of agencies for economic action that collaborate with the prefectoral administration. This reflects as much its lack of means to do otherwise as it does its interest in compensating for its inferiority with regard to the region and to the department of the Nord.[49]

Interestingly enough, neither department participated much in the elaboration of the first regional plan, concerned that the region would encroach on the department's domain and become a *tuteur*, or tutor, rather than remain a mediator. They therefore waited to see what programs would be adopted in the final plan before deciding on the extent of their participation, thus controlling the amount they would contribute.[50] By 1984, though, the departments had already overcome some of their reticence with regard to the region, participating with it in a variety of local development initiatives.[51] In other regions, however, such fears of a regional *tutelle* were much less apparent even initially, with numbers of departments participating by developing departmental plans to be incorporated into the regional plan.[52]

Departments' fears of a regional *tutelle* are not without foundation. Jean-Marie Auby characterized this *tutelle* as one of *l'englobant,* or the all-encompassing, over *l'englobé,* or the all-encompassed.[53] He argued that the fact that the departmental plan, where it existed, had to integrate itself into the regional plan was an important mechanism of *tutelle*.[54] Even the Planning Commission, in its report on the regional planning process, found such fears about the possible encroachment of the region on the department's territory well taken, noting: "Experience shows that it is easy to pass from a relationship of mediation to an attitude of tutelage."[55] Although some regions were careful not to overstep their boundaries in the regional planning process, as in the case of the Franche-Comté, which resisted state urgings to do so in environmental matters, others appeared quite eager to include in their regional planning contracts, over state objections, projects in domains specifically transferred to the departments and the communes (for example, social services and

---

[49]Gérard Marcou, "Les rapports entre la région et les départements dans le cadre de la nouvelle décentralisation: L'exemple du Nord-Pas-de-Calais." Paper presented at a conference sponsored by the Nord-Pas-de-Calais regional section of the Institut français des sciences administratives (Lille, March 12, 1984).

[50]Quoted in Masse, Koni, and Hennion, "La participation," p. 5.

[51]Deplanque et al., "Le Développement."

[52]See Part II, Chapter 8, "The new decentralized *dirigisme* in local economic development."

[53]Jean-Marie Auby, "La décentralisation fait-elle naître de nouvelles tutelles?" *Actualité Juridique. Droit Administratif* (July–Aug. 1984): 412.

[54]Ibid., pp. 416–17.

[55]Ibid., p. 18.

water supply).[56] In other cases, the state and regions together exercised something of a financial *tutelle* over the local collectivities in cases of joint financing with the communes and departments by setting up commissions composed mainly of representatives of the state and the region to evaluate dossiers that used local governments' monies without taking into account their development priorities.[57]

The departments, in short, were quite wary of the regions with regard to their potential *tutelle* in the area of economic development. In many cases, their answer to this was to remain members of the regional council. Thus, François Poncet, although focused almost exclusively on his duties as president of the general council of the Aquitaine, nevertheless felt the need to participate in the region because otherwise, as he explained, one is excluded from decisions that affect one's department.[58] The limitation of the *cumul des mandats,* however, has closed off this option to a large extent. And the increasing differentiation of the urban-focused regional elites from the more rural-dominated departmental elites, as discussed previously, suggests that the departmental officials will continue to worry about the regions.[59]

Even when local elected officials continue to sit on both the departmental and the regional councils, however, there appears to to be a reasonable amount of role differentiation, with elected officials finding that a measure they voted for at one level of local government may very well be something they must oppose at another.[60] One can see this quite clearly in the parting of the ways of departments and their region in cases in which the overlap in membership would suggest the contrary. In the Nord-Pas-de-Calais, for example, where fifty-nine regional councilors were also general councilors during the departmental debates on the first regional plan, the departments nevertheless went their own way, refusing for the most part to participate in the plans themselves.[61]

Whereas departmental council members feel a need to protect their interests by sitting on the regional council, regional councilors have not felt the comparable need to sit on the departmental council. This may very well have to do with the clear sense of role of those on the regional council – to focus on economic development alone – by contrast with the department, where the actions of the region will have an impact on their own economic action. Thus, the regions tend to worry primarily about

[56]Ibid., p. 30.
[57]Ibid., p. 32.
[58]*Le Monde,* Jan. 24, 1985.
[59]See the discussion in Part II, Chapter 8, "New elites and new rules of the game?"
[60]Pierre Kukawka, Sylvie Biarez, Maurice Croisat, et al., "Les action économiques des collectivités territoriales." Report prepared for the Commissariat Général du Plan (Grenoble: CERAT, 1985), p. 155.
[61]Masse, Koni, Hennion, "La participation," p. 4.

the state with regard to any potential *tutelle,* whereas the departments are concerned not only about both the regions and the state with regard to a *tutelle* in the economic development area, but also about the state with regard to the social services area, albeit to a much lesser extent. All of these fears, however, are likely to recede as regions and departments become more comfortable with their new functions and work out their relationships with one another as well as with the state. The fears of the rural communes with regard to the encroachments on their freedom by the departments and the state, by contrast, are less likely to recede very quickly.

The communes and the "reform at two speeds"

Decentralization, although in principle applying uniformly to all communes, in practice consecrated what Yves Mény has called a "reform at two speeds."[62] At the same time that decentralization legitimated the informal rules already in operation in the big cities, it entailed a seeming return to the status quo ante for rural communes, especially in the light of recent revisions of the laws affecting the rural communes. As a result, the urban and rural communes together experienced the least amount of organizational change with the passage of the Socialists' decentralizing reforms. Although decentralization also left the mayors of the larger communes with only slightly different interrelationships from before, because the region has become a small source of concern, it has left rural mayors frantic, worried about the likely *tutelle* not only by the departments but also by the prefects, despite the changes in their role and demeanor.

The urban communes. The urban communes remain least affected by decentralization, mainly because it simply formalized the informal rules and relationships already in operation. Thus, they continue to represent independent systems much like those described by systemic scholars, with the caveat that the prefect is no longer much of a player in this system. One study found that whereas, in some spheres, the municipal system follows the model Thoenig outlined, in which local administrators appeal to local politicians for help in resolving problems within the administrative hierarchy – in particular in municipal services concerned primarily with technical matters or with *animation* (that is, with the life of the city including culture and sports) – in other spheres such as municipal social assistance services, the pattern of interaction is much more closed to

[62]Yves Mény, "Le sort de la décentralisation, 1982–1987." Paper presented at the New York University and Columbia conference, A France of Pluralism and Consensus? (New York, Oct. 9–11, 1987).

political actors and much more similar to Crozier's model of the vicious bureaucratic cycle, in which the administrators fall back on national rules and regulations to avoid outside pressures.[63] Regardless of the pattern, however, civil servants depend on their own contacts with outside influential individuals to reinforce their positions in local administration, rendering them less subject to the authority of higher level administrators as well as to the pressures of politicians.[64]

The municipal system itself, of course, is not completely closed to the outside, given the necessary relationships with the departments and the regions. But here, the relationship is more one of coexistence and complementarity, in which functions overlap, than it is one of *tutelle*. There is little to suggest that the urban communes will lose out to the departments, the regions, or the prefects even in areas of activity that encompass their primary functions. The city with its mayor is still the first place the local citizen considers when needing social assistance or the like, mainly because the city is closer to the problems affecting the local population, and often better able to deal with them. The city is even more independent than before, due to the new laws on top of its mayor's continued direct access to Paris (usually as a result of the *cumul des mandats*) and its own technical services; it therefore need not turn to the department or the prefect for advice or assistance. The city even continues to have its own funding sources for economic development – often through a direct link with Paris, although in the area the city must depend much more on the region than it did in the past.

The big-city mayors' main concern has been the reduction of their financial resources because of the switch to block grants from the myriad subsidies provided by different Paris ministries and the reduction in revenue from the local business tax. The mayors now recognize that the region has become more important to them as a new source of funding – and a potential rival.[65] (This helps explain the colonization of the regions by urban-based elected officials, themselves often vice-mayors.) On this score, though, it is the mayors of the midsize cities who have been most concerned, for they can turn for help neither to the departments – the traditional ally of the rural communes – nor to the regions – the natural ally of the big cities.

The mayors of midsize communes also complain about the possibility of *tutelle* from the intermediate bodies. Philippe Séguin, echoing the views of most mayors of midsize communes, argued that decentralization has produced a new kind of *tutelle* by the intermediate bodies in ex-

---

[63]Dion, *Politisation*, pp. 130–41.
[64]Ibid., pp. 143–9.
[65]Christian Lalu, director of the Association of Big City Mayors, interview with author, Paris, May 2, 1985.

change for a limited decrease in the state *tutelle*. According to Séguin, a regional *tutelle* is evident, for example, in the fact that although the regions are allegedly solely responsible for the *lycées,* the region demands contributions from the commune. And the state *tutelle*, he insists, has come in the requirement that cities must sign agreements with, or set up plans approved by, a given ministry in exchange for what are essentially camouflaged subsidies granted by the *fonds* established by the ministry. For example, only if you have a contract for local transportation development or sign an agreement with the Ministry of Culture for cultural development do you get a subsidy, otherwise not.[66]

All in all, however, even the midsize cities benefit from decentralization, because they have the formal powers they exercised only informally in the past. In any event, they are not subject to the kind of *tutelle* experienced by the rural communes.

The rural communes. Even though the bulk of the population lives in the larger urban communes, the rural communes are much more numerous. Out of the thirty-six thousand communes, close to twenty-three thousand communes have fewer than five hundred inhabitants. By failing to reduce the number of communes, decentralization left the rural communes, in particular, with new powers and freedoms that they were hard pressed to take advantage of, lacking as they were in the necessary resources. At the same time, however, decentralization broke the system of complicity with the prefect that many rural mayors continued to need and to want.

In their new-found freedom, the mayors of rural communes can no longer count on the delicate balance or compromise of the past in their relations with the prefect to ensure their tenure in office. Because they now have final (rather than first) signatory power over construction permits, for example, they can no longer blame the prefect or the technical field services of the state for unpopular decisions.[67] But they do nevertheless try. The old patterns of interaction tend to persist here. Often, the mayors continue to run to the subprefects for help at the same time that they accuse the prefects of continuing centralization.

One mayor of a small commune of forty-seven hundred inhabitants in the Finistère, one year after the transfer of executive power, saw little change in his relations with the prefectoral corps, finding that despite the a posteriori *tutelle,* mayors had a tendency to call the subprefect for an opinion before the municipal council deliberated on an issue. Another mayor from this department agreed that matters were decided "*à l'amiable,*" ahead of time, and that this was why no matters had been

---

[66]Séguin interview.
[67]Charles Vial, "Haute-Loire: La fin du préfet alibi," *Le Monde,* May 15, 1985.

sent to the administrative courts. Another mayor from an equally small commune in the Lozère insisted that nothing had changed, that excellent relations continued with the prefectoral administration, with no increase in conflict although perhaps less intensity in the interactions. He admitted that "the subprefects sometimes have difficulty in forgetting their role of tutor, but they play the game."[68]

For all this amiability, rural mayors often complain about continuing centralization as a result of the prefect's a posteriori judicial recourse, which they claim is far worse than the former a priori prefectoral review of their decisions. The threat of court proceedings alone, they maintain, is enough for them to capitulate to the prefects' demands. Although they would have to agree that only a very small percentage of their decisions actually wind up in the administrative tribunal or regional accounting courts (less than 1 percent), they would insist that this is because they tend to go to the prefects for the approval a priori of any matter they feel might be open to question. There may be some truth to this, according to Michel Besse, secretary-general of the prefecture of the Bouches-du-Rhône, who found that mayors are going to the prefects for an a priori go-ahead in order to avoid a posteriori judicial recourse. And yet, he admitted that prefects see much less of the mayors of the communes than before, thus suggesting that this new kind of *tutelle* must be found only where there are ticklish issues.[69]

The other side of this, however, is that the prefects themselves feel pressure to resolve issues without going to the administrative tribunals, for fear that they will not win and thus somehow lose face. This explains, for instance, the prefects' reluctance to refer matters involving questionable economic interventions for judicial review – especially once they have lost a certain number of cases (for example, in the Doubs in 1983, when local government won against the prefect in two out of four cases).[70]

The outside reviews by administrative law judge have not been the dreaded actions by impersonal replacements for the prefect that the rural mayors initially made them out to be. The administrative law judge has not become a replacement for, or an agent of, the prefect, but rather acts as a regulator of the system in a variety of ways, depending on the modus operandi of the judge.[71]

Although the view of the administrative law judge changed, that of the regional accounting chambers did not. The smaller communes in particular saw them as a threat, especially because they began going beyond

[68]Marcel Parini, "Droits et libertés des communes: L'avis des maires," *Vie Publique* (Apr. 1983): 40.
[69]Besse interview.
[70]Plan, *Interventions économiques*, pp. 40–1.
[71]Rondin, *Le Sacre*, pp. 232–48.

simple reviews of communal budgets to criticisms of communal administrative practices. Their severest criticisms, however, were directed at the intercommunal syndicates, at overly ambitious investment policies that did not take account of their indirect costs, and at financial assistance to attract new enterprises.[72] In any event, although the regional accounting courts had been taking action in fewer and fewer cases (in 1983, they took action in only 1,667 cases; in 1986, 1,195 as a result of a decrease in the number of late budgets voted),[73] this did not stop the opposition that returned to power in 1986 from exempting all smaller communes from such reviews, much to their relief.

The return to the old system of budgetary review by the treasurer-paymaster general for communes with fewer than two thousand inhabitants (80 percent of the communes), from the new a posteriori review by the regional accounting courts, however, did not in any way signify less control from outside, only different. Instead of review by an independent regional body, it represented in some sense a return to the previous financial *tutelle* by the state, with all the concomitant dangers of recentralization.[74] This was not the only way in which the rural communes' freedom in financial matters has been limited. The revision of the *Dotation globale d'équipement* (DGE), or the block grant for capital investment projects gives the prefect charge of disbursing investment funds to rural communes on a case by case basis on the advice of a commission of local elected officials. The rural mayors can thus claim that recentralization is occurring, minus the benefits of the old system that made the prefects more dependent on local officials and therefore more willing to consider their needs first.

The state has retained its influence in other ways as well. In urban planning, for example, although the communes gained substantial powers, they were still limited by the state, not only because it established the framework within which the communes had to operate but also because it retained certain functions such as housing policy and the protection of the national heritage and historic sites, which could interfere with the commune carrying out its duties.[75] In order to make independent deci-

---

[72]See Yves Jegouzo and Christophe Sanson, "Décentralisation: La pause, pourquoi et comment?" *L'Année administrative 86* (Paris: Institut international d'administration publique, 1987), pp. 46–7.

[73]Jean-François Larger and Charles Deconfin, "Les chambres régionales des comptes: 1983–1987, cinq années de fonctionnement," *Revue Française des Sciences Politiques* no. 22 (1988): 172.

[74]See, for example, Christophe Perron, "La revanche du 'monstre froid,'" *Le Monde*, June 25, 1987.

[75]For the intricacies of the new land-use planning system for the communes, see André Terrazzoni, *La Décentralisation à l'épreuve des faits* (Paris: Librairie générale de droit et de jurisprudence, 1987), pp. 155–68.

sions, for example, in issuing building permits, communes had to have an approved *Plan du occupation du sol* (POS), or land-use plan, (which are zoning documents that outline plans for population growth, industrial expansion and the financial needs to meet the changes, and community needs). Although at the time of decentralization, three-fourths of the population was covered by a POS, only one-third of French communes had them, with the smaller communes inevitably being the ones without. As a result, many communes remained for a time under the *tutelle* of the state, in some cases by choice, simply by not having a POS.[76] In most cases, however, the reason for the delay was that the technical services of the state were overloaded as requests piled in (the number of POS delivered went from 164 in 1981 to 182 in 1982, to 706 in 1983 and over 800 in 1984).[77]

More recently, however, the state's control over urban planning has loosened further with the measures of the neoliberal government, which eased many of the technical requirements of urban planning, for example, in the cases of communes wishing to issue building permits without an approved POS.[78] But even without this, the state's influence is diminishing, if only because the field services face competition. The communes, after all, have a choice in whom to consult in the granting of building permits and the like: they can use the technical field services of the state (the DDE) for free; of the department where they are set up (the DDE-bis, as it is now called) also for free or for a nominal fee depending upon the department; or of private contractors for the going rate. And this has made a difference.

The technical services of the state tend to be more responsive to the wishes of rural mayors, in large measure because they face competitors from the departmental technical services and even from private contractors, whom the mayors now have the legal right to hire – although they must pay for such services themselves. Now, mayors no longer have the problem of discovering, six months after their request for a replacement for the crumbling wall in the ancient cemetery, that the engineers of the DDE have simply gone in overnight and constructed an ugly concrete wall totally out of keeping with the surroundings, designed without even an on-site visit. Instead, any such ugly wall would first have to be approved by the mayor. But there is more to the new interaction of the field services with the mayors than this. As one mayor of a commune of six

[76]For the complexities of the new urban planning situation, both the benefits and the drawbacks, see Maurice Goze, "La décentralisation de l'urbanisme 1983–1987: Une première synthèse," *Annuaire des collectivités locales 1987* (Paris: Librairies techniques, 1987) pp. 91–110.
[77]Christian Vigoroux, "L'urbanisme aux communes: Dispersion et dynamique," *Échange et Projets* no. 41 (March 1985): 58.
[78]See Jegouzo and Sanson, "Décentralisation," pp. 44–5.

thousand in the Loiret sees it, the big changes are that the construction permits are left in the town hall, rather than being brought to the DDE in Orléans (150 km. roundtrip), even though the agents of the DDE are still the ones evaluating the requests; and the delays have been reduced from two months to three weeks – although this results more from the deconcentration of the DDE than from decentralization.

The technical services of the state, in short, have become more efficient as well as more responsive to the mayors of the small communes. But not all mayors have been happy with this situation, mainly because they have been worried about their new responsibilities. Rural mayors in both the Lozère and Finistère, for example, have expressed concern about their new duties in the area of construction permits, fearful that they lacked the technical expertise, as well as about their new financial responsibilities, asking how a farmer or an artisan as mayor would be able to administer a budget of 20 million francs.[79] For these mayors, the answer has been to hide behind the POS and the DDE or even to go to the department. In the Loiret, for example, one finds almost all roads leading to the departmental seat in Orléans, with mayors going less and less to the prefecture, and almost never to the subprefecture.[80]

The departments, however, represent as much a threat to the independence of the small communes as a promise of help, because their ability to provide financial and technical assistance to rural communes means that they may gain a certain measure of control over the communes even though, legally, no level of local government is to exercise a *tutelle* over any other. Because the departments distribute the credits for rural public services (for example, rural electrification, drinking water, sewage, and garbage collection), and part of the departments' DGE goes to aid the rural communes' infrastructure (for example, water, electricity, funds for land-use planning, hydraulic, power, and leisure), the rural communes have become financially dependent upon the departments and upon the prefects. This helps explain the view of one mayor from a small commune of seven hundred inhabitants in the Lozère who insisted that: "decentralization stops at the level of the department. . . . The general councilors who were already the lords of the new regime appear more and more like real feudal lords."[81]

The threat of a departmental *tutelle* over the rural communes has actually led some mayors to pin their hopes on the counter-powers derived from intercommunal charters, which are the successors of the intercommunal syndicates of assistance. But because these charters, or syndicates, represent financial arrangements of convenience more than

[79]Parini, "Droits et libertés," pp. 41–2.
[80]*Le Monde*, May 14, 1985.
[81]Parini, "Droits et libertés," pp. 40–1.

anything else, they are unlikely to challenge the departments' potential control over rural communes. In the first years of decentralization, moreover, mayors tended to dismiss the possibility of using the intercommunal syndicates to create their own technical services in urban planning.[82] The regions, similarly, could provide some counter to the departments in providing aid to rural communes. But this would be more in the form of industrial development subsidies for small- and medium-sized enterprises as opposed to technical services. It therefore represents less of a challenge to a departmental *tutelle* than another kind of *tutelle* in the area of economic development.

The mayors of rural communes, in short, tend to feel that, at best, they have a choice between *tutelles,* in particular between that of the newly powerful department or that of the state.[83] Whereas the departments can exercise control over rural communes through their own technical services and their financing of rural public services and investments, the state can do so through the technical assistance of the DDE, through the budgetary review of rural communes by the treasurer-paymaster general, through the capital outlay decisions of the prefect, and through the a posteriori review of all communes' actions.

But despite all the potential *tutelles,* the most important elements of reform remain, viz., the mayor is no longer subject to the prefect's a priori administrative and financial control. And, like it or not, this means that rural mayors are in fact facing a different situation. Decentralization has produced significant changes in local government, creating separate systems at every level, with the actors playing new roles, following new rules, and developing new interrelationships. This becomes all the more apparent once we consider the changes in local officials' rhetoric, which reflect the new realities of local politics and administration.

[82]Robert Hertzog, "Grands services publics locaux," *Annuaire des collectivités locales 1984* (Paris: Librairies techniques, 1984) p. 458.
[83]See for example, Abélès, "Chemins," pp. 1414–15, 1419; Jean-Claude Thoenig, "Le grande horloger et les effets de système: De la decentralisation en France," *Revue Politique et Management Public,* no. 1 (1985); and Irene Wilson "Decentralizing or recentralizing the state? Urban planning and centre–periphery relations," in *Socialism, the State, and Public Policy in France,* ed. M. Schain and P. Cerny (London: Frances Pinter, 1985).

IO

A new rhetoric and a new reality in local government: Local politics and administration in the Socialist Fifth Republic and beyond

Despite its limitations, Socialist decentralization has had an important impact on local politics and administration. By altering the executive powers and administrative responsibilities of all major actors in the periphery, it has changed the roles, rules, and interrelationships of all local elected officials and administrators. By turning the heads of every level of local government into powerful, popularly elected officials while limiting the number of offices they can accumulate, it has introduced a new pluralism into local administrative arrangements and a new kind of politics into the periphery, increasing the size of the political class, strengthening party politics, and introducing national cleavages and concerns at every level of local government. The new administrative interdependence and the new politics, in brief, have greatly complicated the lives of the newly powerful local elected officials. They no longer have an easy way out of this situation, given the new transparency of local government that denies them the use of the old rhetorics.

With their new powers and formal responsibility for local government, local elected officials can no longer resort as readily to the rhetoric of centralization that hid their complicity with local administrators from public view and enabled them to avoid taking responsibility for their actions. With the greater politicization of all levels of local government, they can no longer use as convincingly the rhetoric of *apolitisme,* or nonpartisanship, to allay the local population's fears of political patronage, to reconcile their political allegiances with their administrative functions, or to avoid central political interference. But this is not to say that local politicians and administrators have completely changed their ways. Old patterns of interaction die hard. And many local elected officials have sought to create another wall of words to shield themselves from responsibility for their actions.

Deprived of the rhetoric of centralization, many created a new rhetoric focused on the limits of decentralization. Deprived of the rhetoric of nonpartisanship, most turned to a new rhetoric emphasizing good management, because they feared the electorate's response to the increasing politicization of the periphery and to the reality of their own new, clearly political roles within it. Rhetoric, however, now as before, also responds to certain realities. The rhetoric of the limits of decentralization also reflects local elected officials' protests against the real constraints imposed on their actions by the new forms of administrative oversight and by new kinds of financial controls as well as their attempts to gain further concessions from the central government. The rhetoric of good management reflects local elected officials' interest in their new duties and larger administratives roles as well as their attempt to minimize the impact of politics on their performance of those duties.

In the first few years of decentralization, the rhetoric of the financial limitations of decentralization predominated. The discourse in the periphery suggested that the state had not compensated local governments adequately for their newly transferred duties and, therefore, had engaged in a "transfer of unpopularity," because it had left local elected officials with the equally unpopular alternatives of raising taxes or cutting services. The view from the center contradicted this: The actual figures suggest that, overall, local governments did quite well, despite the fact that their resources did not increase as rapidly as in the past and were not distributed as equitably as intended. The regions in particular, although equally vociferous in their complaints, gained significant new human and financial resources for the promotion of local economic development. But perhaps most importantly, as proof that local governments were not impoverished as a result of decentralization, local elected officials themselves resorted less and less to the rhetoric of the limits of decentralization as they became more comfortable with their new administrative roles and responsibilities. In its place, they increasingly turned to the rhetoric of good management, which represents at the same time an affirmation of their new administrative responsibilities and a negation of their new political positions.

With this rhetoric of good management, local elected officials seek to depoliticize local government in the eyes of the public, to convince them that their tasks are more managerial than political. But the public has not been fooled. It is clear to just about everyone that national political divisions are increasingly brought into play at the local level, with politicization apparent not only in the actions and interrelationships of local elected officials but also in their interactions with the prefects. The rhetoric of good management, however, serves not only as a way to downplay this but also as a means of promoting cooperation among political rivals within, as well as between, the different levels of local government. And, finally, it also reflects reality: Local elected officials have in fact become good managers, administering local governments more efficiently and cost-effectively than before decentralization, if not always more democratically.

THE NEW RHETORIC OF THE LIMITS
OF DECENTRALIZATION

The new rhetoric focused on the limits of decentralization was most pronounced in the first few years of the decentralization reform, as local elected officials, who were slowly becoming accustomed to their new roles, sought to avoid public recognition of their new responsibilities. Most quickly adapted the old rhetoric – focused on the financial stranglehold of the state – to the new situation, complaining loudly and often about the financial limitations of decentralization and insisting that decentralization represented a transfer not of administrative duties but of financial *charges,* or costs, to the periphery. Local elected officials protested what they anticipated as decreased state aid to local governments and increased local financial burdens, insisting that these would severely cripple their ability to administer effectively. Although there was some truth to the complaints, especially for the poorer communes and departments, the state actually made certain to compensate local governments adequately and local budgets have continued to grow at a reasonable rate.

Regional elected officials in particular, although just as keen on the rhetoric of the financial limitations of decentralization as officials at the other levels, had no grounds for complaint, because their resources had skyrocketed. Moreover, the regions generally had greater financial power than the means technically at their disposal, given their role as local industrial development brokers. But the rhetoric persisted even here, representing less a protest against the limits of decentralization, however, than an attempt to pressure the central government to provide more resources.

The old rhetoric of the administrative overcentralization of the state, by comparison, was not so readily converted. Departmental officials, in particular, quite readily acknowledged that they could no longer make use of the *préfet-alibi* because, in the words of one official from the department of the Haute-Loire: "If elected officials do silly things, they will have to pay for it themselves."[1] Only the mayors of the rural communes converted the old rhetoric to a new rhetoric of the administrative limitations of decentralization, but with good reason. The rural communes have always had the least administrative means at their disposal, and decentralization did not remedy this. Rural mayors' insistence that the prefect's a posteriori recourse to the administrative law judge is

[1] *Le Monde,* May 15, 1985.

merely a new and more impersonal form of the *tutelle* may be exaggerated, as we have already seen, but rural mayors are not wrong to maintain that a variety of *tutelles,* including administrative oversight not only from the prefect but also from the departments, limits their field of administrative action appreciably. Until they develop a new working relationship with the departments and settle back into the old one with the prefect, rural mayors are going to continue to talk about the administrative limitations of decentralization. Although some rural mayors are certain to use this new rhetoric in the traditional way, to escape responsibility for their actions, many others have already been willing to accept responsibility for their actions; and they are likely to use that rhetoric, instead, as a way of protesting against, or of testing, the limits placed on their actions by prefects and departmental officials.

The financial limitations and the "transfer of unpopularity"

From 1983 to 1985 especially, the constant refrain from ever expanding choruses of *cumulants* (or national politicians who were also local elected officials), primarily from the opposition, was that the state was "unloading its own financial difficulties onto local authorities" (Barre) and that decentralization involved not so much the transfer of *compétences,* or administrative duties, as of *l'impopularité* (Chaban-Delmas, among others), because theirs is a no-win situation: In order to meet their obligations, they must either raise taxes or cut services.[2] For these opposition *cumulants,* moreover, the switch to block grants, instead of a liberating measure, was a way of decentralizing the recession, forcing local elected officials to make the hard decisions Paris could not, or did not want to, make. Many predicted that the reform would fail for lack of adequate resources.

Assessing the validity of these claims is quite complicated, due to the complexities in the financing of the new local government system: It built on the old system at the same time that it altered it in significant ways.[3] In the final analysis, the changes actually provide local government on the

[2]It is pointless to try to list all those who joined in the chorus and the numbers of articles in newspapers and magazines on the topic. A partial list includes: Raymond Barre, "La décentralisation à l'esbroufe, à la hussarde," *Le Monde,* Mar. 24, 1982; Jacques Chirac, "Il faudra revoir la décentralisation," *La Gazette,* no. 19, Oct. 21, Nov. 3, 1985; P. Clément, "Une décentralisation trop hâtive," *Le Figaro,* Nov. 14, 1985; F. Varenne, "LXVIIe congrés des maires sur le thème de la décentralisation," *Le Figaro,* Oct. 24, 1984; Grignancourt, "La décentralisation à rebours," *Aspects de la France,* Mar. 21, 1985; and "Finances: Les elus du M.N.E.L. lancent un S.O.S.," *La Gazette des Communes,* Jan. 1–20, 1984.
[3]For a discussion of the complexities of the new system of local financing and its relationship to the old system, see, Belorgey, *La France,* pp. 53–81.

whole with adequate compensation for their new duties, even though the resources did not increase quite as rapidly as in the past and have not been distributed as equitably as intended. Despite all of the dire predictions, in the end, the transfer was not one of "unpopularity." How then does one explain local elected officials' rhetoric? The view from the center, which focuses on overall resources made available to local governments, provides a somewhat different picture from the discourse in the periphery, where the experience of the urban communes differed from that of the rural communes, and that of the departments from the regions.

The view from the center. For central governmental officials, the explanation for the rhetoric of the financial limitations of decentralization was quite simple: Local elected officials had grown spoiled by the rapid increase in the size of their budgets through the 1970s and into the 1980s and were afraid that this growth would stop or even be reversed. Arguing against the limits of decentralization was a way of putting pressure on the government to continue to fund local governments generously – at the same rate as in the past. Thus, Eric Giuily, head of the *Direction générale des collectivités locales* (DGCL), or local governments department in the Ministry of the Interior, insisted that the financial complaint was a typical response from members of the opposition, part of a ploy to avoid taking responsibility for making hard decisions. He noted that in the transfer of financial resources, the Ministry had made a point of being overly generous, making certain not only that the first year of the transfer of financial resources would provide local governments with complete reimbursement for the costs of their newly transferred duties, but also that they would have sufficient resources to cover the increasing costs of following years.[4]

A quick glance at the amounts and the annual growth rates of local governments' expenditures, taken individually and as a whole, suggests that central government officials were not far off target in their assessments, despite the fact that there were some problems in certain years and for certain local governments. To begin with, total local government expenditures grew at a reasonable average annual rate of approximately 11 percent between 1981 and 1987 (with the ratio of operating costs to investments remaining steady at around 65 percent to 35 percent) to reach an estimated 581 billion francs, which was over 1.75 times the size of the budget in 1981 (Fig. 10.1).

Local governments' expenditures, considered separately, also show a reasonable rate of growth, although for all but the regions the annual percentage increase was lower after the transfer of financial resources

[4]Eric Giuily, interviews with author, Paris, May 21, 1985 and June 26, 1985.

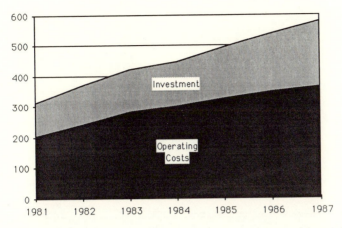

Figure 10.1: The growth of local government expenditures (in billions of francs). Source: Direction générale des collectivités locales. Notes: The 1987 figures are estimates.

than it was before (Fig. 10.2). The regions were the great winners, with their decreasing yearly rate of growth under the previous government (from +20.3 percent in 1978, to +12.3 percent in 1979, and to +8.1 percent in 1980) reversed by the Socialists even before the official transfer of financial resources, rising by an average of +24.35 percent in 1981 and 1982, only to jump to +46.5 percent in 1983, and followed by an average yearly rate of increase of +27.8 percent between 1984 and 1986. The departments, by contrast, had a somewhat bumpier ride, increasing their expenditures by an average yearly rate of +15.6 percent between 1977 and 1983, only to experience a −1.7 percent decline in 1984; but this righted itself in 1985 and 1986, with an average yearly rate of increase of +9.6 percent. The communes, finally, also increased their expenditures before the transfer of financial resources by an average yearly rate of +15.4 percent but, unlike the departments, experienced an +8.5 percent increase in 1984 and a +10.5 percent increase in 1985, only to drop in 1986 to a +6.9 percent growth rate. In 1987, moreover, all three levels of local government experienced a further decline in the growth rate of their budgets, with the regions' expenditures at +16.4 percent, the departments' at +5 percent, and the communes' at 6.7 percent.[5]

Although the annual growth rate of local governments' expenditures did decline somewhat, the increases were nevertheless significant, especially when compared with the growth rate in the expenditures of the state. Between 1981 and 1986, whereas local governments' expenditures averaged 11.4 percent in annual growth, the state's averaged only 9.7

[5]Direction générale des collectivités locales, "Poids économique et financier des collectivités locales" (June 1988), pp. 25–36.

347

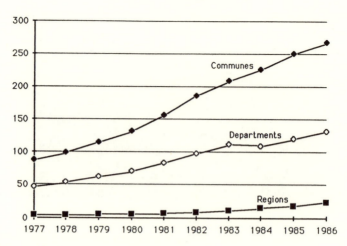

Figure 10.2: The growth in expenditures of local governmental units (in billions of francs).
Source: Direction générale des collectivités locales.

percent. Moreover, whereas in 1982, local government expenditures represented 10.4 percent of the GDP and 45.2 percent of overall state expenditures, they came to 10.7 percent of the GDP and 48 percent of state expenditures in 1986. Finally, despite the economic crisis, whereas local governments' budgets grew at a rate of approximately 2 percent per year in real terms between 1983 and 1987, the budget of the state was reduced by 2 percent per year in volume.[6]

There is every indication that this trend will persist, because of continuing pressure to fund local governments at rates of increase close to previous ones (adjusted, of course, for the slowdown in the rate of inflation). Under the neoliberal government, the Minister of the Interior, Charles Pasqua, angrily defended his constituency against the proposal of the Minister of the Budget, Alain Juppé, who at one point suggested cutting the budget of local authorities by 2 billion francs.[7] The Socialists in opposition, however, were the ones to press hardest for an increase in state transfers. Despite the government's claim that the proposed budget for 1988 was to increase the resources of the local authorities by more than 4.2 percent, they maintained that the neoliberals were "strangling the local governments financially" and that "the state is disengaging itself from the local governments and throwing decentralization into ques-

[6]Ibid.; Patrick Joyeux, Gérard Logié, Joseph Carles, et al., "Les finances locales depuis 1982," *Cahiers français,* no. 239 (Jan.–Feb. 1989), pp. 68–9; and Pierre Richard, "Les finances locales de 1983 à 1987," *Revue Française de Finances Publiques* no. 22 (1988): 126–7.
[7]*Le Point,* Mar. 23, 1987.

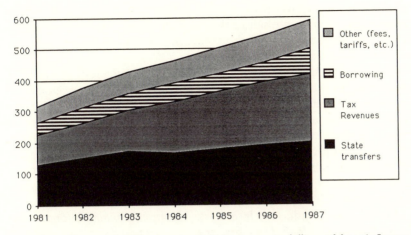

Figure 10.3: The growth of local governmental resources (in billions of francs). Source: Direction générale des collectivités locales. Notes: The 1987 figures are estimates.

tion."[8] Thus, there is every reason to expect that the Socialists in power as of the summer of 1988 will ensure that local authorities continue to experience at least the same level of growth in expenditures as in the recent past.

To speak only of a steady increase in the expenditures of local governments, however, masks the fact that the structure of the resources of local government has changed, specifically in terms of the ratio of state funding to local sources of revenues. In keeping with their pledge to reduce state influence over local governments, the Socialists slowly managed to diminish the percentage of state funding in local governments' overall budgets by transferring certain taxes to local governments while allowing local governments to increase local taxes. The result has been that although state transfers grew at an average annual rate of approximately 14 percent before 1984 and 5.9 percent after, state transfers as a percentage of overall local governmental resources dropped from an average of 40.5 percent between 1981 and 1983 to 36 percent in 1984, 35 percent in 1985 and 1986, and to an estimated 34 percent in 1987 (Fig. 10.3). By contrast, funding from tax revenues has increased not only more rapidly than state transfers, with an average annual rate of +18.2 percent before 1984 and +10.5 percent after, but also as a percentage of total local governmental resources, from 30 percent in 1981 and 1982 to 35 percent in 1984, and down to 37 percent for the following years. Other sources of revenue, moreover, remained at much the same percentage of local resources throughout this period, with fees and other tariffs holding at

[8]*Le Monde,* Nov. 11, 1987.

about 16 percent from 1981 through 1987, while borrowing averaged 13 percent. By 1987, as a result of these changes, local governments gained over half (53 percent) of their resources from local revenue and only slightly over a third from the state.

Although indicative of a greater financial autonomy for local governments, the reduction in the state's percentage of total local governmental resources was at the same time a matter of concern for local officials, who feared that the amount of funding provided through the block grants would be inadequate in the short run and would not keep up with the rising costs of local government in the long run, thus increasing local tax burdens intolerably. But this was not the case in gross terms, even though there admittedly were problems with certain block grants in some years and for certain levels of local government.

Of the block grants, the largest, the *dotation globale de fonctionnement* (DGF), or block grant for current operating expenses, remained steady at approximately 38 percent of all state transfers to local government from 1984 to 1986, although it increased from 62.8 billion francs to 69.9 billion francs in that same period. As with state transfers generally, the DGF itself experienced a decline in its rate of growth: It went from +14.3 percent in 1982 to +6.2 percent in 1985, then stabilized at around +5 percent from 1986 through 1988, when the overall amount of the DGF reached approximately 73 billion francs. This decline in growth rate caused the greatest problems in 1983 and 1984, when the high inflation rate along with the slowdown of the economy decreased local tax revenues while it increased the costs of public services. Subsequent disinflation, however, reduced the severity of the problem.[9] The 1989 DGF stands to help even further, because it is set to rise by 9.28 percent, for a projected 80 billion francs, close to a third larger than the 1984 grant of 62.8 billion francs.[10]

The *Dotation globale d'équipement* (DGE), or block grant for capital investment, also grew between 1984 and 1989 by close to a third, reaching a projected 4.8 billion francs. The *dotation générale de décentralisation* (DGD), or block grant created to pay for the costs of decentralization, by contrast, almost doubled its 1984 size, reaching a projected 13.8 billion francs, mainly as a result of the granting of more money to cover the costs of new administrative duties. For example, with decentralization in the area of culture, the part of the DGD allotted for culture increased by 26 percent from a total of 287.9 million francs in 1986 to

[9]For a full discussion of the technicalities of the DGF, see Alain Guengant and Jean-Michel Uhaldeborde, *Crise et réforme des finances locale* (Paris: Presses universitaires de France, 1988), pp. 148–59.
[10]Direction générale des collectivités locales, *Guide budgétaire communal, départemental, et régional 1989.*

361.25 million francs in 1987, with the budget for the departments' central lending libraries increasing by 16 percent from 145.5 million francs in 1986 to 169.25 million francs in 1987 and the communes' municipal libraries by 45 percent, from 142.4 million francs in 1986 to 192 million francs in 1987, and by 31 percent from 1987 to 1988, to 251.85 million francs.[11]

Through these grants, along with newly transferred taxes, the state made certain to compensate adequately each of the many duties transferred in 1984 and to ensure that this continued in 1985 and later. Thus, for example, the communes received total compensation for their estimated urban planning costs of 53.14 million francs in 1984; this was increased to 55.89 million francs in 1985. The departments were also completely compensated for their estimated 20 billion francs in social assistance costs in 1984, with 8.6 billion francs from the state and 11.4 billion francs in revenue from newly transferred local taxes; in 1985, the state's contribution came to 5.5 billion francs, whereas newly transferred taxes bringing in 3 billion francs only added to the revenue from those taxes transferred the previous year. The regions, in addition, also had the full 1.44 billion francs in costs from their transferred duties in professional development covered, with 1.15 billion francs coming from local revenue and the rest from the state. In 1984, moreover, the amount at the regions' disposal increased to 1.77 billion francs, in 1985 to 1.88 billion francs, and by 1989, it was projected at 2.4 billion francs.[12] Finally, the regions and departments together had the full costs of the transfers in education compensated by the *Dotation régionale d'équipement scolaire* (DRES), or the regional grant for education, and the *Dotation départementale d'équipement des collèges* (DDEC), or the departmental grant for education, to the tune of 3.19 billion francs in 1987. And this was to increase to a projected 3.4 billion francs in 1989.[13]

Revenue from the transferred taxes also increased throughout this period (Table 10.1). The regions' revenue from the *cartes grises* (one-time tax to register title of a new car), given to the regions to compensate for roughly half the cost of their new responsibilities in professional development and apprenticeship (the other half was to come from state grants), increased appreciably, from 2.44 billion francs in 1984 to an expected 3.3 billion francs in 1987, thus reaching a quarter of regional tax revenues by

[11]Pierre Moulnier, "Le ministère de la Culture et ses subventions," *Revue Française de Finances Publiques* no. 23 (1988): 72–3.

[12]Direction générales des collectivités locales, *Démocratie Locale* no. 38 (Apr. 1985); Direction générale des collectivités locales, *Guide budgétaire communal, départemental et régional 1989* (Paris: Documentation Française, 1989).

[13]Richard, "Finances locales," p. 131; Direction générale des collectivités locales, *Guide budgétaire 1989*.

Table 10.1. *Increase in transferred taxes (in billions of francs)*

	1984	1985	1986	1987[a]
Regions				
Cartes grises	2.44	2.96	3.16	3.3
Departments	11.81	18.54	21.65	22.5
Droits d'enregistrement	3.70	9.65[b]	11.66	10.4
Vignette	8.10	8.89	9.99	12.1
Total	14.25	21.50	24.81	25.8

Source: Pierre Richard, "Les Finances Locales de 1983 à 1987," *Revue Française de Finances Publiques* no. 22 (1988): 129–30.
Notes: [a] The 1987 figures are estimates. [b] The increase was due to the additional transfer of the droits de mutations (property transfer fees).

1987. Similarly, the departments' revenue from the *droits d'enregistrement* (various licensing and registration fees) and the *vignette auto,* or automobile sticker (a yearly automobile licensing fee based on the age and value of the automobile), intended to pay part of the costs of the transfer of administrative duties in the area of social services (the rest was to be covered by the DGD and the *droits de mutation,* or property transfer tax) also increased appreciably, from 11.68 billion francs in 1984 to an expected 22.5 billion francs in 1987, representing one-third of departmental tax revenues by 1987.[14]

Local government's increasing revenue did not come only from these indirect taxes. Revenue from the traditional four direct taxes also grew at a healthy rate, for an average annual increase of 13.8 percent (or 5.8 percent in constant francs) between 1980 and 1987. This was made possible by the fact that the state took on an increasing proportion of the burden of local direct taxes to compensate for its reduction of various taxes (for example, the business tax), passing from a net contribution of 6.2 billion francs in 1980 to 34 billion in 1987.[15] Although this did indeed decrease the financial autonomy of local governments, at the same time it gave them increased resources to spend as they saw fit.

In brief, notwithstanding the arguments of local elected officials to the contrary, local governments gained a significant and ever-increasing amount of financial resources from the central government. How then can we explain local elected officials' continued expressions of dissatisfaction with the transfer of financial resources?

[14]Richard, "Finances locales," pp. 129–30.
[15]Ministère de l'économie, des finances, et du budget, "L'évolution récente de la fiscalité directe locale 1980–1987," *Les Note Bleues* no. 2 (Oct. 1988): 29.

The discourse in the periphery. Local elected officials' dissatisfactions stemmed from the particular impact of the transfer of financial resources on their own constituencies and from the differentials in funding levels between the years before decentralization and after. Whereas the poorer communes and departments were distressed over the inequities in the distribution of the block grants, which left them at a distinct disadvantage at least initially, urban communes lamented the change to block grants, which left them less investment funding than under the previous system of subsidizing on a case-by-case basis. Moreover, at the same time that the departments complained about the difficulty of providing social services in an area of skyrocketing costs, the regions maintained that they had insufficient funds to carry out their new responsibilities appropriately. And all were upset about their need to raise local taxes. But few, interestingly enough, complained about the increase in costs related to their own new employees or buildings, even though they used such increases as political fodder against their opponents.

When the DGE was created in 1983, it was the subject of much protest, because numbers of local elected officials, especially from the poorer communes and departments, found their constituencies ill favored by the system. Initially, the problem with the DGE for rural communes was that there were no provisions in the new law for the financing of any long-term projects, and the percentage these communes gained for investment, given the small size of their budgets, meant that they would have to wait for twenty years, if then, to get what they used to get in five.[16] Although helpful financially to the smaller communes, the revision of the law also diminished their financial autonomy by putting the decision-making power back into the hands of the prefect, who was charged with disbursing investment funds on a case-by-case basis to rural communes with the advice of a commission of local elected officials.

Even with this revision, however, the DGE left rural communes, along with the more rural departments, financially worse off than they had been before decentralization. For the communes of fewer than two thousand inhabitants (thirty-two thousand communes), the proportion of the DGE decreased from 40 percent to 35 percent by 1986 and 1987. This was remedied only in 1988 by the neoliberal government in a law requiring that 40 percent of the DGE go to rural communes and the poorest departments.[17] With this, rural communes and poor departments certainly will fare better. But they will always remain behind the larger communes and the richer departments, if only because big spenders are rewarded by the DGE, because it is indexed on the previous year's capital spending, as well as by the DGF, which reimburses value-added tax (VAT)

[16]*Le Monde*, May 14, 1985.
[17]*Le Monde*, May 23, 1987.

on local projects.[18] Moreover, the business tax, which makes up 45 percent of local revenues, favors the largest cities and regions. Despite the fact that the equalization scheme for the business tax did correct approximately 13 percent of the problem, the communes with the richest tax bases and upper middle-class residents nonetheless continue to have proportionately lower taxes than the poorer communes with working-class populations.[19]

The bigger and richer cities, in short, did better with decentralization than the smaller and poorer communes. But this is not to say that the former, too, did not experience some problems with the transfer of financial resources. Mayors in cities of over thirty thousand, in particular, felt that the switch to block grants from the myriad subsidies provided by different Paris ministries left them at a distinct disadvantage, because they could no longer use their influence to gain money for special projects (which even not so nationally important mayors could count on every four or five years). This problem, according to Christian Lalu, the director of the main lobbying group for the large cities, the Association of Big City Mayors, was only made worse by the reduction in revenue from the local business tax, lowered by the Socialists in order to stimulate more business investment. For Lalu, the Socialists' main mistake, however, was to treat all communes equally in the law, with the amount of money provided based on the size of the population, thus failing to take into account the geometrical progression in terms of the problems and the money required in the larger communes.[20]

The communes in general also had some serious concerns about their ability to repay their debts and keep up with rising labor costs and energy prices. Because their debts were incurred primarily from 1979 to 1983 at interest rates of between 12 percent and 17 percent while, given disinflation, local tax revenues since decentralization have been rising an average of only 6 percent to 7 percent in constant francs, local elected officials were very afraid that they would have to struggle under the weight of their indebtedness for years to come. However, in 1986, local governments, much to their own benefit, arranged to renegotiate their debts, refinancing a certain portion of their service of the debt at a lower rate of interest, consolidating certain loans, and gaining the possibility of changing the fixed rates of interest on their debts to variable rates.[21] (Refinanc-

[18]See Ashford, "Decentralizing France."
[19]Jacques Silvain-Klein, *L'Explosion des impôts locaux* (Paris: Documentation française, 1986), pp. 137, 118, 120.
[20]Christian Lalu, Director of the *Association des maires de grandes villes*, interview with author, Paris, May 2, 1985.
[21]Alain Guengant and Jean-Michel Uhaldeborde, "Économie et finances locales," *Annuaire des collectivités locales 1987* (Paris: Librairies techniques, 1987), pp. 289–98.

ing came to 6 billion francs in 1986 and 25 billion francs in 1987.[22])
What is more, disinflation actually devolved to the benefit of local governments by lowering the rate of increase in the cost of labor and of the price
of energy, among other items. Because both labor costs and energy prices
have tended to be below the rate of the real growth in the GDP, whereas
the transfers from the state tend to increase at the same pace as the GDP
(because most transfers are indexed according to the net revenue of the
VAT, which takes into account both the increase in prices and overall
economic growth), all local governments, but especially the communes,
have tended to benefit.[23]

Thus, the communes' complaints about the financial limitations of
decentralization, although justified in terms of the distributive inequities
of certain block grants, turned out to have been less justified in the long
run with regard to the issue of the adequacy of state compensation. There
are studies to suggest, moreover, that even the smallest communes have
done reasonably well financially, lowering their indebtedness and increasing their proportion of capital investment by comparison with the past,
despite the problems with the DGE.

In the Lorraine, for example, the communes with fewer than seven
hundred inhabitants (over three-fourths of the communes in the region)
have invested more per inhabitant than many of the larger communes in
the region (in 1985, 1,187 francs per inhabitant vs. 1,039 francs for
communes from two thousand to five thousand inhabitants). Only cities
with more than twenty thousand inhabitants invested more per inhabitant (at an average of 1,496 francs per inhabitant).[24] In addition,
whereas investment expenditures grew significantly from 1981 to 1985
for an overall 50.6 percent increase (even though inflation accounted for
33 percent of this), local debt, contrary to what might have been expected, went down from a high of 204 francs per inhabitant in 1983 to
179 francs per inhabitant in 1985, and the overall percentage increase in
loans from 1981 to 1985 was a mere 8.5 percent (Table 10.2). This has
two causes: Most importantly, perhaps, government subsidies for investment increased by 52.2 percent during this same period, representing 65
percent of the investment receipts in 1985 as opposed to 58 percent in
1981. But local taxes also increased (+82 percent from 1981 to 1985).[25]
Rural communes, in brief, the rhetoric of the financial limitations of
decentralization to the contrary notwithstanding, have not suffered un-

[22]Richard, "Finances locales," p. 136.
[23]Hervé Huntziger, "Prospective des finances des collectivités territoriales," *Annuaire 1987*, pp. 123–4.
[24]Gilbert Toulgoat, "Petites communes: Une certaine aisance financière," *Économie
Lorraine* no. 56 (Apr. 1987): 10.
[25]Ibid., p. 12.

Table 10.2. *Investment receipts and expenditures in the Lorraine: Communes with fewer than seven hundred inhabitants (in francs per inhabitant)*

	1981	1982	1983	1984	1985	% increase 1981-5
Investment expenditures	788	925	1,002	1,031	1,187	+50.6
Investment receipts	555	649	676	756	745	+34.2
Subsidies	320	389	394	459	487	+52.2
Loans	165	191	204	187	179	+8.5

Source: General Treasury, cited in Gilbert Toulgoat, "Petites communes: une certaine aisance financière," *Économie Lorraine* no. 56 (April 1987): 11.

duly as a result of decentralization. And this has proved equally true for the departments.

Although all complained about the financial limitations of decentralization, local elected officials in the departments were probably the most vociferous, and understandably so. The crisis of *l'État providence,* or the welfare state, affected departmental elected officials most directly, faced as they were with the rising costs of social welfare and the diminishing revenues available to pay for them. They feared that what little flexibility they had would be lost, with the 5 to 10 percent of their resources that were unencumbered likely to be eaten up by rising costs in the services that departments are mandated to supply and that the national government may, or may not, cover in the future. Thus, opposition departmental officials maintained that, given the continuing economic crisis, rising unemployment, and the concomitant rising demands for social assistance – all of which they blamed on the Socialists' economic policies – they were unlikely to be able to do their jobs appropriately. They therefore protested that they were confronted with the equally hazardous political choices of either raising taxes or cutting services to one or another constituency group.[26]

Departmental officials' complaints were the most pronounced early on, with the initial transfer of resources, and with good reason given the 1984 decline in expenditures. The Assembly of Presidents of General Councils expressed their concerns, first, that the new finances did not adequately compensate for expenses incurred in 1983 and, second, that the balance between receipts and expenditures would not be maintained

[26]Echoing the views of departmental opposition figures were: Pierre Costa, director-general of departmental services, Alpes-Maritimes, interview with author, Nice, June 7, 1985; and Jacques Médecin, president of the departmental council of the Alpes Maritimes in addition to Deputy and mayor of Nice, interview with author, Nice, June 7, 1985.

in the years to come.[27] On this latter score, however, the departmental presidents proved unnecessarily pessimistic, judging not only from the figures but also from the remarks of the president of the Assembly of Presidents of General Councils himself, Pierre Salvi (UDF-CDS), president of the general council of the Val-d'Oise, who declared in 1988 that, with the resources at their disposal, the departments had proved better able to master expenditures and put local finances in order than the state ever could have.[28] This is not to say, however, that departmental officials did not have legitimate complaints in the first years of decentralization.

Departmental officials were especially upset with the DGE, which at its inception left twenty departments with less money than in the past, among them the Savoie, whose president at the time, Michel Barnier (RPR), estimated that his department lost 13 million francs in potential state funding.[29] But this was not the only financial problem. In the Vosges, according to Christian Poncelet, former minister and Senator from this department, the department's budget for operating costs (the DGF) in 1983 was reduced by 4 percentage points in relation to 1982, whereas the investment budget (the DGE), at only 3 million francs plus 1 million for the supplementary block grant, was a good deal lower than the average 7 million francs a year received previously. Poncelet was equally concerned that the department didn't get enough money for rural consolidation, leading to higher property taxes to the tune of 11 percentage points, as well as for the promotion of local economic development, leading to the department's likely difficulty in responding to the increased pressures from industry and professional organizations for aid.[30]

The transfer of responsibilities in the area of education, however, produced the most concern in the departments and, for that matter, in the regions. Even the director of the local governments department of the Ministry of the Interior admitted that there might be some problem in this area in the future, as the state left local governments more to their own devices in financing, and as they confronted the need to pay for the upkeep costs of crumbling *collèges* and *lycées*.[31] And the costs have turned out to be even higher than those expected by the state because the school age population has been increasing at the same time as the need to rehabilitate, or in some cases even to replace, the poorly constructed school buildings of the 1960s and 1970s. According to a study by the

[27]Assemblée des présidents des conseils généraux de France, "La décentralisation dans le domaine sanitaire et social depuis le 1er Janvier 1984," *Action Sanitaire et Sociale*, dossier no 3 (June 1984).

[28]*Le Monde*, Sept. 14, 1988.

[29]*Quotidien de Paris*, June 2, 1983.

[30]Christian Poncelet, "Les conditions de la mise en oeuvre de la décentralisation," *Le Courrier du Parlement* no. 697 (Jan. 31–Feb. 6, 1984): 14.

[31]Giuily interviews.

Caisse des dépôts et consignations, regional investment in high schools would almost double in 1987 (+85 percent), while the expenditures of the departments would increase by 36 percent. The problem for the regions is particularly serious. In 1986 alone, 17 percent of their budget went for education-related expenses compared to 3 percent for the departments, despite the fact that the amount they spend is close to equal at 4.4 billion francs for the departments and 4 billion francs for the regions. Unlike the departments, which have had the necessary technical and human resources to take charge of the educational facilities, given their transfer from the prefecture, the regional administration has had to start from scratch in this area.[32] The regions' costs, moreover, are likely only to increase. Whereas the departments are experiencing a leveling off of demand for the *collèges,* the demand for *lycées* is on the rise, especially because the neoliberal government's announced objective of having 80 percent of the population high-school graduates (*bacheliers*) by the year 2,000, as opposed to the 40 percent in 1986, will have required the regions to create an additional 100,000 places between 1986 and 1989.[33] This is no doubt why Jacques Blanc (UDF), president of the region of Languedoc-Roussillon, complained that the state *s'est défaussé,* or unloaded (in the sense of a bad debt), the high schools onto the regions.[34]

The regions, in short, are confronting some serious problems with regard to their responsibility for the high schools, so much so that all twenty-six presidents of the regional councils agreed to request added funds for the high schools from Jacques Chirac at a scheduled meeting in May 1987. They had no intention, though, of giving up their administrative responsibilities in this area, as Olivier Guichard (RPR), president of the regional council of the Loire, recommended at the time.

Education was not the only matter of concern to the regions. Even though regional elected officials could not, of course, justifiably complain as did the other levels of local government about a reduction in resources, they could, and did, about the inadequacy of the new resources, given their new duties. Thus, before 1987, when the ceiling on the amount the region could tax the local population (180 francs per inhabitant) was lifted, regional officials protested their lack of fiscal autonomy as well as their lack of resources. Between the lack of flexibility of their tax vehicles and the increasing administrative expenses resulting from their duties in areas other than economic development, for example, high schools, regional officials worried that they would have trouble meeting their goals in economic development.[35] More particularly, Bernard Stasi, first vice

[32]Philippe Bernard, "Chers collèges, très chers lycées," *Le Monde,* May 24–5, 1987.
[33]*Le Monde,* Nov. 13, 1986.
[34]*Le Monde,* Nov. 13, 1986.
[35]Jegouzo and Sanson, "Décentralisation," pp. 36–7.

president of the CDS, argued that the region was handicapped by its lack of resources, especially because the new receipts from transferred taxes were from sectors in crisis – building construction and automobiles.[36] And Michel Giraud, president of the regional council of the Ile-de-France, in response to a question about whether decentralization was, in the final analysis, a transfer of unpopularity, agreed, insisting that this was "one of the hidden dangers of decentralization, and perhaps even a governmental perfidy." He explained that, in order to respond to the ineluctable increase in expenses in the area of professional training alone, the regional council, which was faced with an insufficient transfer of credit for 1984, had to increase by 19 percent the cost of the *cartes grises* (which, he admitted, however, had not risen since 1982).[37]

Actually, having to raise taxes was the main worry of all local elected officials, and best explains the rhetoric of the financial limitations of decentralization. Most local elected officials found that, because they could not expect revenues to increase as they had in the past given the economic crisis, raising taxes (in particular the newly transferred taxes) was inevitable. (The traditional sources of tax revenue – the four basic taxes on property, housing, and business – did not rise at nearly the same rate because they were much more complicated to raise.) As it turns out, however, these tax hikes were relatively painless, with few political repercussions, even though the local population was quite cognizant of them. In a recent survey for the *Caisse des dépôts,* 56 percent of local leaders agreed that decentralization had greatly increased local taxes (with 37 percent disagreeing), whereas an even larger percentage (63 percent) agreed that it had greatly increased the operating costs of local governments (as opposed to 27 percent who disagreed).[38]

Local elected officials did find, however, that the issue of tax increases served as good political fodder against opponents, in particular the departments against the regions and right- against left-wing local governments. Departmentalists, dismayed by what they saw as lost revenue for the departments, were very quick to note that the local taxpayers' burden had increased most sharply at the level of the region. Jean Cluzel, for example, made a point of arguing that in the Auvergne, the overall increase in direct taxes by inhabitant was quite high at the regional level, especially by comparison with the departments. Whereas the departments in the region raised taxes by no more than an average of approximately 15 percent per year from 1981 to 1985, the region's taxes increased by more than 80 percent in 1982 over 1981, followed by a 31 percent

[36]*Démocratie Moderne,* May 8, 1986.
[37]*Le Figaro,* Sept. 12, 1984.
[38]*Le Monde,* Dec. 4–5, 1988.

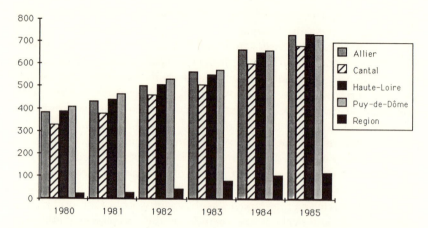

Figure 10.4: Direct taxes by inhabitant in the Auvergne departments by comparison with those of the Auvergne region (in francs). Source: Auvergne regional council, cited in: Jean Cluzel *Les "Anti-Monarques" de la cinquième* (Paris: Librairie générale de droit et de jurisprudence, 1985), p. 69.

increase the next year (Fig. 10.4).[39] A glance at the chart, however, suggests that even though the departments less than doubled their taxes over the same period, these increases placed a lot more of a burden on the local taxpayer than did those of the regions. On average, the local taxpayer paid 139 francs in direct taxes to the region, 813 francs to the department, and 1,832 francs to the commune or urban community.[40] So the departmentalists' accusations are not likely to have the hoped-for impact.

Whereas departmentalists accused the regions of unduly increasing taxpayers' burdens, right-wing regionalists consistently accused the left of the same. Michel Giraud, regional president of the Île-de-France, for instance, claimed indirect taxes (for example, auto licensing and registration fees) to be twice as high in the Socialist regions generally; personnel costs close to three times as high for some regions, for example, 15.90 francs per inhabitant in Provence-Alpes-Côtes d'Azur by comparison with 5.30 francs per inhabitant in Ile-de-France; and operating costs close to double, for example, 9 percent of the budget in the Nord-Pas-de-Calais compared to less than 5 percent of the total budget for Île-de-France.[41] Whether these figures indicate profligacy on the part of left-wing governments, of course, remains open to question. However, if we were to extrapolate from the results of one of the few studies of this topic, a comparative study of the finances of left- and right-wing municipal governments in the 1960s and 1970s in the west and northwest suburbs of

[39]Cluzel, *Les "Anti-Monarques,"* p. 69.
[40]*Le Monde*, Sept. 15, 1988.
[41]*La Croix*, March 5, 1986.

Table 10.3. *The estimated cost of decentralization in selected departments (in millions of francs)*

Department	Cost of buildings[a]	Cost of new employees[b]	1985 Budget
Aveyron	13	4.6	717.6
Calvados	22.7	3.9	1,291
Charente-Maritime	.8	1.4	1,243
Gironde	3	5.1	2,300
Loire	5.7	3.8	1,207
Nord	7.5	22.5	4,900
Rhône	.5	6.6	2,700
Seine-Maritime	30	8.6	2,793
Val d'Oise	53	5.6	1,700
Vienne	2.2	3.8	650

Source: L'Express, Mar. 8-14, 1985
Notes: [a] Money spent since 1982 for refurbishing or constructing buildings to house territorial or prefectoral administration. [b] Only new (not transferred employees) estimated at 125,000 francs salary per person.

Paris, we could conclude that the higher spending levels of left-wing governments had much more to do with the socioeconomic context and the needs of the local population than with ideology.[42] This is not to say, however, that politics does not matter. On the contrary, as a recent study on the impact of politics on municipal expenditures in large cities between 1983 and 1985 shows, political divergences among mayors of different parties within the left and right, as well as between them, lead them to implement different policies with different price tags – the right slightly ahead of the left, the RPR slightly ahead of the UDF, and the PCF ahead of the PS – in response to different pressure groups.[43]

Most importantly, perhaps, despite all these accusations of profligacy by departmentalists against the region and by right- against left-wing local governments, as well as of niggardliness by local elected officials generally against the state, few local elected officials protested the increase in the number and costs of new employees and buildings in their own constituencies. And this was no small matter. As of March 1985, the reforms had already cost a minimum of 1 billion francs, counting the expense of new employees and new or refurbished buildings, with some departments and regions spending a lot more than others in these areas (Tables 10.3 and 10.4). The department of Calvados, for example, with a

[42]See Pierre Limouzin, "Idéologies politiques et politiques municipales," *Revue d'Économie Régionale et Urbaine* no. 3 (1984).
[43]Richard Balme and Vincent Hoffmann-Martinot, "Policy Differences under Centralization: Politics and Municipal Expenditures in France." Paper prepared for delivery for the annual meeting of the American Political Science Association (Atlanta, Ga., Aug. 31–Sept. 3, 1989).

Table 10.4. *The estimated cost of decentralization in selected regions (in millions of francs)*

Region	Cost of buildings[a]	Cost of new employees[b]	1985 Budget
Bretagne	35	3.9	714
Basse-Normandie	49	2.5	300
Poitou-Charente	70	5.8	500
Provence-Alpes-Côtes d'Azur	60	13.8	1,500
Rhône-Alpes	50	14.4	1,149

Source: L'Express, Mar. 8-14, 1985
Notes: [a] Money spent since 1982 for refurbishing or constructing building to house territorial or prefectoral administration. [b] Only new (not transferred employees) estimated at 125,000 francs salary per person.

budget of 1.29 billion francs for 1985, took in 129 prefectoral functionaries and added 31 extra at an estimated cost of 3.9 million francs. The region of Poitou-Charente, with a budget of 500 million francs, took in 25 prefectoral functionaries and added 46 at an estimated cost of 5.8 million francs. The construction costs involved in new or refurbished buildings to house either the prefectoral or territorial services of these two local governments, moreover, were proportionately much higher, reaching 22.7 million francs in Calvados and 70 million francs in Poitou-Charente by 1985. Not all departments and regions spent this much on new buildings, though; but they made up for this in what they spent on new employees. The department of the Nord, for example, only spent 7.5 million francs on building costs since 1982; but it spent 22.5 million francs on its approximately 180 new employees. Finally, even in Gaston Defferre's home region – or perhaps most significantly there – costs went up astronomically. Provence-Alpes-Côte d'Azur, with a 1985 budget of 1,500 million francs, added approximately 110 new employees at a cost of 13.8 million francs and spent nearly 60 million francs on construction since 1982.[44]

Right-wing as much as left-wing departments and regions, in short, showed little restraint in incurring large construction and personnel costs. Among the local elected officials I interviewed in the Lorraine and Provence-Alpes-Côtes d'Azur, none complained about the growth in personnel costs and only one, the construction costs: Philippe Séguin (at the time RPR Deputy and mayor of Épinal, regional councilor of the Lorraine, and general councilor of the Vosges, but subsequently Minister of Social Affairs and Employment for Prime Minister Chirac) condemned the expense of the new walls of the departmental headquarters (approxi-

[44]*L'Express,* Mar. 8–14, 1985.

Table 10.5. *Number of employees in local government*

	1983	1984	1985
All employees (full-time equivalent) [a]	978,300	995,400	1,005,200
Regions	1,669	2,371	2,862
Departments	162,994	163,818	163,683
Communal sector	774,037	788,796	796,373

Source: Pierre Richard, "Les finances locales de 1983 à 1987," *Revue française de Finances publiques* no. 22 (1988): 133.
Notes: [a] This includes syndicates, districts, régies, and other local public establishments in addition to the regions, departments, and communal sector.

mately 60 million francs) and the refurbishing of the regional headquarters (the cloisters of Saint-Clément in Metz at 96 million francs). He did not, however, mention the cost of his own tastefully modernized and refurbished town hall in Épinal.[45]

Local elected officials remained similarly unconcerned about the significant increases in the number and cost of employees (Table 10.5). Regional elected officials in general, for example, did not protest the dramatic increase in their personnel, despite the fact that they posted a 42 percent increase in 1984 over 1983 and a 20.7 percent increase in 1985. Similarly, local elected officials in the communal sector did not seem worried about their more modest increase in personnel, up by 1.9 percent in 1984 and by 1 percent in 1985, for a grand total of 796,373 employees. One might think that because the departments remained quite stable, having only a 0.5 percent increase in 1984 and a 0.1 percent decrease in 1985, their officials were cost-conscious with respect to personnel. In fact, it is more a case of their having inherited from the prefectures all the necessary personnel, and then some, for their new duties. Overall, local government employees increased by 1.7 percent in 1984 and 1 percent in 1985, resulting in personnel costs (salaries + payroll taxes) that, from 113 billion francs in 1983, rose to 154 billion francs in 1987, for an annual increase in volume of 2.4 percent.[46]

Both the departments and the regions, in short, went on a spending spree, with local elected officials intent on consecrating their new powers with the symbols of power: new or refurbished buildings and new or transferred employees.[47] But these were not the only costs to the periphery related to decentralization. The regional accounting courts, which by 1985

[45]Philippe Séguin, interview with author, Épinal, June 18, 1985.
[46]Pierre Richard, "Finances locales," p. 133.
[47]For the costs in the regions, see *Le Point*, Mar. 23, 1987.

counted approximately 880 employees and were scheduled to reach 2,000, have also raised the price of decentralization. In the Lorraine alone, as of 1985, there were eighty-seven magistrates, secretaries, and supplementary employees to be housed in a 24-million-franc building.[48] The overall costs to the locality were estimated by one member of the opposition (former minister of Giscard d'Estaing) at 4 percent of departmental taxes.[49]

Finally, departmental and regional councilors have not been reluctant about having the departments and regions organize and pay for study trips (with the costs to councilors nominal at best). China has been quite popular, visited by councilors from such regions as the Lorraine, the Rhône-Alpes, and the Nord-Pas-de-Calais, as well as from such departments as the Pas-de-Calais (separate from the region's trip). But the United States also did well, with California being visited by departmental councilors from the Pyrénées-Atlantiques and Miami by regional councilors from Haute-Normandie. Other places visited were Kenya (Seine-Maritime) and Japan (Nord-Pas-de-Calais and Provence-Alpes-Côtes d'Azur). Only the regional councilors from Bretagne went nowhere at regional expense.[50]

In brief, local elected officials seemed quite happy to take advantage of all the perquisites of their new powers, even though investments in their physical plants, new human resources, and "study trips" may make it harder for them to pay for the services they are to deliver and, therefore, may lead to further increases in taxes. Only the national government, attacked by the local governments for its lack of generosity, seemed truly distressed by local governments' spending. Balladur, citing the fact that the proportion of local taxes in the GDP went from 4.7 percent in 1980 to 6 percent in 1986, and that local governments' personnel costs increased by 95 percent between 1980 and 1985, suggested that local governments needed to master their expenditures better.[51] As we shall see below in the discussion of the rhetoric of good management, they actually have, even though it does not show up in the figures on construction and personnel costs.

The regions' new resources and the promotion of local economic development

In the context of the promotion of local economic development, as in other areas, local elected officials complained that they did not have nearly the resources they needed to do their jobs appropriately. Quite

[48]*L'Express,* Mar. 8–14, 1985.
[49]*Le Monde,* June 27, 1983.
[50]*Le Point,* Mar. 23, 1987.
[51]Bechtel, Henry-Meininger, and Jegouzo, "Chronique," pp. 157–8.

typical is the view of René Dosière, president of the regional council of
Picardie, who saw the region's budget at 250 million francs as woefully
underfinanced, especially since he felt he needed a minimum of 500 million francs to appear serious on economic projects for which he had only
50 million francs to spend.[52] It is important to note, however, that in the
very nature of things, regional elected officials would have found no
amount of money sufficient for their purposes. At least by comparison
with the past, between their own resources and those pledged by the state
and other levels of local government, they had the necessary financial
means available to fulfill their duties appropriately in the area of local
economic development.

To begin with, despite the rhetoric, most regions did a very good job
with the means already at their disposal in the regional planning effort.
The Lorraine's success in regional planning, for instance, just as that of
regions such as the Nord-Pas-de-Calais and Provence-Alpes-Côte d'Azur,
was due in large measure to the fact that it had the administrative means
and planning apparatus, along with much of the needed personnel, already in place. And yet, there were continual complaints by regional
officials in the right-wing Lorraine about the need for more money and
personnel.

Some regions, though, were justified in their complaints about the financial limitations of decentralization in this area. The left-wing Limousin had
to turn to the field services of the state for help in the regional planning
process because it lacked the administrative means and the personnel to
carry out its functions on its own. The Planning Commission, in its official
evaluation of the regional planning process, found such recourse to the
state perfectly appropriate – as an instance of more decentralized planning
and *concertation* than in cases where the region has all the necessary means
at its disposal to carry out planning without appeal to the state. Its report,
however, did note that dissatisfaction with this need to go to the state could
explain the regions' many complaints about lacking the administrative
means to complete their tasks.[53]

In any event, however justifiable the complaints about the lack of
personnel were in the first few years of decentralization, they are no
longer (Table 10.6). Even the Limousin, where the complaints about
administrative limitations were most pronounced, has seen a sevenfold
increase in the number of its employees between 1982 and 1985. Most
regions, in fact, significantly increased their personnel in response to their
new duties. But there was wide variation here. While Provence-Alpes-

[52]Sylvie Trosa, "Picardie: La naissance d'une région," *Intervention* no. 3 (Mar.–Apr. 1983).
[53]Commissariat Général du Plan, *Evaluation de la planification décentralisée* (Paris: Documentation française, 1986), p. 12.

Table 10.6. *Increase in the number of regional employees (full and part-time)*

Regions	1981	1982	1983	1984	1985
Alsace	9	10	37	49	67
Aquitaine	19	22	88	109	152
Auvergne	11	19	49	68	80
Bourgogne	19	34	61	73	85
Bretagne	16	19	52	66	72
Centre	9	16	34	57	84
Champagne-Ardennes	7	10	36	43	53
Corse	13	13	14	94	96
Franche-Comté	12	12	46	58	80
Ile-de-France	32	32	312	326	347
Languedoc-Roussillon	18	20	90	116	135
Limousin	7	7	24	33	49
Lorraine	29	29	59	82	92
Midi-Pyrénées	15	17	61	89	119
Nord-Pas-de-Calais	16	10	59	273	394
Basse-Normandie	11	17	46	56	72
Haute-Normandie	39	47	34	42	47
Loire	20	26	59	66	78
Picardie	18	24	81	106	114
Poitou-Charentes	33	35	45	60	73
Provence-Alpes-Côte d'Azur	26	50	73	265	299
Rhône-Alpes	34	31	75	96	125
France total (metropolitan)	413	500	1,435	2,227	2,713

Source: Le Point no. 757 (Mar. 23, 1987).

Côte d'Azur had a ten-fold increase in number of personnel, going from 26 in 1981 to 299, the Nord-Pas-de-Calais went from 16 to 394 employees, for an increase of close to twenty-five times the original number. Bretagne, by comparison, was much more conservative, only quadrupling its number of employees, going from 16 in 1981 to 72 in 1985, while the Lorraine was even more conservative, increasing only slightly over three times its initial 29 employees in 1981. In France as a whole, regional employees went from 413 before decentralization in 1981 to 2,713 in 1985, increasing more than six times its original size.[54] But however great the increase, the average operating costs remained a relatively small part of the overall regional budget, at 39 percent in 1984 and 1985, although it did climb in 1986 to 44 percent (Fig. 10.5).

The regions, in fact, had a good deal of money to spend, arguments to the contrary notwithstanding. The regional budgets had themselves been increasing steadily between the years 1981 and 1986. Between 1981 and 1986, the regional budget almost quadrupled, going from 6.3 billion

[54]The differences between the 1983, 1984, and 1985 figures for the number of regional employees in Francs as a whole in Table 10.5 and those in Table 10.6 can be explained by the fact that the former were compiled earlier. The actual numbers are in any case less important than the increases that they demonstrate.

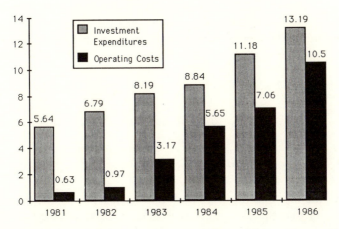

Figure 10.5: Increase in regional expenditures (in billions of francs). Source: Direction générale des collectivités locales.

francs in 1981 to 23.7 billion francs in 1986 (Fig. 10.5). By 1988, the amount in the primitive regional budget was set at 33 billion francs.[55] The amount spent on investment also increased steadily and remained a relatively large portion of the overall budget. In 1984 and 1985, investment expenditures represented 61 percent of the overall budget; in 1986, 56 percent. This contrasts significantly, however, with the investment expenditures of 1982, which represented 87 percent of the overall budget. In 1983, in effect, the year of the transfer of administrative functions, operating expenditures increased over 1982 at the highest percentage rate for the period, at +227 percent. The rate of increase in operating expenditures in 1985 over 1984, by comparison, was only 25 percent; and in 1987 over 1986, an estimated 20 percent.[56] But however fast the rate of increase in operating expenditures, the amount of investment expenditures also increased, remaining quite high by comparison in the overall budget; and even in 1983, the amount spent on investment increased by 21 percent over the previous year. The regions, in other words, were left with a good deal of money to invest in local economic development.

Admittedly, the regions don't have all that much money when compared to the other levels of local government (Table 10.7). In 1986 alone, the regions' operating costs remained significantly lower than those of all the other local authorities; their investment expenditures 7 times smaller than those of the communes; and their overall budget 5.5 times smaller than that of the departments. The difference between the departments and regions appears somewhat less significant, though, once we take into

[55]Direction générale des collectivités locales, *Guide budgétaire 1989.*
[56]Ibid.

Table 10.7. *Local government expenditures in 1986 (in billions of francs)*

	Communes	Departments	Regions	Groupings[a]	Other[b]	Total
Operating costs	177.9	94.3	10.5	33.2	33.1	349.0
Investments	88.9	37.2	13.2	33.0	15.4	187.7
Total	266.8	131.5	23.7	66.2	48.5	536.6

Source: Direction générale des collectivités locales
Notes: [a] Groupings consist of syndicates, districts, and urban communities.
    [b] Other includes *régies* and other local public establishments.

account the fact that there are ninety-nine departments and twenty-two regions, so that the average departmental budget comes to 1.3 billion francs, or only slightly larger than the average regional budget of 1.1 billion francs. What is more, the average region's investment expenditure, at 0.6 billion francs, was close to twice the department's, at 0.37 billion francs.

It is important to remember that the regions have almost complete freedom to spend their resources as they see fit by comparison with the other levels of local government. Whereas the department's budget is 90 percent to 95 percent committed already to nationally mandated programs (for example, social services, roads), the region's budget is 90 percent to 95 percent unencumbered, or at least it was until the region began committing itself to various regional development projects with the cooperation of other units of government and on its own. Olivier Guichard, regional president of the Loire, agreed that he has a great deal of freedom by comparison with the departments because, even though the regional budget at 800 million francs in 1985 was low by comparison with its departments (2 billion francs for the Loire-Atlantique and 1.5 billion francs for Nantes), it was relatively unencumbered, with 80 percent of it free for investment credits.[57]

Moreover, although the departments had a lot more money to perform their own administrative functions (primarily in the area of health and social services), the region far outstripped the departments in the area of local economic activity (Fig. 10.6). In 1985, for example, of the 6.6 billion francs local authorities spent on economic investment, the regions spent 33 percent of the overall budget (2.2 billion francs) by comparison with the departments' 23 percent. What is more, the regions controlled 40 percent of the most significant activity for the promotion of local economic development, that of direct aid, by comparison with the departments' 26 percent. The communes, however, had the largest budgets, at

[57] *L'Express*, Mar. 8–14, 1985.

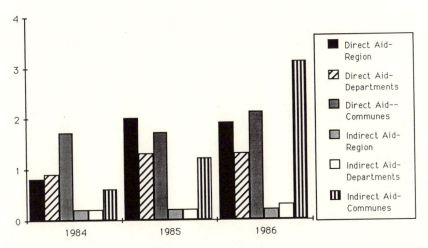

Figure 10.6: Local economic aid (in billions of francs). Source: Direction des collectivités locales, cited in Jean-Claude Némery, "Les collectivités locales, l'économie, et l'emploi" in *Cahiers français*, no. 239 (Jan.–Feb., 1989), Notice 4, p. 4.

44 percent of overall aid, mainly due to their 75 percent share of indirect aid. By 1986, moreover, of the 8.9 billion francs for overall economic aid, the communes had outstripped the regions and departments even in direct aid, with 40 percent compared to the regions' 36 percent and the departments' 24 percent. But the communes' share of local economic aid is likely to diminish, because one of the largest parts of their economic development budgets, loan guarantees, is an avenue of financing now virtually closed to them. And the regions, in any case, did outspend their greatest rival, the departments.

It is not enough, however, simply to compare the regions' actual resources to those of the other levels of local government, because the regions have greater financial power than the means technically at their disposal. In the first place, they gain substantial resources from the state in the context of the regional plans (Table 10.8). To take only one example, the Nord-Pas-de-Calais was to receive 3.95 billion francs from the state for its regional planning contract, in addition to the 2.45 billion francs it pledged (a ratio of 1.67 for the state to 1 for the region). Thus, although the actual amount of money in the region's budget was not great – 2 billion francs in 1985 by comparison with the department of the Nord at 5 billion francs and the urban community of Lille at 4 billion – the amount at its disposal was significant.

The regions, in short, gained a substantial amount of extra funds from the state as a result of the regional plans, in addition to the amounts they were able to borrow – often also from the state as represented by the

Table 10.8. *Planning contracts for the duration of the Ninth Plan--Distribution of financing*

	State's contribution (in millions of francs)	Region's contribution (in millions of francs)	State's contribution by inhabitant (in francs)	Region's contribution by inhabitant (in francs)	State share compared to region (in %)
Alsace	1,100	700	701	446	1.6
Aquitaine	1,470	930	553	350	1.6
Auvergne	775	450	583	338	1.7
Bourgogne	851	601	532	376	1.4
Bretagne	1,804	814	668	301	2.2
Centre	860	610	381	270	1.4
Champagne-Ardennes	850	445	632	331	1.9
Corse	1,100	300	4,580	1,249	3.7
Franche-Comté	847	550	784	509	1.5
Ile-de-France	7,137	8,465	713	846	0.8
Languedoc-Roussillon	1,381	776	716	402	1.8
Limousin	757	308	1,023	416	2.5
Lorraine	2,979	942	1,283	405	3.2
Midi-Pyrénées	1,433	787	616	338	1.8
Nord-Pas-de-Calais	3,950	2,450	1,005	623	1.6
Basse-Normandie	770	450	559	333	1.7
Haute-Normandie	865	523	524	317	1.7
Loire	1,180	883	403	301	1.3
Picardie	1,776	851	1,021	409	2.1
Poitou-Charentes	1,250	630	796	401	2.0
Provence-Alpes-Côte d'Azur	2,796	1,897	706	479	1.5
Rhône-Alpes	2,980	1,520	595	303	2.0
France total (metropolitan)	38,911	25,882	716	479	1.5

Source: DATAR and INSEE, from *Evaluation de la planification décentralisée,* Ministère du Plan et de l'Amènagement du Territoire, Commissariat Général du Plan (Paris: Documentation française, 1986): 33.

nationalized banks. The financing of the regional plans comes from state contributions, the region's share of tax revenues, and regional borrowing from national and international capital markets, for example, through the issuing of regional bonds. And the state's share is generally 1 to 3 times the amount the region consecrates to such efforts, with an overall average of 1.5 times the region's contribution. In 1984 alone, the regions pledged 5 billion francs or 36 percent of their overall budgets (not including administrative costs, that is, personnel and interest payments), whereas the state pledged 7.4 billion francs for the planning contracts in metropolitan France. The overall amount of state funding for the duration of the plan (1984–1988) came close to 39 billion francs, with a contribution per inhabitant of 716 francs, and close to 26 billion francs for the regions, with a contribution of 479 francs per inhabitant.

With the state–region plans, then, the regions substantially increased their financial resources and therefore their ability to promote local economic development. But this is not the only area in which external resources are made available. The regions also arrange the major local cooperative ventures that receive funding from the state, the departments, and the communes, as well as from the nationalized industries and banks and from local chambers of commerce and industry. In brief, regardless of the rhetoric, the regions have a significant amount of finances under their influence, if not their control. And this has been a major contributing factor in the success of the decentralized *dirigisme* in local economic development.

THE NEW RHETORIC OF GOOD MANAGEMENT AND THE POLITICIZATION OF THE PERIPHERY

Although the rhetoric of the limitations of decentralization worked well in the first few years, it was becoming less effective and less appealing to local elected officials as they became more familiar with their new duties and were quite clearly responsible for such in the public eye, whether they liked it or not. And they began increasingly to resort to the rhetoric of good management, which represents as much an affirmation of their new administrative responsibilities as it does a substitute for the rhetoric of nonpartisanship, which, for obvious reasons, can no longer be used to deny the politicization of local governments, given the new politics in the periphery. The rhetoric of good management is not entirely new. The more progressive mayors have turned to it since the 1970s and Communist mayors have used it since the postwar period to allay the electorate's fears of patronage and political favoritism almost as effectively as other mayors had used the rhetoric of nonpartisanship. It has come into its own, however, since decentralization.

With the new rhetoric of good management, local governmental decisions are presented as managerial, not political. Even political campaigns seek to demonstrate the better managerial skills and local development strategies of their candidates and to describe the programs of their future "administrations" in value-neutral managerial terms like efficiency, productivity, and cost-effectiveness. As with the old rhetoric of nonpartisanship, this new rhetoric of good management serves to depoliticize local government in the eyes of the public and to enable local bosses to avoid accusations of clientelism. Again, like the old rhetoric, it tends to facilitate relationships among the major actors in the periphery, allowing mayors, as well as presidents of regions and departments, to build a consensus within politically divided executive bureaus and to promote cooperation between different and potentially rival local governments, thus getting on with the business of government.

At the same time that politicians' rhetoric "depoliticizes" local government, the reality is one of increasing politicization, with partisan politics now much more clearly present at the local level and very much on the minds of local elected officials. By providing for proportional representation on municipal and regional councils and, at least informally for a short time, for minority representation in the executive bureaus of the councils of all three levels of local government, decentralization has encouraged greater politicization along national party lines in the deliberations and actions of local government. National cleavages have opened up in the regions, departments, and big cities, as well as in some of the smaller ones. Even the prefects are now clearly perceived in political terms, regardless of how much they or the Ministry of the Interior try to deny it.

The rhetoric of good management, however is not simply "rhetoric." It responds to the new realities of administrative decentralization as much as to fears about its political consequences. Faced with new roles and responsibilities, this rhetoric also reflects a reality in which local elected officials have been intent on managing local government better than in the past, experimenting with new financing arrangements as well as administrative techniques, and hiring better qualified personnel. What is more, they have been reasonably successful at it.

The rhetoric of good management

Nowadays, one cannot read anything on local government, from newspapers to scholarly articles to publicity brochures, without coming across countless instances of the rhetoric of good management. Numerous articles have appeared detailing the invention of local management.[58] Others have urged local administrators and elected officials to adopt new managerial attitudes and to run local government as they would a business.[59] And even those who argue that local government cannot be run like a business see similarities in role between the mayor and the CEO of a company.[60]

Thus, the departments are now portrayed as "enterprises with their CEOs and experts."[61] For the communes, one reads that "the town hall is an enterprise for which the mayor is the manager."[62] The mayors themselves, as the refrain goes, must manage as best they can and must no

[58]See Hertzog, "Grands services," p. 252.
[59]See the debates from the conference, "Les stratégies de gestion – Doit-on gérer une commune comme une entreprise?" in *Revue Française de Finances Publiques* no. 13 (1986).
[60]Michel Chappat, "Communes et entreprises: Les termes possibles de comparaison," from the conference, "Les Stratégies de gestion," pp. 185–92.
[61]*Le Monde,* Sept. 15, 1988.
[62]Such phrases appeared everywhere in articles on local government. This particular quote is from Daniel Cilla and Martine Pascal, "L'entreprise 'Mairie,' " *Économie Lorraine* no. 10 (Feb. 1983): 4.

longer content themselves simply to administer. The key to this is in the modern management techniques that are all the rage as these *maires managers* talk about "rationalizing their management" and "better mastering their expenditures." Much of their discussion focuses on hiring the best trained personnel (from the A category of the state civil service) to perform the necessary functions and to streamline services, all with an eye on the bottom line, as well as on seeking advice from consultants and getting management audits of their performance from outside experts.[63] In addition, mayors, not only in the large towns, but even in the smaller ones, are engaging in "municipal marketing," producing new logos and new publicity brochures in their efforts to attract new businesses to their communes.[64]

What is more, the rhetoric of good management has been adopted by the left as much as by the right. For instance, René Dosière, PS Mayor of Laon, in describing his relationship with his appointed staff, noted: "The mayors and the vice-mayors give the *impulsion*. . . . Then the heads of the services manage by objectives . . ."[65] The Communist mayor of La Ciotat (Bouches-du-Rhône) prides himself on his good management, which includes ensuring a competitive bidding process for city contracts. He even instituted a personnel evaluation system that the CGT did not like, but as the head of the local union admitted, "We also know that the city cannot act like a socialist island in a capitalist world."[66] A recent survey carried out for *Le Monde* and the *Caisse d'épargne* confirmed this managerial focus in the discourse of the left as much as the right. It noted that all mayors, regardless of political leanings, now tend to discuss their jobs in entrepreneurial terms as they describe local economic development as one of their major tasks and talk about helping businesses that create jobs by lightening their tax burdens, setting up industrial zones or training activities, and even, although much less so, gaining capital in private enterprises. Moreover, although a large majority of mayors remain in favor of public services, a growing number approve of privatization, especially in new sectors such as cable television and modern transportation. Mayors even claim to be open to new financing arrangements, with 79 percent ready to borrow on the European market, although, for 70 percent of them, only at fixed interest rates.[67]

This is not simply rhetoric, however. There is a good deal of evidence to suggest that local elected officials have backed up their words with

[63]François Grosrichard, "Maires: La passion du management," *Le Monde Affaires*, Nov. 14, 1987.
[64]Anita Rudman, "Les villes en campagne," *Les Monde Affaires*, Nov. 14, 1987.
[65]Grosrichard, "Maires."
[66]Francoise Chirot, "Gestion oblige," *Le Monde Affaires*, Nov. 14, 1987.
[67]*Le Monde*, July 3–4, 1988.

actions. In a survey of local leaders, a large majority noted that decentralization had contributed to some improvement in relations between the public powers and the *administrés*, or local population (8 percent saw a lot of improvement, 24 percent enough, 41 percent a little, and only 20 percent none at all). In addition, 48 percent found that in administrative matters decentralization rendered decision-making more rapid than before, against 35 percent who saw no change and 11 percent who saw it as less rapid. A majority of these leaders noted improvement in the delivery of major local public services, whereas no more than between 5 percent and 8 percent saw deterioration in those services. More specifically, 56 percent noted improvement in the case of social assistance and public health as opposed to 24 percent who found neither improvement nor deterioration; 62 percent noted improvement in urbanism and planning as opposed to 20 percent for no change; and 53 percent noted improvement in economic intervention as opposed to 30 percent for no change. Only two areas had less than a majority finding improvement in services and they were, quite predictably, education, at 38 percent for improvement as opposed to 38 percent for no change, and culture, at 47 percent for improvement as opposed to 33 percent for no change.[68]

Local governments, moreover, are beginning to function internally more like enterprises, as they become increasingly sophisticated in terms of their financing. In 1983 only 34 percent of local financing came from the financial markets; by 1987, over 86 percent did. The local government financing market has become increasingly competitive as local governments find themselves courted by French as well as European banks which see this market as attractive because of the relatively small risks and the large numbers of operations to be financed (in 1986, local governments borrowed 54 billion francs; in 1987, 72 billion francs for an increase of 33 percent). As a result, local governments are able to get very good deals, certainly much better than in the past when they were limited to borrowing from the CDC (*Caisse des dépôts et consignations*). Moreover, in addition to the traditional lending institutions (for example, *Caisse des dépôts, Crédit agricole,* and *Caisse mutuel*), the *Caisses d'épargne écureil*, with noncentralized funds from the *Caisse des dépôts*, provided local governments with roughly 15 billion francs in 1987, and banks and brokerage houses were equally willing to do so (estimated at between 6 and 7 billion francs); by 1989 their numbers should include the financial establishment of other EEC countries, if all works out as planned.[69]

Finally and most importantly perhaps, given the rhetoric of the finan-

[68]*Le Monde*, Dec. 4–5, 1988.
[69]Eric Camel, "Les communes courtisées," *Les Monde Affaires*, Nov. 14, 1987; and Richard, "Finances locales," pp. 135–6.

cial limits of decentralization, local governments are in fact "mastering their expenditures." For local governments generally, expenditures increased only 1.8 percent in constant francs between 1983 and 1988, by contrast with 5 percent in preceding years, suggesting that local governments have been becoming more efficient.[70] Therefore, in the words of the neoliberal deputy minister in charge of local governments already in 1986, decentralization "has not been expensive," in particular because, as he found, the expenditures for social assistance had regressed since the state had transferred them to the departments, with local governments having realized economies as a result of the multiplication of services in proximity to the users.[71] As Pierre Salvi, president of the Assembly of Presidents of General Councils, rightly suggested, the departments' mastering of the social assistance budgets was one of the great successes of decentralization.[72]

The departments, in effect, appear to have followed the words of advice of the *Caisse des dépôts et consignations* in 1983 for *moins de béton, plus des gestion,* or less cement, more management.[73] They showed themselves to be good managers from the very first year of the transfer of administrative duties, through savings in the area of social assistance as a result of better oversight in terms of entitlement programs and better management of administrative costs. The overall expenditures in social assistance, coming to 7 percent of operating costs for all local governments (the communes contribute a portion to the departments and have their own services – *Centres communaux d'action sociale* [CCAS], or municipal centers for social assistance – but 50 percent for the departments, increased only moderately: in real terms, −1.5 percent in 1985, −1 percent in 1986, and +1 percent in 1987, going from 21 billion francs in 1984 to 24 billion francs in 1987. From 1979 to 1983, by contrast, the increase was close to one-third.[74]

Saving money was only half the battle for the departments, however; streamlining the delivery of public services, making them more efficient as well as cost-effective, was the other half. There are innumerable examples of this. In the department of the Loire-Atlantique, for instance, the cost of school bus transportation before decentralization increased at a rate of 15 percent, or 4 points above the rate of inflation without any appreciable increase in the number of children transported. Some of the factors contributing to this increase were the Byzantine administrative structures, the system of crossed financing, the lack of any one designated agent clearly in

[70]Richard, "Finances locales," p. 134.
[71]*Le Monde,* Sept. 19, 1986.
[72]*Le Monde,* Sept. 14, 1988.
[73]Cited in Bernard, *L'État,* p. 225.
[74]Richard, "Finances locales," p. 132.

charge, and the absence of a competitive bidding system for contracts. After decentralization, such transportation costs were brought under control at the same time that productivity was improved by computerizing the system, by reducing its Balkanization through a diminution in the number of third-party contracts, and by engineering consensus when possible or managing conflict when necessary. Some order was thereby brought into the system, saving 1 million francs in 1985 in the first area affected, 0.5 million francs in the second area, with 4 zones to follow. In social welfare, similarly, the problems before decentralization, which included a rise in costs at a faster rate than the rate of increase in the price index, were remedied by 1986 with a reduction in expenditures in real terms as a result of better management, albeit without an improvement in productivity (the number of clients was diminished).[75]

The rhetoric of good management, in short, reflects a new reality, in which local governments have in fact mastered their expenditures and streamlined their services, providing the same quantity, and sometimes even higher quality care, for lower costs. This new reality has been accompanied by a reduction in the number of local elected officials resorting to the rhetoric of the financial limitations of decentralization. But they need not worry about losing this earlier rhetoric as an alternative, if their management practices fail. A recent survey suggests that the rhetoric of the financial limits of decentralization has been at least as successful as the rhetoric of good management, because 62 percent of those questioned agreed that local governments did not have sufficient financial means to conduct decentralization (as opposed to 23 percent who disagreed and 15 percent who gave no response), even as they noted significant improvement in most local public services.[76]

There is actually little likelihood of a return to the rhetoric of the limits of decentralization. Local elected officials in general are now completely convinced of the validity of their own rhetoric of good management and their ability to administer local government successfully with the resources in hand. As a matter of fact, local elected officials have become so convincing in their discourse about the importance of their managerial roles that they appear to have persuaded themselves that even their political role is secondary, at best, to the managerial role in the view of the public. In a survey for *Le Monde* and the *Caisses d'épargne* of mayors of communes of more than two thousand inhabitants, 86 percent of the respondents thought that they would be judged on the quality of their administration in the next municipal elections (of March 1989), as opposed to only 7 percent who felt the choice would be made according to

[75]Huntziger, "Prospective," pp. 119–21.
[76]*Le Monde*, Dec. 4–5, 1988.

political label.[77] At least some have been sorely disappointed in this, however, given the Socialists' gains in the 1989 elections. The fact remains that, however much local elected officials seek to "depoliticize" their roles, the periphery is even more politicized today than it was before decentralization.

The politicization of local elected officials

Much as local officials might have tried to deny it, local government has always been politicized.[78] But with decentralization, it stood to increase appreciably, leading many to fear that major decisions would be made along partisan lines and jobs and favors dispensed according to political affiliation. Although some such as Crozier even before decentralization encouraged the introduction of party politics at the local level in order to diminish the power of local elites, others such as Jean-Émile Vié have seen the new politics as promoting only local conflict and the patronage that often goes along with partisan politics.[79] Most fear that the politicization of the periphery will interfere with fair governmental administration, with presidents of regional and departmental councils being tempted to follow the lead of the big-city mayor in exchanging favors for partisan loyalty. But even without this, there are those who are concerned that having political actors at all four levels of local government (including the prefect) will lead to great administrative confusion and perhaps even the stalemates of the past if rival parties control different levels. And they worry, at the very least, that the new politics in the periphery, combined with the new administrative roles, rules, and relationships of local politicians and administrators, will prove to be more of a divisive than a dynamizing and reintegrating force.[80]

As it turns out, decentralization has not produced quite the dire consequences many feared, even though it has brought with it an increased politicization of the periphery. Politics, after all, is quite clearly present at every level of local government, however much local elected officials might try to hide it with the rhetoric of good management. There is no way of avoiding public recognition of the politicization of decision-making and the political significance of local elected officials' party affiliations when changes in majority at the local level bring with them, as they did when the right returned to power in many municipalities, changed street names (for

[77]*Le Monde*, July 3–4, 1988.
[78]See the discussion in Part II, Chapter 7, "The rhetoric of nonpartisanship."
[79]Crozier, *On ne change pas;* and Jean-Émile Vié, "Lacunes et écueils de la décentralisation," in *Décentralisation et politiques sociales: Actes de colloque de Grenoble,* Jan. 18–20, 1983 (Paris: Futuribles/C.E.P.E.S., 1983).
[80]Thoenig, "Le grand horloger"; and Jean-Michel Bellorgey, "De certains aspects du discours," *Échange et Projets* no. 39 (Sept. 1984): 21–3.

example, from rue Salvador Allende to rue Thiers), closed medical and cultural facilities and fired administrators, and new organizations to promote more "appropriate" forms of contemporary culture.[81]

Some of this politicization results, quite naturally, from the fact that decentralization, as Michel d'Ornano put it, has *responsabilisé et personalisé* the roles of local elected officials by making them more personally responsible to the electorate for their actions.[82] The very fact that local elected officials complained that decentralization would lead to their unpopularity, given the fiscal constraints, certainly demonstrates their keen awareness of the political dimensions of their newly powerful roles. And this awareness has translated itself into a politicization that has brought national political divisions increasingly into play in the "management" of local government.

National political cleavages are especially apparent at the regional and departmental levels. The most obvious indication of this is that the regional councils and the general councils of the departments have become forums for national debate. For example, antigovernment speeches by Olivier Guichard, regional president of the Loire when the Socialists were in power, had become so commonplace that the prefect no longer responded to them, let alone left the room.[83] In the Lorraine, where the right-wing majority had been reduced following the Socialist victory in 1981 (forty-four seats for the UDF and the RPR, seventeen for the PS and PC combined), meetings became extremely tense, with the left expressing its opinions more forcefully than before and the right never letting an opportunity go by to criticize the government.[84] In the department of the Alpes-Maritimes, where in 1985 there were five Communists, only one Socialist, and fifty-one opposition members, the president of the general council, Jacques Médecin, was reduced to attacking the Communists as the former collaborators of the Socialist government, whereas it was the lone Socialist who found himself interceding to ask that departmental issues, as the order of the day, be discussed.[85]

Needless to say, partisan politics does not limit itself to pro- or antigovernment positions taken within any given level of local government. It

[81]*Le Monde,* Nov. 3, 1983; Marie-José Chombart de Lauwe, "Les communes sous le règne du libéralisme," *Hommes & Libertés* no. 41 (1986): 16–23, cited in Mark Kesselman, "Restructuring the French state: An end to French exceptionalism?" Paper prepared for delivery at the sixth international conference of Europeanists (Washington, D.C., Oct. 30–Nov. 1, 1987), p. 21.

[82]*L'Express,* Mar. 8–14, 1985.

[83]Ibid.

[84]Jean-Claude Bonnefont, *La Lorraine* (Paris: Presses universitaires de France, 1984), p. 35.

[85]At least, this was the case at the meeting of the general council of the Alpes-Maritimes in Nice, June 6, 1985. I was informed that ever since decentralization, it has been the rule.

also affects the way in which local affairs are managed within the municipal, general, and regional councils. For instance, mayors, departmental presidents, and regional presidents often delegate primary authority to the bureau that contains a majority or even a totality of their own party in order to avoid allowing the municipal, departmental, or regional commissions, which include members of other parties, to have any say. In the Alpes-Maritimes, for example, the Communists were ejected from the all-important bureau of the departmental council because, according to the president of the council, Jacques Médecin, he saw no reason to turn for the execution of the budget to those who did not vote for it.[86]

The political orientation of the local party in power, moreover, has tended to influence the way in which the local council functions. In the municipalities, for example, the parties on the left had as a rule run the municipal council on a more cooperative basis, depending upon other party members for support and delegating responsibility to other elected municipal officials, than the parties on the right, where the mayor tended to be more of a leader who sought to marginalize potential rivals. Where there were alliances between the Socialists and Communists, however, both parties exercised more control over their members than otherwise. For example, in cities in the red belt, alliances between the two major parties of the left put both more on their guard, with each party exercising much greater control over its members in order to present a united front to its allies, and with the minority party members ending up much more restricted in their actions and in the exercise of their duties than majority members.[87]

Funding for local projects and local groups has also taken on a distinctly partisan political character. In Communist municipalities, for example, municipal associations and events linked to the party were funded most generously. And the new channels of communication opened up by the new breed of *notables* have simply provided more opportunities to introduce political messages into the everyday communications of the municipal services with their clientele.[88] Needless to say, in recent years the right has engaged in these practices as much as the left, taking a page from the left's book after 1983, and not only at the municipal level. In the Alpes-Maritimes, for example, the Communists were the ones to complain about the department's funding of ad hoc associations intended to counter the Communists' influence in traditional agricultural milieus.[89]

Party politics, in brief, has managed to intrude itself into the management of local government in a very real way. And this has been extended

[86]*Le Monde*, Sept. 22, 1988.
[87]Dion, *La Politisation*, pp. 75–81.
[88]Ibid., pp. 56–7.
[89]*Le Monde*, Sept. 22, 1988.

to the relationships between levels as well. Where partisans of different parties hold power at different levels of local government, each level may find itself disadvantaged in the area of jurisdiction controlled by its rival. Where this has occurred, the response has been considerable, ranging from bringing the regional council to administrative court, as in the Languedoc-Rousillon, to holding special sessions of the departmental council solely to attack the opposition, as in the Isère, where a special session on the departmental economy in May 1984 became a trial of the Socialist government.[90]

Partisan differences, however, are not the only reason for intergovernmental rivalries: economic differences and history also play an important role. In Provence-Alpes-Côte d'Azur, for example, the Alpes-Maritimes has always wanted to go its own way. The "comté de Nice" had for a long time a strong regionalist, separatist movement beginning in 1860, but gaining force in the first years of the Third Republic.[91] And the latest "count," Jacques Médecin (who, rumor has it, calls himself the count of Médicis when visiting Los Angeles), has sought to create a new region focused on "tourism and the retired," as opposed to "heavy industry and immigrants," consisting of the Alpine departments (Alpes-Maritimes, Alpes de Haute Provence, and Hautes-Alpes) since 1972 (when he claims Pompidou agreed to his request but asked him only to wait a bit to see how regionalization worked before any regional reorganization – Pompidou died, of course, before he righted the situation).[92] The partisan differences here, then, only reinforce divisions based on other issues.

Even where partisan differences based on a left–right divide do not exist, moreover, the politicization of the periphery remains quite evident. Political divisions have been just as intense between rival politicians from different factions on the same side of the left–right divide as well as on opposite sides, whether at the same or different levels of local government. In the Lorraine, for example, there has been a three-way split between members of the UDF, the RPR, and the *parti Radical*. Jean-Marie Rausch, as president of the region, mayor of Metz, a major figure in the UDF, and a minister in Rocard's government as of 1988, was the rival not only of the mayor of Nancy and head of the *parti Radical*, André Rossinot, with their political differences fueled by the traditional rivalry between Metz and Nancy, but also of Philippe Séguin, who, as mayor of

[90]Schlenker, "Industrial strategies," p. 293.
[91]See, for example, Paul Gonnet, "Particularisme et patronage politique dans le comté de Nice depuis 1870," in *Régions et régionalisme en France du XVIII siècle à nos jours*, ed. Christian Gras and Georges Livet (Paris: Presses universitaires de France, 1977), pp. 273–86.
[92]Jacques Médecin, interview with author, Nice, June 7, 1985.

Épinal in the Vosges, member of the RPR, and Minister of Social Affairs and Employment under Chirac, felt completely cut out of the economic largesse of the region divided up between Nancy and Metz.

Partisan politics, then, is likely only to increase and, along with it, decisions responding to national political pressures based along party lines. Therefore, instead of having a prefect as the executive power who seeks to accommodate everyone (the process of *saupoudrage*), the departments and the regions are likely to have presidents who will seek to accommodate primarily their own local political constituency. Although this politicization could translate itself into continued *saupoudrage* when the president does not have a firm majority in the council, it is more likely to become the reason for partisan political decisions about who gets what, when, how, and where. This is especially the case when regional and departmental presidents see themselves in the "presidential" role and use political cabinets that reflect only the views of the majority of the council to direct the affairs of the region or department.

There are, nevertheless, limits as to how much partisan politics can interfere with the equitable distribution of resources. For example, because municipal, departmental, and regional levels all have responsibility for local economic development, the extent to which one level or another can exercise political tyranny may be limited, for tyranny at one level may be offset by help at another. In this context, it is interesting to note that, in a recent survey of local business leaders and others, the respondents were almost evenly divided on whether there has been too much politicization in local economic development, with 43 percent suggesting that there has indeed been too much and 46 percent insisting that there has not.[93]

There are also limits to the freedom the different levels of local government may have to engage in partisan politics. For example, even though the departments have become more politicized, their freedom to follow the dictates of politics or to play political favorites is quite limited, because as discussed above, most of their budget is already encumbered legally by nationally set guidelines and locally necessitated expenses. The regions have more freedom in this regard, but they are mandated to consult with all levels. The communes, though, do have a great deal of freedom to play political favorites. But this is no different from the past. And even here, there have been other, more political reasons for limiting the amount of party politics allowed to influence decisions about hiring, purchasing, letting contracts, and the like.

The Communist mayors, in particular, are sensitive to the widely held view among political opponents, as well as a good portion of the public, that Communist elected officials tended to turn municipal services into

[93]*Le Monde*, Dec. 4–5, 1988.

reserves for party militants and to let contracts only to Communist suppli-
ers. They have generally made a point of recruiting technical staff and
others from outside their own ranks, as well as from within them, and of
allowing for competitive bidding for contracts. This was proof enough,
according to one Communist mayor in the red belt surrounding Paris,
that his pluralism "was not a façade" and that "all these stories of politicization are stories to discredit the Communist party." And they may well
have been. Studies suggest that the Communists as well as the Socialists
found that it made more sense to recruit along clientelistic lines than on
the basis of party favoritism, with an eye to expanding the consensus in
favor of the existing administration.[94]

Good politics, in short, is not always partisan politics. In the future just
as in the past, local elected officials are likely to do the right thing by a
political rival just to avoid the appearance of prejudice or partisanship or,
better yet, simply to follow sound economic policy or "good management." Even someone like Jacques Médecin claims to have been motivated by the dictates of sound economics when he provided economic aid
to the constituency of the lone Socialist on the general council of the
Alpes-Maritimes.[95] The five Communists tell a different story, however,
insisting that since decentralization, outside of legally required assistance,
they have received, with one exception, no favorable response to their
requests.[96]

Purely political considerations, in any event, can lead to seemingly
nonpartisan policies. Because mayors, as well as departmental and regional presidents, are elected by their respective councils, but are subject
to reelection by the population at large, they may very well try for this
reason to avoid even the appearance of engaging in partisan politics and
favoritism, especially where this was traditionally their modus operandi.
And for all of this, of course, the rhetoric of good management serves
local elected officials in good stead.

The politicization of local administrators

With the increasing politicization of local elected officials, the main question for the prefects is whether they are to be neutral mediators – as they
themselves would claim – or political agents of the state – as others,
mainly in opposition, insist that they have become. The question of
whether or not the *commissaire de la République* is political, as we have
already seen, has been raised as much for the previous regime of Giscard
d'Estaing as for the Socialists' regime. The question, then, is whether the

[94]Dion, *La Politisation*, pp. 53–4.
[95]Médecin interview.
[96]*Le Monde*, Sept. 22, 1988.

prefect in role has become more political. The answer, though, is not a simple yes or no. It really depends primarily on the politics as well as on the personalities of the prefects and the local elected officials of the particular region, department, or commune.

For example, when the prefect is seen as a political agent of the state as opposed to simply its representative, politics usually determines the perks. Because the expense allowance of the prefect was to be decided by regional and departmental presidents, as of 1982 until 1986, it was often influenced by political considerations. Thus, in the Calvados in 1985, where the department was to pay the prefect's expenses through 1986, the president Michel d'Ornano (UDF), who was also a Deputy and president of the region of Basse-Normandie, decided to allow the prefect only the expenses he felt were necessary for him to represent the state appropriately – viz., no more meetings with mayors, ribbon-cutting ceremonies, or anything else that could conceivably be of political benefit to the Socialists in power at the time.[97]

When the prefect has clearly identified political affiliations, though, the political problems go much beyond the question of money. For example, in the Meuse, a department with only five left-wing Deputies out of a total of thirty-two at the time, the political uproar was extreme when a Communist, Maurice Siegel, was named prefect in January 1982. The departmental president, Rémi Herment (UDF), also mayor of Vigneulles and Senator, saw it as an indication of the Socialist government's lack of regard for a weak department. The conservative general councilor and mayor of Void Vacon, Jean-Louis Gilbert, insisted that it was a punishment, citing not only the prefect's Communist affiliation but also his nonprefectoral career. Instead of being, as is the norm, a member of the *grand corps* with all the connections and experience that that implies, his previous positions were all in the Ministry of Finance, and in the pension service at that. At the very least, according to Gilbert, a Communist with technical economic credentials should have been chosen.

The response on the left, needless to say, was quite different. Some simply suggested that party affiliation was immaterial. But others such as Jean Bernard, mayor of Bar-le-Duc and a Socialist Deputy, welcomed the change, citing the inappropriateness of the actions of the former prefect, Pierre Costa, who had incessantly attacked the government.[98] It is perhaps significant that Costa, who saw a new and extreme politicization of the prefectoral corps under decentralization, was also one of those who was clearly most active in its politicization.[99] It was immediately after Costa's stay in the Meuse that he left the national civil service to become

[97]*L'Express*, Mar. 8–14, 1985.
[98]*Le Monde*, Feb. 23, 1983.
[99]Pierre Costa, interview with author, Nice, June 7, 1985.

director of departmental services for the Alpes-Maritimes under the ultra right-wing president Jacques Médecin.

As it turns out, the Communist prefect was generally well liked by members of the right and the left, thus suggesting that this prefect's politics, at least, did not affect his performance in role. But this did not in any way alleviate the extreme political polarization in the general council of the department. By February 1983, it was the only department left that had refused to ratify the *convention,* or agreement, for the division of property and expenses between state and department. Decentralization, in this case, led to the increasing politicization of the department and its disaffection from the state. As one of the most anti-Communist of the general councilors (and former Giscardian Deputy), Gérard Longuet, explained: "Because political suspicion of the prefect has been added to the traditional suspicions, the situation has become explosive."[100]

How explosive such situations have become, however, still depends a lot on the politics and personalities of the administrators and politicians involved. For instance, despite the fact that Gaston Defferre himself made clear that one of his main reasons for pushing for decentralization came from his having suffered under the prefects for years, as Minister of the Interior, he appointed as *commissaire de la République* of the region of Provence-Alpes-Côte d'Azur the same person who had been prefect of the Bouches-du-Rhône under Giscard d'Estaing (and thus Defferre's prefect) before becoming prefect of police in Paris while Jacques Chirac was mayor. Defferre's choice of Somveille lends credence to the view of Michel Besse, secretary-general of the prefecture of the department of the Bouches-du-Rhône, that the role of prefect, at least as Somveille played it, had not been completely politicized.[101] It also tends to support the contentions of officials of the Ministry of the Interior such as Michel Cotten, the first director of the DGCL, or local governments department, under the new laws, who argued that the prefects remained neutral, essentially apolitical forces.[102] But this is true only where relationships are established between prefects and local elected officials in which both sets of actors manage to overcome their political differences. And although this may have been relatively easy before decentralization, the increased politicization of the periphery can make it much more difficult now.

In any event, it is quite clear that even now, personality and personal ties can overcome political affiliations, at least when they are not extremely pronounced. When they are, as in the case of Pierre Costa, the

[100]*Le Monde,* Feb. 23, 1983.

[101]Michel Besse, secretary-general of the prefecture, interview with author, Marseilles, June 5, 1985.

[102]Michel Cotten, interview with author, Paris, May 20, 1985.

outcome has been a move into the territorial civil service from the national. Costa, after all, was only the first of seven prefects and forty-five subprefects to move into the territorial service. And this trend is likely to continue, with the *alternance* caused in politics by changes in national government reproducing itself in the upper levels of the civil service for those members of the prefectoral corps who can be more clearly identified politically.

How significant this trend is, however, is open to question. Although much was made of the exodus of *grand corps* members from the national civil service, it really was only fifty-two out of a possible eight hundred members of the prefectoral corps. As a result of the local elections during the first half of the 1980s, during which time the Socialists lost almost all of the periphery to the right, movement out of the national into the territorial civil service has not really been much of an option for left-leaning prefects. Add to this the fact that the new territorial civil service code has not been implemented, and we have a situation in which the *alternance* is likely to occur, if at all, within the confines of national service alone. Here, as in the past, it is probable that decisions on prefectoral appointments will only sometimes involve the political.

Such political considerations, needless to say, occur when there are real shifts in who holds power. Thus, when the Socialists came in, Gaston Defferre changed fifty-three prefects – certainly more than the last big change of 1967, when Christian Fouchet changed forty-one. But although Defferre did replace a large percentage of the prefects, the changes were as much a function of the normal three-year prefectoral rotation as they were of political considerations; and the prefects, as mentioned above, weren't sent to administrative Siberia either; they were quite simply assigned to new posts. It is nevertheless clear, however, that on their way out the Socialists did indeed follow politics. In March 1985, Pierre Joxe changed prefects in eleven regions and twenty-nine departments, affecting sixty-one functionaries and making even the big changes of 1967 and 1981 look modest. With one department out of two changing *commissaire de la République*, Joxe, according to *Le Figaro*, looked more like a minister of elections than Minister of the Interior since it was less than four days before the *cantonales* (the elections for the general councils of the departments) and one year before the legislative elections.[103] The changes were almost as dramatic when the right came back into power after the legislative elections of 1986.

But even if the appointment of prefects has been politicized to some extent, we have already seen that, after appointment, politics does not

[103]*Le Figaro*, Mar. 7, 1985.

always affect the prefects' actions. Thus, there remains some question as to how much politicization there really is at the level of the state's representative in the periphery. By contrast, there is no question that there has been a great deal of politicization at the other levels of local government, especially given the scuttling of the Socialists' territorial civil service reform in favor of the neoliberals' reform, which consecrated such politicization at the upper echelons of the local civil service.

Certainly, the regions have a highly political administration, because the comparatively small number of regional functionaries were themselves recruited only since the Socialists' decentralization reforms and are charged with carrying out the policies of the clearly political regional councils. One complaint of the Socialists about the delay in the elections for regional governments was that the right in power in many of the regions was able to put its own people into positions of responsibility in the regional administration. The much larger, departmental administrations have also become more politicized, in particular at the highest levels, with members of the prefectoral corps moving to the departments for political reasons. But this politicization cannot have been as extensive as in the regions, given the numbers of long-term state civil servants transferred to the locality. Although there are no studies yet that assess the degree of politicization of the departments, it is likely that the experience of the departments is most similar to that of the cities in the previous decade. There, politicization was evident, for instance, not only in the reform efforts by mayors and cabinet members seeking to reinforce their own power as much as to make the bureaucracy more efficient, less bureaucratic, and more responsive to the local population, but also in the resistance of local civil servants to such reform in the name of nonpartisanship. There were limits to politicization even here, however. Often, mayors turned to technocrats to run municipal services in order to minimize the potential influence of political rivals. And even when top administrators were themselves political operatives, they would often seek to respond to politicians' requests while insulating municipal services from political demands.[104]

The politicization in the administration of local governments, in conclusion, only adds to the pluralism evident in the new politics in the periphery, making the rhetoric of good management less effective as a way of allaying the local electorate's fears of the consequences of such politics, while making the reality of good management more of a necessity. That reality has already made the rhetoric of the limits of decentralization less appealing to local elected officials who, in their new roles and with their new responsibilities, may succeed in having the new pluralism in local

---

[104]Dion, *La Politisation*, pp. 95–119.

administrative institutions and processes work to their advantage, making local governments more efficient, less costly, and perhaps even more democratic. In the meantime, we can continue to look for the signs of such change in the rhetoric of local elected officials and administrators, in their evolving interrelationships, and in the developing political and administrative processes in the periphery.

Conclusion

Socialist decentralization represents the end of a very long and not very glorious history. The Revolution of 1789, to begin with, cast a long shadow over all decentralizing reform, both conceptually, by assuming an opposition between national unity and equality on the one hand and local liberty on the other, and institutionally, by consecrating local governmental structures that subsequent generations treated as inviolable. The Revolution also initiated the self-interested pattern of legislative behavior on the issue of decentralization, one in which considerations of political interest almost always took precedence over those of political principle. Although in the first century following the Revolution, such self-interested opposition to local liberty was motivated by a distrust of the general population by those in power, in the second century, it was fueled by a distrust of those in power by local officials who, by now, controlled the periphery.

How then do we explain the success of decentralizing reforms today or of those one hundred years ago? In these two instances alone, political interest combined with the politics of the moment to favor the disinterested politics represented by decentralization. In both cases and each time initiated by the left, legislation promoting local liberty has been associated with a short-term political calculation to retain power at the local level, even if it was lost at the national, as well as with a long-term electoral strategy to gain and retain the allegiance of a changing electorate. At the beginning of the Third Republic, decentralization was linked to a realignment of the emerging electorate of middle-income peasants and shopkeepers behind a center–left coalition; in the Socialist Fifth Republic, it has been linked to what very well may become a realignment of the emerging electorate of middle-level managers and workers behind a center–left *rapprochement* led by the Socialists.

The left, in sum, supported decentralization for pragmatic reasons as much as, if not more than, for principled ones. And this pragmatism was also reflected in the substance of the legislation, helping to explain the

389

reluctance of legislators in both periods to tamper with the organizing principles of local government established by the Revolution and the Napoleonic era. The reforms of the Third Republic remained quite modest in light of this, restricted primarily to changes in the role of the mayor. By contrast, those of the Socialist Fifth Republic were most ambitious, altering the roles of all actors in the periphery, giving the presidents of the councils of the regions and departments new powers and duties, while diminishing those of the prefect, and replacing or revising almost every law related to center–periphery relations. The pragmatism here was focused in the Socialists' consensus-building effort to ensure passage of the reforms. It resulted in the Socialists' failure to solve some of the most pressing problems of French local government – that is, the excessive number of units and levels of local government, the complexity of local finances, the complications in the division of health and social services, and the low levels of direct citizen participation. This leaves open to question whether the new system will be much more efficient and cost-effective, let alone more democratic, than the old.

Whatever the limitations, however, the decentralizing reforms of the Socialist Fifth Republic, as well as those of the Third Republic, have had a profound effect on the politics and administration of local government. The reforms of the Third Republic had their greatest impact on the municipal level of local government, creating a "revolution" in which mayors became members of a new elite that accumulated offices rather than titles and was more representative of, and responsive to, the new electorate of peasants and shopkeepers in the periphery. Moreover, because the mayors' new political role provided them with a counterweight to the prefects' administrative control, it promoted the development of the complicity that was at the basis of the informal, decentralized politico-administrative system that lay behind the formal–legal system of centralization. This new reality engendered by the Third Republic reforms remained obscure, however, hidden by the rhetoric of centralization, which enabled local elected officials to escape responsibility for their administrative actions, and by the rhetoric of nonpartisanship, which helped them dissemble their political leanings.

The decentralizing reforms of the Socialist Fifth Republic transformed this local politico-administrative system, primarily by formalizing local elected officials' informal powers and by creating a new pluralism in local institutions and processes, as well as new roles, rules, and interrelationships in the periphery. Evidence of this transformation can be found not only in what local elected officials and administrators have been doing but also in what they have been saying, in new rhetorics reflective of the new realities.

Conclusion

The Socialists' reforms, more specifically, have had their greatest political impact on the departmental and regional levels of local government. The "revolution" this time affects primarily the presidents of regional and departmental councils, who, along with the mayors, are now members of a political elite who can no longer accumulate so many offices, are increasingly differentiated according to their mandates and their constituencies, and are more representative of, and responsive to, the new electorate of middle-level managers and workers in the periphery. This, in turn, has promoted a new political pluralism, as evidenced by the growing politicization of local elections along national lines and the increased political competition among parties and personalities in the periphery. Local elected officials' new, clearly political role, moreover, has led to a replacement of the rhetoric of nonpartisanship with that of good management, which reflects as much local politicians' continuing attempts to "depoliticize" local government as it does their recognition of the demands of the new administrative realities and their success in rising to the challenge. Local elected officials have, in fact, become good managers, if not always good democrats.

The impact of the Socialists' reforms has been as significant in the administrative arena as in the political. Again, the regions and the departments have undergone the greatest transformation, becoming separate politico-administrative systems in their own right, alongside those of the big cities, and their presidents have become the new potentates in the periphery, taking over from the prefects who have now become mediators, a threat to no one but rural mayors. This transformation has, in turn, engendered a new administrative pluralism based on the new complementarity among different levels and units of local government and the state. This pluralism has particularly affected the regions, in which the exercise of their new interventionist powers in the area of local economic development takes the form of a new "decentralized *dirigisme*" in consequence of the large number of local, national, and even supranational actors also involved. Finally, here too, a new rhetoric of the limits of decentralization has emerged to replace the rhetoric of centralization. It serves as much to express local elected officials' concerns about the financial constraints of the reform as it does to obscure the fact that the state has, in the main, provided adequate compensation for their newly transferred duties.

Socialist decentralization, in short, in addition to being a significant event in France's legislative history, has been a turning point in its local governmental history, changing the rules of the game of local politics and administration. Although some local officials still play the old games with a new twist, most are playing new games with an old twist. The rules of the game have changed as a result of their formalization; and decentralization, in consequence, rather than being a case of attempting to "change society by decree," typical of a "blocked society," has served to "unblock society by decree." The Socialist reforms, in sum, were indeed *la grande affaire du Septennat*, fulfilling one of the last imperatives of the French Revolution and, once and for all, establishing both conceptually and institutionally the compatibility of national unity and equality on the one hand with local liberty on the other.

Bibliography

Abélès, Marc. "Les chemins de la décentralisation." *Les Temps Modernes* no. 463 (February 1985).

Agulhon, Maurice. *La République au village*. Paris: Plon, 1970.

Agulhon, Maurice, L. Girard, J. L. Robert, W. Serman, et al., *Les Maires en France du consulat à nos jours*. Paris: Sorbonne, 1986.

Anderson, R. D. *France 1870–1914*. London: Routledge & Kegan Paul, 1977.

Ashford, Douglas. *British Dogmatism and French Pragmatism*. London: George Allen & Unwin, 1982.

Policy and Politics in France. Philadelphia: Temple University Press, 1982.

Barthélemy, Joseph. *Le Gouvernement de la France*. Paris: Payot & Cie, 1919.

Becquart-Leclercq, Jeanne. *Paradoxes du pouvoir local*. Paris: Presses de la fondation nationale des sciences politiques, 1976.

Bernard, Paul. *L'État et la décentralisation*. Paris: Documentation française, 1983.

Birnbaum, Pierre, Francis Hamon, and Michel Troper. *Réinventer le parlement*. Paris: Flammarion, 1977.

Bodiguel, J. L., et al., eds. *La Réforme régionale et le referendum du 27 Avril 1969*. Paris: Cujas, 1970.

Bordes, Maurice. *L'Administration provinciale et muncipale en France au XVIIIe siècle*. Paris: Société d'Edition d'enseignement supérieur, 1972.

Burdeau, François. *Liberté, libertés locales chéries*. Paris: Cujas, 1983.

Capdevielle, Jacques, Elisabeth Dupoirier, Gérard Grunberg, et al., eds. *France de gauche: Vote à droite*. Paris: Presses de la Fondation Nationale des Sciences Politiques, 1981.

Caroux, Jacques. "The end of administrative centralization?" *Telos,* no. 55 (Spring 1983).

Chapman, Brian. *The Prefects and Provincial France*. London: George Allen & Unwin, 1955.

Charnay, Jean-Paul. *Le Suffrage politique en France*. La Haye: Mouton & Co., 1965.

Chevalier, Jean-Jacques. *Histoire des institutions et des régimes politiques de la France moderne (1789–1958)*. Paris: Dalloz, 1967.

Chevallier, Jacques. "Administration et développement local en France." *Revue Française d'Administration Publique*, no. 34 (Apr.–June, 1985).

"L'Intérêt général dans l'administration française." *Revue Internationale des Sciences Administratives*, vol. 41, no. 4 (1975).

Chevallier, Jacques, François Rangeon, and Michèle Sellier. *Le Pouvoir régionale.* Paris: Presses universitaires de France, 1982.

Cluzel, Jean. *Les Anti-Monarques de la Cinquième.* Paris: Librairie générale de droit et de jurisprudence, 1985.

Commissariat Général du Plan. *Evaluation de la planification décentralisée.* Paris: Documentation française, 1986.

Crozier, Michel. *La Société bloquée.* Paris: Seuil, 1967.

Le Phénomène bureaucratique. Paris: Seuil, 1963.

On ne change pas la société par décrêt. Paris: Grasset, 1979.

Crozier, Michel, and Jean-Claude Thoenig. "La régulation des systèmes organisés complexes." *Revue Française de Sociologie,* vol. 16 (1975).

Debbasch, Charles. *L'Administration au pouvoir.* Paris: Calmann-Lévy, 1969.

Ed. *La Décentralisation pour la rénovation de L'État.* Paris: Presses universitaires de France, 1976.

Diamant, Alfred. "The department, the prefect, and dual supervision in French administration: A comparative study." *Journal of Politics,* vol. 16 (1954).

Dion, Stéphane. *La Politisation des mairies.* Paris: Economica, 1986.

Dosière, René, Jean-Claude Fortier, and Jean Mastias. *Le Nouveau Conseil général.* Paris: Editions ouvrières, 1985.

Ducrocq, Th. *Études sur la loi municipale du 5 Avril 1884.* Paris: Ernest Thorin, 1886.

Dupeux, Georges. *La Société française (1789–1960).* Paris: Colin, 1964.

Dupuy, François, and Jean-Claude Thoenig, *L'Administration en miettes.* Paris: Fayard, 1985.

Ehrmann, Henry. *Politics in France.* Boston: Little, Brown, 1968.

Farago, Bela. "De la décentralisation." *Commentaire,* vol. 6, no. 21 (Spring 1983).

Faure, Marcel. *Les Paysans dans la société française.* Paris: Colin, 1966.

Ferron, H. de. *Institutions municipales et provinciales comparées.* Paris: L. Larose & Forcel, 1884.

Giard, Jean, and Jacques Scheibling. *L'Enjeu régional: une démarche autogestionnaire.* Paris: Éditions sociales, 1981.

Godechot, Jacques. *Les Institutions de la France sous la Révolution et l'Empire.* 2d ed. Paris: Presses universitaires de France, 1985.

Goguel, François. *Sociologie electorale.* Paris: Colin, 1954.

Goubert, Pierre. *L'Ancien Régime.* Vol. 2. Paris: Colin, 1973.

Gourevitch, Peter. *Paris and the Provinces.* Berkeley: University of California Press, 1980.

"Reforming the Napoleonic State: The Creation of Regional Governments in France and Italy." In *Territorial Politics in Industrial Nations,* ed. S. Tarrow, P. J. Katzenstein, and L. Graziano. New York: Praeger Special Studies, 1978.

Gras, Christian, and Georges Livet, eds. *Régions et régionalisme en France du XVIII siècle à nos jours.* Paris: Presses universitaires de France, 1977.

Greffe, Xavier. *Territoires en France.* Paris: Economica, 1984.

Grémion, Pierre. *Le Pouvoir périphérique.* Paris: Seuil, 1976.

Grémion, Pierre, and Jean-Pierre Worms. *Les Institutions régionales et la société locale* Paris: Centre de Sociologie, 1969.

Guengant, Alain. *Équité territoriale et inégalités. Le rôle de la DGF dans la réduction des inégalités financières entre communes.* Paris: Litec, 1983.

Guengant, Alain, and Jean-Michel Uhaldeborde. *Crise et réforme des finances locales.* Paris: Presses universitaires de France, 1988.

Guillermet, Catherine. "Les politiques et stratégies des établissements publics régionaux à travers leurs choix budgétaires." In *Centres et périphéries: Le partage du pouvoir,* ed. Yves Mény. Paris: Economica, 1983.

Halévy, Daniel. *The End of the Notables.* Middletown, Conn.: Wesleyan University Press, 1974.

La République des ducs. Paris: Grasset, 1937.

Hannezo, Guillaume, and Jean Rondin, "La Décentralisation: Une Passion d'opposant?" *Échange & Projets,* no. 41 (March 1985).

Hanotaux, Georges. *Histoire de la France contemporaine.* Vol. 3. Paris: Société d'éditions contemporaines, 1903.

Hauriou, Maurice. *Précis elémentaire de droit administratif.* Paris: Sirey, 1938.

Hoffmann, Stanley. "Paradoxes of the French Political Community." In *In Search of France,* ed. S. Hoffmann, C. Kindleberger, L. Wylie, et al. New York: Harper & Row, 1963.

Jardin, A., and André-Jean Tudesq. *La France des notables.* 2 vols. Paris: Seuil, 1973.

Jegouzo, Yves, and Christophe Sanson. "Décentralisation: La pause, pourquoi et comment?" *L'Année administrative 86.* Paris: Institut International d'Administration Publique, 1987.

Kergoat, Jacques. *Le Parti Socialiste: De la commune à nos jours* (Paris: Sycomore, 1983.

Kesselman, Mark. *The Ambiguous Consensus.* New York: Knopf, 1967.

La Décentralisation en marche, Cahiers français, no. 220 (Mar.–Apr. 1985).

La Décentralisation, Cahiers français, no. 204 (Jan.–Feb. 1982).

Lacorne, Denis. *Les Notables rouges.* Paris: Presses de la Foundation Nationale des Sciences Politiques, 1980.

Legendre, Pierre. *L'Administration du XVIIIe siècle à nos jours.* Paris: Presses universitaires de France, 1969.

Les Collectivités locales, Cahiers français, no. 239 (Jan.–Feb. 1989)

Les Collectivités territoriales, Cahiers français, no. 239 (Jan.–Feb. 1989).

Lewis-Beck, Michael. "France: The Stalled Electorate." In *Electoral Change in Advanced Industrial Democracies: Realignment or Dealignment?* ed. Russell J. Dalton, Scott C. Flanagan, and Paul Allen Beck. Princeton, N.J.: Princeton University Press, 1984.

Mabileau, Albert. *Les Pouvoirs locaux à l'Épreuve de la décentralisation.* Paris: Pédone, 1983.

Mabileau, Albert, and Pierre Sadran. "Administration et politique au niveau local." In *Administration et politique sous la Cinquième République,* ed. F. de Baecque and J. L. Quermonne. Paris: Presses de la Fondation Nationale des Sciences Politiques, 1981.

McCarthy, Patrick, ed. *The French Socialists in Power, 1981–1986.* Westport, Conn.: Greenwood, 1987

Machin, Howard. "All Jacobins now? The growing hostility to local government reform." *West European Politics,* vol. 1, no. 3. (Oct. 1978).

The Prefect in French Public Administration. New York: St. Martin's, 1977.

Machin, Howard, and Vincent Wright, eds. *Economic Policy and Policy-Making under the Mitterrand Presidency 1981–1984.* New York: St. Martin's, 1985.

Mawhood, Philip. "Melting an iceberg: The struggle to reform communal government in France." *British Journal of Political Science,* vol. 2 (1972)

Mény, Yves. "Central Control and Local Resistance." In *Continuity and Change in France,* ed., V. Wright. London: George Allen & Unwin, 1984.

Centralisation et Décentralisation dans le Débat Politique Français. Paris: Librairie générale de droit et de jurisprudence, 1974.

"Partis politiques et décentralisation." In *L'Administration vue par les politiques,* ed. Institut français des sciences administratives. Paris: Cujas, 1978.

Monnet, Émile. *Histoire de l'administration.* Paris: Rousseau, 1885.

Morgand, Léon. *La Loi municipale.* Paris: Berger-Levrault, 1906.

Penniman, Howard R., ed. *The French National Assembly Elections of 1978.* Washington, D.C.: American Enterprise Institute, 1980.

Perrineau, Pascal, ed. *Régions: Le baptême des urnes.* Paris: Pédone, 1987.

Peyrefitte, Alain, ed. *Décentraliser les Responsabilités: Pourqoi? Comment?* Paris: Documentation française, 1976.

Le Mal français. Paris: Plon, 1976.

Philip Cerny and Martin Schain, eds. *French Politics and Public Policy.* New York: St. Martin's, 1980.

Richard, Pierre. "Les Finances Locales de 1983 à 1987," *Revue française de Finances Publiques,* no. 22 (1988).

Roig, Charles. "Théorie et réalité de la décentralisation." *Revue française de Science Politique,* vol. 126 (1966).

Rondin, Jacques. *Le Sacre des notables.* Paris: Fayard, 1985.

Sautel, Gérard. *Histoire des institutions publiques.* Paris: Dalloz, 1974.

Savigny, Jean de. *L'État contre les communes?* Paris: Seuil, 1971.

Schain, Martin. "The National Front in France and the Construction of Political Legitimacy." *West European Politics,* vol. 10, no. 2 (April 1987).

Schain, Martin, and Philip Cerny, *Socialism, the State, and Public Policy in France.* London: Frances Pinter, 1985.

Sharp, Walter Rice. *The French Civil Service: Bureaucracy in Transition.* New York: Macmillan, 1931.

Schmidt, Vivien A. "Decentralization: A Revolutionary Reform." In *The French Socialists in Power 1981–1986,* ed. Patrick McCarthy. Westport, Conn.: Greenwood, 1987.

"Engineering a Critical Realignment of the Electorate: The Case of the Socialists in France." *West European Politics,* vol. 13, no. 2 (April 1990).

"Industrial Management under the Socialists in France: 'Decentralized Dirigisme' at the national and local levels." *Comparative Politics,* vol. 21, no. 1 (Oct. 1988).

"Unblocking Society by Decree: The Impact of Governmental Decentralization in France." *Comparative Politics,* vol. 22, no. 4 (July 1990).

Silvain-Klein, Jacques. *L'explosion des impôts locaux.* Paris: Documentation française, 1986.

Suleiman, Ezra N. "Administrative Reform and the Problem of Decentralization in the Fifth Republic." In *The Impact of the Fifth Republic on France,* ed. William G. Andrews and Stanley Hoffman. Albany: State University of New York Press, 1981.

Tarrow, Sidney. *Between Center and Periphery.* New Haven, Conn.: Yale University Press, 1977.

"Decentramento incompiuto o centralismo restaurato? L'esperienza regionalistica in Italia e in Francia." *Rivista di Scienza Politica,* vol. 9, no. 2 (Aug. 1979).

Terrazzoni, André. *La Décentralisation à l'Épreuve des Faits.* Paris: Librairie générale de droit et de jurisprudence, 1987.

Thoenig, Jean-Claude. *L'Ere des technocrates: Le Cas des Ponts et Chaussées* Paris: Les Editions d'organisation, 1973.

"La politique de l'État à l'égard du personnel des communes." *Revue française d'administration publique,* no. 23 (July–Sept. 1982).

"La relation entre le centre et la périphérie en France: Une analyse systématique." *Bulletin de l'Institut International d'Administration Publique* (Dec. 1975).

Tocqueville, Alexis de. *Democracy in America.* New York: Doubleday, 1969.

Tudesq, André-Jean. *La Démocratie en France depuis 1815.* Paris: Presses universitaires de France, 1971.

Vigier, Philippe. *La Seconde République dans la région Alpine.* 2 vols. Paris: Presses universitaires de France, 1963.

Vigoroux, Charles. "Quelques éléments pour un bilan des E.P.R., C.G.P.," *Service régional urbain* (Nov. 1979).

Virieux, Jean-Marc. "Les tendances longues de la décentralisation." *Futuribles,* no. 56 (June 1982).

Weber, Eugen. *Peasants into Frenchmen.* Stanford, Calif.: Stanford University Press, 1976.

Williams, Philip M., and Martin Harrison. *Politics and Society in de Gaulle's Republic.* New York: Anchor, 1971.

Worms, Jean-Pierre. "La Décentralisation: Un processus, une chance à saisir." *Échange et Projets,* no. 39 (Sept. 1984).

"Le préfet et ses notables." *Sociologie du Travail* 3 (July–Sept. 1966).

Wright, Vincent. "Politics and Administration under the French Fifth Republic." *Political Studies,* vol. 22 (1972).

"Regionalization under the French Fifth Republic: The Triumph of the Functional Approach." In *Decentralist Trends in Western Democracies,* ed. L. J. Sharpe. London: Sage, 1979.

Wright, Vincent, and Howard Machin. "The French regional reforms of July 1972." *Policy and Politics,* vol. 3, no. 3 (March 1975).

Wylie, Lawrence. *Village in the Vaucluse.* Cambridge: Harvard University Press, 1974.

Index

Abel-Durand, M., 82, 203
administration, local
  after Socialist reforms, 266–7, 289–90,
    313–5, 325–6
  before Socialist reforms, 216–9, 235–7,
    259–63
ANCE (national agency to promote creation of business enterprises), 304
ancien régime, 13–15
ANER (national association of regional
  elected officials), 143
ANVAR (national agency for applied research), 298–9
apolitisme, see nonpartisanship, rhetoric of
arrondissements, 23–4, 30–1; *see also*
  conseils d'arrondissements
artisans, 51, 161
associational movement, 150–1, 287
Aubert, Jacques, 97
autogestion (self-management)
  after Socialist Fifth reforms, 149–50,
    151, 157, 162, 266, 286
  before Socialist reforms, 87, 93, 100,
    102, 103, 206

Barnier, Michel, 357
Barre, Raymond, 168, 169–71, 174, 275,
  345
Barrot, Odilon, 30, 34
bassins d'emploi, 297
Baudis, Dominique, 285
Beauquier, Pierre, 64
Bernard, Jean, 383
Besse, Michel, 320, 337, 384
Blanc, Jacques, 358
Blanc, Louis, 30, 36, 53
Blanqui, Louis Auguste, 36
Blum, Léon, 65, 76
Bonapartists, 38–9, 47–8, 52–3, 56, 66

Boulangists, 160
Brisson, Henri, 48
Broglie, Albert, duc de, 38, 47, 53–4, 57
Buffet, Louis, 55
building permits, delivery of, 113, 194,
  229–30
business tax, local, 136, 352, 354

cadres moyens (middle-level managers and
  employees), 152, 154, 157; *see also*
  salariés
candidature officiel, 57
cantons, 16, 22, 23
  cantonal assemblies under Napoleon,
    23–4
  and electoral districts, 92, 140, 141
capacité: as eligibility requirement for voting, 31–2, 199
Capdeville, Robert, 148
Carignon, Alain, 273
Carrère, Gilbert, 320
Cazenove de Pradine, 47
CDS (*Centre des démocrates sociaux*), *see*
  Christian Democrats
cens: as elibility requirement for voting,
  31–2
center, opening to, 165–6, 170–1, 176
centralization, 61, 67–8, 182, 188–98,
  207–10, 235
  rhetoric of 183, 222–4, 225–37, 237–
    47, 342–3
centrists, *see* moderate right
CES (*Comité économique et social*), 94,
  100, 234, 291–2
Chaban-Delmas, Jacques, 284, 345
Chambord, Comte de, 35, 50, 54
chambres régionales des comptes, see regional accounting courts
Chandernagor, André, 95, 108

399

Index

Charles-Brun, Jean, 60
charters, intercommunal, *see* communes
Chevènement, Jean-Pierre, 127, 284
Chirac, Jacques, 93, 95, 96, 99, 120, 169–71, 174
  and centralization, rhetoric of, 225–6
  and economic development, local, 303–4
Christian Democrats, 66, 73, 90, 99
circonscriptions d'action régionale (regional action areas), 78
civil service:
  personnel, 318–19, 324–6, 331–2, 361–3, 364;
  politicization, 261–3, 382–7
  professionalization of, 191, 193, 205
  reform, 113, 130–2
Clemenceau, Georges, 58, 64
Closon, F. L., 73
Club Bretagne et Démocratie, 87
Club Jean Moulin, 85–6
CODER (regional economic development commission), 78, 82, 88, 195–6
"cohabitation," 162
comités d'expansion (expansion committees), 77, 82
Commissaire
  de la République, 33, 69, 73, 74, 112–13
  in Directory, 21, 22
Commissariat général au Plan, 85
communes, 334–41; *see also* mayors; municipal council; Paris
  districts urbains, 79–80
  and economic development, 113, 129, 292–4, 301–4, 368–9
  finances and state subsidies, 245
  financial expenditures, 240, 242–3, 347–8, 367–8
  financial problems, 353–6
  intercommunal charters, 121
  multipurpose syndicates, 79–80
  syndicates, 67
  number of, 93, 110, 197, 336
  personnel, 363
  rural, 113, 337–8
    and decentralization, rhetoric of 344–5
    finances, 135–6, 338, 353–4, 355–6
  and *tutelle,* 229–31, 335–41, 344–5
  taxes, 242, 351–2
  urban, 334–6
Communists, 65–6, 69, 88, 91, 73–4, 103–4
  and good management, rhetoric of, 249, 256–8
  and local government, 234, 276, 278–9, 379, 381–2

complicity, 182, 187, 210–11, 213–14, 215, 227; *see also* elected officials, local
conseils d'arrondissements, 115–16
Constant, Benjamin, 28
Constituent Assembly, during the French Revolution, 17–9
Corbière, Jacques, Comte de, 27
Cormenin, Louis Marie, Vicomte de, 30, 200
corporatism, 53–4, 66, 78, 211, 288
Costa, Pierre, 131, 383, 384–5
costs, local government, *see* finances, local
Cot, Pierre, 74
Cotten, Michel, 384
couche nouvelle sociale, see social stratum, new
Cresson, Edith, 161
culture
  and communes, 336
  decentralization of, 122t, 123t, 127
  in regional planning process, 296
  state transfers for, 350–1
cumul des mandats (accumulation of offices)
  before Socialist Fifth Republic, 72, 83, 89, 91–2, 198, 199, 211
  during Socialist Fifth Republic, 138, 144–9, 277, 279–80, 284–5, 302, 333
cumulants (local elected officials with more than one significant mandate), 175, 218
  see also cumul des mandats; elected officials, local

DATAR (Délégation à l'amènagement du territoire), 77, 85, 196, 299–300
DDE (*Direction départementale d'équipement*), 97, 193–4, 230, 339–40
DDEC (*dotation départementale d'équipement des collèges*), 135, 351
Debarge, Marcel, 145
Debré, Michel, 83, 90, 99, 118, 225–6
decentralization
  laws
    from before 1789 to 1815, 16–25
    from 1815 to 1871, 26, 29–33, 36–7, 39–40
    from 1871 to 1945, 48–9, 56–7, 66–9
    from 1945 to 1981, 93–5
    from 1981 on, 105, 115–17, 140, 144–5
  legislative debates and proposals
    from before 1789 to 1815, 14–20

Index

from 1815 to 1871, 26–8, 30–1, 33–8
from 1871 to 1945, 43–66
from 1945 to 1981, 71, 73–5, 83–4, 89, 94–104
from 1981 on, 109, 110–12, 117–20
of local government
  processes, 187–8, 189, 198–207
  system, 211–21, 310–16
resistance to, 71–2
  before Socialist Fifth Republic, 75–6, 78, 81–4, 90–2, 95, 226
  in Socialist Fifth Republic, 107, 112–14, 117–18, 121–4, 138, 140, 322–5
rhetoric of limits of, 342–6, 348–9, 356–7, 359
and scholarly assessments, 181–2
  before Socialist reforms, 187–192, 200–7, 210–21
  of Socialist reforms, 264–6, 312–6
strategy for passage of Socialist reforms, 106–17, 119, 120–1, 124, 132–3
deconcentration, 34, 37, 67, 129–30, 192–4, 311, 322–5
Defferre, Gaston, 87, 117, 119, 385
  on deconcentration, 129
  and regions, 327
  strategy for reform, 106–12, 124
  support for decentralization, 145, 247, 384
de Gaulle, Charles, 77, 88–90
Delebarre, M., 111
democracy, local
  in conservative Fifth Republic, 206–7, 214, 215–16
  in Socialist Fifth Republic, 140, 149–52, 183–4, 266, 267, 286–9
  in Third Republic, 190
demographic shifts, 92, 154
departmental elections, 98, 141–2, 162; see also cantons, and electoral districts
  politicization along national party lines, 270, 272
departments, 16, 79, 119–20, 330–4
  and economic development, 304–5, 368
  and education, 121–3, 357–8
  finances of, 136
    expenditures, 240, 242–3, 347–8, 367–8, 375–6
    problems for poorer departments, 353–4, 356–7
    state transfers, 134–5, 245
    taxes, 134, 351–2, 359–61, 242
  organization and functions, 115, 121, 124–6, 330

personnel, 363
and prefects, 321–2, 383–4
president, see general council, president of
and regional planning, 292–4, 332–3
and regions, 331–4
and rural land-use planning, 305
and tutelle, 328, 330–1, 340–1
Deschanel, Paul, 61–2
décumul (divestiture of mandates), see cumul des mandats
DGCL (Direction générale des collectivités locales), 132
DGD (dotation générale de dé-centralisation), 134, 135, 350–1
DGE (dotation globale d'équipement), 97, 134, 135–6, 338, 350, 353 .
DGF (dotation globale de fonctionnement), 134, 136, 244, 350
Directory, 21–2
dirigisme
  decentralized, 184, 267, 289–309
  deconcentrated, 291
  and regional planning, 296–7
  state, 191, 299
districts, 16, 21, 22
Dosière, René, 373
DRES (dotation régionale d'équipement scolaire), 135, 351
Dubedout, Hubert, 102
Dufaure, Armand, 46
Durrieu, Yves, 101
Duvergier de Hauranne, J. M., 28

economic development, local, 127–9, 184, 267, 289–309, 364–70; see also dirigisme, decentralized
  before Socialist reforms, 191, 193
  and EEC, 300–1
  financing of, 368–71
  and prefect, 320–1
  and state, 297–301, 324
économie sociale (cooperative movement), 161, 298, 303, 323
education
  costs, 351, 357–8
  decentralization of, 122t, 123t, 126–7
  in regional planning process, 288–9, 296, 306
elected officials, local, 184, 189, 266, 277, 279–86
  and administrators, local, 218, 232–3
  and democracy, local, 287–9
  and economic development, local, 302–4
  politicization of, 377–82

Index

elected officials, local (*cont.*)
and the prefect, 198–201, 203–4, 206–
7, 211–12, 228–9
profile of, 266, 279–85
and role change, 184–316–17
salaries of, 146–7
statute of, 145
elections
European, 162, 164
local, *see* departmental elections; municipal elections; regional elections
national
and extreme right, 175–6
legislative, 162, 164–6, 175
presidential, 162, 164–6
electoral reform
under de Gaulle, 255
in Socialist Fifth Republic, 140–4
electorate, local; *see also* elected officials,
local; parties, local; departmental
elections; municipal elections; regional elections
composition of
from before 1789 to 1815, 14, 18–20,
21, 23
from 1815 to 1871, 26–7, 29, 31–2,
33, 36, 39
from 1871 on, 44, 52
politicization of along national party
lines, 250, 254, 256–7, 269–72
regional versus departmental, 285–6
republicanization of, 51–2
electorate, national
allegiance to Socialists, 153–67
dealignment of, 160
and demographic shifts, 154, 156
and occupational shifts, 142, 156
and penetration by left, 158–9, 163–6
potential of, according to occupation
154–5
realignment of, 139, 152–77
stability of, 176–7
value changes of, 156–7
and variables affecting voting, 156
elites, local, *see* elected officials, local
empereur au petit pied, 24
Empire, Second, 36–9
ENA (École Nationale d'Administration),
261
Ernoul, Edmond, 47
État-providence (welfare state), 106
Europeanists, 85
extreme right, 152–3, 167, 169,
171–6
and alliances, local, 277–8
and decentralization, 172
and electorate, local, 172–4, 276

Fabius, Laurent, 284
farmers, 161, 164, 172; *see also* peasants
FCTVA (compensation fund for the value
added tax), 134
federalism, *see* national unity, threats to
Ferry, Jules, 38, 46, 56
FGDS (*Féderation de la gauche démocrate
et socialiste*), 87
field services of state, 193–5, 205, 232,
317–18, 322–6
Fifth Republic, *see* Republic, Fifth
FIM (fund for industrial modernization),
298
finances, local
borrowing by local governments, 243,
244–5, 302, 354–5, 374
costs
of decentralization, 116, 126, 361–4
of local government, 237–9
expenditures of local governments, 135,
239–43, 346–8, 367–8, 374–5
as compared to state, 347
as percentage of GDP, 348
problems with, 135–7, 353–9
reform initiatives, 80–1
resources of local governments, 349–50
taxes, 133–4, 193, 242, 243, 358–61
as percentage of GDP, 364
revenues from, 349–352
state
financing of local economic development, 297–8
transfers, 134–6, 349–51
subsidies, 242–3, 244–5
FNSEA (*Fédération nationale des syndicats
d'exploitants agricoles*), 161
fonds interrégional de péréquation (interregional equalization fund), 101
Fontaine, Émile, 62
forces vives, see socioprofessionals
Fouchet, Christian, 385
Fougeyrollas, Pierre, 84
Fourcade, Pierre, 133
Fourth Republic, *see* Republic, Fourth
Franclieu, marquis de, 53
French Revolution, 15–22

Gambetta, Léon, 42, 44, 45, 55, 56, 109,
139
GAMs (*Groupements d'action municipale*),
102
Gaullists, 99, 153, 168, 171; *see also* moderate right
general council
president of, 115
in Fourth Republic, 73–4, 75
politicization, 378–82, 384

and prefect, 234, 321–2
role change, 311, 326–7
selection and powers of
from 1789 to 1815, 18, 19–20, 20–1, 21, 24
from 1815 to 1871, 29–30, 32, 33, 36–7, 39
from 1871 to 1981, 49, 67
from 1981 on, 121 (*see also* departments)
general councilors
and nonpartisanship, rhetoric of, 253–4
profile, 281–2, 284
and regions, 333–4
Gilbert, Jean-Louis, 383
Giraud, Michel, 143, 147, 148, 278, 285, 359, 360
Girondins, 19–20, 33
Giscard d'Estaing, Valéry, 93, 98, 167, 168, 247, 225–6
Giuily, Eric, 132, 346
Goblet, René M., 58
Gravier, Jean-François, 76
Guesdes, Jules, 65
Guichard commission, 96–7, 247
Guichard, Olivier, 96, 118, 284, 358, 368, 378

Halévy, Daniel, 42, 54–5, 198, 204
Hanotaux, Georges, 31
Haussonville, viscount de, 49
health services, transfer of, 122–6
Herment, René, 383

IGAMEs (inspectors general of the administration in extraordinary mission), 76–7, 204

Jacobins, 19–21, 35–6
Jeanneney, Jean-Marcel, 89
Josèphe, Noël, 278
Joxe, Pierre, 385
judicial review, system of, 115, 337–8 *see also* tutelle
July Monarchy, 29–33
Juppé, Alain, 168, 348

Kaltenbach, Jean, 285
Krieg, Pierre-Charles, 285

Lafont, Robert, 84
Lalu, Christian, 132
Lamennais, Felicité Robert de, 36
land-use planning, 97, 121, 305, 339–40
Lanesson, Jean-Marie Antoine de, 59
Le Pen, Jean-Marie, 173–4; *see also* extreme right

Lecanuet, Jean, 147
left
noncommunist: in conservative Fifth Republic, 86–8, 91, 100–3
republican; *see also* moderate republicans; Opportunists; Radicals; Socialists
in July Monarchy, 30–1
in Second Empire, 38
in Third Republic, 43–5, 46–7, 48–9, 53
legitimists
in July Monarchy, 31
in Restoration, as ultras, 27
in Second Empire, 37–8
in Second Republic, 35
in Third Republic, 47, 53, 56, 66
Léotard, François, 168, 169
liberals; *see also* Orleanists
in July Monarchy, 29–30
in Restoration, 28, 29
in Second Republic, as conservative republicans, 34–5
listes de notabilités, 23, 24
loi Bonnet, 97–8
loi Frey, 94–5
loi Marcellin, 93
loi Royer, 92
Longuet, Gérard, 384

Madelin, Alain, 169
management, good
reality of, 372, 373–7
rhetoric of, 223, 256–8, 275–6, 343–4, 371–7
managers, middle-level, 70, 92, 139, 165, 172; *see also salariés; cadres moyens*
managers, upper-level, 165
Marcellin, Raymond, 90, 146
Marcère, Émile Deshayes de, 59
Marnot, P., 111
Martignac, proposal of, 26–7, 28
Mauroy, Pierre, 100, 118, 138, 145, 271, 286, 327
mayors, 200–2, 212–3, 215–16; *see also* elected officials, local; municipal council; Paris
and centralization, rhetoric of, 227–8, 244–5
Communist, 257–8
as electoral agents, 44, 46, 52–3, 58
and nonpartisanship, rhetoric of, 249–53
occupational profile, 281
and prefects, 320, 339–40
role of, 233–4, 311–12, 335–7

mayors *(cont.)*
  rural, 25, 336–7, 339–41
  selection and powers of
    from before 1789 to 1815, 18, 21, 23–5
    from 1815 to 1871, 29, 33–4, 36–7, 39, 39–40
    from 1871 on, 44, 54, 55–6, 57, 58–60, 67–8, 80, 189–92
Meaux, Camille, Vicomte de, 47
Mendès-France, Pierre, 87
Médecin, Jacques, 147, 293, 378, 379, 380
Méline, Jules, 63
Mitchell, Robert, 56
Mitterrand, François, 87, 91, 101, 105, 162, 271–2
moderate republicans, 61–3
moderate right, 167–76; *see also* neoliberalism
  and economic development, local, 298, 303–4, 306, 308
  and elections, local, 274–5
  electorate, potential, 155
  and taxes, local, 360–1
modus vivendi, 76, 182, 203–4; *see also* elected officials, local
monarchists, *see* legitimists; Orleanists
Monnet, Émile, 60
Monod, Jacques, 99
Monory, René, 127
Moreau, Jacques, 150
MRG *(Mouvement des radicaux de gauche)*, 100
MRP *(Mouvement républicain populaire)*, *see* Christian Democrats
municipal council; *see also,* communes; elections, municipal; mayors; Paris
  politicization, 379–82
  selection and powers of
    from 1789 to 1815, 18, 19, 21, 23–5
    from 1815 to 1871, 29–30, 31–2, 33, 36–7, 39, 39–40
    from 1871 on, 48, 57, 59–60, 68–9
municipal elections, 81–2, 97, 98, 140, 142, 162
  politicization along national party lines, 254–6, 268, 269–70, 272, 273–5
municipal socialism, 64, 191–2
Murville, Couve de, 88, 90
mutual dependence, 182, 199–201; *see also* elected officials, local

Nancy program, 37
Napoleon I, 23–5
Napoleon III, 38
National Defense, government of, 39–40
National Front, *see* extreme right

national unity, threats to
  by federalism, 12, 73, 74, 75, 88
  by regions, 64, 73, 228
    for Communists, 104
    for Gaullists, 83, 94, 95, 118, 120
    for Socialists, 101
neoliberalism, 152, 167–9, 171
Noir, Michel, 275
nonpartisanship, rhetoric of, 183, 222–3, 247–54, 255–7, 261–3, 342–3
  use by national government, 254–6
notables, la fin des, 198
notables; *see* elected officials, local

Opportunists, 56, 58
ordre moral, 53, 56
Orleanists, 38, 47, 66; *see also* liberals, in July Monarchy, in Restoration)
Ornano, Michel d', 378

Paris
  municipal organization
    from 1789 to 1815, 23, 29, 31–2
    from 1815 to 1871, 37, 39–40
    from 1871 to 1981, 58, 80, 93
    from 1981 on, 115
  and *tutelle,* 231
Paris Commune, 40
Parti radical, 293
parties, local, 266, 267–8, 276–9; *see also* departmental elections; electorate, local; municipal elections; regional elections
  national party influence, 272–6, 278–9
Pasqua, Charles, 169, 175, 348
paysans moyens, see peasants, middle-income
PC *(Parti Communiste), see* Communists
PDP, *Parti démocrate populaire,* 66
peasants, 45, 47, 49–52, 54–5, 92
  middle-income, 42, 45–6, 50–51
Pensec bill, 101
petite-bourgeoisie, see shopkeepers
Peyrefitte, Alain, 94, 96, 226
Pezet, Michel, 279
Pétain, Marshal, 69
Philibert, Louis, 148
Phlipponeau, Michel, 87
Picard, Ernest, 46, 48
Pisani, Edgar, 101
Pléven, René, 203
pôles de conversion (reindustrialization zones), 122, 297, 298–9, 302
politique des chimères, 56
politique des résultats, 56
Pompidou, Georges, 90, 91, 94, 95–6, 99
Poncelet, Christian, 357

Poncet, François, 148, 333
Poniatowski, Michel, 247
POS (*Plan d'occupation du sol*), *see* land-
    use plans
Poujadists, 160
Prax-Paris, Adrien, 47–8
prefects; *see also* subprefect; *tutelle*
    appointment of, 258–61, 385
    from 1789 to 1815, 23–4
    from 1815 to 1871, 29, 37
    from 1871 to 1945, 49, 55, 57, 59, 67,
        68–9, 201–2,
    from 1945 to 1981, 75–6, 81, 94, 201
    from 1981 on, 112–3, 115–20, 121–2,
        195, 201–4, 322–4
    politicization, 63, 247, 258–63, 382–6
    and nonpartisanship, rhetoric of, 248
    regional, 68, 73, 78, 195–6, 203–4
    role change, 184–5, 311, 317–22, 337
prefets à poigne, 37; *see also* prefect, from
    1815 to 1871
procureur général syndic, 18, 21
proletariat, 52, 64–5; *see also* workers
PS (*Parti socialiste*), 87, 100, 103
PSU (*Parti socialiste unifié*), 86, 87, 91,
    100, 103

Racine, Pierre, 99
Radicals, 58, 63–4, 74–5, 99
Raudot, Claude Marie, 35, 49
Rausch, Jean-Marie, 146, 147, 273, 287,
    293, 321, 380
regional accounting courts, 113, 116–7,
    337–8, 363–4
regional council
    politicization of, 378–9, 380–1
    president of, 115
        and prefect, 321–2
        role change, 311, 326–8
    selection and powers of, 94, 115
regional councilors
    and *cumul des mandats*, 284–5
    and departments, 333–4
    profile of, 282–4
regional elections, 141–2
    and extreme right, 277–8
    politicization of along national party
        lines, 271, 273, 274
    timing of, 141–2, 143
regional planning, 196, 288–9, 290–7,
    305–6
    financing, 295, 364–5, 369–71
    and national plan, 291, 294–6
    and prefects, 295, 320–1
regionalists, ethnic, 84–5, 100–1
regions
    after Socialist reforms, 143, 327–30

    and economic development, 304–7
    and education, 121–3, 357–8
    expenditures of, 347–8, 366–9
    financing of economic development of,
        368–71
    organization and functions of, 115,
        121, 128, 140, 290–1, 305, 327
    personnel, 363, 365–6
    taxes, 351–2, 358–61
    and *tutelle*, 231, 328–30, 328, 332–3
    before Socialist reforms, 67, 68–9, 76–
        9, 93–5, 194–7, 234–5
        expenditures, 240–3
        finances, 245
        and state subsidies, 245
    and departments, 118–20, 142, 203–4,
        283–6
    referendum of 1969, 88–91
    support for
        in Conservative Fifth Republic, 84–6,
            100–1, 228
        in Fourth Republic, 76–7
        in Socialist Fifth Republic, 118–19,
            142–3
        in Third Republic, 43, 47, 60–1, 66
    as threat to national unity, *see*, national
        unity, threats to
rénovateurs, 171
Republic
    Fifth
        Conservative, 77–104
        Socialist reforms of, 105–38
    Fourth, 72–7
    Second, 33–6
    Third, 41–68
        Electoral coalition of, 92, 139, 159,
            169, 170, 172, 184; *see also* peas-
            ants; farmers; shopkeepers; artisans
Republican party, 99
republicanism, spread of, in Third Repub-
    lic, 51–2
Resistance, 69
Restoration, 26–9
République de droit, 49
République des ducs, 51, 55
Révolution des maires, ("revolution of the
    mayors"), 42, 54, 204
rhetoric: *see* centralization, rhetoric of;
    decentralization, rhetoric of; man-
    agement, good, rhetoric of; nonparti-
    sanship, rhetoric of
right, *see* extreme right; legitimists; moder-
    ate right; Orleanists
Robespierre, M.F.I. de, 18
Rocard, Michel, 86, 271–2, 276
Rossinot, André, 293
Rouher, Eugène, 38–9, 47

Index

RPR (*Rassemblement pour la république*), see Gaullists

salariés (wage earners), 70, 92, 109, 154
in local politics, 184, 285–6
in Socialist electoral strategy, 139, 142, 152, 157–8, 170, 176
Salvi, Pierre, 357, 375
saupoudrage, 238–9
Savary, Alain, 95
Schmitt, Dominique, 131
Second Empire, see Empire, Second
Second Republic, see Republic, Second
Servan-Schreiber, Jean-Jacques, 96, 99, 244
Séguin, Philippe, 111, 145–6, 273, 293–4, 302, 335–6, 380–1
on costs of decentralization, 362–3
SFIO (*Section française de l'internationale ouvrière*), 74
shopkeepers, 32, 42, 45–6, 51–2, 92
Siegel, Maurice, 383
Siegfried, André, 51, 76, 199
Sieyès, Emmanuel Joseph, abbé, 14, 23
Simon, Jules, 38
SIVOM (*syndicats intermunicipales à vocation multiple*), see communes, multi-purpose syndicates
social services
transfer of, 122t, 123t, 124–6
division of, between state and department, 330–1
costs, compensation for, 351–2
social stratum, new, 42, 44, 55, 139, 204
Socialist Fifth Republic, 105–177; see also Republic, Fifth
parallels with the Third Republic, 139, 153, 166–7, 177
Socialist–Communist alliance, 92
Socialists
before Socialist Fifth Republic, 64–5, 69, 74, 87–8, 91, 100–3
in Socialist Fifth Republic, 109, 117–8
and economic development, local, 298, 303
electoral strategy of, 139, 140–1, 152, 154, 157–9
and good management, rhetoric of, 275–6
and government, local, 276, 278–9
and governmental policies, 161

ideological flexibility of, 153, 160–1, 162–3
and taxes, local, 360–1
socioprofessionals (*forces vives*), 70, 78, 82, 274, 275
Soisson, Jean-Pierre, 273
Stasi, Bernard, 278, 285, 327, 358
subprefect, 24, 319, 336
Sue, Eugène, 35
syndicates, see communes
taxes, local, see finances, local

Thiers, Adolphe, 30, 35, 38, 46, 47–9
Third Republic, see Republic, Third
Tocqueville, Alexis de, 10, 15, 31, 34
Tolain, Henri Louis, 48
trésorier-payeur général (treasurer-paymaster general), 194, 338
tutelle
from 1789 to 1815, 18–19, 23
from 1815 to 1871, 29, 37
from 1871 to 1945, 57, 58, 59, 189
from 1945 to 1981, 72, 74, 75, 93, 229–33, 235
from 1981 on, 112, 115–18, 185, 311–12, 328–34

UDF (*Union pour la démocratie française*), 167–8
UGSC (*Union de la Gauche et des Clubs Socialistes*), 101
ultras, see legitimists
UNR (*Union pour la nouvelle République*), 81
urban communities and districts, see communes
urban planning, 193, 247, 338–9, 351; see also municipal socialism

Valfons, marquis de, 56
Vichy regime, 68–9
Vigoroux, Robert, 279
Villèle, Jean Baptiste, Comte de, 27–8
Vivien, Alexandre François Auguste, 34, 38

wage earners, see salariés
workers, 70, 92, 139, 165, 172; see also proletariat; salariés
Worms, Jean-Pierre, 102, 145, 210, 286

zones d'entreprises (enterprise zones), 298